A Culture of Discontinuity?

CULTURAL HISTORY AND LITERARY IMAGINATION

EDITED BY CHRISTIAN J. EMDEN & DAVID MIDGLEY

VOL. 34

A Culture of Discontinuity?

Russian Cultural Debates in Historical Perspective

Olga Tabachnikova (ed.)

PETER LANG
Lausanne - Berlin - Bruxelles - Chennai - New York - Oxford

Bibliographic information published by the Deutsche Nationalbibliothek. The German National Library lists this publication in the German National Bibliography; detailed bibliographic data is available on the Internet at http://dnb.d-nb.de.

A catalogue record for this book is available from the British Library.

Library of Congress Control Number: 2023912548

Cover image: Erik Boulatov «Russian XX century I» (1990), © Erik Boulatov / ADAGP/ UPRAVIS 2023.
Cover design by Peter Lang Group AG

ISSN 1660-6205
ISBN 978-1-78997-937-4 (print)
ISBN 978-1-78997-993-0 (ePDF)
ISBN 978-1-78997-994-7 (ePub)
DOI 10.3726/b17524

Published by Peter Lang Ltd, Oxford, United Kingdom
info@peterlang.com - www.peterlang.com

This publication has been peer reviewed.

Contents

A Note to Reader

This volume was written before 24 February 2022 and has not undergone any changes since. This is because a multifaceted evaluation of the questions of Russian cultural continuity presented herein should only increase in value in light of the tragic events that have unfolded since. We hope that the material presented in the book will help to elucidate many cultural underpinnings of the current geopolitical catastrophe.

Acknowledgments

I hereby gratefully acknowledge the support for this project by the University of Central Lancashire Research Centre for Migration, Diaspora and Exile (MIDEX). I am also very grateful to all the contributors, translators and copyeditors of this volume for their hard work, patience and perseverance.

Figures

OLGA TABACHNIKOVA

Introduction: Continuity behind Rupture

В России нужно долго жить,
А в ней всё больше умирают.
Отечество не выбирают,
Где вечно ворону кружить,
Где после смерти воскресают
И ткут связующую нить.

И оттого горит окно,
И свет от Бога до порога,
С того и дышится глубóко,
Что здесь в предание одно
Вплелись, кто умерли до срока,
И ниткой стелется дорога
Одна от Пушкина до Блока,
И крутится веретено.

(2021)

In Russia, you need long life,
But people die instead.
You don't choose a homeland
with a crow ever overhead,
where after death you rise again
and weave a binding thread.

That's why a window is lit,
with a candle that always burns,
and it beams all the way to God.
Breathe deep, for the premature dead
are woven into one myth.
The same thread is the path
stretching from Pushkin to Blok,
and the spindle turns and turns.

(Translated by Peter Daniels)

A culture of discontinuity? Setting the scene

Studies of cultural continuity are important for any country, as it is vital for the spiritual health of a nation to be self-aware in terms of the foundations on which its cultural life is based and to distinguish the sustainable and essential from the fleeting and transient. The task is especially fascinating in the case of Russia, whose culture has often been referred to as a culture of explosions, which is to say, of discontinuity and abrupt rifts, so much so that it is hardly possible to speak of Russian culture as a homogeneous, unified whole. Thus, Yuri Lotman, the prominent literary scholar and cultural historian, famously stated that 'the history of Russian culture sees itself as a chain of explosions',[1] and similarly the poet and artist Maximilian Voloshin in his poem *Neopalimaia kupina* wrote, 'Europe went via a culture of fire, while we carry in ourselves a culture of explosion'.[2] An essentially revolutionary consciousness led to the country more often than not denying and rewriting its past, be it the drastic turn to the West under Peter the Great at the brink of the eighteenth century, or a Futurist passion to do away with classical Russian literature at the dawn of Bolshevism, or post-Soviet attempts to obliterate the Soviet period. Every turn of Russian history was accompanied by great cultural turmoil and facilitated fierce cultural debates. Continuing polemics between Slavophiles and Westernizers, Eurasian and anti-Eurasian sentiments, and a search for a national idea are just some examples.

The destiny of Russia in the context of its geopolitical position and its cultural role on the domestic as well as international fronts have been fundamental to these debates. At the same time, such discussions always went deeper, and invariably acquired an existential dimension, probing into the human condition, into the 'cursed questions of existence'. The same phenomena can be observed in Russia today, amid the complexities of the modern world. Can Russian culture be characterized as discontinuous, or has there always been a solid kernel that is invariably carried

1 Yuri Lotman, 'Collection of works:' Yuri Lotman i tartusko-moskovskaia semioticheskaia shkola, ed. A. D. Koshelev (Moscow: Gnozis, 1994), p. 409.

2 Maximilian Voloshin, *Neopalimaia kupina*, <http://az.lib.ru/w/woloshin_m_a/text_0096.shtml> (Accessed 10 July 2023). 'Lib.ru/Классика: Волошин Максимилиан Александрович. Неопалимая купина'.

forward, providing a common ground for the life of the nation? Moreover, what do we mean when we talk about 'Russian culture' from our historical position of today? How can we trace the problem of continuity/discontinuity of Russian culture through Russian cultural debates? This is the range of questions addressed by a major international conference held at the University of Central Lancashire in Preston, England, in May 2016, which subsequently gave rise to the current volume.

The chapters in this volume, while covering a broad chronological range, focus predominantly on the past 200 years, when Russian literature came of age and Russian thought found its most vocal and conceptual expression. Thematically, the material is organized into three sections that move from the study of Russian history as an ideological narrative to the problems of continuity and breaks in literature, which is followed by other art forms. The chapters, diverse in scope and approach, are nevertheless woven together as the links of one continuous chain, creating a complex tapestry of Russian cultural history where continuities visibly emerge from behind the ruptures, and where the conceptual and general are illustrated by the particular and concrete.

It is precisely this vision of the wood behind the trees that unites the contributions into a coherent whole greater than the sum of its parts. No doubt, every culture exemplifies both continuities and ruptures; the question, however, is what prevails and how we can trace cultural continuity, whose manifestations vary, take on diverse disguises and often evade identification. The chapters of this volume attempt to defy the challenge, and end up sharing the realization that behind the tectonic shifts of Russian history and the irreversible ruptures some stable cultural patterns can invariably be discerned. In other words, for all its breaks and rifts, there is indeed continuity in Russian cultural development, and it is this continuity that every chapter ultimately traces.

But how do we tackle the problem of Russian cultural continuity in conceptual terms, and what are the generic approaches to studying cultural evolution?

Russian cultural debates and civilizational characteristics

The revival of a civilizational approach to cultural studies is not accidental, but 'linked to a broader cultural turn in the human sciences'[3] with its acknowledgment of the primacy of culture. The processes of globalization which are taking an increasingly strong grip on the world have brought the questions of national cultures into sharp focus. Yet, rather expectedly, the very definition of culture remains constantly contested, not least because the 'study of culture itself belongs to culture'.[4] On the one hand, cultural determinism has outlived itself, replaced with the ideas initiated by Clifford Geertz, in his seminal *The Interpretation of Cultures* (of 1973), who argued that scholars should look not for substantive identities, but rather relationships among diverse phenomena. On the other hand, in the same work, Geertz claimed, reformulating Max Weber, that 'man is the animal suspended in the webs of significance he himself has spun',[5] as if acknowledging the room for a creative and subjective approach to the cultural field. In the half a century that has passed, the situation with studying culture in historical perspective has not become any simpler, and there is currently 'no consensus paradigm for how to approach cultural evolution.'[6]

In their famous 'Perepiska iz dvukh uglov' (Correspondence across a Room) of 1920 (since then translated into many languages), Mikhail Gershenzon and Viacheslav Ivanov, two distinguished representatives of the Russian Silver Age (a cultural renaissance on the brink of the twentieth century), throw into question the very concept of culture. Their dialogue is symptomatic of the time of tectonic sociopolitical changes in Russia and

3 Johann Arnason, 'The Cultural Turn and the Civilizational Approach', *European Journal of Social Theory*, Vol. 13, No. 1 (March 2010), pp. 67–82; p. 67.

4 Simon During, *Cultural Studies: A Critical Introduction* (Abingdon: Routledge, 2005), p. 7.

5 Clifford Geertz, *The Interpretation of Cultures* (New York: Basic Books, 1973), p. 5.

6 William C. Wimsatt, 'Articulating Babel: A Conceptual Geography for Cultural Evolution', in *Beyond the Meme: Development and Structure in Cultural Evolution*, ed. A. C. Love and W. C. Wimsatt (Minneapolis: University of Minnesota Press, 2019), pp. 1–41; p. 40.

the world, with the crumbling of old biblical truths and the Nietzschean sentiment that 'God is dead', leading to a shift in the entire cultural paradigm. The two correspondents voice, respectively, cultural optimism, with its belief in perpetual cultural development through creativity and spirituality (Ivanov), and cultural nihilism, which castigates cultural values as subversive of the free human will and denigrates modern culture as too abstract and suffocating (Gershenzon). Significantly, the very understanding of culture by these two protagonists differs; in Ivanov's words, Gershenzon perceives it 'not as a living treasury of gifts, but as a system of most subtle constraints'.[7] As Boris Schloezer noted in connection with this debate, Russian polemics about culture cannot be reduced to explaining it, as in Western Europe, but is always a question of justifying it. In this sense, the Russian idea is always, at least partly, transcendental with respect to culture because it judges culture.[8]

Father Alexander Schmemann makes an even stronger statement: of culture being altogether violated in the Russian context owing to maximalist tendencies that stem from Russia's relationships with Byzantium. Indeed, having joined the Christian world so belatedly, Russia inherited a maximalism of Christian faith, which was not – in contrast to the situation in Byzantium itself – attenuated by centuries of cultural development. In other words, religious passion lacked the protective layer of cultural foundation. Instead, Russia had taken wholeheartedly to the religious revelation of Jerusalem, to the world of prayer rather than that of wisdom and ratio. As a consequence, culture was sacrificed for the sake of religion and then subsumed by pragmatic goals and social utopia. The concept of boundaries, of measure, which largely characterizes culture as a whole, was violated in the Russian case.[9]

7 Viacheslav Ivanov and Mikhail Gershenzon, *Perepiska iz dvukh uglov* (St. Petersburg: Alkonost, 1921), p. 13.

8 Boris Schloezer, 'Russkii spor o kul'ture: Viacheslav Ivanov i M. O. Gershenzon, "Perepiska iz dvukh uglov"', *Sovremennye Zapiski*, Vol. 11 (1922), pp. 195–211; p. 211.

9 For an eloquent description of this process, see, for instance, lectures on Russian culture by Father Alexander Schmemann, *Osnovy russkoi kul'tury: Besedy na Radio Svoboda*, 1970–1971, compiled by E. Yu. Dorman (Moscow: Russian Orthodox Sviato-Tikhonovsky University for the Humanities, 2017).

At the same time, Russian culture in many ways came of age through its complex encounter with Western Europe, which has been tainted by ambivalence, by an explosive fusion of apprenticeship with rivalry. Indeed, Europe in the eyes of Russia was, on the one hand, 'the country of sacred miracles' and, on the other, the source of petty-bourgeois mentality and excessive rationality. For Europe, Russia has remained in cultural terms its perpetual opponent – the West's 'Other', often frightening and always enigmatic. Winston Churchill's definition of the country as 'a riddle wrapped in a mystery inside an enigma' can serve as a more universal perception of Russia in the West. Paradoxically perhaps, Russia remains enigmatic to its own self as well and, traditionally immersed in introspection, forever tries to identify its most fundamental cultural features.

Though we agree that cultural determinism 'in its extreme form [...] encourages one to string vastly diverse social facts on a single conceptual cord and to look for a cultural continuity impervious to historical change'[10] and is thus unlikely to be productive, there exists, nevertheless, a tendency that – with full self-awareness and thus not without caution about its relativity – admits the validity of certain 'cultural constants'. Thus, it is hard to disagree with the outstanding Russian thinker Sergei Averintsev in his conclusion about an increased role in Russian cultural consciousness of an individual tour de force as opposed to any institutional order.[11] Similarly, in the poetic realm, Fedor Tyutchev famously argued for the irrational character of Russian culture saying that Russia cannot be comprehended by reason.[12] Although it is only a poetic metaphor, it has been fervently embraced as quintessential both within and outside the country. Moreover, a hundred years on, another Russian poet, Aleksandr Yeremenko, echoed the same sentiments: 'It is a horizontal country, indescribable by qualifiers. Here

10 Dmitrii Shalin, 'Introduction: Continuity and change in Russian culture', in *Russian Culture at the Crossroads: Paradoxes of Postcommunist Consciousness*, ed. D. N. Shalin (New York: Routledge, 2018 [1996]), pp. 1–10; p. 2.

11 Sergei Averintsev, *Sviaz vremen* (*Sobranie sochinenii*), 2004, <http://www.fedy-diary.ru/html/042011/11042011-05a.html> (Accessed 17 January 2022).

12 Fedor Tyutchev, 'Umom Rossiiu ne poniat', 1866, <http://rupoem.ru/tyutchev/all.aspx#umom-rossiyu-ne> (Accessed 10 February 2022). In Russian: 'Умом Россию не понять ... в Россию можно только верить'.

a diagonal and a side are forever incommensurable.'[13] Fedor Dostoevsky, in his turn, spoke of the universal compassion of Russian mentality, while Nikolai Berdyaev noted a profound ambivalence and contradictory nature of Russian national character (thus implicitly validating this very concept and its legitimacy and meaningfulness): 'On the same grounds the Russian people may be characterized as imperial-despotic and anarchic freedom-loving, as a people inclined to nationalism and national conceit, and a people of a universal spirit, [...] cruel and unusually humane; inclined to inflict suffering and illimitably sympathetic.'[14]

Among such national cultural traits, Tatiana Chumakova points out a specific ontological epistemology, characteristic not only of Old Russian thought but also of Russian religious philosophy, which results in the concept of the 'suffering reason' – reason involved with the heart ('the heart with thought') – that is clearly demonstrated in the works of Tsar Ivan IV (Ivan the Terrible).[15] Hence, the Russian striving to 'animate' reason, to deal with it only in the context of 'living life' and to reject abstractions, has deep roots.

In other words, in the Russian case, we may be dealing with a different kind of reason, one that is inseparable from feelings and that craves the heavenly truth, the ideal, but within the shell of the 'living life'. Ivan Kireevsky, for instance, argued that a Russian Orthodox believer can arrive at atheism, but not (in contrast to a Western Christian) through a natural evolution of mind.[16]

13 Aleksandr Yeremenko, 'Gorizontal'naia strana', 1987, <http://modernpoetry.ru/main/aleksandr-eremenko-gorizontalnaya-strana#erema98> (Accessed 10 February 2014). In Russian: 'Горизонтальная страна. Определительные мимо. Здесь вечно несоизмеримы диагональ и сторона'.

14 Nicolas Berdyaev, *The Origin of Russian Communism*, translated from the Russian by R. M. French (London: Geoffrey Bles, 1948 [1937]), p. 17.

15 Tatiana Chumakova, 'Irrationalism in Ancient Russia', in *Facets of Russian Irrationalism between Art and Life. Mystery inside Enigma*, ed. Olga Tabachnikova (Leiden: Brill, 2016), pp. 72–93; p. 72.

16 See Ivan Kireevsky, 'O neobkhodimosti i vozmozhnosti novykh nachal dlia filosofii' (1856), in I. V. Kireevsky, *Polnoe sobranie sochinenii v dvukh tomakh*, ed. M. Gershenzon (Farnborough, Hampshire: Gregg International, 1970 [Moscow, 1911]), p. 250.

Continuing on this path, Olga Shemiakina, in the spirit of Dostoevsky's sentiments, assigns Russia to the civilization of the 'boundary type' that is most conducive to the dialogue with the outside world, thanks to the qualities of plasticity, tolerance and positive orientation to the 'Other'. In her view, behind the 'obvious ruptures, a stable continuity of reproducing the system of the main forms of life and creation of meaning is concealed'.[17] She distinguishes the concept of 'cardiognosis' (cognition by heart, that is, through emotional rather than logical perception of the world) as being the primary method of cognition for the Russian cultural consciousness, and she talks of a myth creation inherent in Russian cultural history.

Notwithstanding the above opinions about Russian cultural invariants and national characteristics, there exist diametrically opposite views according to which such cultural constants are regarded merely as self-fashioning national mythology. For example, there is a striking difference in the interpretation of Russia's adoption of Christianity on the part of the Russian academician Dmitry Likhachev and Western scholar Dean S. Worth. The former interpreted the famous legend about Prince Vladimir's choice of faith for the country as determined above all by aesthetic considerations ('beauty determined the nature of Orthodoxy in Russia'),[18] while the latter drew a much more pragmatic conclusion ('one suspects that politics and diplomacy played more of a role than a beautiful church').[19] Similar examples, from both Russian and foreign sources, are in abundance.

At the same time, a qualitative classification that legitimizes contested concepts such as 'national character' is not alien to scholarly tradition beyond Russia, as can be seen, in particular, in Western studies that operate with this terminology (by Margaret Mead, Clyde Kluckhohn, Geoffrey Gorer, Henry Dick and other social scientists, to name but a few), linking culture with psychology and nation-building. The emergence of terms

17 Olga Shemiakina, 'Razryv i preemstvennost' v russkoi kul'turnoi traditsii: Opyt dialoga', *Obshchestvennye nauki i sovremennost'*, Vol. 1 (2001), pp. 106–116; p. 106.

18 Dmitry Likhachev, 'Religion: Russian Orthodoxy', in *The Cambridge Companion to Modern Russian Culture*, ed. Nicholas Rzhevsky (Cambridge: Cambridge University Press, 1998), p. 40.

19 Dean S. Worth, 'Language', in *The Cambridge Companion to Modern Russian Culture*, p. 24.

such as 'cultural identity', 'modal personality', 'collective unconscious' and 'ethnic mentality', in addition to the notorious 'national character', basically results from the attempts to bind together in a meaningful way the subjective and objective.[20]

However, in historical terms, cultural studies methodology has been distinguished by its social, political, ideological and economic engagement. From cultural hegemony analysis, the field ultimately evolved into the politics of representation, where 'culture and identity were regarded as constructed, as artificial, malleable, and contestable artefacts, and not as natural givens',[21] before seeing a shift to postmodern theories. The rise of structuralism and semiology, involving, in particular, Roland Barthes's *Mythologies*, marked a move within cultural studies toward the realm of literature, when culture and society started to be treated as texts amenable to analysis in terms of their structures, significance and effects.

Along these lines, Lotman's theory of the semiosphere argues that 'culture as a whole can be viewed as text'.[22] Moreover, it is 'a complexly arranged text that breaks down into a hierarchy of "texts within texts" and forms a complex interweaving of texts'.[23] This gives rise to the unpredictable element, conducive to and characteristic of cultural 'explosion', which, in turn, is responsible for cultural and historical evolution as well as its opposite (or its double): a gradual, predictable development. In semiotic terms,

> both gradual and explosive processes in a synchronized structure perform important functions: some provide innovation, others continuity. In their assessment by contemporaries, these tendencies are experienced as hostile, and the struggle between them is interpreted in the categories of a military battle leading to destruction. In reality though, these are two sides of a single, connected mechanism, its synchronous

20 Aleksander Etkind, 'Psychological Culture: Ambivalence and Resistance to Social Change', in *Russian Culture at the Crossroads*, pp. 99–126; p. 99.

21 Douglas M. Kellner and Meenakshi Gigi Durham, 'Adventures in Media and Cultural Studies: Introducing the Key Works', in *Media and Cultural Studies: Key Works*, ed. D. M. Kellner and M. G. Durham (Oxford: Blackwell, 2006), pp. ix–xxxviii; p. xxxiii.

22 Yuri Lotman, *Kultura i vzryv* (Moscow: Gnozis, 1992), p. 121.

23 Ibid.

> structure, and the aggressiveness of one of them does not drown out, but stimulates the development of the opposite one.[24]

Jointly with B. A. Uspensky, Lotman defined culture as the genetically non-inherited memory of a collective and, at that, a supra-individual mechanism for storing, transmitting and generating new texts that constitute collective memory. The latter can be of two types: 'informative', which is linearly synchronized with modernity and only interested in the production of the final result, erasing all prior information; and 'creative', which is instead in a constant dialogue with the past, whereby all the accumulated potential of culture in the historical continuum is active simultaneously, with temporal layers influencing one another.[25] Thus, cultural memory is understood as 'a cultural text, the content of which is the cultural experience of the past as a result of the adaptation of an ethnos to the conditions of existence. Experience tends to reproduce and reactivate.'[26] This interpretation powerfully links the concept of cultural continuity with the life of tradition, which is 'a certain form of structuring cultural experience, a way of existence of a cultural text, its preservation and reproduction. Cultural continuity is a mechanism for the movement of tradition in the space–time continuum.'[27]

According to Dmitry Likhachev, it is tradition that ultimately sustains national culture as a 'way of facilitating continuity that integrates those tendencies of the creative activity of the past which matter for the contemporary development'.[28] For him, 'tradition is not merely a preservation and transmission of values. It assumes a productive type of communication

24 Ibid., p. 26.

25 O. V. Pervushina, 'Kul'turnaia preemstvennost', kul'turnaia pamiat' i traditsiia: sootnoshenie poniatii kak kul'turologicheskaia problema', *Mir nauki, kul'tury, obrazovaniia*, Vol. 26, No. 1 (2011), pp. 324–328; p. 327.

26 Ibid.

27 Ibid.

28 A. S. Zapesotsky and V. G. Lukianov, 'Dmitri Likhachev: O sushchnosti kul'turnoi traditsii', *Voprosy kul'turologii*, Vol. 7 (2007), pp. 4–12; p. 4.

between cultures, when the old passes into the new and actively works in it.'[29] Thus, cultural continuity is perpetuated by the dialogue of the ancient culture with modernity, and 'cultural history is not only the history of changes, but also the history of the accumulation of values that remain living and effective elements of culture in its subsequent development'.[30]

With culture understood as a 'tree' of traditions, the latter work as a 'stabilizer' of culture, a basis and foundation of its dynamic development. The dialogue of cultures, as Likhachev argued, is a form of continuity that ensures the inheritance and use of cultural values accumulated by our ancestors, contributing to the creative processing of these values and further cultural development.[31] According to Likhachev, 'the binary character of cultural oppositions of preservation and change, imparting a certain drama to cultural life, at the same time acts as a guarantee of the sustainability of the development of culture'.[32] It then follows that tradition and innovation can be treated as dialectically interlinked opposites, whereby culture evolves as a result of their continuous cyclical interaction.[33]

The chapters of this volume in their diverse ways illuminate the above ideas, reflecting the continuous, yet cyclic, movement of cultural waves, the alternation and dialectic interaction of explosive as well as gradual developments, the life of tradition and creative collective memory. The sheer breadth of existing theories and approaches as well as their polemical character demonstrate the unabating rich controversy of cultural debates about Russia in historical perspective, and they signify the need for further study of Russian culture and its evolution – the field to which this book aspires to contribute.

29 Ibid.

30 Dmitrii Likhachev, *Izbrannye raboty*, 3 vols (Leningrad: Khudozhestvennaia literatura, 1987), p. 26.

31 Zapesotsky and Lukianov, 'Dmitri Likhachev', p. 8.

32 Ibid., p. 5.

33 Ibid.

The current volume in context

The very need to study one's national culture is perpetual because cultures, just like languages that mirror and manifest them, can be viewed as living organisms. But there are times that mark turning points in history, and it is then that the urge to revisit the cultural canon becomes particularly pressing. In the case of Russia, the latest major upheaval was that of *perestroika* in the late 1980s. It caused a serious reevaluation of values and brought about new ideologies and new perspectives on the country's past – and with it, on its future. It was then that books appeared explicitly addressing Russian cultural continuity as dominant rather than a theme (as do, for instance, various introductions and companions to Russian culture). In English, it was, most notably, Dmitri Shalin's collective volume *Russian Culture at the Crossroads: Paradoxes of Postcommunist Consciousness* of 1996, with its comprehensive approach. However, as the title suggests, its investigations gravitate more toward a sociopolitical agenda, to which other discourses converge. Not surprisingly, there is a similar title of that era, with even more explicit emphasis on politics: 'Continuity and Change in Russian Political Culture', by Jeffrey W. Hahn (*British Journal of Political Science*, 1991), not to mention several analogous publications of previous as well as subsequent years: for instance, 'Continuity and Change in Soviet Political Culture: An Emigre Study' by Stephen White (*Comparative Political Studies*, 1978) or 'Continuity in Russian Strategic Culture: A Case Study of Moscow's Syrian Campaign' by Dmitry Adamsky (The George C. Marshall European Center for Security Studies, 2020). Other studies, which focus on culture per se, are more restricted in their thematic scope: see, for example, the recent collection edited by Pauline Fairclough and Philip Bullock titled *1917 and Beyond: Continuity, Rupture and Memory in Russian Music* (2019).

Our volume does neither of the above. It has no claim to be comprehensive, either conceptually or thematically, neither does it gravitate toward politics or focus on any particular narrow aspect of culture or art form. Instead, it offers fresh ideas in a broad range of Russian life, literature and arts, often focusing on the under-researched, connecting particular with the general, exposing some unexpected connections (such as, for instance, between literature, cultural ideologies and economic theory), and thus sheds some new light on Russian cultural distinctiveness. In doing that, it attempts to answer the questions asked above – of what sustains Russian cultural development across centuries and how Russian culture has evolved to this day. Importantly, it addresses the topic from the contemporary frame of reference, which has moved on significantly from the *perestroika* years, and sets the debates in historical perspective, as the title of the volume stipulates. It thus fills a gap in existing research on Russian culture, while enriching our understanding of Russia and its never-fading enigma in ways that are both conceptual and concrete.

The section opening the volume unravels the ideological underpinnings of Russian history and thus provides a conceptual background to the rest of the book. It is, if you like, a system of ideological coordinates that gives coherence to the subsequent essays – a framework within which they can be meaningfully unlocked.

The first chapter, 'Historical Background of Russian Literature', by Olha Chervinska and Aleksandr Sych, offers an overview of Russian history as a backdrop for Russian culture, presenting it as a polemical territory, with often conflicting views on past events, and keeps the question of cultural continuity in sharp focus. While tracing all the dramatic upheavals of Russian historical development, the authors argue that at every drastic historical turn, behind the shattered patterns and dismissed cultural paradigms of the past, Russian culture retained an 'excess' of the previous experience as a foundation for the subsequent development. The continuity has been based on allotropy whereby different, even contrasting, forms coexisted, and every new developmental stage retained among its compositional factors a localized remainder of the Other. Regeneration of cultural tradition is then, in turn, conditioned by the conversion of allotropic forms that are influenced by deformations of the familiar context.

The chapter concludes that 'the complex Russian historical experience shows that all the previous cultural breaks, which led to almost catastrophic spiritual losses and mental deformations, and the subsequent difficult and sometimes painful experiences, ended with a subsequent submersion in their own historical landscape. Following the misunderstood and unconditionally denied achievements of the previous era, after a certain time at a new turn in history, when rejected values are understood in a new way, they can turn out to be claimed back'.

The subsequent chapters, in many ways, can be viewed as an illustration of this premise. Furthermore, the historical overview presented by the first chapter serves as a springboard for the other essays in this section that discuss the specifics of Russian cultural consciousness as responsible for the country's explosive development. Thus, Aleksandr A. Medvedev's chapter, 'Athena versus Gaia: Ideology and Being in Russian Literature of the Nineteenth and Twentieth Centuries', distinguishes a typically Russian ideology-driven mental attitude to life as one of the key reasons for the discrete development of Russian history.

Medvedev draws extensively on Russian literature that traditionally warned against such over-ideological attitude to existence that would subsume and destroy the real fullness of life. He thus highlights the phenomenon of Russian nihilism of the nineteenth century and its literary reflections, most notably in the works of Turgenev and Dostoevsky, and demonstrates that Russian literature not only was acutely aware of the ontological failure of the ideology-driven type of personality but also offered to society a national type of a supra-ideological character, in whom the ideological level would not suppress the ontological one. Such a type of character, wherein the existence of a person is deeper than any of its ideas, can be defined as humanist. The chapter then moves to the Soviet epoch and focuses on two of its major artists who exemplify such a humanist type: the writer Mikhail Prishvin and film director Andrei Tarkovsky. Both chose contemplative attention, non-intrusive observation, as the key creative principle that opposes any ideocratic 'super-reality'.

Notably, among various historical examples of ideologically driven consciousness in Russia, Medvedev discerns the seventeenth-century schism, where (just as in the subsequent ideocracies such as nihilism and Bolshevism) 'humanity was fanatically sacrificed to a dogmatically understood truth (without discussion, a ready-made idea), and the present was sacrificed to a utopian project of the past or future. In fact, there was a rejection of history, which, from the point of view of the Old Believers, was mastered by the Antichrist [...] The reason for this ideologized perception of Christianity, with its inherent fanaticism and dogmatism' Medvedev sees, quite in the spirit of Father Shmeman, in 'the lack of an ancient intellectual culture, a culture of dialogue and debate'. By the same token, 'the ideology-driven mental attitude was also manifested in the phenomenon of the Russian intelligentsia (from Belinsky through the Narodniks to the Bolsheviks). Having comprehended its history, G. P. Fedotov, in 1926, formulated the key feature of the intelligentsia as groundless idealism – a theoretical worldview, constructed rationally and applied to life forcefully as a norm and canon.'

Indeed, as Alexander Herzen wrote, in Russia, 'it is not the man but the idea that the people respect'.[34] Such opting for ideology at the expense of ontology is closely related to the dangers, passionately flagged up by Russian classics, of an abstract, rationalist mind, divorced from feelings and morality. Dostoevsky was perhaps the champion of the battle against excessive rationality and dogmatic reason, while Chekhov, as Lev Shestov argued, was emancipated entirely from ideologies and abstract ideas.[35] Of the same root are Saltykov-Shchedrin's words from his novella *Protivorechiia*, 'to remain the same student, the same fiery admirer of an abstract entity, to speak only of mankind and forget about a particular man is stupid, and not only stupid, but also vile'.[36] A century later, Vasily Grossman's character from his epic *Life and Fate* essentially repeats the same sentiment: 'I do not believe in good, I believe in kindness'.[37]

However, interestingly, the same phenomenon that is responsible for the discontinuity of Russian history, for its explosive development, can serve as an indication of cultural continuity, for it reflects a stable national

34 Alexander Herzen's letter to Jules Michelet of 22 September 1851. See <http://altheim.com/lit/herzen-ftos.html> (Accessed 17 December 2021).

35 See Lev Shestov, 'Anton Chekhov. Creation from the Void', <https://www.angelfire.com/nb/shestov/all/pw_1.html> (Accessed 12 February 2022).

36 Mikhail Saltykov-Shchedrin, 'Protivorechiia', in *Sobranie Sochinenii v 20 tomakh* (Moscow: Khudozhestvennaia Literatura, 1965), Vol. 1, pp. 73–74.

37 Vasily Grossman, *Zhizn' i sud'ba*, <http://lib.ru/PROZA/GROSSMAN/lifefate.txt> (Accessed 10 February 2022).

mental pattern: the propensity for taking ideas to their logical extreme and putting them into practice with essentially religious fervor and dedication. As Lev Shestov has famously written, 'we have always taken over European ideas in such fantastic forms. Take the sixties for example. With its loud ideas of sobriety and modest outlook, it was a most drunken period. Those who awaited the New Messiah and the Second Advent read Darwin and dissected frogs. It is the same today.'[38]

In his chapter, Medvedev usefully traces these threads of the ideological suppressing the ontological to Soviet times and illustrates how artistic resistance is achieved through adopting the role of a creative observer.

In the next chapter of the volume, 'Political Terrorism of the Early Twentieth Century in the Context of Russian Cultural Consciousness', Lidia I. Shishkina discerns the same ideological underpinnings behind such a phenomenon of Russian history as political terrorism on the brink of the twentieth century. The exaltation of an idea, of being ideologically driven, suits the unattenuated religious-cum-revolutionary temperament of Russian cultural consciousness, with its uncompromising maximalist tendencies. As Shishkina observes, Russian political terrorism flourished not least because of the remarkable popular support. 'The surprising phenomenon of support that the activities of the Socialist Revolutionary "militants" received from the "advanced public" can be explained by the fact that, in their propaganda, the terror theorists touched upon certain root features of the Russian cultural consciousness.' The idea of retribution, of divine justice, was traditionally prevalent in the Russian popular imagination and opposed to the power of the law. The perpetrators of this idea acquired the spectacular aura of martyrdom, and became romantic heroes of self-sacrifice, which overshadowed the violent and bloody nature of terrorism.

Importantly, Shishkina points out that 'the category of victimhood also defined another important component of terrorism – the combination of terror and religion, in which many cultural figures of the early twentieth century also saw the root features of the Russian national character,

38 Lev Shestov, 'All Things Are Possible' ('Apotheosis of Groundlessness'). <https://www.angelfire.com/nb/shestov/all/all_23.html> (Accessed 26 January 2022).

for which, in the words of Leonid Andreev, "rebellion was a religion, and religion was a rebellion"'. This was linked to the intelligentsia's interest in sectarianism and equating contemporary terrorists to the first Christian martyrs. A paradoxical fusion of religious consciousness and revolutionary violence determined the heroic behavior of the terrorists, earning them a widespread respect.

Notably, the decline of this movement was largely due to the end of the self-sacrificial myth when the exposure of the notorious provocateur Azef brought home a realization of a 'moral chasm [...] between the young people, who were enthusiastically going to their doom, and their commanders-in-chief, for whom the revolution had long been a gamble and a "commercial matter"'.

'Economic Thought as a Mirror of Cultural Debates: The Ideology of Westernism and Slavophilism in Modern Russia', the concluding chapter of this section, by Olga Tabachnikova and NataliaVinokurova, continues the discussion of the role of ideas in Russian history and its cultural implications. A most tangible battle of ideologies, which in many ways shaped the development of Russia, has been that between the two schools of thought traditionally known as Slavophiles and Westernizers. The chapter demonstrates the relevance of this opposition of the two camps, in their contemporary form, to Russian modernity, with a focus on the country's economic development. Through tracing the evolution of these two intellectual movements up to 2020, the authors argue the case for Russian cultural continuity.

They start by illustrating how, growing from Russian literary culture, these two strands infiltrated Russian economic thought, giving rise to two camps of contemporary economics: 'economic liberalism' and 'economic conservatism'. The authors then trace the main contradictions between Slavophiles and Westernizers based, on the one hand, on Russian philosophical literature of the nineteenth century, and, on the other, on the convictions of some contemporary Russian economists concerning Russia's ways of development, and demonstrate an impact of ideology on economic convictions. To this end, they first give an extensive account of the historical background to this ideological opposition with a reference to Russian literature and philosophy, and then address the results of recent sociological surveys of Russian youth concerning the respondents' attitudes to the above two schools. In the concluding part of the chapter, views of leading Russian economists (as derived from original interviews with the latter, conducted between 2010 and 2020) on the ways of development of the country in the context of modern Westernism and Slavophilism are presented.

The next section of the volume, rooted in Russian literary history, in many ways echoes the premises set out in the first section, on Russian history as ideology, extending and illuminating them through concrete examples. The semantic nods of Russian cultural evolution and its most abrupt rifts, including the Golden and Silver ages as well as the transition from Tsarist to Soviet form of political reality, all find expression in the chapters of this section, demonstrating continuity behind rupture.

The first chapter of this section, 'Rift versus Attraction as the Receptive Motivators of Russian Culture ', by Olha Chervinska, discusses the concept of a rift, break and discontinuity in conceptual terms, focusing on the Russian cultural context. In doing so, it points out the important distinction between a rift and disintegration. 'All cases we are dealing with are about a split of a hitherto undivided entity, where the most important thing is to accurately determine the so-called bifurcation point and the condition preceding it [...] Rift and disintegration are not the same, because "long-term disintegration", which leads to the irreversible collapse of a certain integrity, and "rift", which occurs according to a different formula, are not only far from being synonymous in this sense, but they are fundamentally opposite conditions.'

Chervinska explains that rift is linked to gravitation and attraction, and constitutes its corollary; it completes a particular stage of the preceding cultural development, as can be seen from Russian artistic culture and philosophical thought. However, their perception by other cultures remains contradictory due to the multiple differences in historical and cultural parameters.

Chervinska explores a variety of typological examples of rifts in Russian cultural history, showing that destruction need not mean regression as breaks with a tradition can be perceived as leading to a redeeming innovation. Furthermore, based on the philosophy of Alexei Khomyakov, a dichotomy can be marked between unity and freedom, as two poles between which

Russian culture oscillates. The chapter ultimately argues that 'a break does not in any case necessarily mean a radical destruction of integrity, because a broken integrity can, in many cases, preserve itself in fragments. This means overcoming the negative trend toward irreversible disintegration.' Russian culture thus turns into a palimpsest, where a particular experience is subsequently retained, even if in a latent state, and prepares the grounds for a brand new cultural stage.

This connection to the past at a deeper level, beneath an apparent superficial break, can be observed in the next chapter of the section, 'Marina Tsvetaeva's Poetry as an Embodiment of Russian Cultural Dialectic of Rupture and Continuity', by Sarah Ossipow Cheang. It is devoted to Marina Tsvetaeva, a great Russian poet of the twentieth century, and focuses on her understudied poem 'The Bolshevik' (1921) as an embodiment of rupture that conceals continuity. The chapter points to the 'presence of an explosive impulse, typical of Russian culture, in Tsvetaeva's poetry' that is 'counterbalanced by a very strong attachment to the classical and older traditional forms of literature'. It studies their interaction in Tsvetaeva's oeuvre as epitomized by 'The Bolshevik'. The latter, which is a by-product of Tsvetaeva's work on the epic poem 'Egorushka' (which remained unfinished), is based on the spiritual verses about the folkloric figure Egory the Brave, defender of the people.

The poet's turning to national folklore with its unruly elemental force seems hardly accidental at the time of the tectonic political changes that released the primordial energy of the people. Notably, while Tsvetaeva's leanings were unambiguously with the White Army, she was capable of admiring, in her own words, 'some impeccable living communists'.[39] By this she meant, in particular, the prototype for her 'Egorushka' and 'Bolshevik' – the romantic truth-seeker, Civil War hero, young and handsome communist Boris Bessarabov (1897–1970). Tsvetaeva's ability to rise to the humane principle, having overstepped the boundaries of her sociopolitical class and convictions, is quite remarkable and sends us back to Pushkin's *The Captain's Daughter*, in which exercising this exact principle is what ultimately saves the protagonists. 'Boris, I love it when trees grow straight – you too should

39 Marina Tsvetaeva, from the letter to A. V. Bakhrakh of 9 June 1923, see M. Tsvetaeva, *Sobranie sochinenii v 7 tomakh* (Moscow: Ellis Lak, 1994), Vol. 6, p. 559.

grow into the sky. It is one and the same for all: for the Reds and for the Whites' are her own words addressed to Bessarabov.[40] Furthermore, 'The Bolshevik' evokes many wild rebels of the Russian past as well as folkloric legendary figures, such as Emelian Pugachev, Stepan Razin, Saint George, Sadko, Svyatogor and Ilya Muromets, among others. Tsvetaeva's admiration for the character's natural might and his archaic rootedness in the Russian heroic folklore are combined with portraying the menacing and unconscious power of destruction that he inevitably brings, with the 'prevalence of an elemental and natural principle over a cultural one', as Ossipow Cheang notes in her chapter (which returns us to the aforementioned idea on the violation of culture in the Russian context).

In fact, Tsvetaeva's poem seems a perfect poetic (verbalized) illustration of Boris Kustodiev's 1920 painting of the same name with its ambivalent fusion of mighty power and mass destruction.

As Ossipow Cheang writes, by Tsvetaeva's own admission, she saw in the prototype of the poem's hero 'not only an embodiment of the radically new ideology but also features of the Old Russia', thus creating an 'apparently incompatible mix of the traditional and revolutionary'. In other words, Tsvetaeva, through mythical folkloric allusions, bridged the gap between the country's past and present, and exposed continuity (even if ambivalent and disturbing) in the otherwise explosive and disruptive narrative of a new modernity.

The focus of the next chapter of the volume, 'Creative Personality as an Indicator and Formula for the Discontinuity/Continuity of Culture: Yevgeny Zamyatin' by Larisa V. Polyakova, is another cultural hero of that era, Yevgeny Zamyatin (as it happens, Kustodiev's good friend, who was among the first to see and appreciate the aforementioned ambivalent painting that resonates so strongly with Tsvetaeva's poem). Using Zamyatin's creative path and artistic legacy as a case study leads Polyakova to conclusions of a more general character. The chapter argues that a true artistic discovery is resilient and withstands even an 'explosion' caused by a precise and heavy 'blow' from innovators, by third-party 'attacks' and by

40 *Marina Tsvetaeva–Boris Bessarabov: Khronika 1921 goda v dokumentakh; Dnevniki Ol'gi Bessarabovoi (1915–1925)* (Moscow: Ellis Lak, 2010).

sociopolitical upheavals. Furthermore, it is artistic discoveries, relatively scarce, that stimulate the evolution of literature and create the 'pulse of poetic epochs', while between the extremes of literary history, there are always transitional points of a diverse nature. Polyakova asserts that this seismography, of rare but tangible renewing tremors, is thus not destructive, but constructive.

Methodologically, as the chapter stresses, since creative writing is 'polymorphic and polysemantic, and by its very nature it is doomed to debatable assessments and a priori hypothetical discussions of its history', and 'due to the specific nature of the "cryptogram" of the artistic language', it is hardly possible to write 'authentic, scientific literary history, the history of the art of writing'. However, any work of art is 'a synthesis of previous individual and historical-literary influences' and as such is a result of a collective historical endeavor. This, if you like, ensures continuity par excellence. Thus, as Polyakova writes, 'the history of literature as a cultural phenomenon not only corresponds to the general law of cultural development but also confirms it: discontinuity has a relative, even visible character; continuity is absolute, universal, basic for the dynamics of movement and the accumulation of new aesthetic values', and 'the law of continuity in the art of speech also works in extreme situations'.

Notwithstanding the importance of the cumulative effect of previous artistic generations in cultural history, the chapter insists on the leading role of individual artists in cultural evolution. It is precisely the artistic individuality that is an 'indicator, a tool and a formula, even an emblem; according to Spengler, it is a symbol of the processes of discontinuity/continuity in culture as a whole or at a certain historical stage. It is, in addition to being an intermediate phenomenon in cultural history, the most reliable "island of salvation" from the destruction of culture.'

Zamyatin's life ended in exile from Bolshevik Russia, among other leading cultural figures of Russian emigration who were 'on a mission' to preserve Russian culture in its untarnished form to serve as guarantors of Russian cultural continuity. One of the most famous Russian émigré writers was Vladimir Nabokov, whose novel *Pnin*, perhaps lesser known than many others, resulting from a collection of individual essays, is discussed in the next chapter of the volume, ' "Ah, they'll be driven off to the steppes, my

Harlequins…": Pnin the Wanderer as an Incarnation of Russian *Fin de Siècle* Culture Abroad', by Elena Tchougounova-Paulson.

As Tchougounova-Paulson points out, Nabokov, in his fiction, was forever reinventing his Russianness and resurrecting the old idyllic world of his childhood years in the country that was lost forever after 1917. 'Based upon recollection and relinquishing', she notes that '*Pnin* as a novel is a perfect example of this reinvention'. Importantly, in this novel, 'as in a droplet of water, one can see the interplay of the old and the new or, more precisely, how the cultural offshoots of the Old World find their way in the new one'. As such, we can precisely trace how 'culture perpetuates itself, surviving and perishing at the same time'. The protagonist of this novel, Russian professor Timofey Pavlovich Pnin, working in an American college, is 'an individual with the overwhelming burden of the (crumbling) Old World on his shoulders, who is wandering around the new lands, recollecting – and reinventing – himself altogether, and rebuilding those parts of the fallen universe into something unquestionably new'.

In Tchougounova-Paulson's view, *Pnin* is 'one of the best (if not *the* best) intimate portrayals of the complex metaphysics of the first wave of Russian emigration'. The hero is 'the epitome of a Russian émigré who left his *Oekumene* (i.e., pre-revolutionary Russia) in order to preserve its enduring value in his most precious, long-lasting memories, which can be quite challenging'. Thus, despite all the hardship and emotional martyrdom, despite the need to adjust and conform, the emigrant Pnin, like his creator Nabokov, carries within him the universe of Old Russia and its culture that proved the ultimate personal treasure.

Curiously, the cultural loyalty to the lost Old Russia on the part of the first wave of Russian emigration can be mirrored by processes within the country where a new political regime prevailed. The shredded pieces of the cultural past stealthily found their way into the new reality in a transfigured form, hiding behind the revolutionary changes. One such way of preserving the ethos of the previous epoch was in the transformation of the cultural loci of country estates – traditional hearths of the life of family and friends, those 'gentry nests' elegized by Ivan Turgenev – into new entities compatible with existence under the Soviet regime. They eventually turned into summer houses (*dachas*), popular and common among the Russians – the cultural islands of privacy, if not freedom, close to the elemental forces of nature, full of fresh air, and at the same time giving an illusion of private property in a country where everything was nationalized. Simple folk would enjoy this escape into the countryside, from the urban environment to a peasant-like existence, and for the Soviet *nomenklatura* it was also their exclusive territory of wealth and a mark of high status, separating them from ordinary mortals (recall Aleksandr Galich's and Gennady Shpalikov's lines 'in the countryside there are fences, behind which there are our leaders').[41]

'The Russian estate, as a semiotic phenomenon, is unique. On the one hand, this phenomenon is unparalleled; on the other hand, it undoubtedly exists within the framework of the Western European tradition', as Elena Glukhova writes. Her chapter Cultural Transfer and Continuity: Gothic in the Russian 'Estate Text' examines a specific subset of literary representations of Russian estate culture in transition from the pre-revolutionary to post-revolutionary Russia – namely, it studies the special status of Gothic plots and motives in the 'estate text' of Russian modernism, and explores the mechanisms of adaptation and assimilation by Russian cultural tradition of Gothic-related literary characters and themes, borrowed from Western Europe. In other words, it studies the cultural transfer of Western European Gothic to Russian estate text, thus engaging with the Russian tradition of persistent and complex cultural interactions with Western Europe through the creative appropriation of Western European patterns to be adjusted to the Russian context.

Interestingly, while there are nostalgic portrayals of estate narrative in cinema, most notably in Nikita Mikhalkov's films, they are not drawing on Western European examples, and thus are not of Gothic nature, and in Soviet literature, the Gothic in the country estate depictions largely migrates to detective story genre, mostly for children. However, a different picture can be observed in the Russian émigré literature, which the chapter also explores, where the elements of the Gothic mode of estate text are preserved.

41 A. Galich and G. Shpalikov, 'Za sem'iu zaborami', see <http://www.bards.ru/archives/part.php?id=4162> (Accessed 12 February 2022).

The chapter thus traces the transformations of the country estate Gothic during the last two centuries, when it absorbs folklore together with nobility's esoterics, in line with Russian psychological novel, while simultaneously following the literary trends of the time. From Romanticism to Symbolism, through plots of mass literature about vampires and ghosts to the children's detective stories of the Soviet time, it finally transforms into a contemporary meta-historical novel.

The last chapter of this section, 'Continuities and Discontinuities of Russian Culture through the Prism of Turgenev's *Fathers and Sons*', by Vladimir Golstein, essentially takes us back to the roots of the Russian country estate culture and rounds up the discussion of cultural continuity theme in Russian literature by exploring the generational conflict and its resolution in Turgenev's *Fathers and Sons*.

Notably, Golstein provides an assessment of Turgenev's classical work from a modern historical-literary perspective, where the Silver Age perception of Russian classical literature plays a major role. As he argues in his multifaceted analysis of the novel, a real, genuine cultural continuity is achievable only through a profound rift, a revolt of a Prodigal Son against his parents, which ultimately leads one back to the parental hearth, but only via a path of suffering and hardship, by learning one's lessons 'the hard way'. In other words, one cultural wave necessarily has to give way to a counter-wave, before the pendulum swings back and allows for further development. The choice of Turgenev is significant here, in the debate about culture, as this writer 'after Pushkin is almost the sole genius of measure and, therefore, a genius of culture',[42] in the words of Dmitry Merezhkovsky (a major figure on the Silver Age scene) that Golstein cites. In the footsteps of Merezhkovsky (and the Silver Age more generally), Golstein also refers back to the Golden Age of Russian culture, with Aleksandr Pushkin as its epicenter. Using the poet as an ultimate cultural standard, he proceeds to demonstrate the covert presence of Pushkin in Turgenev's work and in his entire worldview, and considers Pushkin's role as a symbol of cultural continuity, of harmony and natural rhythms.

42 D. S. Merezhkovsky, *Vechnye sputniki* (Moscow: Nauka, 2007), p. 692.

Within the study of the generational conflict, Golstein uncovers a whole network of polemical discussions, including the writer's relationship with his artistic fathers and with the cultural tradition in general. He demonstrates that Turgenev, similar to his character Arkady Kirsanov, 'chooses the continuity of tradition over the discontinuity of rebellion' and feels obliged 'to highlight the obvious and fundamental link that connects generations, namely, language and culture'. At the same time, Golstein emphasizes Turgenev's own uneasy oscillations between Romanticism and Realism, individualism and 'holism', and the novelist's ambivalence with respect to nihilism, radicalism and individualism more generally: his sympathy toward an individual heroic tour-de-force, and yet his profound doubts about 'the very ability of individualist heroes to function within a complex social and cultural framework, a network of mutual obligations and creative reworking of tradition'.

The reference to Pushkin in the chapter on Turgenev as a guarantee of harmony and cultural continuity resonates with the next chapter titled 'The Problem of Continuity in S. I. Taneev's Views on the Future of Russian Music', by Galima Lukina, on the composer Sergei Taneev, where a similar reference is made to Glinka. Indeed, both Aleksandr Pushkin and Mikhail Glinka are often regarded as two commensurable Russian geniuses: one in literature, the other in music. Both drew on Western European patterns, enriching these with specifically Russian national spirit. Such Russian synthesis resulting from creative appropriation was also at the center of Taneev's musical preoccupations, as Lukina points out, emphasizing that 'Taneev considered himself to be as good as a successor of the work started by Glinka who put together a "program" for creating national music'. For Taneev, 'the distinguishing characteristic of the Russian style should be a harmonious combination of Russian and European principles, possible, for example, in the form of a "Russian fugue" or an "Orthodox cantata"'.

Lukina's chapter opens the concluding section of the volume that moves from literature to performing arts in an exploration of cultural continuity, and in the case of music such continuity is perfectly embodied in the teaching and creative legacy of Sergei Taneev, as the chapter persuasively demonstrates. In the composer's striving to the eternal spiritual values and overcoming what he saw as European hedonistic tendencies that lead to civilizational crisis, he 'developed a concept according to which Russian composers can "on the one hand, contribute to the growth of the European tree, but on the other hand, cultivate [their] own crops"'.

Taneev's ideas highly resonate with the cultural theories of many Russian philosophical thinkers of the time and echo the Slavophile–Westernizer debates. Active in the cultural sphere like many of his contemporaries, Taneev wished to strengthen and develop the national basis of Russian art, to preserve its spiritual sources, which, in the musical realm, he saw in church music. As Lukina puts it, 'Through his selfless devotion, Taneev preserved and strengthened the ethos of Russian culture in order to keep art connected with its innermost spiritual source – namely, the creativity of the Russian people.' At that, he echoed the ideas of the early Slavophile Alexei Khomyakov who believed that 'the artist does not create on their own; it is the spiritual power of the nation in the artist that creates'.[43]

The example of Sergei Taneev, as presented by Lukina, can be usefully juxtaposed to the conclusion of the previous chapter by Golstein that 'true continuity is achieved only by overcoming discontinuity', as modifying its restrictive character. Indeed, as Lukina demonstrates, Taneev, at the risk of being viewed as outdated, quite consciously adhered to traditional forms, seeing in them some universal principles that by themselves ensure cultural continuity. His alleged 'non-modernity' with respect to the innovative Silver Age aesthetics can thus be explained by his striving to the eternal, by the conviction that human salvation is concealed precisely in preserving the traditional, in 'preservation of traditions and transfer of artistic achievements across generations, due to which deep transcendental connection of cultural experience is translated through time'.

The theme of the Silver Age is continued in the next chapter, 'Silver Age Aesthetics versus New Conceptions of Soviet Time in Music: Continuity or Discontinuity with the Past?', by Elena Artamonova, which propels it to early Soviet times, uncovering some unexpected cultural parallels, in the realm of music and beyond, between these two periods, usually deemed as culturally disjoint. Indeed, the post-revolutionary Russia that drew a

43 Alexei Khomyakov, 'O vozmozhnosti russkoi khudozhestvennoi shkoly' (1847), *Polnoe sobranie sochinenii* (Moscow, 1861), Vol. 1, p. 414.

sharp line over the past and craved new aesthetics to celebrate the birth of a new – proletarian – state did not welcome the art of the Silver Age, which was created by the condemned social class and deemed decadent. In the musical sphere, as Artamonova writes, 'this formal renunciation of everything connected to the past laid foundations for the appearance of new tendencies and experiments in music, which in the words of one of the most unconventional composers of the avant-garde, Nikolai Roslavets, "dreamt of new unheard worlds of sound" '.[44] In her chapter, she seeks to answer the question of whether composers really broke with the pre-revolutionary tradition or skillfully adjusted and modified their language according to the requirements of the new musical era.

Drawing on unpublished and little-researched materials from Moscow archives, including the under-researched writings of Alexei Losev on music, Artamonova reveals a common conceptual ground between the aesthetics of the Silver Age and the avant-garde, and traces how the old was adopted by the new. Artamonova finds a 'striking resemblance between the ideologies of the classes in Russian society' and argues that it was 'the main reason why many scholars, writers, composers and musicians initially supported the Socialist Revolution or at least maintained political neutrality, despite the unprecedented scale of brutality of that time'.

Artamonova's chapter concludes that the legacy of the previous generations of artists, including writers, musicians and philosophers, 'guided and directed new ideas as well as modified and reshaped conceptions that had a great impact on the Russian cultural heritage' of the post-revolutionary period.

This, often non-obvious, even covert, continuity between the two artistic worlds – of Tsarist and Bolshevik Russia – is also the focus of the next chapter, by Natalia Skorokhod, who demonstrates how a play by the popular pre-revolutionary writer Leonid Andreev (d. 1919) influenced a cinematic production by the legendary Soviet film director Sergei Eisenstein.

44 Nikolai Andreevich Roslavets, 'N.A. Roslavets o sebe i svoem tvorchestve' [Nikolai Roslavets on Himself and His Creativity], *Sovremennaia muzyka*, No. 5 (14 January 1924), p. 133.

She reiterates how the Soviet avant-garde of the 1920s (the so-called October Age) was for a long time erroneously associated with denying the heritage of both classical Russian culture and the Silver Age. As she writes, 'today there is no doubt that the political and social revolution, which interrupted the natural development of the art of the Silver Age, in fact, could not protect artists from the influence of certain previously created ideas and works'. Her chapter, which is appropriately entitled 'The Old Roots of the New Era: From Leonid Andreev to Sergei Eisenstein, the Unknown Connection', reveals some remarkable links between the play by Leonid Andreev *Tsar Golod* (King Hunger, 1907) and the first full-length film by Sergei Eisenstein *Stachka* (The Strike, 1925). Building on the idea from film studies with her own theatre research results and illuminating archival findings, Skorokhod makes a convincing case by uncovering similarities between the two works at multiple levels.

More generally, as the chapter argues, it was not only Futurism but also Symbolism and Acmeism – of the Silver Age artistic movements – that strongly influenced the theatre and literature of 1920s Soviet art. Furthermore, the idea of *sobornost* (a spiritual community), developed by Russian nineteenth-century philosophers from Alexei Khomyakov to Vladimir Solovyov, was in fact borrowed by the theoreticians of the new proletarian culture. Skorokhod's chapter, which can be viewed as another contribution to modern research in 'Russian Expressionism', demonstrates that 'the aesthetic foundation of revolutionary Soviet art began to form long before the historical cataclysm of 1917', thus providing one more argument for Russian cultural continuity concealed behind the evident rupture.

What emerges from the above is the idea of art developing in accordance with its own intrinsic inner laws rooted in national as well as international traditions rather than springing from the imposed political-ideological agenda. As a result, art proves more resilient to political change than it may seem, even though it does respond to ideological pressures in a variety of ways.

The next chapter, 'The Phoenix's Rebirth from Its Ashes: Russian Dance in the Twentieth Century', by Elena Yushkova, engages with this theme by studying the interplay between art and politics in connection with the Russian history of dance. As she explains, 'interactions between dance and politics became an object of study for academic research in the 1990s', yielding substantial results in 'conceptualizing how such relations work' and 'analyzing many examples from world dance history'. However, in Russia, dance studies became a separate discipline only in the last decade, and a thorough examination 'of relationships between politics and dance in Russia and the Soviet Union' is still in the making. Yushkova's chapter elucidates the validity and promise of such research, and sets conceptual frameworks for it. In particular, she refers to different periodizations of dance history in Russia, depending on the chosen approach, and distinguishes between the treatment of the subject by ballet historians and those studying non-classical dance, as well as various social and cultural studies theories, where dance is studied, in particular, as a means of resistance or compliance. In order to trace 'how traditions and breaks have created such unique phenomena as Russian classical and non-classical dance', the chapter then provides a brief analytical overview of the history of classical ballet, non-classical (free) dance and contemporary dance in the Russian context.

Yushkova concludes that 'dance history in Russia in the twentieth century is a great example of cultural continuity that, despite all attempts of the state to break traditions in favor of ideology or state interests or to establish new aesthetic norms and canons, has never been really interrupted. Like a phoenix, it has always risen from the ashes and continues to develop.'

Her chapter, which illuminates the ideological pressures on art in the Russian cultural history of the last century, lays bare the role of the state in artistic development not only domestically, but also internationally. It is perhaps commonplace that any state politics uses art for cultural diplomacy, not to say cultural expansionism. In pragmatic terms, Lyudmil Dimitrov, the author of the next chapter, 'Russian Drama of the Twentieth Century as an Imported Commodity: The Transgression of Transfer', which focuses on Russian theatre, writes, 'the purpose of the nation is to create and reproduce a common cultural identity for all citizens of the country for the benefit of their political interests, and the drama – according to Hegel's definition – is "a product of the already developed national life within itself"'.[45] In the case of Russia, due to its size, imperial history and impressive artistic potential, Russian art has been exported to the world on a massive scale and has made a distinctive cultural impact on other countries near and far.

Such an encounter, however, is invariably a double-edged sword, and Russian culture, though strategically facilitating such cultural transfer, would simultaneously be shaped by it. In order to research the process of Russian cultural interaction with the outside world through exporting its artistic products, Dimitrov is preoccupied with the question of how international theatre managed to indirectly problematize the notions of Russian-as-one's-own and one's-own-as-Russian at the close of the twentieth and beginning of the twenty-first centuries, in interpreting nineteenth-century plays, mainly by Chekhov.

In particular, he is interested to see why it is predominantly Chekhov (from several Russian playwrights) who seems to survive such cultural transfer most successfully, while in the field of literature, there are at least two more names – of Tolstoy and Dostoevsky – that remain equally popular worldwide. Operating within the contemporary post-drama theatre amid the crisis of personal and group identities, Dimitrov constructs a framework of conceptual premises to do with cultural transfer more broadly, while keeping Russian theatre in focus, and then applies these to the case studies of Bulgarian, Hungarian and Croatian theatrical productions.

The theme of turning to the nineteenth-century Russian classical canon in twenty-first-century reality is continued in the last chapter of the volume, 'Russian Classics in the Mirror of Vasily Sigarev's Remakes', by Margarita Odesskaya, who explores the tendency for producing remakes of Russian classical literature for the modern Russian stage. The case study for her analysis is the work by the contemporary Russian playwright and stage director Vasily Sigarev, born in 1977.

Popular and successful on the Russian cultural scene of today, Sigarev is nevertheless a rather controversial figure and in many ways an instructive symptom of modern culture, not only in Russia but globally as well. In his case, we are dealing with a tendency, with an opposition of two fundamental

45 G. W. F. Hegel, *Sochineniia* (Moscow, 1940), Vol. 13, p. 331.

movements: of 'traditionalists' and 'innovators', in line with the theories of cultural evolution described above. This opposition in the Russian context is as powerful as that between Slavophiles and Westernizers (although distinct from it, but not necessarily disjoint). While crucial for ensuring cultural continuity, tradition can become stifling without the fresh blood of renovation. However, the avant-garde experimentation can be deceptive and even harmful if its nature is self-serving rather than culturally enriching. In scholarly terms, it is important to problematize this phenomenon, to ensure that a voice is given to a diversity of opinions (which also increases the appeal of such a discussion to the readers – with whom after all the ultimate judgment on the cultural production lies).

Between the old and the new: Dangerous traps of modernity

Literary history is akin to history per se, where studying the past helps humankind understand and make sense of its present. This is especially pertinent during times of abrupt historical rifts accompanied by profound changes in cultural paradigms and reassessment of the old values. In this sense, as Odesskaya notes, 'literary remake appears to be one of the ways of reevaluating the cultural inheritance of the past, of demythifying'. Drawing on the ideas of Yuri Lotman, mentioned above, she views remake as representing 'the structural model of a text within a text', where 'a new contemporary text [...] intervenes in the old canonized text of one particular era', facilitating the 'transfer from one system of semiotic realization of the text into another', leading to generating new meanings. She remarks that at the end of the twentieth century when the 'socialist' paradigm rapidly collapsed, literary remakes have played 'a significant role in reactualizing cultural values, interpreting and reinterpreting classical examples in modern times'.

One can recall in this connection famous literary remakes of previous epochs – for instance, Ivan Krylov's creative appropriation of La Fontaine's and Lessing's fables as a conscious opposition to the rationalism of the Enlightenment, where Krylov, who 'favoured instead a cheerful scepticism of the folk worldview',[46] 'opposed the wisdom of a proverb to the wisdom of ideologues'.[47] If for La Fontaine the moral was the soul of a fable that he tried to free from banality, Krylov, on the contrary, made fun of the very banality of the moral, thus overcoming 'not only La Fontaine's rationalism, but a rational logic of the global cultural development as such'.[48] Stretching it, one could even venture to say that Pushkin's borrowings from European literature and acculturating them on Russian soil could also be attributed to remakes (of European literary patterns). The keyword for such endeavors, however, is the aforementioned generating of new meanings, while adapting – with a touch of genius – the old texts to the new/different sociocultural contexts. The danger of postmodernism is that more often than not it has served to destroy the old meanings and ideals just for the sake of destruction, without any positive, redeeming agenda, without any 'motion of one's soul' that alone deserves to be made into art.[49] In post-Soviet Russia, with the total collapse of the communist ideology that discredited itself by all-pervasive hypocrisy, the tendency for humiliation, skepticism and grotesque in artistic and other discourses became overwhelming. Such a tendency is not new and often accompanies great political turmoil with the inevitable paradigmatic cultural shifts. As Vladimir Tunimanov wrote about Aleksandr Blok's essay 'Irony' of 1908, for Blok 'the age was marked by a universal epidemic of destructive irony', the irony that is 'the bite of a vampire'.[50]

What is more, in post-Soviet Russia, this dangerously coincided with the market economy, commercializing literature and the arts, and resulting in the devaluation of old values. High artistic standards were no longer the leading criterion, having been replaced by commercial mechanisms and often resulting

46 *Russkaia poeziia 1801–1812*, ed. A. Arkhangelsky and A. Nemzer (Moscow: Khudozhestvennaia Literatura, 1989), pp. 369–370.

47 Averintsev, *Sviaz vremen*.

48 Ibid.

49 These are the words of Fazil Iskander. The precise quotation reads thus: 'Only a motion of the soul is worthy of words, only that deserves to be expressed by the means of art'. See <http://www.sergeydovlatov.ru/?cnt=1> (Accessed 11 February 2022).

50 Vladimir Tunimanov, 'Yevgeny Zamiatin: The Art of Irony', in *Reflective Laughter: Aspects of Humour in Russian Culture*, ed. Lesley Milne (London: Anthem, 2004), p. 110.

in creative poverty. This paradox of having the ability to produce masterpieces under a totalitarian regime and displaying artistic impotence under political liberty has been noted numerous times in scholarship.[51] Amplifying the dark, low facets of life in Russia became a profitable trend in the early perestroika years, bringing its authors international fame and prestige, and lucrative awards. An array of talented Russian artists fell prey to this easy temptation, dragging the artistic down to the profane, to catering for basic instincts. In addition to such self-serving sensationalist behavior there was also a new trend of seemingly noble orientation: to simplify the artistic sphere in order to attract the new generation, debauched by the commercial (as well as – nowadays – virtual) reality, back to culture. In this vein, the works of Russian classics were sometimes modified to suit the new 'lowered', taste, as a compromise alternative to their total oblivion. However, deliberately lowering your standards is a risky business, as art does not forgive a betrayal of its high ideals.

In this respect, Vasily Sigarev has an ambiguous reputation. His plays and films are filled with obscene vocabulary, and present the 'dark reality' of contemporary Russia, namely, the depictions of the downside of life. By Sigarev's own admission, his first encounter with literature was through reading Stephen King, whose works, he now believes, should be taught in Russian school instead of those by classical writers.[52] Similarly, his first encounter with theatre was through attending his own staged play (a remake of Pushkin's *Blizzard* discussed in Odesskaya's chapter), while by the time of entering the Theatre Institute in Ekaterinburg he had read only a single play – Chekhov's *The Cherry Orchard*.[53] Sigarev interprets such innocence as a bonus that helps him not to be swayed by the old cultural patterns. It is, however, clear that he has at least read enough to create remakes. Such a bravado of ignorance fits in well with his authorial image of deliberately low aesthetics and exploiting the bleak lumpen themes. He thus consciously

51 See, for example, one of the first such works: Aleksander Ivashkin, 'The Paradox of Russian Non-Liberty', *The Musical Quarterly*, Vol. 76, No. 4 (1992), pp. 543–556.

52 See Vasilii Sigarev, Interview, 31 October 2013: 'Obychnaia levitatsiia', <https://seance.ru/articles/sigarev_interview/> (Accessed 11 February 2022).

53 See Vasilii Sigarev, Interview, 21 May 2003: 'Ya prosto rasskazyvaiu o strastiakh i bedakh chelovecheskikh', <http://www.teatr.ru/docs/tpl/doc.asp?id=605> (Accessed 11 February 2022).

propagates literary discontinuity while engaging in remaking the old and traditional classical works – the focus of Odesskaya's chapter. At the same time, Sigarev, as she notes, is 'one of the leading Russian playwrights and stage directors' of contemporary Russia, distinguished by many prestigious awards, and, one might add, with a huge following of admirers. However, another cult figure of the contemporary Russian literary scene, Zakhar Prilepin, who constantly fights for preserving the traditional moral and aesthetic values while expressing controversial political views, criticized Sigarev precisely for exploiting low truths in order to pursue his (Sigarev's) own selfish ends. In Prilepin's opinion, Sigarev belongs to the multitude of contemporary artists who are to blame for destroying the very foundations and principles on which art rests and who quite deliberately ruin the traditional values and violate human dignity: 'An attempt to lower the bar as much as possible and condone collective vulgarity seems to me disgusting, and insulting to the role of the creator in art. You cannot do it this way! I find this deeply immoral and vile. What's going on in our film industry? Some of the leaders condone the so-called Western awards system – and all this black bile of Sigarev begins. Others indulge in the meanness of human nature – all these dialogues, all these scenes, all this "junk food" of base comedy just twists the mind, I begin to physically hate the people who do it.'[54]

More examples of bitterness and anger in the face of the new Russian cultural reality, as opposed (paradoxically) to the artistic paragons of the Soviet era, despite its ideological constraints, can be found on the part of many artists of the older generation. Thus, Yuri Solomin, famous Russian actor and director, and former Russian Minister of Culture, laments the current state of affairs in art, exclaiming, 'I am a categorical opponent of distorting classical works on stage. You cannot crush the classics to adjust their works to suit yourself [...] Respect them, try to understand, and it's not so easy! Staging classical works and adjusting them to suit your own needs is your choice, but this is rape, and it should be punished as a criminal

54 Zakhar Prilepin, 'My ne dolzhny rastit' kollektivnogo khama...', Interview, 2 March 2021, <https://www.mosfilm.ru/news/?ELEMENT_ID=49860> (Accessed 15 February 2022).

offence.'[55] Such highly charged rhetoric demonstrates the burning nature and extreme relevance of these debates in contemporary Russia, and is, in fact, indicative of similar processes worldwide.

However, the very fact that Russian classical literature continues to serve as the foundation of Russian culture – even if possibly in a distorted way, even if for entertainment rather than contemplation, and even as a material for irony and ridicule – is still a sign of cultural continuity, an indication that, one way or another, we are not parting with our cultural pillars. As the latter have acquired a sacred status in Russian cultural history, the situation with the above distortion may seem reminiscent of that with Russian laughter culture, which can be viewed as an opposition to the sacred, a conscious defiance of religious values, that is, a deliberate sin committed without losing piety.[56] As L. A. Trakhtenberg writes in this connection, 'this is a conscious sacrilege which does not disavow the sacred, but instead only confirms its immutability'.[57]

***

Taken collectively, the chapters of the volume, in their different ways, reveal a complicated picture of Russian cultural continuity, rediscovering it behind the rupture in the country's entangled and seemingly explosive cultural history. It is hoped that this collective effort will meaningfully contribute to the continuing development of this complex but rewarding field of research. As Anton Chekhov wrote in one of his most cherished stories: 'The past [...] is linked with the present by an unbroken chain of events flowing one out of another. And it seemed to him that he had just seen both ends of that chain; that when he touched one end the other

55 Interview given by Yurii Solomin to the journal *Teatral*, 4 July 2012, No. 7–8 (96), <https://teatral-online.ru/news/7097/> (Accessed 12 February 2022).

56 See on this Yurii Lotman and Boris Uspensky, 'Novye aspekty izucheniia kultury Drevnei Rusi', *Voprosy literatury*, Vol. 3 (1977), p. 156.

57 Lev Trakhtenberg, 'K istorii izucheniia russkoi smekhovoi kul'tury', in *Russkoe literaturovedenie XX veka: imena, shkoly, kontseptsii*, ed. Oleg Kling and Alexei Kholikov (Moscow: Nestor-Istoriia, 2012), pp. 163–171; p. 168.

quivered.'[58] The work on this book has given us the opportunity to experience this magic connectedness, and we are thrilled to share this experience with our readers.

Bibliography

Adamsky, Dmitry, 'Continuity in Russian Strategic Culture: A Case Study of Moscow's Syrian Campaign', The George C. Marshall European Center for Security Studies, 2020, <https://www.marshallcenter.org/en/publications/security-insights/continuity-russian-strategic-culture-case-study-moscows-syrian-campaign-0> (Accessed 25 February 2022).

Arnason, Johann, 'The Cultural Turn and the Civilizational Approach', *European Journal of Social Theory*, Vol. 13, No. 1 (March 2010), pp. 67–82.

Averintsev, Sergei, *Sviaz vremen* (*Sobranie sochinenii*), 2004, <http://www.fedy-diary.ru/html/042011/11042011-05a.html> (Accessed 17 January 2022).

Berdyaev, Nicolas, *The Origin of Russian Communism*, translated from the Russian by R. M. French [1937] (London: Geoffrey Bles, 1948).

Chekhov, Anton, 'The Student', <http://www.free-short-stories.org.uk/anton-chekhov-the-student.htm> (Accessed 14 February 2022).

Chumakova, Tatiana, 'Irrationalism in Ancient Russia', in *Facets of Russian Irrationalism between Art and Life. Mystery Inside Enigma*, ed. Olga Tabachnikova (Leiden: Brill, 2016), pp. 72–93.

During, Simon, *Cultural Studies: A Critical Introduction* (Abingdon: Routledge, 2005).

Etkind, Aleksander, 'Psychological Culture: Ambivalence and Resistance to Social Change', *Russian Culture at the Crossroads*, ed. D. N. Shalin, 2012, pp. 99–126, <https://digitalscholarship.unlv.edu/russian_culture/5> (Accessed 14 March 2023).

Fairclough, Pauline, and Philip Bullock, *1917 and Beyond: Continuity, Rupture and Memory in Russian Music*, MHRA *Slavonic and East European Review*, Vol. 97, No. 1 (2019).

Galich, A., and G. Shpalikov, 'Za sem'iu zaborami', <http://www.bards.ru/archives/part.php?id=4162> (Accessed 12 February 2022).

58 Anton Chekhov, 'The Student', <http://www.free-short-stories.org.uk/anton-chekhov-the-student.htm> (Accessed 14 February 2022).

Geertz, Clifford, *The Interpretation of Cultures* (New York: Basic Books, 1973).

Grossman, Vasily, *Zhizn' i sud'ba*, <http://lib.ru/PROZA/GROSSMAN/lifefate.txt> (Accessed 10 February 2022).

Hahn, Jeffrey W., 'Continuity and Change in Russian Political Culture', *British Journal of Political Science*, Vol. 21 (1991), pp. 393–421.

Hegel, G. W. F., *Sochineniia* (Moscow, 1940), Vol. 13.

Herzen, Alexander, Letter to Jules Michelet of 22 September 1851, <https://pages.uoregon.edu/kimball/Hzn-Michelet.htm> (Accessed 27 January 2022).

Ivanov, Viacheslav, and Mikhail Gershenzon, *Perepiska iz dvukh uglov* (St. Petersburg: Alkonost, 1921).

Ivashkin, Alexander, 'The Paradox of Russian Non-Liberty', *Musical Quarterly*, Vol. 76, No. 4, 1992, pp. 543–556.

Kellner, Douglas M., and Meenakshi Gigi Durham, 'Adventures in Media and Cultural Studies: Introducing the Key Works', in *Media and Cultural Studies: Key Works*, ed. D. M. Kellner and M. G. Durham (Oxford: Blackwell, 2006), pp. ix–xxxviii.

Khomyakov, Alexei, 'O vozmozhnosti russkoi khudozhestvennoi shkoly' (1847), *Polnoe sobranie sochinenii* (Moscow, 1861), Vol. 1.

Kireevsky, Ivan, 'O neobkhodimosti i vozmozhnosti novykh nachal dlia filosofii' (1856) in I. V. Kireevsky, *Polnoe sobranie sochinenii v dvukh tomakh*, ed. M. Gershenzon [Moscow, 1911] (Farnborough, Hampshire: Gregg International, 1970).

Likhachev, Dmitry, *Izbrannye raboty*, 3 vols (Leningrad: Khudozhestvennaia literatura, 1987).

——— 'Religion: Russian Orthodoxy', in *The Cambridge Companion to Modern Russian Culture*, ed. Nicholas Rzhevsky (Cambridge: Cambridge University Press, 1998).

Lotman, Yuri, *Kultura i vzryv* (Moscow: Gnozis, 1992).

——— and Boris Uspensky, 'Novye aspekty izucheniia kultury Drevnei Rusi', *Voprosy literatury*, Vol. 3 (1977).

Merezhkovsky, D. S., *Vechnye sputniki* (Moscow: Nauka, 2007).

Pervushina, O. V., 'Kul'turnaia preemstvennost', kul'turnaia pamiat' i traditsiia: sootnoshenie poniatii kak kul'turologicheskaia problema', *Mir nauki, kul'tury, obrazovaniia*, Vol. 26, No. 1, pp. 324–328.

Prilepin, Zakhar, 'My ne dolzhny rastit' kollektivnogo khama…', Interview, 2 March 2021, <https://www.mosfilm.ru/news/?ELEMENT_ID=49860> (Accessed 15 February 2022).

Roslavets, Nikolai Andreevich, 'N.A. Roslavets o sebe i svoem tvorchestve' [Nikolai Roslavets on Himself and His Creativity], *Sovremennaia muzyka*, No. 5 (14 January 1924).

Russkaia poeziia 1801–1812, ed. A. Arkhangelsky and A. Nemzer (Moscow: Khudozhestvennaia Literatura, 1989).

Saltykov-Shchedrin, Mikhail, 'Protivorechiia', in *Sobranie Sochinenii v 20 tomakh* (Moscow: Khudozhestvennaia Literatura, 1965), Vol. 1, pp. 73–74.

Schloezer, Boris, 'Russkii spor o kul'ture: Viacheslav Ivanov i M. O. Gershenzon, "Perepiska iz dvukh uglov"', *Sovremennye Zapiski*, Vol. 11 (1922), pp. 195–211.

Schmemann, Father Alexander, *Osnovy russkoi kul'tury: Besedy na Radio Svoboda. 1970–1971*, compiled by E. Yu. Dorman (Moscow: Publishers of the Russian Orthodox Sviato-Tikhonovsky University for the Humanities, 2017).

Shalin, Dmitrii, 'Introduction: Continuity and Change in Russian Culture', in *Russian Culture at the Crossroads: Paradoxes of Postcommunist Consciousness*, ed. D. N. Shalin (New York and Abingdon: Routledge, 2018 [1996]), pp. 1–10.

Shemiakina, Olga, 'Razryv i preemstvennost' v russkoi kul'turnoi traditsii: Opyt dialoga', *Obshchestvennye nauki i sovremennost'*, No. 1 (2001), pp. 106–116.

Shestov, Lev, 'All Things Are Possible' ('Apotheosis of Groundlessness'), <https://www.angelfire.com/nb/shestov/all/all_23.html> (Accessed 26 January 2022).

——— 'Anton Chekhov. Creation from the Void', <https://www.angelfire.com/nb/shestov/all/pw_1.html> (Accessed 12 February 2022).

Sigarev, Vasilii, 'Obychnaia levitatsiia', Interview, 31 October 2013, <https://seance.ru/articles/sigarev_interview/> (Accessed 11 February 2022).

——— 'Ya prosto rasskazyvaiu o strastiakh i bedakh chelovecheskikh', Interview, 21 May 2003, <http://www.teatr.ru/docs/tpl/doc.asp?id=605> (Accessed 11 February 2022).

Solomin, Yurii, Interview, 4 July 2012, *Teatral*, No. 7–8 (96), <https://teatral-online.ru/news/7097/> (Accessed 12 February 2022).

Trakhtenberg, Lev, 'K istorii izucheniia russkoi smekhovoi kul'tury', in *Russkoe literaturovedenie XX veka: imena, shkoly, kontseptsii*, ed. Oleg Kling and Alexei Kholikov (Moscow: Nestor-Istoriia, 2012), pp. 163–171.

Tsvetaeva, Marina, *Marina Tsvetaeva–Boris Bessarabov: Khronika 1921 goda v dokumentakh; Dnevniki Ol'gi Bessarabovoi (1915–1925)* (Moscow: Ellis Lak, 2010).

——— *Sobranie sochinenii v 7 tomakh* (Moscow: Ellis Lak, 1994), Vol. 6.

Tunimanov, Vladimir, 'Yevgeny Zamiatin: The Art of Irony', in *Reflective Laughter: Aspects of Humour in Russian Culture*, ed. Lesley Milne (London: Anthem, 2004).

Tyutchev, Fedor, 'Umom Rossiiu ne poniat', 1866, <http://rupoem.ru/tyutchev/all.aspx#umom-rossiyu-ne> (Accessed 10 February 2022) (Russian: 'Умом Россию не понять…').

Voloshin, Maximilian, *Neopalimaia kupina*, <http://az.lib.ru/w/woloshin_m_a/text_0096.shtml> (Accessed 10 July 2023). Lib.ru/Классика: Волошин Максимилиан Александрович. Неопалимая купина).

White, Stephen, 'Continuity and Change in Soviet Political Culture: An Emigre Study', *Comparative Political Studies*, Vol. 11, No. 3 (1978), <https://journals.sagepub.com/doi/10.1177/001041407801100305> (Accessed 25 February 2022).

Wimsatt, William C., 'Articulating Babel: A Conceptual Geography for Cultural Evolution', in *Beyond the Meme: Development and Structure in Cultural Evolution*, ed. A. C. Love and W. C. Wimsatt (Minneapolis: University of Minnesota Press, 2019), pp. 1–41.

Worth, Dean S., 'Language', in *The Cambridge Companion to Modern Russian Culture* (Cambridge: Cambridge University Press, 1998), pp. 19–37

Yeremenko, Aleksandr, 'Gorizontal'naia strana,' 1987, (Accessed 10 February 2014) (Russian: 'Горизонтальная страна').

Zapesotsky, A. S., and V. G. Lukianov, 'Dmitri Likhachev: O sushchnosti kul'turnoi traditsii', *Voprosy kul'turologii*, Vol. 7 (2007), pp. 4–12.

PART I

Russian History as Ideological Narrative: Continuities and Breaks

OLHA CHERVINSKA AND ALEKSANDR SYCH

1 Historical Background of Russian Literature

The distinctive character of Russian history is determined primarily by its geographical location between different poles of civilization and by the choice of its own ideological path, which is rightly recognized as 'a constantly acting factor that determines the ways of its development, sometimes spontaneously and unconsciously even for culture, and sometimes openly and even emphatically'.[1] In the first centuries of its Christian history, which is covered in the 'Tale of Bygone Years' (about 1113) with the description of the so-called test of faith[2] and a great awareness of the geography of the lands of the Russian principalities, the country was in the zone of influence of the Byzantine civilization, which, according to Archpriest John Meyendorff, 'always lacked the consistency and dynamism inherent in both Western scholasticism and the Western Renaissance.[3] The main cultural achievement of this period, as is known, was the assimilation of the book tradition on the basis of Cyrillic writing, which resulted in the emergence of a culture of chronicling (see numerous works of Dmitry Likhachev and the school of his followers),[4] while a detached and, perhaps, quite a skeptical

1 Yuri Lotman, 'Modern Times between the East and the West', *Znamya*, Vol. 9 (1997).
2 'The Tale of Bygone Years', in *Ipatiev Chronicle: Complete Collection of Russian Chronicles* (St. Petersburg, 1908), Vol. 2, col. 89–112.
3 John Meyendorff, *Byzantine Theology: Historical Trends and Doctrinal Themes* (Minsk: Luchi Sofii, 2007), p. 79.
4 For instance, D. A. Balovnev, 'The Tale of "the Initial Spread of Christianity across Rus". An Attempt at Critical Analysis', in *The Church in the History of Russia* (Moscow, 2000), Vol. 4, pp. 5–46.

view of the borrowed heritage was already present at this stage of culture.[5]

After the gradual disintegration of Byzantium over many centuries in the confrontation with the Ottomans and the fall of Constantinople on 29 May 1453, which has been depicted almost minute by minute by historical scholarship,[6] Russia readily accepted the mantle of the Byzantine heritage, considering itself its spiritual successor, conceptually expressed by the well-known formula 'Moscow – the third Rome'. The main aesthetic principles of the Byzantine church tradition (long before the beginning of the Christianization of Rus in 988) were formulated by the fathers of the Eastern Church, first of all, St. Augustine, John of Damascus and the Greek psalmists;[7] for a long time its influence predetermined all the main directions of the future forms of Russian classical art – from the architecture of church buildings to literature as such, the beginning of which was laid by the spiritual associate of Yaroslav the Wise, the first Russian Metropolitan of Kievan Rus', Hilarion (second half of the eleventh century)[8] through his works, in particular 'the Sermon on Law and Grace' that exists in numerous copies. In the future, the ethnic traces of the Russian culture remained exclusively in the sphere of folklore, the influence of which on Russian culture became more active only at the turn of the eighteenth to nineteenth century, most openly and programmatically visible in the culture of modernity, leaving a trace in the music of the early twentieth century under the name 'new folklore wave'.

5 G. V. Markelov, 'Humorous Postscripts in the Manuscripts of Pushkin House Archives', *Proceedings of the Department of Old Russian Literature*, Vol. 41 (Leningrad: Nauka, 1988), pp. 444–446; p. 446.

6 See Steven Runciman, *The Fall of Constantinople, 1453* (Cambridge: Cambridge University Press, 1965); translated from English by L. B. Petrusheva (Moscow, 2008).

7 See John of Damascus, *An Exact Explanation of Orthodox Faith* (Moscow: Lodiya, 2002); Archbishop Filaret (Gumilevsky), *Historical Review of Psalmists and Chanting of Ancient Greece*, Reprinted edition (Sergiev Posad: Holy Trinity Sergius Monastery, 1995); P. A. Florensky, *Iconostasis* (Moscow: Iskusstvo, 1995).

8 Hilarion, 'Sermon on Law and Grace by Metropolitan Hilarion', ed. with commentaries by A. M. Moldovana, trans. Deacon Andrei Yurchenko, RAN Institute of Russian Literature, *Library of Ancient Rus Literature*, Vol. 1: *XI-XII Centuries* (St. Petersburg: Nauka, 1997), pp. 26–61.

Since the first centuries of its history, the country has experienced the sociocultural impact of Eastern civilizations and, over time, Western European cultures. This impact was not always unambiguous. It is generally believed that the so-called Tatar-Mongol period of the historical existence of the Russian people seriously and permanently slowed down its socio-economic and cultural development, although at one time Lev Gumilev proposed a different point of view, most fully expressed in his work 'Ancient Rus' and the Great Steppe'. In particular, Gumilev put forward a hypothesis about the formation of a military alliance between the Golden Horde and Russia, created by Aleksandr Nevsky and Batu. It should be noted that this version gained a lot of supporters, but most historians considered it untenable and subjected it to detailed and substantive criticism.[9]

However, abstracting from the discussions of historians, we can state that the obvious and terrible result of the Tatar-Mongol invasion was the death of a huge number of the population of Russia; according to various estimates, it decreased by 40–60 percent. Kiev, Vladimir, Suzdal, Ryazan, Tver, Chernigov and many other cities of Kievan Rus' were destroyed; according to archaeologists, out of the 74 cities of the twelfth to thirteenth centuries, known by the results of excavations, 49 were completely destroyed by the Batu invasion, 14 of them never rose from the ashes and another 15 became ordinary villages. Many cities could not be reborn for a very long time. For example, archaeological excavations of Chernigov show that after the layer of the thirteenth century there is a layer of the seventeenth. For several decades of the sixteenth century, construction using stone in Russian cities practically stopped – that is, for the next 50 to 70 years, not a single stone building or church was built in Russia. The developed urban culture of ancient Russia suffered very significant damage. Complex crafts, such as the production of glass ornaments, cloisonné enamel, blackware, polychrome irrigation ceramics and so on disappeared. In total, only between 3 and 6 of the main 60 crafts were preserved.

The southern Russian lands lost almost all the settled population. And the surviving inhabitants went to the forest northeast, concentrating in

9 See, for instance, V. A. Kuchkin, *Rus' under the Yoke: What Was It Like?* (Moscow: Panorama, 1991).

the interfluve of the Northern Volga and the Oka, located, moreover, far from the trade routes. Here the soil was poorer and the climate colder than in the completely devastated southern regions of Russia, and, therefore, the conditions for farming and cattle breeding were much less favorable. Analyzing that period, the historian A. Shestakov has summarized the opinion of many researchers that 'if there had been no Mongol yoke, our ancestors would not have been divided into Russia, Ukraine and Belarus.[10] Ancient Rus' by the time of the Tatar-Mongol invasion was divided into 18 large state entities, including a number of apanage principalities; correspondingly, their military forces were not united, which determined the outcome of the clash with the Horde. In fact, in just four years of the Tatar-Mongol campaigns against Rus' (from the end of 1237 to 1241), most of the Russian princes recognized the supremacy of the great Mongol Khan and his representative Batu, Khan of the Golden Horde (formed in 1243). The main reason for radical changes in the structure of government – the borders of the conquered principalities and their number – was that they were obliged to replenish the treasury of the Horde and received edicts for the reign from the Khan. The new situation forced people to settle in remote lands. Chronicles, handwritten documents, cartographic descriptions of the possessions and archaeological research allow us today to fully restore the historical picture of this tragic period.

The Tatar-Mongol invasion and more than two centuries of the Horde rule became a national and cultural disaster for the Russian lands, which is considered to be the main reason for their noticeable civilizational lag behind European countries. When Europe entered the era of the initial accumulation of capital and the formation of the foundations of a post-industrial society, Russia had to recover, that is, to repeat part of the historical path that it had already made before Batu.

The first attempts to overcome this lagging behind occurred in the early years of the reign of a very ambiguous historical figure Ivan IV the Terrible (1530–1584),[11] who overtly turned to the West, opened a transit

10 See Andrei Shestakov, *The Mongol Invasion of Russia and Europe* (Moscow: Veche Vsemirnaia Istoriia, 2017).

11 See E. M. Eliyanov, *Ivan the Terrible – Creator or Destroyer?: Research into the Subjectivity of Interpretations Problem in History* (Moscow: Editorial URSS, 2004).

route to profitable (duty-free) markets for Europeans, carefully studied European forms of statehood, entered into correspondence with European royal courts and personally communicated with their diplomatic missions, and even, according to researchers, attempted to woo the English Queen Elizabeth I (in 1567)[12] – the only woman with whom he corresponded until his death (the letters have been preserved). His activities also aroused no less attention in the West, causing wariness.[13] Interestingly, in his era, Russia had a well-developed industry and crafts that were on par with Europe's (e.g., metalworking, the production of furniture, tableware, linseed oil, etc.); some of the products were even exported.[14] With regard to armaments, Russia was in the lead.[15] In fact, the regular army was formed and equipped with small arms produced in Russia[16] – it numbered about 12,000 people (at the end of the sixteenth century the *Streltsy* army numbered up to 25,000 people). However, all these achievements were later destroyed during the Times of Trouble.

The first Zemsky Sobor convened by Ivan the Terrible (1549) marked the beginning of a class-representative monarchy in Russia; a new collection of laws was compiled – the *Sudebnik* of 1550, a system of so-called *prikaz* (specialized central departments – the prototype of future ministries) was created; the governorate (*zemstvo*) reform was completed, which led to the emergence of deputies from nobility and *zemstvo* elders from wealthy peasants, in *volost* and *uyezd*. In 1553, by the tsar's order, a printing yard was founded, the first Russian paper factory was built,[17] and

12 See Yu. V. Tolstoy, *The First 40 Years of Relations between Russia and England, 1553–1593* (St. Petersburg: Tranzschel, 1875) and *English Travellers in the Muscovite State in the XVI Century* (Ryazan: Aleksandria, 2007).

13 See L. Yu. Taimasova, *A Potion for a King: English Espionage in Russia in the XVI Century* (Moscow: Veche, 2010).

14 N. Rozhkov, *Historical-Comparative Treatment of Russian History (Basics of Social Dynamics)* (Leningrad, 1928), Vol. 4, pp. 24–29.

15 R. Dupuy and T. Dupuy, with commentaries by N. Volkovsky and D. Volkovsky, 'All Wars in World History', in *The Harper Encyclopedia of Military History* (St. Petersburg, 2004), Vol. 3, pp. 142–143.

16 Ibid., pp. 136.

17 M. Pokrovsky, with N. Nikolsky and V. Storozhev, *Russian History since Ancient Times* (Moscow, 1911), Vol. 3, p. 117.

many churches were erected – in five years (by 1561) the Cathedral of the Intercession of the Most Holy Theotokos (St. Basil's Cathedral) was built. Ivan the Terrible's personality as an intellectual tsar is associated with the myth of the legendary Liberiya, the library of Sofia Palaiologos[18] that he inherited, and there is also a register of rare publications that actually belonged to him (154 units), compiled by N. Zarubin in the last century.[19] A very revealing analogy to the bibliophilism of Ivan the Terrible is the interest in the enlightenment of Peter I by whose order the first state library was created and opened in 1714 with free access for all.

The initially progressive nature of the reign of Ivan the Terrible and the modernization process that began on his initiative were interrupted by two circumstances: the unsuccessful Livonian War (1558–1583), which cost the country many lives and resources, but ended in the status quo ante bellum, as well as the collapse into the bloody *Oprichnina* (the state policy of mass repressions by the first political police in Russia, special administrative elite). Various opinions have been expressed regarding the historical meaning of the latter. For example, the historian D. N. Alshits believed that the *Oprichnina*, as a 'precisely calculated and completely successful political action', had a pragmatic purpose and was quite deliberately introduced by the tsar in order to consolidate autocracy.[20] But, on the other hand, its costs and dire consequences were quite obvious and played a role in the sociopolitical crisis that Russia plunged into at the beginning of the seventeenth century, known as the Time of Troubles (1598–1613). In addition to the three-year heptarchy (which recognized the Polish king Vladislav as the Russian tsar and led to the power of the False Dmitry),

18 A. I. Sobolevsky, 'The Library and Archives of Ivan the Terrible', *Knigovedenie*, No. 4 (1894), pp. 17–20. Public commission session on inquiry of the library of Ivan the Terrible, April 1963: Stenograph. Typewriting. Archives from USSR AS, Holding 693, List 3, No. 85.

19 N. I. Zarubin, *The Library of Ivan the Terrible: Renovations and Bibliographic Description* (Leningrad: Nauka, 1982).

20 Daniil N. Alshits, *The Beginning of Absolutism in Russia* (Leningrad: Nauka, 1988), p. 111. See also Daniil Al', *Ivan the Terrible: Known and Unknown Facts* (St. Petersburg: Neva, 2005), p. 155.

the tragic situation was aggravated by the great famine of 1601–1603[21] under the rule of Boris Godunov, which pushed the starving not only to riots but also to the rapid resettlement to the southern and eastern lands of the country and even to Siberia. The consequences of this time in the Russian mentality have never been completely outlived: in particular, the famous Russian historian E. F. Shmurlo also saw the sad consequences of the *Oprichnina* in the steady practice of bribery, denunciations and lobbying established at the state level.[22]

From the second half of the seventeenth century, the ruling elite again tried to embark on the path of transforming the country in the European spirit, trying, first of all, to adopt from the West (and especially from Holland, the most advanced in this regard) new forms of organizing economic life, including military-technical support for the defense of the state. This explains the appearance of the first manufactories (however, by their nature very far from European ones), the establishment of the so-called regiments of the foreign system, the transition to a policy of mercantilism and the like.

The trend toward the West began with a change in educational guidelines. Traditionally, Russia followed the Byzantine models of the Constantinople Pandidakterion (a higher school founded in the ninth century on the basis of an older Hellenic tradition), in which the initial training was given by psalm teachers at the temple. During the sixteenth and seventeenth centuries, the organization of Orthodox education in the eastern lands of Europe became more active in the polemical confrontation with the non-Orthodox. The first Orthodox university, the Ostrog Slavonic Greek and Latin Academy, was founded in 1576;[23] this was followed by the Lvov Brotherhood School (1585), arising at the Assumption Cathedral, which

21 S. O. Kozlovsky, 'The Great Famine and Times of Trouble: On the Issue of the Influence of Climate and Nature Factors on the Sociopolitical Crisis in Russia in Second Half of the Sixteenth – First Half of the Seventeenth Centuries', *Proceedings of the History Department of St Petersburg University*, Vol. 10 (2012).

22 E. F. Shmurlo, *Russian History: Controversial and Unexplained Issues of Russian History*, Vol. 4, Second edition (St. Petersburg: Aleteya, 2000).

23 *Ostrog Academy in the Sixteenth and Seventeenth Centuries: Encyclopedia* (Ostrog: National University of Ostrog Academy, 2011).

finally began its activities and gave rise to a number of similar brotherhoods in other places; the Kiev-Mohyla Academy (1632), which commenced its activities; and later the Slavonic-Greco-Latin Academy in Moscow (1687), which was established on the initiative of the poet Simeon of Polotsk.

This period coincides with an important event that helps to understand Russian culture, and the consequences of this event up to the twentieth century were largely determined in a hidden form by internal contradictions among Russian writers and artists. This is about the activities of Patriarch Nikon and his reforms of 1653–1654 that were aimed at unifying the Russian church tradition with the Greek one (making the sign of the cross with three fingers, checking service books against Greek publications – the so-called *knizhnaya sprava* [amendments of church books], checking icons against the Greek canon, etc.) and the subsequent schism in Russian Orthodoxy.[24] Again persecution pushed a huge number of dissenters (called Old Orthodox/Old Believers) to relocate. This page was stained with a lot of blood: it was effectively a civil war on religious grounds, especially tragic in its consequences was the resistance of cultural strongholds – monasteries. First of all, in 1674, the Solovetsky Monastery, which withstood a six-year siege, was brutally suppressed by the *Streltsy* and ended with executions. This was also associated with the uprising of the Old Believers in Moscow in 1681 with the pogrom in the Kremlin churches and subsequent executions; followed by the *Streltsy* riot of 1682 and the execution by burning on Good Friday in 1682. Four people were named in history as Pustozersky sufferers together with the famous Protopope Avvakum (see 'The Life of Protopope Avvakum'),[25] and the list of these historical atrocities can be continued. Knowing about them is indispensable, in particular, for understanding some works of Russian literature (the

24 Nikon (Patriarch), *The Tragedy of Russian Schism: Collected Essays* (Moscow: Dar, 2006); V. S. Rumyantseva, *Patriarch Nikon and Spiritual Culture in Seventeenth Century Russia: From the Manuscript Legacy of Patriarch Nikon's 'Commandments of Christian Life' ('Monumental Commandments')* (Moscow: Russian Academy of Sciences Institute of Russian History, 2010).

25 'Materials from the Archives of Pustozyorsk Martyrs', in *Significant Sites of Old Believers' Literature* (St. Petersburg, 1998).

characters of F. Dostoevsky, P. Melnik-Pechersky, N. Leskov, V. Nabokov and a number of others), which otherwise can remain incomprehensible.

Against the background of such an acute situation, the dispute with Catholicism paradoxically contributed to attracting more of attention to its culture, developed according to non-Orthodox principles, which perhaps explains the process of secularization of public consciousness in Russia. New (private) schools, in which teaching was focused on Western European education and cultural values, were organized. Works of European scientists were translated and published (e.g., Copernicus). Also, in Russian painting, for example, such a genre as *parsuna*, an intermediate form of portrait painting between icon painting and a realistic portrait not previously recognized by the church, was approved.[26] Against the background of the schism in 1672, the first court theatre appeared – showing evidence of the complete misunderstanding and alienation of the aristocratic elite from the traditional culture of the popular environment. In everyday life, European customs and living conditions were now more and more noticeable. The political system of Russia itself had evolved toward the establishment of an absolute monarchy, following the example of the countries of Europe.

However, any attempt to focus on internal transformations was thwarted by the constant military threats from outside and the difficult geopolitical situation of the country. These circumstances hindered the process of necessary transformations, undoubtedly affecting the nature of modern culture and the themes of art. So, in the sixteenth century, Muscovy fought against the Polish-Lithuanian Commonwealth, the Livonian Order and Sweden for a total of 43 years, and, without a single year of interruption, the struggle with the Tatars on their southern and eastern borders continued. The seventeenth century was even more ridden with military conflicts, which continued for 48 years; in fact, every second year the country lived in a state of war or even several wars, which led to large human losses, complicated daily life and undermined the economy and treasury. In the centuries that followed, this trend continued and even intensified. Russia

26 N. I. Komashko, 'The Artist Bogdan Saltanov in the Art Life of Moscow in the Second Half of the Seventeenth Century', *Ancient Rus*, Vol. 2, No. 12 (2003), pp. 44–54.

in the eighteenth century fought for almost 60 years, and in the nineteenth century, for 67 years.[27] Hence, the permanent need to ensure its security (and eventually to conduct external expansion, including the return of the once-lost Russian lands) becomes the dominant and, in a certain sense, the driving force of state development, defining the specifics of the political evolution of the country toward increased internal centralization, the excessive influence of state power on the life of society.

These circumstances led to such a feature of the civilizational path of Russia as its mobilizational (catching up) type of development – in contrast to the evolutionary-type characteristic of Western civilization (the theory of N. Morozov).[28] This type is characterized by the acceleration of evolutionary processes due to the deliberate intervention of the state (mainly due to external circumstances) in the economic and social development of society. In the context of Russian history, the state has repeatedly used its monopoly on coercive violence and non-economic coercion to gradually destroy the traditional society that existed for centuries.

The first of the overt and significant examples of such a role of state power should be considered the necessary and quite overdue modernization of Russia during the reign of Peter the Great. This took place against the background of the 20 years of the Northern War for the Baltic against the Swedish Kingdom by the European coalition with the participation of Russia, ending in 1721 with the victory and the return of the lands lost a hundred years before, and the transformation of the Russian Kingdom into the Russian Empire.[29] Thus, modernization was carried out in extreme conditions that required the exertion of all national resources.

However, a consequence of Peter's transformative activity, carried out as is well known by very radical methods, was the deep cultural split, previously

27 V. A. Volkov, V. E. Voronin and V. V. Gorsky, *Military History of Russia from Ancient Times up to the End of the Nineteenth Century* (Moscow: Ministry of Education and Science of Russia, 2012); *War, Conflicts, Campaigns and Combat Actions of the Russian Army, 860—1914: A Handbook*, 2 vols (Moscow: Runivers, 2018).

28 N. M. Morozov, 'The Mobilization Development of Russian Civilization', *Tomsk State University Journal of History*, No. 2 (2011), pp. 175–184.

29 See *History of the Great Northern War 1700–1721*, ed. I. I. Rostunov (Moscow: Nauka, 1987).

outlined and now finally realized, of the previously unified Russian society, as evidenced by the presence of two capitals: patriarchal Moscow and the 'construction of the century', European-oriented St. Petersburg. Thus, the tsar, in accordance with the European calendar tradition, issued a decree in 1699 to introduce a new chronology 'from the Birth of Christ', and not 'from the creation of the world'. The difference between these events in the church tradition was calculated as 5,508 years, and the year henceforth began with 1 January, instead of 1 September.

Perfectly reflecting the reformist spirit of the era, the well-known 'Peter's stories', printed and handwritten, were most typical and popular – 'The Story of Aleksandr the Russian Nobleman', 'The Story of the Russian Sailor Vasily' and 'The Story of the Russian Merchant John'. 'The first two of them reflect elements of the life and customs of the Russian nobility at the beginning of the eighteenth century, the third – that of the merchants.'[30] Reading of that era, according to the research of V. Kuzmina, was rather succinct: it consisted of the many times rewritten lives of saints (e.g., the life of Alexei, the man of God, the life of Peter and Fevronia of Murom), Old Russian military stories (the story of the Mamaev massacre, the Story of the Kazan Kingdom) and stories of didactic character (the story of Akir the Wise, about Basarga, about Barlaam and Joasaph), from translated texts – mainly chivalrous stories (about Brunzvik, Peter of the Golden Keys, Vasily Goldilocks, Bove Korolevich).[31]

The so-called cultural landscape of the eighteenth century was ably reproduced by the active representative of the literary environment of the post-revolutionary emigration P. Muratov[32] in the historical novel *Igeria* (1922), where the love story, resurrected in the memories of an artist, not understanding the background of the events, develops against the

30 V. D. Kuzmina, 'Tales of Petrine Times', in *History of Russian Literature*, Vol. 3: *Literature of the 18th Century* (Moscow: Academy of Sciences USSR, 1941–1956), ch. 1, pp. 119.

31 Ibid., p. 118.

32 I. G. Ivanova, 'Muratov P. P. and His Contribution to Development of Ideas about cultural Landscape', *Heritage and Modern Times*, Vol. 1 (1998).

background of a real political intrigue involving the Swedish King Gustav III and the Rosicrucians.[33]

Yuri Lotman conceptually commented on this turn to the West: 'The attitude to the Western world was one of the main issues of Russian culture throughout the post-Petrine era. We can say that the alien civilization acts as a kind of mirror and reference point for Russian culture, and the main meaning of interest in the "alien" in Russia is traditionally a method of self-cognition.'[34]

At the same time, European education and culture, in reality, became the property of only a narrow stratum of privileged classes, primarily the nobility, while the peasantry, the middle urban strata and the merchants for the most part remained adherents of Old Russian cultural values and moral norms, and this split only deepened over time, putting forward its ideologists. So, in the nineteenth century, it was embodied in a powerful confrontation between Slavophiles[35] and diverse Westerners (among them were adherents of religious, liberal and socialist ideas); the traces of their struggle are clearly visible in the works of all the literary masters of this century. However, according to Lotman, 'The "East" and "West" in the cultural geography of Russia invariably appear as saturated symbols, based on geographical reality, but in fact imperatively dominating it.'[36]

The complex and contradictory historical path of Russia could not but affect the development of its culture. The Russian thinker and commentator Vadim Kozhinov noted: 'In the movement through socio-cultural catastrophes, the decisive denial of the previous stages of its development is the peculiarity of the historical path of Russia and its culture.'[37] A. S.

33 P. P. Muratov, *Egeria: A Novel; and Short Stories from Various Books* (Moscow: Terra, 1997).

34 Lotman, 'Modern Times between East and West'.

35 V. A. Kupriyanov, 'Russia and Europe in Early and Late Slavophilism' (A. S. Khomyakov and V. I. Lamansky), *Solovyov Research*, No. 2 (2018), pp. 21–33; A. Valitsky, 'Encircled by Conservative Utopia: Structure and Metamorphoses of Russian Slavophilism', *New Literary Review* (2019); S. O. Shidlovsky 'From Projects by I.S. Aksakov on Socio-cultural Development of the North-West Region of the Russian Empire', *Slavic Studies* No. 5 (2013), pp. 78–85.

36 Lotman, 'Modern Times between East and West'.

37 V. Kozhinov, *Sins and Sacredness of Russian History* (Moscow: Exmo: Yauza, 2010).

Akhiezer, the author of the concept of sociocultural evolution, has fully justified the idea that a characteristic feature of the historical development of Russia is a constant split of culture, directly affecting social relations.[38] The era of Peter the Great once again confirmed the obvious significance of systematic and almost unpredictable situations, a kind of iconic 'rift' in the development of Russian history and culture, which, together with the denial of previous experience, can cause a dramatic turn of the country's path – such as the time of the baptism of Russia, the Mongol period, the policy of individual rulers, 1917 and 1991. Such splits or, more precisely, breaks in culture occurred, as a rule, in those periods of history when natural disasters, the political situation or the 'innovations' that came from outside led to a radical rejection of the established foundations of being and consciousness.

How such cataclysms affected the fate of culture, destroying it or, on the contrary, stimulating the search for new forms and meanings, and whether this is good or bad, is in fact one of the most difficult questions, to which two opposite answers are possible and both will represent someone's subjective position. This is a question to which Lev Gumilev tried to give a scientifically based answer with his theory of the '*passionarnost*' (passionarity) of ethnogenesis,[39] which at one time caused a violent polemic criticism in the Soviet scientific community, the rejection by foreign experts on Russian history[40] and which is still ambiguously perceived. However, the rational grain of this theory germinates: it is associated with continuity, which can be interpreted as the 'excessive' previous experience that survived the destruction of the old, and remained intact, or, as Lotman aphoristically described it, 'what defines itself as "having never existed until today" very often turns out to be as "having always existed" – a constantly active model'.[41]

Thus, after the October Revolution, one way of life was replaced not just by another, but by a radically different system. The new way of life

38 A. S. Akhiezer, *Russia: Criticism of Historical Experience (Sociocultural Dynamics of Russia)*, Vol. 1: *From Past to Future* (Novosibirsk: Sibirsky Chronograph, 1998).

39 L. N. Gumilev, *Ethnogenesis and the Biosphere of Earth* (St. Petersburg: Kristall, 2001).

40 L. Graham, *Natural Science, Philosophy, and the Sciences of Human Behavior in the Soviet Union* (translated) (Moscow: Publishing House of Political Literature, 1991).

41 Lotman, 'Modern Times between East and West'.

carried the idea of uniting people on the basis of common goals and meanings. At the same time, the old things (including culture) were destroyed very decisively, often crudely and cruelly. Entire scientific fields of a humanitarian nature were curtailed.[42] The pre-revolutionary past (the noble and bourgeois cultures) was declared alien to the people, and historians were required to justify its 'harmfulness' – its hopeless isolation from the interests of the working people. A major role in the approval of this approach was played by the position of Lenin's colleague, the historian M. Pokrovsky, the author of a new concept of historical science, according to which the function of history should be seen in the 'correct change of human society'. It is significant that almost immediately after his death in 1932, the 'red academician' was accused of being mistaken, of having scientific beliefs that did not correspond to genuine Marxism, and, in addition to his followers, even his opponents were attributed to his 'school' and then repressed.[43] At the ideological level, the historical and cultural past was filtered in terms of its usefulness as a cementing element in the construction of a new building – according to the famous aphorism of the same M. Pokrovsky: 'history is politics, capsized into the past'.

Along with the formation of a new culture, the country lost many outstanding philosophers, writers, artists, musicians and actors. This historical precedent of the twentieth century gave a rich variety of directions to Russian émigré culture, which continued to exist in its own way for several generations. They were the creators of the phenomenon of Russian culture in emigration, which had existed in a different sociocultural environment for several generations in an original and fruitful way. At the same time, the so-called internal emigration remained in the USSR and held an invisible defense of the classical heritage (the Acmeists; the first landmark in a series of subsequent dystopias – the novel *We* by E. Zamyatin; *The White Guard* by M. Bulgakov, historically true and in some ways coinciding with

42 I. P. Medvedev, *Byzantine Studies of Saint-Petersburg: Chapters of History* (St. Petersburg: Aleteya, 2006).

43 A. N. Artizov, 'M.N. Pokrovsky: Career Finale – Success or Defeat?', *Russian History*, Nos 1 and 2 (1998), pp. 77–96 and pp. 124–143; A. N. Artizov, 'The Fate of the Historians of the School of M. N. Pokrovsky (Mid-1930s)', *Questions of History*, No. 7 (1994), pp. 34–48.

Bunin's *Cursed Days*; and the body of repressed literature, still far from being fully restored).

All this indicates that the fundamental condition for preserving the historical integrity of culture was the allotropy factor, which is a situation of coexistence in a single contour of different, sometimes even contrasting, forms. In each new time frame, along with various innovations, there remain persistent (obvious or latent) compositional factors: awareness of these requires the localized remainder of the Other/Different. The special cultural situation in the post-colonial and post-Soviet world today allows us to constitute this important, though unidentified, component of the historical movement in all the significance of its general historical meaning (although, possibly, such incidents have always taken place). The conversion of allotropic forms is carried out under the influence of the deformation of the usual context, due to its polyfunctional specificity, and plays a primary role in the regeneration of cultural tradition. With regards to the culturological aspect, any of the conditionally homogeneous cultures – or, taking up P. Sorokin's expression, 'sociocultural bodies' – in the context of their development inevitably have faced, face or will face in the future, a situation where this homogeneity ceases to be obvious.[44]

Destruction in the name of creating a new society made a gaping hole in the culture, but at the same time, the Soviet government began to intensively fill it with an alternative system of values, its own moral imperatives and an entirely original art, united by the ambiguous marker 'Social Realism', which absorbed and melted down, in essence, the most heterogeneous forms. The so-called proletarian, and then the Soviet culture was created, and millions of people protected by the Iron Curtain from the rest of the world – and most effectively, young people – were introduced to it in a new, well-thought-out educational and repressive format. The concept of 'Nation' (national character, national ethos), brought to outright vulgarism, was cultivated (the author of this paradigm, I.-G. Herder, once put a completely different meaning into it). Popular songs, poems, revolutionary prints, posters (to which in the post-revolutionary years such

44 See O. Chervinska, 'The Scientific Term "Allotropy" in Modern Literary Use', *Mirgorod* (Lausanne, Siedlce), Vol. 2, No. 8 (2016), pp. 90–99.

giants as Mayakovsky also got involved), films and festive parades formed a pantheon of selfless heroes of a new type – both real contemporaries (Chapaev, Shchors, Kotovsky, etc.) and fictional ones (Pavka Korchagin of N. Ostrovsky, children's characters of A. Gaidar, A. Barto and S. Marshak). In the early years, there was even sharp satire (the famous 'Bathhouse' and 'Bedbug' by V. Mayakovsky), but in the 1930s, it was already concerned exclusively with remnants of the past ('The Twelve Chairs' and 'The Golden Calf' by the partnership of I. Ilf and E. Petrov) or enemies. At the same time, according to the remark of the modern theologian A. Osipov, the official guidelines in the field of culture could be reduced to one denominator: namely to make a person better, more humane and kinder, which echoed with and was, in fact, borrowed from the commandments of early Christianity.

The spirit of the Soviet era, at once ascetic and triumphant, was embodied visibly in the architecture of Soviet Constructivism, in the music of I. Dunaevsky and, almost painfully, in D. Shostakovich. A special theme is the breakthrough in cinema (expressive film language from Eisenstein, A. Dovzhenko, Vs. Pudovkin, Dz. Vertov). M. Sholokhov writes *And Quiet Flows the Don*, M. Bulgakov – *The Master and Margarita*, A. Platonov – *Chevengur* and A. Akhmatova – *Poem without a Hero*. As we can see, even in the era of Socialist Realism, there is a diversity of literary techniques in different genres.

The rehabilitation of the idea of continuity began with the revival of the cult of Pushkin – in 1937, the country mourned the centenary of the poet's death, the blame for which was laid on tsarism. Thus, the poet's patriotism changed its inner meaning and was interpreted as belonging to the people and defending national interests, and thus turned into an ideological weapon. Pushkin's love for Russia no longer had the right to be Lermontov's 'strange love', as it was for the emigrants. And, of course, in the Great Patriotic War, the newly formed understanding of patriotism played an extremely important, key role. In the Soviet country, this feeling was brought up according to an authoritarian ideological scheme on the example of Sholokhov's *Virgin Soil Upturned*, the heroic and cheerful paintings of A. Deineka, M. Grekov, I. Grabar, A. Laktionov and many others; and of such films as *Aleksandr Nevsky*, *Minin and Pozharsky*, *Kutuzov*,

Suvorov, *Nakhimov* and *Admiral Ushakov*. The art of the word remained the most vulnerable.

The classical heritage of Russian culture was again in demand and organically incorporated into the cultural policy of the Soviet state, whose official ideological attitudes became very close to or even repeated – of course, in the style of modern terms and concepts – many components of the Russian cultural code and values (patriotism, statehood, respect for historical traditions, loyalty to traditional family values, etc.).

After the death of Stalin, interest in classics acquired a new political meaning, and therefore publishing activity in this regard, although with great caution, was also intensified in relation to writers 'forgotten' by the Soviet government (e.g., Blok, Yesenin, Dostoevsky). Theatrical life revived, although great playwrights of the standard of Chekhov did not appear. Russian classics began to be actively adapted (*The Idiot*, *The Lady with the Dog*, *War and Peace*, *Anna Karenina*, *The Brothers Karamazov*, etc.).

Thus, a restoration of historical continuity in the development of Russian culture was gradually carried out, and conversation about its value orientations, moral traditions and universal meanings began again. And, once again, opinions radically diverged: in defiance of the apologists of conservative Socialist Realism, the young generation of the 'nineteen sixties' (*shestidesiatniki*) came out, offering a completely new poetry (Bella Akhmadulina, Yevgeny Yevtushenko, Andrei Voznesensky); a new prose appeared – 'urban' (Yu. Kuznetsov, Yu. Trifonov, V. Makanin) and 'rural' (V. Belov, V. Shukshin, V. Rasputin) – while cheerful short-story writers matured (F. Iskander). Some went abroad, successfully joining the ranks of the Russian emigration, and giving it a new coloring, or preserving their personal space like Joseph Brodsky did, not joining any groups. It was at this time that Venedikt Yerofeev wrote his brilliant postmodern text *Moscow-Petushki* (an inverted remake of *A Journey from St. Petersburg to Moscow* by Radishchev), a sign of a radical twist and reincarnation of the entire style of the Soviet era, which ended with the collapse of the USSR only 20 years later.

Another break in Russian culture occurred at the turn of the twentieth and twenty-first centuries with the country's transition to the Western model of social development. The market, private property, predatory privatization, the emergence of a greedy oligarchy, unprecedented corruption, spiritual degradation, colossal social stratification, impoverishment of the majority of the population against a background of democratic slogans and ideological pluralism – for Russia all this was, in essence, a 'well forgotten past'. Under these conditions, the commercialization of culture took place, when the measure of creative achievements was primarily the commercial success of the created work or, as they began to say, of the 'cultural product', as well as the orientation toward the mass consumer and the fascination with Western – or rather, American – Hollywood 'aesthetic' standards. This period is not yet complete, although forecasts can be made. However, such a state of culture has already been analyzed in other historical material by José Ortega y Gasset back in 1930 in the treatise *Revolt of the Masses*, which has not lost its relevance.

Periods of Russian cultural break were expressed in a radical rejection of the cultural canons and achievements of the previous stage, through tough confrontation with opposite trends (their own traditions and other people's experience). D. Granin, describing in an interview in 1994 the state of culture as a result of the collapse of the Soviet Union and the beginning of liberal reforms, aphoristically defined the situation as barbarism turned against itself: 'The chain of time has been broken, and culture has turned out to be defenseless. A new utterance is expected from it, but the new word does not appear in the cemetery, it is carried in the womb of the departing one [...] History does not tolerate breaks.'[45] Neither does culture.

The complex Russian historical experience shows that all the previous cultural breaks, which led to almost catastrophic spiritual losses and mental deformations, and the subsequent difficult and sometimes painful experiences, ended with a subsequent submersion in their own historical landscape. Following the misunderstood and unconditionally denied achievements of the previous era, after a certain time at a new turn in history, when rejected values are understood in a new way, they can turn out to be claimed back. Thus, V. Rasputin, an outstanding representative of 'rural prose', a connoisseur of the Russian boondocks, who was suffering from the virtually agonizing state of the country as a result of the hard times

45 Cited in Kozhinov, *Sins and Sacredness of Russian History*, p. 340.

of the 1990s, nevertheless did not have doubts about the future: 'I believe in recovery. Such spiritual resources, such cultural wealth, such national power, as we have, cannot be buried.' So far, Russian society continues to stand at a crossroads – reformatting of (already digital) public consciousness is a reality. In fact, the question arose of changing the civilizational vector of development of the Russian orthodox ethnos, but the path to the optimal form of social life will always remain a topical issue on the agenda.

Bibliography

Akhiezer, A. S., *Russia: Criticism of Historical Experience (Sociocultural Dynamics of Russia)*, Vol. 1: *From Past to Future* (Novosibirsk: Sibirskii Chronograph, 1998).

Al', Daniil, *Ivan the Terrible: Known and Unknown Facts* (St. Petersburg: Neva, 2005).

Alshits, Daniil N., *The Beginning of Absolutism in Russia* (Moscow: Nauka, 1988).

—— *Ivan the Terrible: Known and Unknown Facts* (St. Petersburg: Neva, 2005).

Artizov, A. N., 'The Fate of the Historians of the School of M. N. Pokrovsky (Mid-1930s)', *Questions of History*, No. 7 (1994), pp. 34–48.

—— 'M.N. Pokrovsky: Career Finale – Success or Defeat?', *Russian* History, Nos 1 and 2 (1998), pp. 77–96; pp. 124–143.

Balovnev, D. A., 'The Tale of "the Initial Spread of Christianity across Rus". An Attempt at Critical Analysis', in *The Church in the History of Russia* (Moscow: Institut Rossiiskoi Istorii RAN [Institute of Russian History of the Russian Academy of Sciences], 2000), Vol. 4, pp. 5–46.

Chervinska, O., 'The Scientific Term "Allotropy" in Modern Literary Use', Mirgorod (Lausanne, Siedlce), Vol. 2, No. 8 (2016), pp. 90–99.

Dupuy, R., and T. Dupuy, with commentaries by N.L. Volkovsky and D.N. Volkovsky, 'All Wars of World History', in *Harper Encyclopedia of Military Biography* (St. Petersburg: Harper Collins, 2004), Vol. 3, pp. 142–143.

Eliyanov, E. M., *Ivan the Terrible – Creator or Destroyer?: Research into the Subjectivity of Interpretations Problem in History* (Moscow: Editorial URSS, 2004).

English Travellers in the Muscovite State in the XVI Century (Ryazan: Aleksandria, 2007).

Filaret (Gumilevsky), Archbishop, *Historical Review of Psalmists and Chanting of Ancient Greece*, Reprinted edition (Sergiev Posad: Holy Trinity Sergius Monastery, 1995).

Florensky, P. A., *Iconostasis* (Moscow: Iskusstvo, 1995).

Graham, L., *Natural Science, Philosophy, and the Sciences of Human Behavior in the Soviet Union* (translated) (Moscow: Publishing House of Political Literature, 1991).

Gumilev, L. N., *Ethnogenesis and the Biosphere of Earth* (St. Petersburg: Kristall, 2001).

Hilarion, Metropolitan (Hilarion of Kiev), 'Sermon on Law and Grace by Metropolitan Hilarion', in *Library of Ancient Rus Literature*, Vol. 1: *XI-XII Centuries*, ed. with commentaries by A. M. Moldovan, trans. Deacon Andrei Yurchenko (RAN Institute of Russian Literature) (St. Petersburg: Nauka, 1997), pp. 26–61.

Ipatiev Chronicle: Complete Collection of Russian Chronicles (St. Petersburg: Tipografiia M.A. Aleksandrova, 1908), Vol. 2 col. 89–112.

Ivanova, I. G., 'Muratov P.P. and His Contribution to Development of Ideas about Cultural Landscape', *Heritage and Modern Times*, Vol. 1 (1998).

John of Damascus, *An Exact Explanation of Orthodox Faith* (Moscow: Lodiya, 2002).

Komashko, N. I., 'The Artist Bogdan Saltanov in the Art Life of Moscow in the Second Half of the Seventeenth Century', *Ancient Rus*, Vol. 2, No. 12 (2003), pp. 44–54.

Kozhinov, V., *Sins and Sacredness of Russian History* (Moscow: Exmo: Yauza, 2010).

Kozlovsky, S. O., 'The Great Famine and Times of Trouble: On the Issue of the Influence of Climate and Nature Factors on the Socio-political Crisis in Russia in Second Half of the Sixteenth – First Half of the Seventeenth Centuries', *Proceedings of the History Department of St Petersburg University*, Vol. 10 (2012).

Kuchkin, V. A., *Rus' under the Yoke: What Was It Like?* (Moscow: Panorama, 1991).

Kupriyanov, V. A., 'Russia and Europe in Early and Late Slavophilism' (A. S. Khomyakov and V. I. Lamansky) *Solovyov Research*, No. 2 (2018), pp. 21–33.

Kuzmina, V. D., 'Tales of Petrine Times', in *History of Russian Literature*, Vol. 3: *Literature of the 18th Century* (Moscow: Academy of Sciences USSR, 1941–1956), Ch. 1.

Lotman, Yu., 'Modern Times between East and West', *Znamya*, Vol. 9 (1997).

Markelov, G. V. 'Humorous Postscripts in the Manuscripts of Pushkin House Archives', *Proceedings of the Department of Old Russian Literature*, Vol. 41 (988), pp. 444–446.

'Materials from the Archives of Pustozyorsk Martyrs', in *Significant Sites of Old Believers' Literature* (St. Petersburg: Izdatelstvo RKhGI, 1998).

Medvedev, I. P., *Byzantine Studies of Saint-Petersburg: Chapters of History* (St. Petersburg: Aleteya, 2006).

Meyendorff, John, *Byzantine Theology: Historical Trends and Doctrinal Themes* (Minsk: Luchi Sofii, 2007).

Morozov, N. M., 'The Mobilization Development of Russian Civilization', *Tomsk State University Journal of History*, No. 2 (2011), pp. 175–184.

Muratov, P. P., *Egeria: A Novel; And Short Stories from Various Books* (Moscow: Terra, 1997).

Nikon (Patriarch), *The Tragedy of Russian Schism: Collected Essays* (Moscow: Dar, 2006).

Ostrog Academy in the Sixteenth and Seventeenth Centuries: Encyclopedia (Ostrog: National University of Ostrog Academy, 2011).

Pokrovsky, M., with N. Nikolsky and V. Storozhev, *Russian History since Ancient Times* (Moscow: Mir, 1911).

Rozhkov, N., *Historical-Comparative Treatment of Russian History (Basics of Social Dynamics)* (Leningrad: Kniga, 1928).

Rumyantseva, V. S., *Patriarch Nikon and Spiritual Culture in Seventeenth Century Russia: From the Manuscript Legacy of Patriarch Nikon's 'Commandments of Christian Life' ('Monumental Commandments')* (Moscow: Russian Academy of Sciences Institute of Russian History, 2010).

Shestakov, Andrei, *The Mongol Invasion of Russia and Europe* (Moscow: Veche Vsemirnaia Istoriia, 2017).

Shidlovsky, S. O., 'From Projects by I.S. Aksakov on Socio-cultural Development of the North-West Region of the Russian Empire', *Slavic Studies*, No. 5 (2013), pp. 78–85.

Shmurlo, E. F., *Russian History: Controversial and Unexplained Issues of Russian History*, Vol. 4, Second edition (St. Petersburg: Aleteya, 2000).

Sobolevsky, A. I., 'The Library and Archives of Ivan the Terrible', *Knigovedenie*, No. 4 (1894), pp. 17–20.

Taimasova, L. Yu., *A Potion for a King: English Espionage in Russia in the XVI Century* (Moscow: Veche, 2010).

Tolstoy, Yu. V., *The First 40 Years of Relations between Russia and England, 1553–1593* (St. Petersburg: Tranzschel, 1875).

Valitsky, A., *Encircled by Conservative Utopia: Structure and Metamorphoses of Russian Slavophilism* (Moscow: Novoe Literaturnoe Obozrenie, 2019).

Volkov, V. E., V. E. Voronin, and V. V. Gorsky, *Military History of Russia from Ancient Times up to the End of the Nineteenth Century* (Moscow: Ministry of Education and Science of Russia, 2012).

War, Conflicts, Campaigns and Combat Actions of the Russian Army, 860–1914: A Handbook, 2 vols (Moscow: Runivers, 2018).

Zarubin, N. I., *The Library of Ivan the Terrible: Renovations and Bibliographic Description* (Leningrad: Nauka, 1982).

Translated by Nikita Khmarenko

ALEKSANDR A. MEDVEDEV

2 Athena versus Gaia: Ideology and Being in Russian Literature of the Nineteenth and Twentieth Centuries (Turgenev, Dostoevsky, Prishvin, Andrei Tarkovsky)[1]

In exile, in 1946, N. A. Berdyaev pointed out the discontinuous, catastrophic development of Russian history, highlighting five periods in it (Kievan Rus', Russia during the Tatar yoke, Moscow Russia, Petrine Russia and Soviet Russia).[2] In our opinion, one of the key reasons for an unstable, discrete development of Russian history is an ideology-driven mental attitude toward life, as P. Chaadaev noted at the time, linking the lack of 'natural progress' in Russia with borrowing 'ready-made ideas' from abroad, which are perceived dogmatically, without proper critical reflection:

> We have no internal development, no natural progress at all; the old ideas are swept away by the new ones, because the latter do not come from the former, but they come from nowhere. We perceive only completely ready-made ideas, so those indelible traces which are comprehended by the minds in the course of consecutive thought development do create mental power and do not furrow our consciousness [...] We are like those children who have not been forced to reason themselves, so that when they grow up, there is nothing of their own in them; all their knowledge is superficial, their whole soul is outside of them.[3]

1 The author is grateful to Yana Grishina, Head of the Department «House-Museum of M.M. Prishvin in the village of Dunino» (the State Museum of the History of Russian Literature named after V. I. Dal, Moscow) for Prishvin's photos that she has kindly provided.

2 N. A. Berdyaev, *The Russian Idea* (St. Petersburg, 2008), p. 32.

3 P. Y. Chaadaev, *A Complete Set of Essays and Selected Letters*, 2 vols (Moscow, 1991), Vol. 1, p. 326.

The cultural gap between pre-revolutionary and Soviet Russia caused by ideology was noted by A. Besançon, who emphasized its paradoxical nature:

> Ideology is also responsible for locking Russia in itself and reinforcing the most caricatured features of the Old Order, and it is also responsible for a radical break with the former Russia, much deeper than the natural distance between the past and the present that exists in modern nations.[4]

The features of ideology-driven mentality were described by R. Barth and, as we will see later, they correspond to the Russian experience, too; ideology is always 'partial' in relation to the whole; but at the same time it claims to have 'imperial' domination and universality; hence its aggressiveness; it possesses a coercive character – 'it seeks to suppress personal consciousness and alienate the responsibility of the individual'; it is represented as a phenomenon of 'nature', that is, as something natural, and not as a product of culture; it is stereotypical –'ideology tries to abolish any ingenuous vision of the world, its demiurgic "discovery" in acts of individual experience, offering a routine "recognition" of ready-made clichés and topoi instead'; it seeks to create a 'stable', permanent image of the world, 'developing for this purpose Norms, Rules and Schemes, which a mobile, infinitely changeable Life is adjusted to'.[5]

We also think that the options of ideology identified by K. S. Gadzhiev are significant: creating the image of an external and internal enemy as a 'powerful catalyst for the crystallization' of the interests of the followers of ideology; intolerance, fanaticism, dogmatism, monologism (confidence in possession of the absolute truth); isolation – the desire to 'squeeze real life into the Procrustean bed of abstract and artificial one-dimensional constructions'; theocratic would-be religion – ideology as 'the state religion with its dogmas, with its sacred books, saints, apostles, with its man-gods (embodied in leaders, Fuhrers, Duces, etc.), liturgy, etc.'; utopianism – 'The

4 A. Besançon, *Intellectual Origins of Leninism* (Moscow, 1998), p. 26.

5 G. K. Kosikov, 'Ideology, Connotation, Text': Roland Barthes, *S/Z* (Moscow, 2001), pp. 8–30, pp. 10–11.

eternal dream of people for a perfect social order.'[6] Thus, the goal of ideology, in the words of Besançon, who continues the thought of J. Michelet, is that it 'rejects reality in order to put in its place the super-reality imposed by ideology'.[7]

A Russian ideology-driven mental attitude to life has been reproduced in Russian history as a stable component in various forms – in the messianic idea of the Orthodox Empire – 'Moscow, the Third Rome';[8] in the Russian schism of the seventeenth century; in Uvarov's triad 'Autocracy, Orthodoxy, Nationality'; in nineteenth-century nihilism; and in the 70-year-old Bolshevik ideology of the twentieth century – 'The Third International'. The religious nature of this ideology was clearly felt by M. Voloshin in 1924:

> In everything Russia only needs faith:
> We believed in the two-finger cross, in the tsar,
> In dreams, in sneezes, in dissecting frogs,
> In socialism, and the International.[9]

The Russian schism was based on rite-based belief and on the belief that Russia has a Messianic mission.[10] As in subsequent ideocracies (nihilism, Bolshevism), during the schism, humanity was fanatically sacrificed to a dogmatically understood truth (a ready-made idea, not amenable for discussion), and the present was sacrificed to a utopian project of the past or future. In fact, there was a rejection of history, which, from the point of view of the Old Believers, was mastered by the Antichrist (the

6 K. S. Gadzhiev, 'Political Ideology: Conceptual Aspects', *Philosophical Questions*, No. 12 (1998), pp. 3–20, pp. 5–6, 8.

7 Besançon, *Intellectual Origins of Leninism*, p. 84.

8 For more details on the ideology of Russian Messianism and its ideology model in Russia during the First World War, see A. A. Medvedev, ' "A Russia of Xerxes or of Christ?": The Critique of Messianism in the Russian Émigré Community in a Historical-Cultural Perspective, from Vladimir Solov'ëv to Ol'ga Sedakova', in *Russian Classical Literature Today* (Newcastle upon Tyne, 2014), pp. 205–219; and A. A. Medvedev, 'La mythologie de la guerre dans les articles de Vassili Rozanov', *La Revue russe*, No. 47 (2016), pp. 117–130.

9 M. Voloshin, *Collected Writings* (Moscow, 2003), Vol. 1, p. 376.

10 N. A. Berdyaev, *The Russian Idea*, pp. 40–41.

myth of the city of Kitezh). The reason for this ideologized perception of Christianity, with its inherent fanaticism and dogmatism, was the lack of an ancient intellectual culture, a culture of dialogue and debate.

The ideology-driven mental attitude was also manifested in the phenomenon of the Russian intelligentsia (from Belinsky through the Narodniks to the Bolsheviks). Having comprehended its history, in 1926, G. P. Fedotov formulated the key feature of the intelligentsia as groundless idealism – a theoretical worldview, constructed rationally and applied to life forcefully as a norm and canon:

> the 'idea' does not rise from life, from its irrational depths, as its highest rational expression [...] Athena versus Gaia – in this myth (an episode from the gigantomachy) is the meaning of Russian tragedy, that is, the tragedy of the Russian intelligentsia [...] Groundlessness is a rejection: from everyday life, from the national culture, from the national religion, from the state, from the class, from all organically grown social and spiritual formations.[11]

In Fedotov's mind, an exception from the ideology-driven intelligentsia is the humanist Herzen, whose conflict with the revolutionary Democrats and the Narodniks is explained exactly by Herzen's humanistic position:

> What is striking about Herzen's writings is that man is always ahead, he is always more important than his ideas. He is not a sceptic and never toys with ideas. But he also does not kneel before them [...] More freedom. More humanity. Less servitude to formulas, to doctrines. Politics regarded not as a pseudo-science and false religion, but as an expression of men's moral and social conduct.[12]

According to Fedotov, the dogmatic system of the Russian intelligentsia is incapable of development because of its groundless idealism: 'It is dying violently, being displaced by a new system of dogmas, and this death of

11 G. P. Fedotov, 'The Tragedy of the Intelligentsia', in *Fate and Sins of Russia: Selected Papers on Philosophy of Russian History and Culture*, 2 vols (St. Petersburg, 1992), Vol. 1, pp. 66–101; pp. 70–71.

12 G. P. Fedotov, 'The Lost Writer A. I. Herzen (1812–1870)', in *Works*, 12 vols (Moscow, 2014), Vol. 7, pp. 86–89; p. 88.

ideas usually corresponds not to the metaphorical, but to the literal death of an entire generation'.[13]

'He who does not possess the idea, but he who is obsessed with it': The nihilism ideologist in Russian literature of the nineteenth century (Turgenev, Dostoevsky)

In the nineteenth century, the ideology-driven life attitude was manifest in the phenomenon of Russian nihilism. A classic image of the *raznochinets* hero was Turgenev's Bazarov (*Fathers and Sons*, 1862), whose nihilistic ideology denies the fundamental humanistic values – morals, respect, faith, tradition – 'he does not believe in principles, but believes in frogs';[14] spirit, individuality – 'it is not worth the effort to study individual personalities. All people are similar to each other both in body and spirit';[15] nature – 'Nature is not a temple, but a workshop, and a man is a workman in it';[16] arts – 'Raphael is not worth a brass farthing';[17] 'Your father plays the cello? [...] Bazarov suddenly burst out laughing [...] Have mercy! At the age of forty-four, a man, pater familias, in – parish plays the cello!';[18] friendship, love, marriage and family – 'no friendship can withstand such collisions for long';[19] 'love in the ideal sense, or, as he put it, in the romantic sense, he called gibberish, unforgivable nonsense';[20] 'You still attach importance to marriage; I did not expect this from you';[21]

13 Fedotov, 'The Tragedy of the Intelligentsia', p. 70.

14 I. S. Turgenev, *Fathers and Sons*, in *Complete Essays and Letters*, 30 vols (Moscow, 1981), Vol. 7, pp. 7–188; p. 26.

15 Ibid., p. 78.

16 Ibid., p. 43.

17 Ibid., p. 52.

18 Ibid., p. 43.

19 Ibid., p. 123.

20 Ibid., p. 87.

21 Ibid., p. 42.

As a result, Bazarov contrasts these humanistic values with materialism and force – his constant reference is *Stoff und Kraft* (Force and Matter), 1855, by the German vulgar materialist L. Buchner: 'We break because we are a force'.[22]

For another iconic nihilist of the nineteenth century, Raskolnikov (*Crime and Punishment*, 1866), 'the end justifies the means': for the sake of an idea that will save all humankind, he is ready to destroy 'the present in the name of the best', ready with a clear conscience to step 'through corpses, through blood'.[23] In his personality, as in Bazarov's, there are such attitudes of ideology-driven consciousness as dogmatic, unquestioning perception of the truth, the monopoly on the truth and the perception of an opponent as an enemy (a heretic). In Raskolnikov's famous dream, it is this ideological 'inflexibility of the truth' that infects the entire society, destroying the basic values and foundations of humanity (morals, the idea of justice, crafts, farming and so on), leading eventually to wars and the apocalyptic collapse of the world:

> They never considered their judgments, their scientific conclusions, their moral convictions and beliefs more unshakable [...] they did not understand each other, everyone thought that in him alone lies the truth [...] They did not know who and how to judge, could not agree what to consider evil, what to consider good. They didn't know who to blame, who to justify. People killed each other in a kind of senseless anger [...] They abandoned the most ordinary crafts, because everyone offered their thoughts, their corrections, and could not agree; agriculture stopped [...] Fires started, famine started. Everything and everyone perished.[24]

It is significant that Dostoevsky's ideologue heroes become murderers or people who order the hit (Raskolnikov, Verkhovensky, the Grand Inquisitor, Ivan Karamazov).

Bear in mind that M. M. Bakhtin defined the hero of Dostoevsky as an 'ideologue hero'. Bakhtin relied on the concept of the 'man of ideas' from B. M. Engelhardt who earlier, in 1924, had shown that the idea took

22 Ibid., p. 51.

23 F. M. Dostoevsky, *Crime and Punishment*, in *Complete Works*, 30 vols (Leningrad, 1973), Vol. 6, pp. 5–422; p. 200.

24 Ibid., pp. 419–420.

possession of the hero of Dostoevsky as a dominant in his image (instead of the traditional biographical one), defining his entire personality. Engelhardt justified this type of hero in Dostoevsky with three quotations, the writer's diary for May 1876, the novel *Demons* and *Materials* for it, in which the overwhelming idea that captured the Russian person ('the norm that determines the volitional impetus') is compared with the stone that crushed the person (in this case, Shatov):

> He was one of those ideal Russian beings who can suddenly be so struck by some strong idea that it seems to crush them then and there, sometimes even forever. They are never strong enough to master it, but they are passionate believers, and so their whole life afterwards is spent in some last writhings, as it were, under the stone that has fallen on them and already half crushed them.[25]

Engelhardt projects the characterization of Stavrogin in his *Materials to the Demons* onto Dostoevsky's other heroes (Raskolnikov, Svidrigailov, Arkady Dolgoruky, Kirillov, Verkhovensky, Ivan Karamazov):

> The idea captures him and possesses him, but it has the property that it dominates him not so much in his head as by incarnating in him, passing into personality, always with suffering and anxiety, and, having already settled in personality, requires immediate application in life .[26]

Probably with this thought in mind, M. M. Prishvin in his diary (28 October 1919) gave the exact formula of the Russian intellectual according to Dostoevsky – 'he doesn't possess the idea, he's obsessed with it'.[27]

Engelhardt's portrait of Dostoevsky as a deracinated ideologue strongly resembles the one by Fedotov. The hero is detached from his native soil (he is alien to the 'rules', 'duty and honor' sanctified by tradition); he is not rooted in existence; and he cannot absorb the Western tradition: 'the tradition and ritual of a historically formed cultural existence is never

25 B. M. Engelhardt, 'The Ideological Novel of Dostoevsky', in *F. M. Dostoevsky: Essays and Materials*, Sb. II (Moscow, 1924), pp. 71–109; p. 86.

26 Ibid.

27 M. M. Prishvin, *Diaries 1918–1919* (St. Petersburg, 2008), p. 434.

adopted: it is created, it survives in continuous cultural creativity'.[28] As a result, only 'piles of ideas and abstract principles', 'syllogism, thought frozen in discursive detachment', 'idea-force', which is 'completely unhindered and mercilessly destroys traditional rules and norms, unceremoniously taking their place, assuming their functions and becoming the absolute mistress of the individual',[29] are easily adopted and grasped by his empty consciousness. The idea, as a 'power-hungry and cruel being', 'deforms and mutilates', 'empties' the hero who is obsessed with it and eventually kills him: 'exhausted, decomposing, it comes to self-denial, to a refined irony of itself, and finally perishes in a disfigured, incinerated inquiry, dragging him to death'.[30]

Russian literature did not only warn about the ontological and ethical collapse of the ideological type of hero but also offered society as an alternative supra-ideological type of personality, in which the ideological level does not suppress the ontological one (Raskolnikov in the epilogue,[31] Myshkin, Zosima, Alyosha Karamazov, etc.). Thus, Myshkin (*The Idiot*, 1868) is not so much an ideologist of the 'Russian world', Christian love, as a person who can first of all experience and survive the 'here-and-now' ontological reality of a human:

> I know you think me Utopian, don't you – an idealist? Oh, no! I'm not, indeed – my ideas are all so simple… […] 'Listen – I know it is best not to speak! It is best simply to give a good example – simply to begin the work. I have done this – I have begun, and – and – oh! can anyone be unhappy, really? Oh! what does grief matter – what does misfortune matter, if one knows how to be happy? Do you know, I cannot understand how anyone can pass by a green tree, and not feel happy only to look at it! How anyone can talk to a man and not feel happy in loving him! Oh, it is my own fault that I cannot express myself well enough! But there are lovely things at every step I take – things which even the most miserable man must recognize as beautiful.

28 Engelhardt, 'The Ideological Novel of Dostoevsky', p. 87.

29 Ibid., pp. 86–87.

30 Ibid., p. 87.

31 'Instead of dialectics, there came life, and something completely different had to be developed in the consciousness.' Dostoevsky, *Crime and Punishment*, in *Complete Works*, Vol. 6, p. 422.

> Look at a little child – look at God's day dawn – look at the grass growing – look at the eyes that love you, as they gaze back into your eyes.[32]

This type of hero, in whom the existence of the individual is deeper than any of his ideas, we define as humanistic. S. L. Frank wrote about the Christian humanism discovered by Dostoevsky, referring to the Gospel (Mark 2:27): '"Man is not made for the Sabbath, but the Sabbath for man." All – even the most ideal – standards of goodness, truth, and reason pale before the greatness of the ontological reality itself of the human being. This defines the deep, touching humanity of Dostoevsky's moral worldview.'[33] During the Soviet period, this humanistic 'message' of the Russian classics was subjected to ideological distortion in favor of the political conjuncture.[34]

32 F. M. Dostoevsky, *The Idiot*, in *Complete Works*, Vol. 8, pp. 5–510; pp. 458–459.

33 S. L. Frank, 'Dostoevsky and the Crisis of Humanism', in *About Dostoevsky: Works of Dostoevsky in Russian Thought 1881–1931; A Set of Essays for the Fiftieth Anniversary of Dostoevsky's Death* (Moscow, 1990), pp. 391–397; p. 396.

34 Ideologization of Russian classics was touched upon by A. I. Solzhenitsyn in his story 'Nastenka' (1995), in which a student at the Department of Languages and Literature of the Rostov Pedagogical Institute, who experienced the Russian classics and fell in love with them before the revolution, does not recognize the classics when presented with their works in a vulgar-sociological interpretation at the institute lectures: "Although Pushkin was recognized in passing for his melody of poetry (although the limpid lucidity of worldview was not mentioned), it was strongly pointed out that he expressed the psycho-ideology of the middle nobility during the beginning of the crisis of Russian feudalism. This social class needed depictions of the well-being of the landowners estate and displayed a fear of a peasant revolution, as *The Captain's Daughter* clearly demonstrates. 'It is some kind of algebra rather than literature – and where has Pushkin himself gone from this?'" A. I. Solzhenitsyn, *Selected Works*, 30 vols (Moscow, 2006), Vol. 1, p. 359.

'The Leviathan' or 'infallibility of ideas': The phenomenology of the Soviet Man

M. M. Prishvin continued to contemplate the issue of ideological consciousness secretly in his diary.[35] In the1930s, when the Bolshevik project to create new anthropological human species reached its culmination, Prishvin brought into light the phenomenology of the new Soviet Man and the new Soviet realities from inside Soviet life, yet describing ~~bsently~~ the ideologically-driven mindset and behavior of the Soviet man in an estranged and dispassionate manner (comparing the similarities and differences between him and the pre-revolutionary Russian).

The 44-year-old Prishvin faced the revolution of October 1917 as a mature personality;[36] he did not accept it personally, comprehending the revolution as 'a fundamental depreciation of personality' (21 September 1917).[37] Already on 30 October 1917, he wrote in his diary: 'we fell out of the pan into the fire, from the tsar-and-church iron fist to the socialist one, bypassing the freedom of the individual'.[38] Prishvin calls Lenin's articles in *Pravda* as 'examples of logical madness': 'I do not know whether there is such a disease – logical madness, but a Russian chronicler will not call our time by any other name' (1 March 1918).[39]

In the diary entries of the 1930s, observing the new Soviet reality Prishvin sees in it the embodiment of Bazarov's nihilism, but in such a concentration that Bazarov, as the proto-hero of the Soviet man, appears only as a weak reflection of it: 'this is a Bolshevik as if he were from under

35 The writer kept his diary for half a century, from 1905 to 1954. The release of his diary in its complete and uncensored state (18 volumes) could be accomplished only in post-Soviet times and took 26 years (1991–2017).

36 On Prishvin's criticism of October 1917, see A. A. Medvedev, 'The Russian disaster of 1917 and "great times" (M. Prishvin, V. Rozanov, A. Blok)'. *Studi Slavistici. Rivista dell'Associazione Italiana degli Slavisti*, Vol. 15, No. 1 (2019), pp. 143–154.

37 M. M. Prishvin, *Diaries 1914–1917* (St. Petersburg, 2007), p. 513.

38 Ibid., p. 528.

39 Prishvin, *Diaries 1918–1919* (St. Petersburg, 2008), p. 48.

the pen of Turgenev [...] now that everything has come true, Bazarov is not a man, but a faint smudge' (25 February 1935).[40]

According to Prishvin's diary of this period, one can comprehend the agenda of Soviet Bazarovs. Let us consider its main provisions. The starting point of the revolution as seen by Prishvin is dogmatism and ideological intolerance toward other opinions:

> In my mind, it began when, in a certain (I don't remember which one) theatre, a sailor in a gallery shot an artist for mentioning the name of Christ[41] in some poem. In fact, the trigger was not pulled to shoot at the actor, but to shoot at Christ, or at personality, personal opinion. After that, a single general view was created, whereas dissenting opinions of individuals were cut away like leaves, like twigs of a tree. Earlier power was essentially created by the victory of some idea. But back then the idea was hidden behind someone's personality (Ivan the Terrible, Peter), now it is not a personality that triumphs, but an opinion that excludes all other individual ones. (12 December 1941)[42]

The writer states that with the change of a sovereign (Lenin, Stalin), the dogmatic infallibility of ideas of a new dictator is established in the Soviet system:

> The characteristic feature of the revolution is that victory of one or another contender immediately establishes infallibility of his ideas and compulsoriness for all. I won and it's over, and here are our bellies, our lives! Here are our bellies, and our heads, and everything. (1 November 1930)[43]

One loses identity, one blends in the public and thrall worship of the 'leader': 'a formless mass has emerged, and now it is spread around

40 M. M. Prishvin, *Diaries 1932–1935* (St. Petersburg, 2009), p. 608.

41 Z. N. Gippius recalled that at the end of 1917 'in the midst of night robberies, murders and the undeniable victory of Lenin' during one particular literary soirée in Petersburg, 'when some actor read the poetry of D. S. Merezhkovsky "Christ is risen" (very old, but very popular at that time), somebody from the audience, indeed a soldier, shot an actor'. This poem (1887) was popular due to the romance composed by S. V. Rakhmaninov (1906). See Z. N. Gippius-Merezhkosvkaya, *Dmitry Merezhkovsky* (Paris, 1951), p. 231.

42 M. M. Prishvin, *Diaries 1940–1941* (Moscow, 2012), pp. 723–724.

43 M. M. Prishvin, *Diaries 1930–1931* (St. Petersburg, 2006), p. 266.

the personality of the leader, like filings around a magnetic pole' (25 November 1936).[44] During the party congress, Prishvin observes how 'everyone with utmost praise, clapping his hands, seemed to deliberately try to silence, to drown the voice of his own personality': 'There seemed to be something sinister and unprecedented in these talking and clapping puppets' (13 November 1936).[45] A person turns into a mechanically controlled thing ('puppet'), manipulated by a 'puppeteer'. 'A military speaker, a young man, was so adept in oratory that by simply raising his voice at an appropriate time during his speech, he kind of pressed a button, after which hundreds of mechanical hands, without the slightest participation of inner spirit in a citizen, were set in motion and clapped.'[46]

'Never in the history of mankind has the Leviathan reached such power as in the USSR' (undated);[47] the total dictatorship of the state over the individual forms a person of the state: 'A communist is certainly a Leviathan, a quadrupedal state animal' (17 June 1937).[48] Therefore, the individual is not treated as a self-valuable individual, but is treated 'expediently', with the utilitarian self-interests of the state coming first:

> the SPD plenipotentiary sneaks everywhere. He's frigid. And in general, the type of such a pure statesman is outlined: he does not care about you, as a person, at all. A cold, inexorable creature. In a tsarist prison, as I remember, there was the same mood from the comrade prosecutor. (8 January 1930)[49]

Such a vision of a person as 'the quadrupedal Leviathan' is in contrast to the 'bipedal personality', which means 'being independent of any benefits, and corruption, and satisfaction with its own futility' (17 June 1937).[50]

The negation of an identity is also expressed in the destruction of the feminine principle: 'The revolution creates a woman of the kolkhoz

44 M. M. Prishvin, *Diaries 1936–1937* (St. Petersburg, 2010), p. 367.
45 Ibid., p. 355.
46 Ibid.
47 Prishvin, *Diaries 1938–1939*, p. 562.
48 Prishvin, *Diaries 1936–1937*, p. 636.
49 Prishvin, *Diaries 1930–1931*, p. 8.
50 Prishvin, *Diaries 1936–1937*, p. 636.

[collective farm]' (10 July 1930).[51] Seeing the revolution as an 'ideological', masculine principle, Prishvin notes that it 'rushed with extreme hatred into the destruction of the feminine world, love, motherhood', since it is in them where origins of a personality are – 'differences among people, and, of course, ownership and talent';[52] it was mothers who brought up the sense of ownership as 'the cornerstone of the entire community' in the pre-Soviet system (8 July 1930).[53] Prishvin is outraged by the nihilistic denial of motherhood and love:

> Why, for example, does the author of the article 'socialist city' mock maternal feeling? Why are 'childhood', 'love', etc., for example, the veneration of the elderly, father and mother – all this is forbidden in our country [...] This is how the beehive state is created, in which love, motherhood, etc., the nursery of individuality, interfere with communist labour. (8 July 1930)[54]

The ideology-driven approach to man replaces conscience as a universal ethical value with a narrow class concept: 'Someone (Ognev) tries to repent of their intellectual conscience in the hope of reaching the proletarian one, but they will never succeed, because there is nothing in the proletarian conscience – just emptiness' (7 November 1932).[55] Soviet 'ethics' is defined by the state's 'expediency' ('the end justifies the means'):

> A conscientious person now shudders at the thought that is now imposed on him on a daily basis: that the most incredible crime, lies, the most brazen deceptions, systematic violence against personality – all this can not only go unpunished, but even be a good lever of history, of the future. (24 January 1930)[56]

The Soviet project is based on the replacement of the present with a utopian future, to which a person is sacrificed: 'Sometimes it seems to me that under the pretext of the future, there is a denial of the current life

51 Prishvin, *Diaries 1930–1931*, p. 149.
52 Ibid.
53 Ibid., p. 150.
54 Ibid., p. 147.
55 Prishvin, *Diaries 1932–1935*, p. 230.
56 Prishvin, *Diaries 1930–1931*, p. 15.

in our time, and this is exactly where disdain of the individual somehow comes from' (17 June 1937).[57] And 13 years later, Prishvin conceives the same idea more clearly: 'Soviet life is precisely given to the future, all of us are sacrificed to this "eternity" and are so devoted to it that there is nothing in the present for any one of us' (10 July 1950).[58]

The negation of identity is also associated with the negation of ownership. For Prishvin, ownership is not a confined economic concept, it is directly related to an individual:

> Communism has scraped out all personal attachment of our people to their belongings, all personal skills of craftsmen, all public practices. Thus a formless mass has been formed, and now it is spread around the personality of the leader, like filings around a magnetic pole. (25 November 1936)[59]

As noted by Y. Grishina and N. Poltavtseva, from Prishvin's perspective, the state should not convey messages. The function of the state is to

> arrange the life of human society ('Individuals can have principles [...] the state should not have [...] a predilection for ideas'), cooperation should not be an idea ('cooperation [...] should be [...] an activity, and the public activity must proceed from personal gain'), neither love nor literature can be ideology-driven.[60]

And the Soviet system is doomed precisely because ideology has supplanted life in it ('Marxists who call themselves materialists [...] they are completely devoid of perception of the material world: they are the purest idealists'; 'The bourgeoisie was the historical tentacle of matter, and socialism will only make a step forward when it recognizes the bourgeoisie as its father – matter').[61]

57 Prishvin, *Diaries 1936–1937*, p. 636.

58 M. M. Prishvin, *Diaries 1950–1951* (St. Petersburg, 2016), p. 145.

59 Prishvin, *Diaries 1936–1937*, p. 367.

60 Y. Grishina and N. Poltavtseva, 'Commentaries', in M. M. Prishvin, *Diaries 1923–1925* (St. Petersburg, 2009), pp. 481–507; p. 494.

61 Ibid., 494–495.

'True inquisition', or 'the Purge': Prishvin and RAPP

In a letter dated 19 April 1933, Prishvin writes to S. Dynamov about the spirit of hostility and creative bankruptcy in Soviet literature created by the ideology of the RAPP:[62]

> The RAPP group dominates, dividing the sphere of writers through a vulgarized understanding of class struggle as enmity. This policy has led to the impoverishment of the creativity of writers (it is terrible to write, so as not to make a mistake, guns are aimed at every new idea). This policy led the leaders themselves to tendentiousness, abstraction, and scholasticism. Obviously, one enmity is not enough for creativity. For two years I could not write a single line, understanding the creativity of this time as the architecture of emptiness. To fill this void with something, I went to the Far East and then began to process the collected manuscripts, opposing this materially valuable stuff of mine to scholastic disputes.[63]

As G. A. Belaya notes, the RAPP representatives, as supporters of 'egalitarian socialism' and 'barracks communism', sought 'to create a new anthropological human species, caught this idea and this trend in the Stalinist regime early on, and worked with strength and passion for it'.[64] To achieve this goal, they believed that the writer should 'illuminate, electrify the huge damp basement of the subconscious', forcibly invading the subconscious in order to 'consciously direct it'.[65]

The thinking of RAPP representatives was characterized by extreme dogmatism, the search for the 'enemy', and violence against reality and the soul of man. In the Procrustean bed of Soviet ideology, they subjected the

62 RAPP (also known as Russian Association of Proletarian Writers) was a Soviet literary association (1925–1932) whose goals were to carry out a rigid party policy in literature: the creation of a class (proletarian) culture and the rejection of classical literature as bourgeois; it was distinguished by an irreconcilable struggle with other literary associations and, in fact, carried out ideological repressions against fellow writers. RAPP was a direct instrument of Stalin's policy in the field of literature.

63 G. A. Belaya, *Don-Quixotes of the Twentieth Century: 'Pereval' and the Fate of Its Ideas* (Moscow, 1989), p. 364.

64 Ibid., p. 126.

65 See Ibid. G. A. Belaya, *On the Literary Post*, No. 6 (1929), 19.

diversity of living reality and the living complexity of the individual to a rigid vulgar-sociological schematization. Thus, Prishvin notes that, from the standpoint of class (proletarian) ideology, RAPP representatives grossly distorted the personality of A. Grigoriev:

> They discovered that Ap. Grigoriev was an ideologue of the commercial bourgeoisie. For us, this 'discovery' does not reveal anything, you can be an ideologue of the bourgeoisie and give the world a lot of valuable things, and this valuable thing should be revealed by a critic. But the Marxist critic discovered the 'ideologue' and that's it. [...] the class struggle is the particularity of our common daily struggle, the particularity taken for everything (*pars quo totum*)[66] [...] [T]his discovery of the root causes or 'clarification' (of the writer) throws out the living person and condemns him to inactivity and often starvation; if you look at life more broadly, then we will see that is philosophy has turned there into a real inquisition, which is called a 'purge'. The life of a state farm consists of constant purges, denunciations, intrigues, and an incessant change of faces. (22 December 1931)[67]

As we can see, in accordance with Barthes's concept of ideology-driven mental attitude, in Grigoriev's RAPP perception, the 'personal' (class relations) is presented as the 'whole'; the living personality is replaced by a scheme that is aggressively imposed on the reader.

It is significant that the radical RAPP ideology first of all sought to destroy humanistic values. Even a 'socialist humanism' compromise was unacceptable to the RAPP. Thus, L. Averbakh wrote in 1929: 'People come to us with the propaganda of humanism, as if there is anything more truly human in the world than the class hatred of the proletariat'.[68] In M. Bochacher's article (1930), humanism and morality were openly replaced by 'revolutionary violence', 'the class struggle of the proletariat' and 'revolutionary expediency'.[69] M. Gorky, who became the ideologist of class

66 Prishvin clearly meant here the Latin expression *pars pro toto* (a part taken for the whole).

67 Prishvin, *Diaries 1930–1931*, p. 580.

68 Belaya, *Don-Quixotes of the Twentieth Century*, p. 312.

69 Ibid., p. 313. In the aforementioned Solzhenitsyn story, a 'napostovets' (a member of a literary association – 'Na postu') Shurka Gen justifies the struggle against the '*Pereval*' association 'that has agreed to neo-Slavophilism, to Kulak humanism', to 'love for man in general', 'beauty is universal'. Solzhenitsyn, *Selected Works*, Vol. 1, p. 362.

humanism, also contributed to the discrediting of humanism and to the creation of the image of the class enemy.[70]

During this period, Prishvin himself was subjected to ideological harassment for 'humanism' by Soviet 'nihilists' represented by the LFA,[71] RAPP and critics close to them (Osip Brik, Vladimir Kirshon, Arkady Glagolev, Mikhail Grigoriev). In his diary, Prishvin quotes a speech by one of the leaders of the RAPP, V. Kirshon,[72] at the Sixteenth Congress of the CPSU(b), calling it 'vile'. Kirshon attacked the *Pereval* group ('The Pass', which Prishvin had joined), accusing it of responding to the slogan of eliminating the kulaks as a class by putting forward 'the slogan of humanism and humanity', the perception of Soviet literature as a 'single stream' and

70 In the article 'Proletarian Humanism' (*Pravda*, 12 May 1934, No. 140), Gorky contrasted the 'falsehood and hypocrisy of bourgeois "humanism"' with the 'truly universal, proletarian humanism of Marx-Lenin-Stalin-humanism, the goal of which is the complete liberation of the working people of all races and nations from the iron clutches of capitalism' and justified with this 'revolutionary humanism' the historical right to 'merciless struggle against capitalism, the right to demolish and destroy all the most abominable foundations of the bourgeois world' (M. Gorky, *Collected Essays*, 30 vols (Moscow, 1953), Vol. 27, pp. 234, 235). In his letter, Gorky noted that this article was 'very much approved by Comrade Stalin' (Ibid., p. 558). It was within the framework of this class concept of humanism that the famous slogan 'If the enemy does not surrender, then it is destroyed' appeared in Gorky's article of the same name (*Pravda*, 15 November 1930, No. 314), in which he wrote about internal enemies – kulaks and pests in the food industry (the writer supported the execution of 48 'organizers of food hunger'), which, in fact, became the ideological basis for all further fabricated campaigns against 'enemies of the people'. In the article 'To Humanists' (*Pravda*, 11 December 1930), Gorky refused to cooperate in the 'International Union of Democratic Writers', as its members (Albert Einstein, Heinrich Mann) signed a protest of the German 'League for the Protection of Human Rights' against the execution of these 48 people.

71 LEF, also known as «Levyi Front Iskusstv» (Left Front of the Arts), was a Soviet literary association (1922–1930); the Goal of LEF was submission of art purely to propaganda and production tasks. The theorists of LEF advanced a utopian conception of art as formation of a new person. Speaking against the development of easel art, they advocated the production art and 'social order', and cultivated propaganda and documentary, photography, film, literature-report, and the actual essay.

72 Vladimir Kirshon (1902–1938), one of the RAPP leaders.

the rejection of the demand for 'political restraint' from writers (8 July 1930).[73] Kirshon saw in *Pereval* 'the class enemy', 'the ideological agents of the kulaks and the bourgeoisie in our country, the emigrants and the imperialists abroad'.[74] From the standpoint of class proletarian ideology and proletarian art, Kirshon demanded that 'fellow writers' (which included Prishvin)

> more resolutely break with the old traditions, caste isolation, intellectual individualism. They need to rush into the thinking of construction work; they need to go to the countryside, go to construction, leave their city offices and literary houses, so that together with the proletariat, among them, they can get material for creativity, re-educate themselves.[75]

In the same record dated 8 July 1930, Prishvin sharply reacts to his accusations of a 'biology-driven orientation', in which the critic Glagolev sees 'one of the essential ideological vices of the view of the *Pereval* group', since it is free 'from any "infusion" of literary sociologism'.[76]

73 Prishvin, *Diaries 1930–1931*, p. 147.

74 Ibid., p. 214.

75 Ibid., pp. 214–215. The spirit of this irreconcilable struggle with fellow poets, characteristic of the 1920s, as 'ideology antipodes' can be heard in the accusing speech of the Komsomol organizer Shurka Gen ('a convinced *Napostovets*', who quotes the words of the *Napostovets* members: 'We are proud of the title "literature *chekists*" and that the enemies call us informers!') (Solzhenitsyn, *Selected Works*, Vol. 1, p. 362). From the already mentioned Solzhenitsyn story:

'fellow poets are the writers of our enemies of yesterday and of the dead men of tomorrow, they have reactionary guts, and they slanderously distort the revolution, and the more talented the more dangerous they are. And literature is not an object of pleasure, but a field of struggle. All this *Pilnyakovism*, *Akhmatovism*, all these little Serapions and Scorpions must either be made to look up to proletarian literature or be swept out with an iron broom, there can be no reconciliation' (Ibid., p. 360). 'Shurka Gen believes that proletarian literature needs no psychologism or artistic reincarnation, but a "proletarian cause": "Psychologism only hinders our victorious progress, and the so-called reincarnation into a character blunts the class"' (Ibid., p. 361).

76 A. Glagolev, 'On the Artistic Appearance of "*Pereval*"', *Novyi Mir*, No. 5 (1930), p. 161.

The greatest absurdity of this ideological perception of literature and reality is achieved in the criticism of Prishvin by LFA representative O. Brik,[77] who accused the writer of missing the 'Soviet spirit' in his story about nature:

> But your story lacks something which is called … Yes, yes, the spirit, the Soviet spirit … Don't smile, please … Here, for example, you write about a crow, and you do not feel like this is our, Soviet, crow […] [As the other speakers spoke, Mikhail Mikhailovich grew more and more flushed. He began to understand what was happening: it was a thoroughly devised, carefully considered harassment of the writer.][78]

After these and other attacks against him in the press, which Prishvin calls a 'purge' (7 December 1930),[79] he is forced to distance himself from the *Pereval*, realizing that otherwise he would be 'left behind' as a writer by this campaign (8 July 1930).[80]

'Blest everyday life of the world': Being and routine

In 1917, during a period of extremely ideology-driven life, nihilism and destruction, Prishvin discovers the value of ordinary, everyday life – both domestic and natural (Ivan Karamazov's 'little sticky leaves that come out in the spring') – about which 20 years later he writes: 'through the empty everyday life of the revolution, I saw blest everyday life of the world and combined my poetry with these sacred sticky leaves' (23 August 1937).[81] Prishvin sees the loss of a sense of living everyday life due to being captured

77 Osip Brik (1888–1945) was an ideologist of LEF (literary group Left Front of the Arts, 1923–1929) and creator of the theories of social mandate (servicing the proletariat and revolution by poet), industrial art and literature of facts.

78 A. N. Varlamov, *Prishvin* (Moscow: Molodaia gvardiia, 2003), pp. 325–326.

79 Prishvin, *Diaries 1930–1931*, p. 296.

80 Ibid., p. 147.

81 Prishvin, *Diaries 1936–1937*, p. 724.

by the 'big ideology' of the Russian schism, Romanticism, Bolshevism and Stalinism:

> Losing interest in everyday work due to the global catastrophe was the main feeling of the student revolutionaries of our time. Thousands of possible engineers gave up their teaching because of this and became clandestine people. This feeling is related to the 'end of the world' mood, be it of the Old Believers' type or the generally defeatist one, and, perhaps, 'world sorrow' is of the same origin (because of something big, I do not want to do something small). This is where the Russian intelligentsia and all its nihilism grew up, and hence the Stakhanovite as the antithesis.[82]

Later, the writer will come to the key idea that the values of simple, everyday life in Russia are threatened by two extremes – 'the slavery of rationalism that reigns in our revolutionary thought' and 'the slavery of irresponsible mysticism that reigns in religion'.[83]

The life-giving source of the ontological sense of the 'blest everyday life' while being under ideological pressure Prishvin found in the Russian classics. In 1918, Prishvin wrote out a phrase of Arkady about the beauty of an ash tree from *Fathers and Sons*: 'Don't you think that the ash has been very well named in Russian *Yasen*: not a single other tree is so light and translucently clear (*yasno*) against the sky' (27 July 1918).[84] Arkady says it when he sits with Katya Lokteva on a bench in the shade of a tall ash tree, a dog is lying next to him gracefully ('like a hare'), and Katya feeds a 'family of sparrows'. Turgenev seems to freeze for an instant, contemplatively admiring the beauty of simple, everyday life:

> A faint breeze, stirring the ash leaves, kept gently moving pale gold patches of sunlight up and down across the shady path and over Fifi's back; an unbroken shadow fell on Arkady and Katya; only from time to time a bright streak gleamed in her hair.[85]

82 Ibid., 723.

83 V. D. Prishvina, 'From "Intermediary Chapter" (Our Idea)', in *From Russian Thought*, 2 vols (Moscow, 1995), Vol. 2, pp. 178–193; p. 191.

84 Prishvin, *Diaries 1918–1919*, p. 201.

85 Turgenev, *Fathers and Sons*, p. 155. See https://www.ibiblio.org/eldritch/ist/fas25.htm (Accessed 10 May 2023).

Rereading the novel in 1935, he again discovers the experience of the ontological fullness of simple, everyday human life – in the episode when Katya sits on a garden bench, 'surrounded by shade and coolness',

> she used to read and work, or give herself up to that sensation of perfect peace, known probably to everyone, the charm of which consists in the half-conscious mute listening to that vast current of life which uninterruptedly flows both around us and within us.[86]

This experience of existence above ideology, in the present, 'here and now', is continued by Prishvin who recorded in 1951: 'Long did we wait for such a May, and only the Easter week could give us such a May, as if God would forgive the Soviet regime' (1 May 1951).[87]

Prishvin rehabilitates the contemptible concept of a 'common man' from the perspective of ideological intellectuals, as he believes that being is ethical behavior, the most important 'culture of personal relationships':

> Yes, I am a common man![88] I understand my being as the improvement of personal relations to people and things, I understand everyday existence as the constant improvement of personal relations, as their culture. Everyday life is a culture of personal relations to people and things. Certainly to things, because a person who considers it a sin to litter on the floor and trample on the particles of solar energy contained in bread crumbs, undoubtedly treats people better than a careless person who litters on the floor. (2 June 1922)[89]

In this spirit of everyday life, Prishvin follows in the footsteps of his teacher V. V. Rozanov, who answered the ideological question in the title of Chernyshevsky's famous nihilistic novel with the need to live a real life: '"What is to be done?" asked the impatient Petersburg youth. – What do you mean, "What is to be done"? If it's summer – prepare berries and

86 Ibid., p. 164; Prishvin, *Diaries 1932–1935*, pp. 607–608.

87 Prishvin, *Diaries 1950–1951*, p. 393.

88 Prishvin uses the Russian word *obyvatel'* which cognates with the verb 'to be' (*byt'*) and the term for an everyday humdrum existence (*byt*) – and makes a point (and a pun) out of this.

89 M. M. Prishvin, *Diaries* (Moscow, 1990), p. 11.

make the jam; if it's winter – drink tea with this jam'.[90] Prishvin wrote as early as 1914 about the nature that saves one from 'ideological emptiness', again in connection to Rozanov: 'The fear of a nightmare (brain crash) and gratitude to nature that saves from it bring me closer to Rozanov' (10 February 1914).[91]

'Pure observation': Prishvin and Tarkovsky

In his diary of 18 March 1979, the film director Andrei Tarkovsky writes out the following of Prishvin's diary entries ('He's smart. He has wonderful ideas about cinema'),[92] finding in them similar thoughts that cinema art should proceed from its own principles, and not be an illustration of literary ideas: 'It is necessary in cinema, as in photography, to use their own means ... And if there are no ideas in these resources, then it is better to have a movie without ideas, like American films, than to get these ideas from fictional literature. Cinema must come from the document' (31 March 1934).[93]

Tarkovsky considered the main principle of cinema art to be observation – 'the observation of vital facts in time, organized in accordance with the forms of life itself and with its temporal laws'.[94] The film image, according to Tarkovsky, should be as organic as possible (lasting in time and not broken up with montage) and express the very fluidity of being in

90 V. V. Rozanov, 'Embryos', in *Selected Works: Religion and Culture; Articles and Feature-Stories 1902–1903* (Moscow, 2008), pp. 211–218; p. 211.

91 Prishvin, *Diaries 1914–1917*, p. 39.

92 A. A. Tarkovsky, *Martyrology: Diaries 1970–1986* (Florence, 2008), p. 200.

93 Prishvin, *Diaries 1932–1935*, p. 372. Probably, the source of these notes for Tarkovsky was in the book *Context-1978*, which contained Prishvin's diary entries of 1930–1934. M. M. Prishvin, 'Notes on Works', in *Context-1978: Literary and Theoretical Research* (Moscow, 1978), pp. 268–296; pp. 287–288.

94 A. A. Tarkovsky, 'Imprinted Time' (1967), in *Archives, Documents, Memories* (Moscow, 2002), pp. 155–184; p. 168.

the frame. Tarkovsky saw the most ideal expression of this principle in art ('purity, subtlety and unity of observation of life') in the Japanese haiku:

> Fishing rods on the tide
> Gently touched by the full moon
> On the run.
>
> Or:
>
> Dew descended,
> And on every sloe's thorn
> Droplets hang.
>
> After all, this is sheer observation! [...] The poetry of the film is born from pure observation of life – this, in my opinion, is the real path of cinematic poetry. Because the film image is essentially an observation of a fact that flows through time.[95]

In a diary entry dated 9 June 1980, Tarkovsky regrets that modern artists have, above all, forgotten how to observe:

> If we could completely ignore all the rules and generally accepted ways in which films, books, etc. are made, what wonderful things could be created! We have completely forgotten how to observe. We have replaced observation with making clichés. It is not for nothing that Castaneda and his Don Juan often come to mind.[96]

In the artistic image, the director appreciated spontaneity in the perception of the world: 'The image is an impression of the Truth, which the Lord allowed us to look at with our blind eyes'.[97] Such an image has a metaphysical, apophatic infinity:

> Infinity is immanent in the very structure of the image [...] the image rushes to infinity and leads to God. And even what is called the 'idea' of the image in its actual multidimensionality and polysemy,[98] is fundamentally impossible to express in words. The very idea of infinity cannot be expressed in words – art does it.[99]

95 Ibid., pp. 167–168.

96 Tarkovsky, *Martyrology*, p. 286.

97 Ibid., 196.

98 In his concept of the artistic image of Tarkovsky, he relied on the perception of Vyacheslav Ivanov as a symbol that is 'inexhaustible and unlimited in its meaning', 'ineffable and inexplicable'. V. Ivanov, 'Poet and Rabble', in *Complete W*orks, 4 vols (Brussels, 1971), Vol. 1 pp. 709–714; p. 713.

99 Tarkovsky, 'Imprinted Time', pp. 217, 211, 213.

In Prishvin's diary for 1933, in which Tarkovsky uncovered thoughts close to him about cinema, the writer also reflected on ideology in art. Thus, the departure of Gogol, Tolstoy and Dostoevsky from the sphere of art to religious teaching is perceived by Prishvin as 'demonism' that seduces the writer, believing that he must remain an artist until the end:

> The artist does not give himself up to the power of ideas that lure him out of the sphere of art, but, on the contrary, as soon as the idea begins to lure him, to seduce him, to tear him off the ground, he throws the idea away and for that, by descending, he receives a new detail (this is how 'The Homeland of the Crane' is designed). On the same path is to resolve all issues only by means of art and to remain an artist to the end. (25 January 1933)[100]

Prishvin perceives his tears on the death of Leo Tolstoy as ideological and selfish ('religious and revolutionary ideals'): 'It seems to me that [...] we are not crying about Tolstoy, but about ourselves ... orphaned we are ... the intelligentsia is still in us: *we live by ideas*' (20 September 1933).[101]

In the same Prishvin publication of 1978, Tarkovsky could also find an entry that is pure observation: 'The moon has fallen, somewhere quietly, very timidly, for the dearest friend, water was gurgling, and what a gentle sky and stars ... all the old best turned out to live with me, and I think: this is the meaning of life, so that a person flying 300 kilometers per hour retains within him all the experience of a pedestrian' (17 March).[102] In this contemplative attention, according to Prishvin, the essence of personality is contained: 'And I realized at that moment that this feeling is the feeling of being a personality and a sense of ownership comes from that, is born within it: I want to live and make everything my own' (1 October 1932).[103]

The ability to contemplate the world, to merge in direct observation (not only phenological but also social) with the very being in its temporal fluidity, is Prishvin's main creative principle, which is opposed to any ideocracy: 'attention is the placement of the whole in a part, the

100 Prishvin, *Diaries 1932–1935*, p. 283.
101 Ibid., p. 285.
102 Ibid., p. 287.
103 Ibid., p. 208.

universe – in the sparkling dewdrop of the morning iris' (15 June 1950).[104] The principle of flowing time is most accurately expressed in Prishvin's image of a forest stream, the flow of which he carefully observes and devotes a detailed entry to this: 'If you want to understand the soul of the forest, find a forest stream and go up or down its bank [...] The entire passage of the stream through the forest is the path of a long struggle, and so time is created here. And so the struggle continues, and in this duration life and my consciousness manage to be born' (1940).[105] As we will see later, Tarkovsky's favorite image of water in his films has the same function of reflecting existence and time as Prishvin's.

In fact, this phenomenological principle is manifested not only in Prishvin's prose but also in his art photography,[106] which is a visual analogue of his work with the word: 'the value of photography lies in the accurate transmission of the image of the world, as a result of which we get a belief in its existence, as if completely independent of our perception' (5 September 1929).[107] In the macro photographs (gossamer, drops, buds), we see how Prishvin captures the usually unnoticed beauty, the 'wonderful moment' of everyday life – two drops of water on the buds of twigs that reflect the trunks of trees going up into the sky (see Figure 2.1), or a forest spider web decorated with shining dew drops (see Figure 2.2) – 'a carpet of pearls, enchanted, like a magic carpet' (13 August 1949).[108] In this way, Prishvin reveals to the indoctrinated consciousness, which monologically objectifies nature and personality, a direct vision of the world, in the words of M. M. Bakhtin – 'self-revealing being'.[109]

104 Prishvin, *Diaries 1950–1951*, p. 128.

105 M. M. Prishvin, *Selected Works*, 8 vols (Moscow, 1983), Vol. 5, p. 35.

106 Prishvin had been photographing since 1906 (his book about the North *In the Land of the Undaunted Birds* he illustrates with his own photos) and does not part with his camera in his travels in Russia until the end of his life: he worked in a variety of genres (street photography, portrait, landscape, industrial landscape), angles and plans (macro photography, close-ups).

107 M. M. Prishvin, *Diaries 1928–1929* (St. Petersburg, 2004), p. 453.

108 M. M. Prishvin, *Diaries 1948–1949* (Moscow, 2014), p. 787.

109 M. Bakhtin, 'Towards the Philosophical Origins of Humanities', in *Collected Writings* (Moscow, 1996), Vol. 5, pp. 7–10; p. 8.

Figure 2.1 Mikhail Prishvin, *Drops*, 1930s, b&w photo from the archive of Liliya A. Ryazanova.

The principle of 'pure observation' can also be seen in Tarkovsky's polaroid photographs. An instant polaroid image directly captures a particular moment in time, as does an instant impression reflected in our minds. Over time, the image fades, and this further enhances the sense of time in it. In this sense, the polaroid image is the most adequate to the nature of human consciousness in its temporal fluidity; it becomes an imprint of human memory. Tarkovsky's pictures are built on the same principles as the frames in his films – tricks of light, rays, fog, water, the color and texture of grass, foliage … they capture the time itself and the beauty of ordinary, everyday life.[110]

Let us pay attention to how the visuals, audio and words interact in Tarkovsky's films in episodes in which the problem of ideology is addressed in one way or another. In the first shots of *Solaris* (Mosfilm, 1973), we see

110 'Mystery of Everyday Life – Andrei Tarkovsky', *Le vagabond des étoiles*, <https://www.vagabond-des-etoiles.com/arts/photographie/mystery-of-everyday-life-andrei-tarkovsky-1979/> (Accessed 4 January 2017).

Figure 2.2 Mikhail Prishvin, *Gossamer*, 1930s, b&w photo from the archive of Liliya A. Ryazanova.

the flow of being that exists independently of our perception – a smooth stream of gurgling water with green algae, an autumn leaf floating in it, reflections on the water, the sounds of birds, green grass stalks, gently swaying algae stalks in the stream, fog,[111] huge burdock leaves, tall thick grass with

111 In a 1974 questionnaire, when asked about his favorite landscape, Tarkovsky called it 'summer, dawn, fog' (*Martyrology*, p. 109). Tonino Guerra, noting that Tarkovsky 'managed to be embodied in nature, as in another dimension, and nature always helped him', recalled the director's words: 'I, Tonino, now imagine my house, which, as you know, is three hundred kilometers from Moscow, with a small river, over which a band of fog is like a white saddle on a running horse'

bushes of pubescent thistles, the trunk of an old tree, water, a house, a gracefully running horse, green duckweed in the water where Chris washes his hands; Chris,[112] whose image grows out of this natural space, is opposed by a fanatical 'ideologue hero' – the scientist Sartorius, who says in Bazar's way: 'Man is created by nature to know it. Moving endlessly toward the truth, a person is doomed to knowledge. Everything else is a whim.' For Sartorius, who proposes to annihilate the ocean of Solaris with powerful radiation, living life is an object, a project of radical alteration.[113] In this 'ideologue hero', Tarkovsky expressed the attitude to the monological objectification of life, which, in the words of Bakhtin, turns a living person into a voiceless object of conclusive understanding (a dead thing).[114] Tarkovsky emphasizes the aberration of this objective and seemingly unbiased vision of the world (in particular, a metaphor for this aberration can be seen in the fact that Sartorius's lens falls out of his glasses during an argument).

For Sartorius, 'truth', not a man, is the highest value, for which he is ready to commit violence. Paraphrasing Dostoevsky's well-known dilemma about 'truth and Christ',[115] we can say that Sartorius prefers to stay with

(P. Volkova, 'Nostos', No. 3 (October 2012), <http://magazines.russ.ru/october/2012/3/v9.html> (Accessed 4 January 2017).

112 In the name of the hero, there are obvious Christian connotations and allusions: the English Chris is a diminutive form of the name Christopher (from the Greek Χριστόφορος – 'carrying Christ') or Christian (from Latin Christianus – 'Christian'). In the Western tradition, the legend of St. Christopher is popular (third to fourth centuries), who carried Christ on his shoulders across the river when he was a child.

113 The idea of reworking is symbolically reflected in his name (from Latin sartor, -oris – 'tailor').

114 M. Bakhtin, 'The Poetics of Dostoevsky and Its problems', in *Collected Writings* (Moscow, 2002), Vol. 6, pp. 5–300; pp. 80, 69.

115 In a well-known letter to N. F. Fonvizina in 1854: 'If someone proved to me that Christ is outside of the truth, and it really would be that the truth is outside of Christ, then I would rather stay with Christ than with the truth.' In such a posing of the question, Tarkovsky, of course, refers to Dostoevsky, whose religious and philosophical tradition was very important to him. Tarkovsky planned to make a film about Dostoevsky, as well as film adaptations of his novels (*The Raw Youth*, *The Idiot*, *Crime and Punishment*). These plans were not realized, but Dostoevsky's polyphonic poetics, dialogical search and testing of truth, 'eternal questions' about faith, God, immortality, and so on were implicitly included in his films.

'truth' (scientific fact), rather than with a living person. The absurdity of this nihilistic ideology is particularly striking in the scene in the library when Snout asserts that 'A man needs a man!', and Sartorius at the same time denies the existence of Hari[116] in her presence: 'You are neither a woman nor a man! Do you understand, if you can understand anything at all! Hari's gone! She's dead! And you, you are only a repetition of it. Mechanical repetition! A copy! The matrix!' The fiasco of this ideological personality type is expressed in the words of Snout, who calls Sartorius a Faust who 'seeks a remedy against immortality'.

In the same scene, Tarkovsky introduces Hari's detailed contemplation of the Dutch Renaissance painter Pieter Bruegel the Elder's painting *Hunters in the Snow* (1565). From a high hill, a 'cosmic' panorama opens, covering the micro- and macrocosm, in all their diversity, in dynamics and peace, in everyday specificity and metaphysics: a withered bush in snow, hunting dogs, ice skating, a winter landscape, a bird soaring in the sky, a dark crown and a tree trunk, hunters walking through the snow … Ordinary everyday life with all its details expands to a cosmic scale, acquiring a metaphysical dimension. This is followed by a shot of a real winter landscape from the hero's childhood, which is a description of the Bruegel panorama. In the words of Bakhtin, Hari's contemplation of the Bruegel landscape reveals not only the infinite world (macrocosm) but also reflects her soul in its infinity and incompleteness (microcosm).[117]

Then, in the zero-gravity scene, the organ version of J. S. Bach's Chorale Prelude *Ich ruf zu Dir, Herr Jesu Christ* (I Cry Out to Thee, Lord Jesus Christ, BWV 639) is played, interspersed with shots from the Bruegel landscape – the smooth, unhurried tempo of the prelude further reveals the depth of the infinite Bruegel space. The episode ends with a childhood memory of a bonfire in the snow and the living waves of the Ocean. Bruegel's painting and Bach's music are characterized by a detached perception of the world (a view from the outside), its 'supernal' contemplation. In his *Martyrology*, Tarkovsky wrote out Mahler's words about Bach's great polyphony: 'In Bach all the vital seeds of music are gathered, just as the world

116 From the Greek χάρις – 'charm, grace, beauty, mercy, joy'.

117 Bakhtin, 'The Poetics of Dostoevsky and Its problems', p. 80.

is in God'.[118] In the music of Bach (as in the painting of Leonardo da Vinci) Tarkovsky saw 'independence' from ideology, 'Olympian art', 'the highest sense of form', reflecting the very flow of being: 'They see the world as if for the first time, as if not burdened by any experience. Their independent gaze is like the gaze of aliens!'[119] At the same time, Tarkovsky noted that for him Bach's music is a natural expression of the 'idea of humanity'.

Thus, in these episodes of direct contemplation of being (as well as its pure contemplation in art – in the landscape of Bruegel, in the music of Bach), there is a meeting with reality, which destroys ideology at the level of form.

As an example, fitting Prishvin's worldview, we will cite an episode from Tarkovsky's last film *Sacrifice* (Svenska Filminstitutet, Sandrew, Sweden; Argos Films, France; Film Four International, Great Britain, 1986), in which Aleksandr tells the story of the garden (it is preceded by a fragment of Bach's organ prelude and fugue BWV 539 performed by the hero). Aleksandr recalls how he decided to give his dying mother a pleasant surprise – to secretly cultivate her overgrown garden, which she liked to look at out of the window:

> When the weather was fine, she often sat at the window and looked out into the garden. She even had a special chair there. One day I decided to put everything in order, I mean, in the garden. Mow the lawns, burn the grass, prune the trees. In general … create something … according to your taste, with your own hands. And all in order to please the mother. For two weeks in a row I walked around the garden with scissors, with a scythe, digging, cutting, sawing, cleaning. Literally, plowing the ground with my nose. I worked hard to get everything done as quickly as possible. […] when everything was done, I washed, put on clean underwear, a new jacket, even a tie. I sat down in her chair to see everything through her eyes. Yes … I … took a look out the window and saw … yes, what did I see? Where has all that was beautiful, all that was natural, disappeared?! It was so disgusting! All these signs of violence!

The hero realizes that out of good intentions, rationally reorganizing nature, he destroyed its natural beauty and harmony. Contemplation, admiring the garden, is destroyed by the idea of 'order' and monologistic

118 Tarkovsky, *Martyrology*, p. 176.

119 Tarkovsky, 'Imprinted Time', pp. 216, 223.

violence against natural beauty (the hero does not consult with his mother about her own garden).

In both Prishvin and Tarkovsky, the ideologized consciousness is opposed to the encounter with reality in pure observation – the direct vision of the world, in its creative 'discovery' by the individual, 'discovery', which ideology seeks to abolish, replacing it with easily 'recognizable' cliches.

Thus, from a historical and cultural perspective, we see that the ideological 'super reality' was reproduced in Russia in various historical forms (the Messianic idea of the Orthodox empire, the rite of schism of the seventeenth century, the Uvarov triad, nineteenth-century nihilism and twentieth-century Bolshevism) and that in it a person was sacrificed to a dogmatically understood truth, and the present was sacrificed to a utopian project of the past or future, as a result of which the 'apocalyptic breakdown' of history periodically occurred. The predominance of ideology in the life of society has led to the discrete and 'explosive' development of Russian history.

In the Russian literature of the nineteenth century, the conflict between two types of consciousness (ideological and supra-ideological, humanistic) is a constant. Bazarov and Raskolnikov present an ideological type of consciousness with its inherent attitudes (fanatical faith, dogmatic, unquestioning perception of truth and monopoly on it, the image of the enemy, the devaluation of human life, sacrificing it to an idea, utopianism, etc.). Turgenev and Dostoevsky not only warned about the ontological and ethical collapse of this type of personality, about its disastrous social consequences for the whole society but also offered to society as an alternative a supra-ideological, humanistic type of personality (Katya Lokteva, Arkady, Myshkin, Zosima, Alyosha Karamazov, etc.), discovering the ontological reality of being and man.

The ideological type of consciousness continued to be studied by M. Prishvin in his secret diary of the 1930s, recording from within Soviet everyday life the program of the Soviet Bazarov – intolerance (the image of the enemy); dogmatism, the dissolution of the individual in the collective worship of the 'leader'; the substitution of conscience as a universal ethical value by a narrow class concept (class ethics); the replacement of the present with a utopian future; the substitution of classical humanism with class humanism and so on. Prishvin also points to this ideology being socially doomed, because it displaces reality itself.

In our opinion, the writer was able to see and reflect on these ideological attitudes because he belonged to a humanistic, supra-ideological type of personality formed in the culture of the Silver Age, which, unlike the vertical monologism of the Stalinist system, was permeated with the spirit of personalism, dialogue and discussion ('Religious and Philosophical Society').[120]

Continuing Turgenev, Dostoevsky, and Rozanov, in their humanism and ontological experience of the completeness of the 'blest everyday life' of being ('here-and-now'), Prishvin also finds a way to overcome the nihilistic dictate of the Idea over Being and Everyday Life, characteristic of Russian history – in sheer observation, in contemplative attention to being, in which the individual meets the ontological reality. Phenomenological observation, direct vision of the world (nature and society) in Prishvin's prose and photographic works, is his main creative principle, which is opposed to any ideocracy.

The difference between the two types of consciousness is manifested in the *Martyrology*, films and photographs of Andrei Tarkovsky in the 1960s and 1980s. The director perceives this problem through the tradition of Russian classics (Dostoevsky's question about 'Christ' and 'truth') and through Prishvin's diary. In Tarkovsky, as in Prishvin, the indoctrinated consciousness (which monologically objectifies nature and personality) is opposed by sheer observation – the direct contemplation of being (as well as its vision and experience in the landscape of Bruegel, in the music of Bach), in which there is a meeting with reality ('self-revealing being') – a meeting that destroys the ideological 'super reality' at the level of form.

120 Prishvin was a member of the Religious and Philosophical Society in St. Petersburg (1907-1917), alongside with such philosophers and writers as V.V. Rozanov, D.S. Merezhkovsky, N.A. Berdyaev, S.L. Frank, and many others. At the meetings of the Society its members gave lectures and engaged in discussions.

Bibliography

Bakhtin, M., 'The Poetics of Dostoevsky and Its Problems', in *Collected Writings* (Moscow: Russkie slovari; Iazyki slavianskoi kul'tury, 2002), Vol. 6, pp. 5–300.

——— 'Towards the Philosophical Origins of Humanities', in *Collected Writings* (Moscow: Russkie slovari, 1996), Vol. 5, pp. 7–10.

Belaya, G. A., *Don-Quixotes of the Twentieth Century: 'Pereval' and the Fate of Its Ideas* (Moscow: Sovetskii pisatel', 1989).

Berdyaev, N. A., *The Russian Idea* (St. Petersburg: Azbuka-klassika, 2008).

Besançon, A., *Intellectual Origins of Leninism* (Moscow: MIK, 1998).

Chaadaev, P. Y., *A Complete Set of Essays and Selected Letters*, 2 Vols (Moscow: Nauka, 1991), Vol. 1.

Dostoevsky, F. M., *Crime and Punishment*, in *Complete Works*, 30 vols (Leningrad: Nauka, 1973), Vol. 6, pp. 5–422.

——— *The Idiot*, in *Complete Works*, 30 vols (Leningrad: Nauka, 1973), Vol. 8, pp. 5–510.

Engelhardt, B. M., 'The Ideological Novel of Dostoevsky', in *F. M. Dostoevsky: Essays and Materials*, Sb. II (Moscow; Leningrad: Mysl', 1924), pp. 71–109.

Fedotov, G. P., 'The Lost Writer A. I. Herzen (1812–1870)', in *Works*, 12 vols (Moscow: Sam 8c Sam, 2014), Vol. 7 pp. 86–89.

——— 'The Tragedy of the Intelligentsia', in *Fate and Sins of Russia: Selected Papers on Philosophy of Russian History and Culture*, 2 vols (St. Petersburg: Sofiia, 1992), Vol. 1, pp. 66–101.

Frank, S. L., 'Dostoevsky and the Humanism Crisis (For the Fiftieth Anniversary of Dostoevsky's death)', in *About Dostoevsky: Works of Dostoevsky in Russian Thought 1881–1931; A Set of Essays* (Moscow: Kniga, 1990), pp. 391–397.

Gadzhiev, K. S., 'Political Ideology: Conceptual aspects', *Philosophical Questions*, No. 12 (1998), pp. 3–20.

Gippius-Merezhkosvkaya, Z. N., *Dmitry Merezhkovsky* (Paris: YMCA-Press, 1951).

Glagolev, A., 'On the Artistic Appearance of "Pereval"', *Novyi Mir*, No. 5 (1930), pp. 157–170.

Gorky, M., *Collected Essays*, 30 vols (Moscow: Gosudarstvennoe izdatel'stvo khudozhestvennoi literatury, 1953), Vol. 27.

Grishina Y., and N. Poltavtseva, 'Commentaries', in *M. M. Prishvin. Diaries 1923–1925* (St. Petersburg: Rostok, 2009), pp. 481–507.

Ivanov, Vyacheslav, 'Poet and Rabble', in *Complete Works*, 4 vols (Brussels: Foyer oriental chrétien, 1971), Vol. 1 pp. 709–714.

Kosikov, G. K., 'Ideology, Connotation, Text', in Roland Barthes, *S/Z* (Moscow: URSS, 2001), pp. 8–30.

Medvedev, A. A., 'La mythologie de la guerre dans les articles de Vassili Rozanov', *La Revue russe*, No. 47 (2016), pp. 117–130.

——— 'The Russian Disaster of 1917 and "Great Times" (M. Prishvin, V. Rozanov, A. Blok)', *Studi Slavistici. Rivista dell'Associazione Italiana degli Slavisti*, Vol. 1, No. 26 (2019), pp. 143–154.

——— '"A Russia of Xerxes or of Christ?": The Critique of Messianism in the Russian Émigré Community in a Historical-Cultural Perspective, from Vladimir Solov'ëv to Ol'ga Sedakova', in *Russian Classical Literature Today: The Challenges/Trials of Messianism and Mass Culture* (Newcastle upon Tyne: Cambridge Scholars Publishing, 2014), pp. 205–219.

'Mystery of Everyday Life – Andrei Tarkovsky', *Le vagabond des étoiles*, https://www.vagabond-des-etoiles.com/arts/photographie/mystery-of-everyday-life-andrei-tarkovsky-1979/ (Accessed 4 January 2017).

Prishvin, M. M., *Diaries* (Moscow: Pravda, 1990).

——— *Diaries 1914–1917* (St. Petersburg: Rostok, 2007).

——— *Diaries 1918–1919* (St. Petersburg: Rostok, 2008).

——— *Diaries 1928–1929* (St. Petersburg: Russkaia kniga, 2004).

——— *Diaries 1930–1931* (St. Petersburg: Rostok, 2006).

——— *Diaries 1932–1935* (St. Petersburg: Rostok, 2009).

——— *Diaries 1936–1937* (St. Petersburg: Rostok, 2010).

——— *Diaries 1938–1939* (St. Petersburg: Rostok, 2010).

——— *Diaries 1940–1941* (Moscow: ROSSPEN, 2012).

——— *Diaries 1948–1949* (Moscow: Novyi khronograf, 2014).

——— *Diaries 1950–1951* (St. Petersburg: Rostok, 2016).

——— 'Notes on Works', in *Context-1978: Literary and Theoretical Research* (Moscow: Nauka, 1978), pp. 268–296.

——— *Selected Works*, 8 vols (Moscow: Khudozhestvennaia literatura, 1983), Vol. 5.

——— *Selected Works*, 8 vols (Moscow: Khudozhestvennaia literatura, 1984), Vol. 7.

Prishvina, V. D. 'From "Intermediary Chapter" (Our Idea)', in *From Russian Thought*, 2 vols (Moscow: Roman-gazeta, 1995), Vol. 2. pp. 178–193.

Rozanov, V. V., 'Embryos', in *Selected Works: Religion and Culture; Articles and Feature-Stories 1902–1903* (Moscow: Respublika; St. Petersburg: Rostok, 2008), pp. 211–218.

Solzhenitsyn, A. I., *Selected Works*, 30 vols (Moscow: Vremia, 2006), Vol. 1.

Tarkovsky, A. A., 'Creation of a Film and the Artist's Responsibility', in Andrei Tarkovsky, *Twentieth Century and an Artist (Beginning)*, 1984, <http://www.tarkovskiy.su/texty/Tarkovskiy/London01.html> (Accessed 4 January 2017).

——— 'Imprinted Time', in *Archives, Documents, Memories* (Moscow: Podkova; Eksmo-press, 2002), pp. 155–184.

———*Martyrology: Diaries 1970–1986* (Florence: Mezhdunarodnyi institut imeni A. Tarkovskogo, 2008).

Turgenev, I. S., *Fathers and Sons*, in *Complete Essays and Letters*, 30 vols (Moscow: Nauka, 1981), Vol. 7. pp. 7–188.

Varlamov, A. N., *Prishvin* (Moscow: Molodaia gvardiia, 2003).

Volkova, P., 'Nostos', October, No. 3, 2012 <http://magazines.russ.ru/october/2012/3/v9.html> (Accessed 4 January 2017).

Voloshin, M., *Collected Writings* (Moscow: Ellis Lak, 2003), Vol. 1.

Translated by Nikita Khmarenko

LIDIA I. SHISHKINA

3 Political Terrorism of the Early Twentieth Century in the Context of Russian Cultural Consciousness

Modern studies have repeatedly noted that Russian history and culture have moved in pendulum swings. This was the case in the era of Peter's reforms, which marked a sharp break in theocratic tradition and establishment of a well-rounded Western type of mindset; the revolution of 1917, which proclaimed the idea of a global reorganization of the world, the cult of the future and denial of the past; as it was in the 1990s, with their decisive rejection of the Soviet legacy.

Russia has never developed progressively by evolution: it has moved forward with social upheavals, explosions and revolutions. Hence the existence of extremist phenomena in its history, to which, in particular, political terrorism of the late nineteenth and early twentieth century can be attributed. First of all, it is connected with the era of '*Narodnaia Volia*' (People's Will), which ended with the assassination of Emperor Aleksandr II on 1 March 1881. But it reached critical mass in the 1900s with the activities of the Militant Organization of the Socialist Revolutionary Party. Proclaiming itself the ideological heir of the 'Narodnaya Volya' and taking the 'heavy sword of retribution' from the hands of the latter, this party made its task to force the government to give up power by physically destroying individual political figures.

Among the causes and conditions of the origin and existence of terrorism, various aspects can be distinguished, such as socioeconomic, cultural-historical and civilizational; but one of the most important is the sociopsychological aspect associated with the specifics of public consciousness, because, without the moral assistance of the environment, any movement would fade away.

The surprising phenomenon of support that the activities of the Socialist Revolutionary 'militants' received from the 'advanced public' can be explained by the fact that, in their propaganda, the terror theorists touched upon certain root features of the Russian cultural consciousness.

The main argument of party theorists and publicists in favor of terror was the idea of a response to power and its cruelty, directed not against a particular statesman, but against the social function he performed. 'As such', wrote the leader of the Socialist Revolutionaries V. Chernov in a manifesto, 'this act is completely cleansed of any personal element'.[1]

The second argument was the idea of the inevitability of retribution, which correlated with the idea of 'eternal justice', resonant with Russian popular thinking. All the victims were chosen as symbols of state repression and did not cause public sympathy. Some of the high-profile murders included, among others, those of the Minister of Internal Affairs V. K. von Plehve, the Ufa governor N. M. Bogdanovich and the Moscow Governor-General Grand Prince Sergei Aleksandrovich, and – during the First Revolution – the suppressor of the Moscow armed uprising General Min, military prosecutor Pavlov and the head of the St. Petersburg prison Gudim.

This made it possible for the head of the *Boevaya Organizatsiya* (Militant Organization) of the Socialist Revolutionaries, G. Gershuni, to assert that 'public opinion indicates the target for terror'. In his speech at the Second Congress of the Socialist Revolutionaries (1907), he proclaimed that the path to terror opens only when public hatred is concentrated on some government person who becomes a symbol of violence and despotism. 'And when there is a bomb explosion, a sigh of relief escapes from the people's chest. Then it is clear to everyone: the people's judgment has been accomplished.'[2]

Leonid Andreev, a writer who was rightfully considered a 'barometer of the era', reproduced the public mood accurately in the story 'The Governor'

1 V. Chernov, 'Eshe o kritikakh terroristicheskoi taktiki' [Further Discussions on Terrorism Tactics]; 'Po voprosam programmy i taktiki' [On the Issues of Tactics and Agenda]. Collection of Papers, *Revolutionary Russia* (Geneva, 1903), p. 183.

2 O. Budnitsky, *Terrorism v rossiiskom osvoboditel'nom dvizhenii* [Terrorism in the Russian Liberation Movement] (Moscow, 2000), p. 173.

(1906), which became an artistic response to the murder of Bogdanovich by members of the Socialist Revolutionary Militant Organization – G. Gershuni and E. Dulebov. In the original version, which bore the demonstrative title 'God of Vengeance', the story reproduces in psychological detail the atmosphere when everyone – the governor, who gave the order to shoot the workers' demonstration, and the whole city – expect the inevitable retribution for the crime committed and are relieved to receive the news of the murder.[3] The writer explains this not by social hatred but by a certain eternal Law of Revenge, relying on the ethical constructs of A. Schopenhauer, who, criticizing Kant's theory of punishment as retribution for the sake of retribution, spoke of 'eternal justice' standing outside the world of phenomena. 'If we understand the spirit of this thirst for retribution', Schopenhauer reasoned,

> it turns out to be very different from ordinary revenge, its goal can be called not as much revenge as punishment, because the intention here is to influence the future by the power of example, and moreover there is no self-serving calculation for the avenging individual (for he dies in this case).

Schopenhauer saw the embodiment of the idea of 'eternal justice' in a separate avenger, who

> wants to frighten every future villain with an example of inevitable revenge [...] This is a rare, significant and exalted trait, because of which individuals sacrifice themselves, wishing to become the hand of eternal justice, the true essence of which they do not understand.[4]

Thus, in 'The Governor', someone who is not named and does not reveal his face becomes an instrument that fulfills the will of the Law of Retribution.

The Russian consciousness, in which the opposition of 'truth-verity' [*pravda-istina*] (law) and 'truth-justice' [*pravda-spravedlivost*] (God's judgment) was originally laid, was ready to perceive the terrorist as an instrument of 'response' – punishment, namely, executing its victim according

3 Leonid Andreev, 'The Governor', *Complete Works and letters, 23 vols*. Moscow: Nauka, 2017, Vol. 4. P.117–163.

4 A. Schopenhauer, *Collection of Essays*, 5 vols (Moscow, 1992), Vol. 1 p. 336.

to the 'verdict of the people's court' for the act that the official law does not want to punish.

Russian society at the beginning of the twentieth century readily responded to the spectacular aura of martyrdom, the romance of selfless feats and sacrifice, which attracted hundreds and thousands of young people who became the 'cannon fodder' of the revolution. It was these qualities that were persistently emphasized by the revolutionary press, which created a mythologized image of 'terror fighters'. In revolutionary publications, a kind of iconostasis of martyrs and saints was formed: lengthy obituaries and memoirs were printed. The figures of S. Balmashev, E. Sozonov and I. Kalyaev, who became banners of terror, were a striking psychological type of killer and victim in one person.

'Heroes of Terror' were presented as the embodiment of the best human qualities, the focus of physical and spiritual beauty. A sublime and poetic image arose from memories of Lydia Stura, a member of the Flying Combat Detachment of the Northern Region, executed for an assassination attempt on the Minister of Justice I. Shcheglovitov in February 1908: 'A slender girl, full of wonderful, spiritual beauty';[5] 'Tender, fragile, perfect child.'[6] With delight, contemporaries wrote about the leader of this detachment, V. Lebedintsev, admiring his aristocracy, beauty, academic talent and career, which he sacrificed for the sake of 'the triumph of total justice', describing him as 'one of the rare moral people'.[7] Vladimir Mazurin was a Socialist Revolutionary maximalist who was hanged in 1906 – one whose very name would invoke horror in people. Remembering him, M. Osorgin quoted a policeman guarding Mazurin: 'He killed people, and yet he was himself akin to either a child or a saint. These words [...] are understandable to anyone who knew Volodya, a charming blue-eyed young man full of love for humanity, for which he raised his hand to man. His portraits, published in large numbers by maximalists, were hung out like icons'[8] .

5 N. Morozov, *Stories of My Lifetime*, 2 vols (Moscow, 1965), Vol. 2, pp. 520–521.

6 V. Figner. *Zapechatlenni trud* [Depicted Works], *Collected Works*, 3 vols (Moscow, 1932), Vol. 3, p. 56.

7 M. Osorgin, 'Neizvestnyi po prozvishchu Verner' ['A stranger nicknamed Verner'], in *Na chuzhoi storone* [In a Foreign Country], (Berlin-Praga, 1924), No. 4, p. 203.

8 M. Osorgin, 'Venok pamyati malykh' [Wreaths in Memory of the 'Poor'], in *Na chuzhoi storone* [In a Foreign Country] (Berlin, 1926), No. 6, p. 118.

In the atmosphere of social exaltation and revolutionary neurosis, the abhorrent side of terror – the blood and pieces of human flesh that remained after the 'acts' of highly moral ascetics armed with bombs and brownings – was 'forgotten'.

The idea of sacrifice became crucial to the psychological motivation of most members of the Combat Organization. This is evidenced, in particular, by the memoirs of B. Savinkov, one of the most prominent figures of the Socialist Revolutionary movement, the organizer of many high-profile assassination attempts. 'He came to terror in his own special way and saw in it not only the best form of political struggle, but also a moral, decisive sacrifice':[9] this was how he characterized Ivan Kalyaev, the murderer of the Grand Prince Sergei Aleksandrovich. The same was written about Dora Brilliant: 'Terror for her, as for Kalyaev, was colored primarily by the sacrifice that terrorism brings.'[10]

Selfless sacrifice became a moral justification for violence in the eyes of society. Thus, the public and religious figure V. Sventsitsky, in his report 'Terror and Immortality', argued that the sin of murder will be justified because 'Kalyaev, and Balmashev, and Spiridonova, and dozens of others like them, killing officials – they themselves go to certain death [...] These are martyrs – and their sin will be forgiven for this great holy love, which pushed them to commit a crime.'[11] At the beginning of the century, a common point of view was formulated by the famous writer M. Osorgin, who was close to the most radical wing of the party, the Socialist Revolutionary maximalists. Pointing out the need to distinguish between the terror of power and the heroism of Davids 'who go with a sling against a heavily armed Goliath almost always to certain death', the writer justified revolutionary violence by the sacrificial martyrdom of those who committed it:

> And when history or human memory summons those big and small 'jugglers with bombs and lives' to their court, let the judges take into account not only the motive of the defendants' activities, not only their position as Davids in the fight against

9 B. Savinkov, *Memoirs of a Terrorist* (Kharkov, 1926), p. 36.

10 Ibid., p. 40.

11 B. Sventsitsky, 'Terror i bessmertye' [Terror and Immortality], in *Matters of Religion* 2 (Moscow, 1908), p. 26.

> Goliaths, but also the entire amount of retribution they have already suffered, both from the hand of the triumphant victor, and from the most terrible executioner: the shaken soul of a man who killed a man.[12]

The category of victimhood also defined another important component of terrorism – the combination of terror and religion, in which many cultural figures of the early twentieth century also saw the root features of the Russian national character, for which, in the words of L. Andreev, 'rebellion was a religion, and religion was a rebellion'. Hence the fascination of the intelligentsia with sectarianism (the hero of L. Andreev's story 'Darkness' is a bomber, Alexei – a native of the cult environment), which was seen as 'the inextinguishability of the people's element', and the identification of modern terrorists with the first Christian martyrs.

Many figures of terror deliberately introduced their activities into the Christian context, making the Gospel commandments the basis of their sacrificial asceticism. Their motto was a saying from the Gospel of John: 'There is no greater love than to lay down your life for your friends' (John 15:13). At the beginning of the twentieth century, striking personalities appeared who combined religious consciousness and revolutionary violence in an extraordinary way. For example, there is a distinctive figure of Maria Benevskaya. 'A believing Christian who did not part with the Gospel, she somehow came to the assertion of violence and the need for personal participation in terror in an unknown and complex way',[13] as Savinkov characterized her. When he asked her about her motives for terror, she replied with a quote from the Gospel: 'For whoever would save his life will lose it; and whoever loses his life for my sake, he will save it' (Luke 9:24). A prominent figure of the Socialist Revolutionary Party, V. Zenzinov, confirmed in his memoirs: 'Marusya was a Christian believer and went to terror, as in the Middle Ages believers went to the stake.'[14] A similar person was Ivan Kalyaev who, before the attempt on the Moscow Governor-General, prayed in front of the icon of the Iberian Mother of God, holding a bomb in one hand, and making the sign of the cross with the other. The concept of the

12 Osorgin, 'Venok pamyati malykh', p. 118.
13 Savinkov, *Memoirs of a Terrorist*, p. 196.
14 V. Zenzinov, *Perezhitoe* (New York, 1953), p. 280.

religiosity of Russian terror was also confirmed in the public consciousness. It was advertised, first of all, by the Merezhkovsky circle, in a collection of articles by Z. Gippius, D. Merezhkovsky and D. Filosofov *Le Tzar et la Révolution*, published in 1907 in Paris, and D. Merezhkovsky's book *Not Peace, but a Sword* (1908), which largely repeated its main provisions. This interpretation was based on an understanding of the theocratic essence of autocracy. Philosophers in the article 'Tsar-Pope', focusing on the extremes in the confrontation between power and society, explained them by identifying the power of the Pope – that is, the church – in the West, and the sacralization of the power of the tsar in the East. If in the West the policy of the government depended on public opinion, and the opponents fought through messages and speeches, then in Russia, deprived of such an opportunity, brownings and bombs came to take the floor as it is the only way to influence power. Based on the fact that autocracy is a kind of religion, the struggle against it was also given a religious meaning. Merezhkovsky's progeny accepted the shedding of blood 'in the name of' the revolutionary sacrifice and spoke of its sanctity. 'The Russian Revolution is not only politics, but also religion', Merezhkovsky proclaimed:

> The revolutionaries are the least aware of this. In their minds, they are godless. But if you look at what they do, you can't help but see that these atheists are sometimes saints. Since the time of the first Christian martyrs, there have been no people who would die like this; according to Tertullian, 'they rush toward death as bees rush to a honey pot'.[15]

Z. Gippius likened the terrorists to the first Christians in the catacombs:

> Their life is the life of ascetics who have given up everything for the sake of an idea. They obey the stern principle of obedience; sacrifice and struggle are sweet to them. The main psychological motivation of most of them, and especially women, is: 'I want to suffer, I want to suffer for the truth' – the motto is purely Christian, even too Christian.[16]

15 D. Merezhkovsky, *Not Peace, but a Sword* (Moscow, 2000 [Saint-Petersburg, 1909]), p. 206.

16 Zinaida Gippius, 'Revolution and Violence', in *Le Tzar et la Revolution*, ed. Z. Gippius, D. Merezhkovsky and D. Filosofov (Moscow, 1999 [Paris 1907]), p. 117.

In this interpretation, the terrorist act turned into a crown of thorns, the path of the terrorist – into Calvary and their death on the scaffold – into redemption.

Merezhkovsky's progeny tried to introduce their own religious understanding of revolutionary extremism into the minds of its representatives: first of all, B. Savinkov, whose novel *The Pale Horse* was created under the influence of their ideas. Largely autobiographical, reflecting the concrete realities of the preparation of the assassination attempt on Prince Sergei Aleksandrovich, it is permeated with themes, motives as well as explicit and hidden quotes from the Apocalypse. Its main character is the terrorist Vanya, a type of 'ideal revolutionary' for which the prototype was I. Kalyaev, who goes in for the terrorist act as if he is going to a cross .

The obligation of sacrifice was determined by the behavior of the 'heroes of terror' who did not seek to avoid death, but, on the contrary, longed for it. The final death was the resolution of the moral dilemma between the desire to bring good to the people and the need to shed blood 'in the name of', which tore apart the consciousness of the most deeply thinking participants. Death was a moral and philosophical justification for the act of murder. One of his contemporaries described Kalyaev as follows: 'Terror-murder became possible for him only because it was both victimhood and self-sacrifice. And I do not know whether a terrorist attempt would have been possible for him if it had not entailed execution'.[17]

The most important thing was not the readiness to die at the scene of a terrorist attack, which was described, for example, by the head of the St. Petersburg security department A. Gerasimov, speaking about the arrest of V. Lebedintsev:

> He was surrounded by dynamite cords all over his body. The terrorists intended to throw a bomb into the minister's carriage. If this failed or the bomb did not explode, Lebedintsev intended to throw himself under the minister's carriage in the form of a live bomb and die with him.[18]

17 M. Mogilyanksy, 'In the 90s', *The Past*, No. 24 (1924), p. 131.

18 A. V. Gerasimov, *Na lezvii s terroristami* [On the Edge with Terrorists] (Moscow, 1991), p. 122.

Most important was the ability to consciously meet the day and hour of his execution. V. Zenzinov claimed: 'To die in a heroic fit with others is not so difficult, [...] it is much more difficult to die alone, to keep self-control until the last moment.'[19]

Death on the scaffold was considered by terrorists as a mandatory final part of the ritual and the highest point of their fate. 'I often think about the last moment', I. Kalyaev reflected:

> You can die on the spot-flash brightly and burn without a trace [...] Yes, this is an enviable happiness. But there is a happiness even higher – to die on the scaffold [...] Death at the moment of the act seems to leave something unfinished. There is still an eternity between the deed and the scaffold – perhaps the greatest thing for a man [...] Only here you will know, feel all the power, all the beauty of the idea. You will unfold, blossom, and die in full bloom.[20]

It is this psychological attitude that explains why Kalyaev refused the offer of the widow of the murdered Moscow Governor-General, Grand Duchess Elizabeth Fedorovna, to write a petition for clemency. It was not a crazy decision of a mentally unbalanced person, as it is sometimes interpreted, but a fully conscious and consistent acceptance of death on the scaffold as the mandatory completion of an 'act' that is fundamentally declarative and designed for public resonance.

The well-known terrorist Anna Rasputina-Shulyatikova objected to her accusers who claimed that it was potential suiciders who would go in for terror because their instinct of life is suppressed and therefore they do not value the lives of other people or their own. To this she replied before the execution: 'This is not so! It is the death instinct which is suppressed in us, just as it is suppressed in a brave officer going into battle.'[21]

Such self-consciousness, in which political murder was colored in the tones of a Christian feat, and death was associated with a crown of thorns, determined the heroic behavior of terrorists who willingly went to their

19 Zenzinov, *Perezhitoe*, p. 274.

20 Ibid., p. 273.

21 G. A. Ivanishin, 'Notebooks of Colonel G. A. Ivanishin', in *The Past: Historical Almanac*, ed. A. Margolis, N. Gerasimov and N. Tikhonova (Moscow, 1994), Vol. 17, p. 497.

deaths, met death with a smile on their lips and aroused the respect of even their political opponents. The head of the St. Petersburg security department, A. V. Gerasimov, recalled the statement of the prosecutor, who, on duty, was present at the execution of members of the Flying Combat Detachment of the Northern Region: 'How these people died! No sigh, no regret, no pleading, no sign of weakness. With a smile on their lips, they went to the execution', and he had to admit that 'the heroism of these young people [...] attracted sympathy in society.'[22]

Public opinion saw the romance of terror and contributed to the creation of an atmosphere of exaltation, under the influence of which hundreds of young people went in for terror, carried away by the legends of the fallen heroes. In this atmosphere, there were no warnings about the moral responsibility of the intelligentsia. This is largely because those who positioned themselves as theoreticians and practitioners of terrorism were heirs to the anti-individualism of populist ethics that perceived 'all or nothing' as a typical trait of the Russian character and Russian mentality with its sacramental setting: 'Give him God, truth-verity [*pravdu-istinu*], that he may love Him more than himself, and may perish every moment for Him; or give him truth-justice [*pravdu-spravedlivost*] on earth. This hero is happy and alive only in the feat of self-denial, sacrifice.'[23] Thus wrote the neo-Platonic philosopher and follower of V. Solovyov, K. F. Zhakov, in his review of 'The Story of the Seven who were Hanged' by L. Andreev,[24] whose prototypes were the terrorist members of the Flying Combat Detachment of the northern region, executed in February 1908 for the failed assassination attempt on the Law Minister I. D. Shcheglovitov.

At the same time, the analysis of the psychology, ethics and 'aesthetics' of Russian political extremism demonstrates common typological features inherent in this phenomenon in different countries and in different epochs. In this sense, we can talk about the actualization in modern conditions of

22 Gerasimov, *Na lezvii s terroristami*, pp. 122–123.

23 K. F. Zhakov, *Leonid Andreev and His Works: Philosophical Experience* (St. Petersburg, 1909), pp. xxi; xxiii.

24 L. Andreev, 'The Story of the Seven Who Were Hanged', in *Complete Works and Letters*, 23 vols (Moscow: Nauka, 2013), Vol. 6.

the historical experience that Russia experienced at the turn of the nineteenth and twentieth centuries. It is worth remembering that the extinction of terror is connected with the exposure of the provocateur activities of Yevno Azef, who was both a member of the Central Committee of the Socialist Revolutionary Party, the organizer of high-profile terrorist 'acts' and a hired agent of the secret police, betraying their perpetrators. The myth of the selfless sacrifice of revolutionary asceticism collapsed. The ethics of intellectual heroism was debunked in the eyes of society. A moral chasm was revealed between the young people, who were enthusiastically going to their doom, and their commanders-in-chief, for whom the revolution had long been a gamble and a 'commercial matter'. Therefore, it was not only the uncompromising policy of P. A. Stolypin, and not only the security department's professionalism of which its head A. V. Gerasimov was proud, considering the end of terror his personal merit; it was above all that the attitude of society dramatically changed, as it saw the wrong side of high ideals, and turned away from the combat activities of many ordinary participants who had experienced a severe mental crisis. This led to the ideological collapse of terror and its gradual fading.

Bibliography

Andreev, Leonid, 'Gubernator' ['The Governor'], *Complete Works and Letters*, 23 vols (Moscow: Nauka, 2017), Vol. 4.

—— 'The Story of the Seven Who Were Hanged', in *Complete Works and Letters*, 23 vols (Moscow: Nauka, 2017), Vol. 6.

Budnitsky, O.V., *Terrorism v rossiiskom osvoboditel'nom dvizhenii: ideologiia, etika, psikhologiia (vtoraia polovina XIX - nachalo XX veka)* [Terrorism in the Russian Liberation Movement: ideology, ethics, psychology (second half of the XIX–beginning of the XX century)] (Moscow: ROSSPEN, 2000).

Chernov, V., 'Eshe o kritikakh terroristicheskoi taktiki' [Further Discussions on Terrorism Critics]; 'Po voprosam programmii taktiki' [On the Issues of Tactics and Agenda], Collection of papers, in *Revolutionary Russia* (Geneva, 1903).

Figner, V.N., *Zapechatlennyi trud* [Depicted Works], Collected works, 3 vols (Moscow: Izdatelstvo vsesoiuznogo obshchestva politkatorzhan i ssylno-poselentsev [Publishing House of the All-Union Society of Political Prisoners and Exiled Settlers], 1933), Vol. 3.

Gerasimov, A. V., *Na lezvii s terroristami* [On the Edge with Terrorists] (Moscow: Tovarishchestvo russkikh khudozhnikov [Association of Russian artists], 1991).

Gippius, Z.N., 'Revolutsiia i nasilie' ['Revolution and Violence'], in *Le Tzar et la Revolution*, ed. Z. Gippius, D. Merezhkovsky and D. Filosofov (Moscow: Izdatelstvo OGI, 1999 [Paris, 1907]), p. 117.

Ivanishin, G. A., 'Zapisnye knizhki polkovnika G. A. Ivanishina' ['Notebooks of Colonel G. A. Ivanishin'], in *The Past: Historical Almanac*, ed. A. Margolis, N. Gerasimov and N. Tikhonova (Moscow and St. Petersburg: Atheneum; Feniks, 1994), Vol. 17, p. 497.

Merezhkovsky, D.S., *Ne mir, no mech* [*Not Peace, but a Sword*] (Moscow: ACT, 2000 [St. Petersburg, 1909]), p. 206.

Mogilyanksy, M.M., 'V devianostye gody' [In the 90s'], *Byloe* [*The Past*], No. 24 (1924), p. 131.

Morozov, N.A., *Povesti moei zhizni* [*Stories of My Lifetime*], 2 vols (Moscow: Nauka, 1965).

Osorgin, M.A., 'Neizvestnyi po prozvishchu Verner' ['A stranger nicknamed Verner'], in *Na chuzhoi storone* [In a Foreign Country], (Berlin-Praga, 1924), No. 4.

Osorgin, M.A., 'Venok pamyati malykh' [Wreaths in Memory of the 'Poor'], in *Na chuzhoi storone* [In Foreign Country] (Berlin-Prague, 1926), No. 6.

Savinkov, B.V., *Vospominaniia terrorista* [*Memoirs of a Terrorist*] (Kharkov, 1926).

Schopenhauer, A., *Collection of Essays*, 5 vols (Moscow: Moskovskii klub, 1992), Vol. 1, p. 336.

Sventsitsky, B.P., 'Terror i bessmertie' [Terror and Immortality], in *Voprosy religii* [*Matters of Religion*], issue 2 (Moscow, 1908).

Zenzinov, V.M., *Bygone* [*Perezhitoe*] (New York: Izdatelstvo imeni Chekhova, 1953).

Zhakov, K. F., 'Leonid Andreev i ego proizvedeniia: opyt filosofskoi kritiki' ['Leonid Andreev and His Works: Experience of Philosophical Criticism'] in Leonid Andreev, *Rasskaz o semi poveshennykh* [The Story of the Seven Who Were Hanged'] (St. Petersburg: Shipovnik, 1909).

Translated by Nikita Khmarenko

NATALIA VINOKUROVA AND OLGA TABACHNIKOVA

4 Economic Thought as a Mirror of Cultural Debates: The Ideology of Westernism and Slavophilism in Modern Russia

Introduction

Although Russian culture is considered to be one of explosions, qualitative leaps and abrupt turnabouts toward unexpected historical movements, certain core issues are clearly traced that are periodically barely distinguishable, but continue to create some eternal and key conflicts for Russia that have a direct impact on its fate.

One such core issue is the relationship between Russia and the West, which gave birth to two camps, two movements, or we can say two outlooks: Slavophilism and Westernism. Voluminous research is dedicated to this issue, and we do not tend to contribute to it as well. We are concerned with a rather confined matter: the impact of this issue on the economic life of modern Russia, leading to 2020.

Why is it essential? Why does it require attention and investigation? What are the ties between literature and culture, and this issue?

As Fazil Iskander wrote:

> in my opinion, the main mistake of our new democratic state from which all other mistakes originate is that the authorities repeat the mistake of Marxism without noticing it: the economy is the basis, and everything else is a superstructure. The state that lives by this law is doomed to perish, it already carries the larva of death in itself. That is why the Soviet state died [...] The paradox is that the state in which the economy is the basis, first of all, is doomed to perish economically [...] The basis of man and human society is conscience, and the economy is one of the most important

> superstructures. At the same time, the economy can work well with a more or less healthy basis – the human conscience.[1]

Perhaps this writer's thoughts may seem utopian to some, but there is no denying the deep relationship between economics and ideology, economics and worldview. To study this connection in the cultural and historical context of Russia is the purpose of this chapter, which is based on the opinions, solicited between 2010 and 2020, of leading Russian economists about the ways of development of the country. At the same time, if we agree with Iskander's position, then Russian literature, traditionally preoccupied with spiritual questions, turns out to be decisive in the economic choices of Russia since it would seem that purely economic debates are in fact rooted in much deeper cultural layers. And it is not for nothing that in Russia it is literary discourse that has traditionally absorbed all the other ones, including politics, economics and philosophy.

In the field of economics, the ideas of 'Westernizers' and 'Slavophiles' are reflected in two directions of modern economic science (and practice), which, again, can be called economic liberalism and economic conservatism. The ideas of liberals and conservatives in economics were expressed in numerous interviews by the Russian economists E. G. Yasin, V. M. Polterovich, B. G. Saltykov, V. A. Volkonsky, N. M. Rimashevskaya, V. L. Makarov, V. L. Kvint and D. S. Chernavsky. These interviews revealed significant differences in assessments of the socioeconomic situation in the country as it transpired by 2020, as well as views on future development.

Historical background

But before we turn to the discussion of these views, let us briefly recall the history of Westernism and Slavophilism in Russia. The starting point in this discussion was the famous 'First Philosophical Letter' (1829) of Petr

1 Fazil Iskander, 'Esse i publitsistika' [Essays and Journalism], <http://www.kulichki.com/moshkow/FISKANDER/isk_publ.txt> (Accessed 15 November 2016).

Chaadaev, a brilliant thinker who is considered to be the most radical Westernizer. However, predecessors of Westernizers of sorts are found even in pre-Petrine times, although it was Peter the Great who turned Russia to the West in a number of ways. Even the new capital of Russia, St. Petersburg, is a Western city, as opposed to the Asian golden-domed Moscow. The ambivalent figure of Peter is still a matter of controversy. As Dmitry Likhachev wrote:

> Peter made it clear that he himself assumed the functions of the patriarch and that he would rule by force. It was Peter the Great who introduced absolutism to Russia; earlier autocracy was limited by councils and an assembly of boyars, the duma, which at times did not submit to the monarch. Strange as it may seem, true despotism came to Russia along with Westernization and Peter was the medium for both one and the other.[2]

However, the ideas of Westernizers and Slavophiles received their theoretical framework only in the 1830s and 1840s. As already noted, the formation of Westernism and Slavophilism was initiated by the escalation of ideological disputes after the publication in 1836 of Chaadaev's 'Philosophical Letter' of 1829.[3]

Interestingly, according to Osip Mandelshtam, Chaadaev's thoughts about Russia remained a mystery,[4] although, in the popular understanding, the philosopher saw Russian history as a series of ominous misunderstandings: 'first a brutal barbarism, then crude superstition, after that fierce, degrading foreign domination by strangers, whose spirit was later inherited by the national government – that is the sad history of our youth'.[5]

2 Dmitrii Likhachev, 'Religion: Russian Orthodoxy', in *The Cambridge Companion to Modern Russian Culture*, Second edition, ed. Nicholas Rzhevsky (Cambridge: Cambridge University Press, 2012), p. 49.

3 P. Chaadaev, *Filosoficheskie pisma* [Philosophical Letters], see <http://www.vehi.net/chaadaev/filpisma.html> (Accessed 15 October 2016). In English, see, for example, *The Major Works of Peter Chaadaev*, Translation and Commentary by Raymond T. McNally (London: University of Notre Dame Press, 1969).

4 O. Mandelshtam, 'Chaadaev', <https://rvb.ru/20vek/mandelstam/slovo_i_kultura/01text/01text/10.htm> (Accessed 25 November 2021).

5 *The Major Works of Peter Chaadaev*, pp. 29–30.

Chaadaev, as is well known, believed that all European nations were going the same 'correct' way, while Russia remained aloof from this path: 'placed, as it were, outside of the times, we have not been affected by the universal education of mankind'.[6]

> We have never advanced along with other people; we are not related to any of the great human families; we belong neither to the West nor the East, and we possess the traditions of neither [...] In a sense, it can be said that we are an exceptional people. We are one of those nations which does not seem to form an integral part of humanity [...] Alone in the world, we have given nothing to the world, taken nothing from the world [...] We have something or other in our blood that alienates any real progress.[7]

In contrast to hopeless Russia, in the West, according to Chaadaev, the fulfilled hopes of humanity are revealed:

> Despite all that is incomplete, vicious, evil, in European society as it stands today, yet, it is nonetheless true that God's reign has been realized there in some way, because it contains the principle of indefinite progress and possesses germinally and elementarily all that is needed for God's reign to become established definitely upon earth one day.[8]

Chaadaev very categorically formulated the idea that the Western path is one of progress, while Russia was left behind, out of progress. It is significant that he reduced all the advantages of the West to those of Catholicism compared to Orthodoxy. S. N. Karamzina, daughter of the famous Russian historian N. M. Karamzin, in a private letter dated 3 (15) November 1836, gave a different title to this work of Chaadaev, directly calling it 'The Advantages of Catholicism over the Greek Confession'.[9] The discussion was thus conducted in a religious key; Chaadaev was called a 'Catholic' and accused of 'kissing the Pope's shoe'.[10] It is exactly in these

6 Ibid., p. 27.
7 Ibid., pp. 27, 32, 37, 38.
8 Ibid., p. 47.
9 S. N. Karamzina, *Pushkin v pismakh Karamzinykh* [Pushkin in Karamzin's Family Letters], Letter 3, 15 November 1836, 1836–1837 (Moscow: Publ. Academy of Sciences USSR, Institute of Russian Literature (Pushkin House), 1960), p. 128.
10 N. M. Yazykov, Poems: 'K Chaadaevu' [To Chaadaev], <http://www.stihi-xix-xx-vekov.ru/yaziykov115.html> (Accessed 12 October 2016).

terms that the radical Slavophile Yazykov, who considered a total separation from the Westernizers to be good, expressed himself in his poems. And his poem 'To Strangers' ('K nenashim') appeared even before the poem 'To Chaadaev': 'Oh, ye who seek to transform us, to spoil us and Germanize Russia, hark to my frank outburst!'[11] In this connection, Yazykov wrote the following seminal lines to his brother:

> These verses have done the job, they divided what should not have been together, separated the sheep from the goats, the benefit is great! Hardly the spirit of the party is action, whatever it may be, against those who want to prove that they have not only the right but also the duty to despise the Russian people, by proving that the Russians are corrupted, whereas this corruption was born and nurtured, and is still born and nurtured, by exactly what they call their conviction![12]

Of course, Yazykov was opposed by well-known Westernizers – for example, by Belinsky, who, among others, was supported by Herzen. Note that all these individuals were primarily literary figures, which once again emphasizes the deep connection of Russian literature with all other facets of Russian life. And it is only natural that the English literary scholar and critic Richard Peace called Russian literature a magic mirror, which, as in Pushkin's fairy tale, not only reflects but also shapes reality, actively responding to it.[13]

The role of Orthodoxy

What were the key beliefs of the Slavophiles on whose behalf the poet Yazykov, among others, spoke? Their demands are well known, but we would like to mention some of the points most important in our context.

11 N. M. Yazykov, Poems: 'K nenashim' [To Strangers]. See <http://yazykov.lit-info.ru/yazykov/stihi/k-nenashim.htm> (Accessed 13 October 2016).

12 N. M. Yazykov, see Biographical Index, <http://www.hrono.ru/biograf/bio_ya/jazykov_nm02.php> (Accessed 13 October 2021).

13 Richard A. Peace, *Russian Literature and the Fictionalisation of Life* (Hull: University of Hull, 1976), p. 2.

First of all, it is, of course, the role of Orthodoxy as the core of all Russian culture. The Slavophiles hoped for *sobornost'* that grew out of a spiritual community, for communality in all spheres of life, and for the family as the bearer of traditional morality and values. 'The peculiarity of Russia was only in the very completeness and purity of the expression that Christian teaching achieved in it – in the entire scope of its public and private existence', wrote one of the main ideologists of Slavophilism, Ivan Kireevsky.[14]

The Slavophiles' way of development

Further on, the Slavophiles saw Russia's identity, traditions, values and own behavioral patterns as their own way of development and, therefore, criticized blind imitation. Thus, they were against borrowing Western ideas and recipes for development. 'Where there is no independence of the spirit, there is slavery of the spirit, and imitation', wrote another ideologist of Slavophilism, K. Aksakov.[15]

Why were the early Slavophiles so opposed to the influence of Western Europe? To put it briefly, and therefore rather simplistically, we can say that they saw the West as too rational and soulless, and their criticism of the foundations of Western culture was directed against the Western fascination with 'law' in contrast to Russian culture that they perceived as focused above all on justice, mercy, love and conscience. Interestingly, two centuries later, Fazil Iskander expressed essentially the same idea through the mouth of his hero:

14 I. V. Kireevsky, 'O kharaktere prosveshcheniia Evropy i ego otnoshenii k prosveshcheniiu Rossii' [On the Character of European Enlightenment and Its Relation to Russian Enlightenment] (Letter to E. E. Komarovsky, 1852), <http://lib.pravmir.ru/library/readbook/292> (Accessed 21 October 2016).

15 K. S. Aksakov, 'Peredovye statii gazety *Molva*' ('Uchenie slavianofilov') [Leading Articles of the Newspaper *Molva* (The Teaching of the Slavophiles)], <http://dugward.ru/library/aksakovy/kaksakov_peredovye.html> (Accessed 25 October 2016).

> If the law becomes life's pivotal principle, conscience wanes. But no matter how much laws are developed and govern the life of society, there have always been, are and will be occasions in life where a person must act in accordance with their conscience. But how can they act in accordance with their conscience when it has withered away? And it withered away precisely because the laws developed well and people became used to restricting themselves only by the law.[16]

It is generally believed that this hierarchy of spiritual values, where legality is given a secondary place due to the primacy of conscience, goes back to Metropolitan Hilarion (the first Russian head of the Kiev metropolis), who argued that the law is only a phantom of truth, and not the truth itself, because it is established by the state, and not by divine authority, and therefore has only legal, not moral content.[17] Kireevsky explained such differences between Russia and the West by tracing these to dissimilarities in the origins of the enlightenment: the Western one from Rome; the Russian one from Byzantium. He argued that Russian enlightenment differs from the Western one not in terms of the degree of development, but in quality and in spirit, because Roman culture, relying on formal logic and laws, overlooks the essential. He believed, quite in the spirit of Hilarion, that the laws are often accidental and unfair, that they are often set by the victors in their favor and that the natural and moral relations of people are distorted: 'the harmony of external formality is brought to such an amazing logical perfection, with an amazing lack of internal justice'.[18]

These thoughts are also in tune with the words of Nikolai Mikhailovsky, which were written at the end of the nineteenth century: 'it seems that only in Russia the truth and justice are called by the same word and seem to

16 Fazil Iskander, 'Dumaiushchii o Rossii i amerikanets' [One Dwelling on Russia and an American], <http://www.lib.ru/FISKANDER/isk_amer.txt> (Accessed 25 October 2016).

17 Hilarion, 'Sermon on Law and Grace', <https://azbyka.ru/slovo-o-zakone-i-blagodati-mitropolita-ilariona> (Accessed 11 November 2016).

18 Kireevsky, 'O kharaktere prosveshcheniia'.

merge into one great whole. Truth – in the great sense of this word – has always been the goal of my strivings.'[19]

A little later – at the beginning of the twentieth century – the artist Vasily Kandinsky seems to have repeated the same thoughts in his memoirs about studying at the University's Law Faculty:

> I was attracted to Roman law by the finesse of conscious and polished construction, but in the end it did not satisfy my Slavic soul with its too schematically cold, too reasonable and inflexible logic. As opposed to Roman law, the history of Russian law and customary law aroused feelings of surprise and love in me, as it was a free and fortunate resolution of the matter of law application.[20]

Kireevsky expressed himself more bluntly, directly stating that the foundations of the European enlightenment were eroded by a destructive 'self-moving knife of reason', 'an abstract syllogism that recognizes nothing but itself and personal experience'.[21] Catholicism was also accused of adhering to a syllogism that disregarded the life of the spirit: 'Roman theologians were especially concerned with the side of practical activity and the logical connection of concepts', without paying attention to the inner life of man.[22]

For the Slavophiles, as for Hilarion in his time, the law was Christianity. For in the origins of law there is the Old Testament law, an eye for an eye, while the New Testament is love and a behest to turn the other cheek. Therefore, when religious people deny the law, it is not just a denial of some legal secular rules in the Slavophile tradition.

In other words, in the development of Russian religious and philosophical thought up to the beginning of the twentieth century, the torments of conscience are more important than the law. Later, in the second half of the twentieth century, Iskander, through the mouth of his hero, concisely summarized and developed this:

19 Nikolai Mikhailovsky, cited in V. V. Zenkovsky, *Istoriia russkoi filosofii* [History of Russian philosophy], Vol. 1, Second edition (Paris, YMCA Press, 1989), p. 19.

20 V. V. Kandinsky, *Tekst khudozhnika. Stupeni* [Artist's Text: Stages] (Moscow, 1918), pp. 16–17.

21 Kireevsky, 'O kharaktere prosveshcheniia'.

22 Ibid.

> a Russian person is strong in his ethical striving, but weak in obeying the ethical laws. A mighty ethical striving perhaps results from a horror of encountering ethical lawlessness. What are the results of all this? Great literature and feeble statehood.[23]

The different understanding of progress

Finally, another key point in the differences between Slavophilism and Westernism was in their respective understanding of progress. Here too, as already noted, Orthodoxy was given a special role. It is the Orthodox faith, as the Slavophiles believed, that points the way to a conscious choice between good and evil, to moral improvement, which in their understanding is the true purpose of man, or, in other words, progress. The Slavophiles associated progress and development primarily with the search for 'spiritual meaning', and not with revolutionary transformations of the social structure. To quote Mikhail Katkov: 'Our so-called progressives imagine that the more we break, beat and destroy, the more progress there will be. Alas, they are wrong!'[24]

There was another reason why the early Slavophiles rejected the West and even in a certain sense grew angry at it: namely, the well-known arrogance of Western Europe toward Russia. As Ivan Aksakov wrote, 'in the concept of the European West, Russia is a barbaric country, it is a terrible, solely material force that threatens to suppress freedom of thought, enlightenment, and the prosperity (progress) of peoples'.[25] It is interesting that the Russian Westernizers who welcomed Europe and sought to merge with it were also perceived in the West as being outside of European development.

23 Fazil Iskander, 'A Poet', <http://lib.ru/FISKANDER/iskan_poet.txt_with-big-pictures.html> (Accessed 23 October 2016).

24 Mikhail Katkov, 'Literary Review and Notes', *Russian Messenger*, Vol. 35 (October 1861), pp. 107–127, <http://dugward.ru/library/katkov/katkov_koe_chto_o_progresse.html> (Accessed 20 October 2016).

25 Aksakov, 'Peredovye statii gazety *Molva*'.

Several decades later (in 1867), Fedor Tyutchev gave a concise poetic assessment of this state of affairs:

> They can't be brought to reason – not a chance,
> The more they're liberal, the more they're vulgar,
> Civilization's their fetish dance,
> But its idea dodges them, no wonder!
> It doesn't matter, gents, how low you bow
> Before Old World: it'll never recognize you,
> For in its eyes you'll always be lowbrows,
> But not the kindred servants of enlightenment.[26]

It is significant that the Westernizers themselves seemed to take on the arrogant European view of their own people. In any case, this is the position that the Slavophiles accused them of. Thus, according to Aksakov, Westernism means 'the division of the people into leaders and followers. Just as the power of exhortation is given to some, the power of attention is bestowed upon others; but it is not men who distribute it, but Providence'.[27] Ivan Kireevsky spoke more generally on this matter: 'All the false conclusions of rational thinking depend only on its claim to a higher and complete knowledge of the truth.'[28]

And yet, for all the fundamental differences in views on Russia and the West, Westernizers and Slavophiles of the early nineteenth century had a lot in common. Both were educated and appreciated Western culture. Moreover, many ideas of Western philosophers, especially Schelling and Hegel, were close to the Slavophiles. Alexei Khomyakov called the West 'the land of Holy miracles',[29] and Ivan Kireevsky admitted: 'Yes, to be honest, I still love the West, I am connected with it by many indissoluble sympathies. I belong to it by my upbringing, my habits of life, my tastes,

26 Fedor Tyutchev, *Poems*, <http://www.ruthenia.ru/tiutcheviana/stihi/bp/291.html> (Accessed 12 November 2016).

27 Aksakov, 'Peredovye statii gazety *Molva*'.

28 I. V. Kireevsky, 'On the Necessity and Possibility of New Principles in Philosophy', <http://knleontiev.narod.ru/context/kireevsky1.htm> (Accessed 21 October 2016).

29 Alexei Khomyakov, 'Dream', 1835. See <http://libverse.ru/homyakov/mechta.html> (Accessed 12 November 2016).

my controversial mindset, even my deep-hearted affections.'[30] In regard to Westernizers, as Archpriest Georges Florovsky wrote, although

> Chaadaev is usually called the first Westernizer, and the history of Westernism is considered to begin with his name, he can only be called the first figuratively – in his generation everyone was a Westernizer, often there were only Westernizers. And he was a peculiar Westernizer. It was religious Westernism.[31]

In addition, both camps were characterized by a rejection of serfdom and autocratic despotism; both supported the destiny of Russia, consistently contrasting it with Western Europe, although they saw the country's development paths differently.

In the letters of Nikolai Gogol addressed to Vissarion Belinsky, Gogol is open for dialogue and is able to unite Slavophiles and Europeanism followers in Pushkin's manner: 'They both speak of different sides of the same subject, without realizing that they are by no means arguing with or contradicting each other.'[32] However, Gogol calls to abandon pride and behold the truth of the opponent, while Belinsky is prone to monologize, he sees progress in external, revolutionary transformations but not in internal, spiritual ones.[33] As a result, his revolutionary theory of socialism

30 I. V. Kireevsky, 'V otvet Alekseiu Stepanovichu Khomyakovu', 1839 [In Response to Alexei Stepanovich Khomyakov], <http://dugward.ru/library/nikolay1/kireevski y_otvet_hom.html> (Accessed 10 November 2016).

31 Georges Florovsky, 'Ways of Russian Theology', <http://umozak.ru/puti-russk ogo-bogosloviya-prot-georgij-florovskij-v2/index4.html> (Accessed 14 November 2016). Be it noted that Florovsky points out further on that 'the mainstream of Russian Westernism goes already in those years into atheism, "realism" and "positivism", and that's what makes it different from Slavophilism'.

32 N. Gogol, 'Spory' [Debates] (from the letter to L***), in N. V. Gogol, *Polnoe sobranie sochinenii* (*PSS*) in 14 vols (Moscow-Leningrad: Izd-vo AN SSSR, 1952), Vol. 8, p. 262.

33 See the interpretation by Aleksandr Medvedev of A. N. Burmeister's work *Dukhovnost i prosveshchenie: u istokov russkogo samopoznaniia* [Spirituality and Enlightenment: At the Origins of Russian Self-Awareness] (Tiumen: TSUABCE, 2010); A. Medvedev, 'Sviatoi Vlamidir i Petr Velikii: russkoe samosoznanie v poiskakh edinstva' [Saint Vladimir and Peter the Great: Russian Self-Consciousness in Search of Unity] in *Russkaia filosofiia: istoriia, personalii, metodologiia* [Russian

and atheism determined the path of external, violent transformations in Russia: 'I am beginning to love humanity in Marat's way: to make the smallest part of humanity happy, it seems that I would destroy the rest with fire and sword.'[34] As A. N. Burmeister writes, the gap between enlightenment and spirituality turned out to be fatal for Russia; Belinsky's exclamations were perceived as 'an extreme political manifesto that opens the way to nihilism, i.e. radical rejection, total negation of the heritage of both Westernizers and Slavophiles'.[35] Subsequently, the Slavophiles became immersed in Orthodox metaphysics, while the Westernizers turned into a radical intelligentsia that led the country to Bolshevik terror.[36]

But there was also a more balanced middle position, the most prominent representative of which was Pushkin, who remained in the memory of the people not only as a poetic genius but also as the herald of the Russian 'spirit'. His famous response to Chaadaev appeals to history rather than to religion. 'There is no doubt', Pushkin wrote,

> that the Schism separated us from the rest of Europe and that we have not participated in any of the great occurrences which have agitated it. But we have had our own special mission. Russia, in its immense expanse, was what absorbed the Mongol conquest. The Tatars did not dare to cross our Western borders and to leave us at the rear. They withdrew to their deserts, and Christian civilization was saved. To achieve this goal, we had to lead a very special existence, which, although retaining Christianity in us, made us utterly alien to the Christian world, so that by our martyrdom the vigorous development of Europe was freed from all hindrances.[37]

And then Pushkin strongly objects to Chaadaev about the 'historical insignificance' of Russia:

Philosophy: History, Personalia, Methodology], *Collected Scientific Papers* (Tiumen: TSUABCE, 2011).

34 V. G. Belinsky, A letter to V. P. Botkin dated 28 June 1841, in V. G. Belinsky, *Complete Collection of Essays*, 13 vols (Moscow, 1956), Vol. 12. No. 179.

35 Burmeister, *Dukhovnost i prosveshchenie*, p. 388.

36 Medvedev, 'Sviatoi Vlamidir i Petr Velikii', p. 73.

37 A. S. Pushkin, Letter to P. Ya. Chaadaev, *Collected Essays*, Vol. 10 (Moscow: Literature, 1978), pp. 285–288. Translation is largely (but not fully) drawn from https://archive.schillerinstitute.com/fid_97-01/993_Pushkin.pdf (p. 58) (Accessed 29 April 2023).

> Are the awakening of Russia, the development of its power, its march toward unity […], is all this to be not history, but a pallid and half-forgotten dream? […] And (cross your heart) do you find nothing impressive in the present-day situation of Russia, nothing which will strike the future historian? Do you believe that he will place us outside Europe?[38]

While acknowledging the correctness of Chaadaev's criticism of public life and the political structure of the country ('while arguing with you, I must say that much of your message is deeply true'), Pushkin, nevertheless, utters his famous phrase, as if echoing his immortal lines about 'love for our home to ashes perished, love for our fathers' sacred graves':

> I am far from admiring all that I see around me […]. But I swear to you on my honor that not for anything in the world would I be willing to change my fatherland, nor to have any other history than that of our ancestors, such as God gave it to us[39]

As is well known, Pushkin decided not to send his letter to Chaadaev, and the latter saw it many years later. V. A. Zhukovsky conveyed Pushkin's words explaining the reason for this decision: 'A raven never pecks a raven's eye'.[40] Chaadaev had a tough time. And this gesture of friendly love and care seems especially organic in the context of Pushkin's position.

What was the proportional division of Russian society into Westernizers and Slavophiles at the beginning of the nineteenth century?

The Slavophiles understood that Peter's reforms affected only the top of society, a small part of the nobility and the tsar's bureaucracy, but did

38 A. S. Pushkin, Letter to P. Ya. Chaadaev. See https://archive.schillerinstitute.com/fid_97-01/993_Pushkin.pdf (p. 58) (Accessed 29 April 2023).

39 Ibid.

40 See *Russkii arkhiv* [Russian Archive], No. 4 (1884), p. 453; *Russkaia starina* [Russian Antiquity] (October 1903), pp. 185–186, ed. A. N. Veselovsky and V. A. Zhukovsky (St. Petersburg, 1904), p. 395.

not reach the bottom, the 'big' peasant Russia, the peasant community. Aksakov calls the Pro-Western society elite 'a separate layer of the Russian people',[41] urging them to return to the 'real Russia'. Perhaps, the Russian aristocrats were close to the Western aristocrats, and therefore they were more inclined to Westernism. Also, the intelligentsia was more committed to Western ideas because they considered themselves educated and thinking. As the Slavophile Katkov, who became a famous reactionary, ironically put it: 'Our intelligentsia is trying to show itself as little Russian as possible, believing that this is what Europeanism is about.'[42] He wrote:

> In our country true barbarism doesn't wear grey armiak, but it wears a tailcoat and even white gloves [...] Our barbarism does not consist of the lack of education of our masses: masses are masses everywhere on earth, but we can admit with dignity and conviction that nowhere else there are people who possess so much spirit and strength of faith as our people do, and this is no longer barbarism.[43]

It should be noted that the staunch Westernizer Ivan Turgenev also criticized and ridiculed the thoughtless craving for Europe among the Russian intelligentsia and tried in vain to depict an ideal image of the Russian European. However, despite the relatively small number of Westernizers, the authorities were more Westernized and thus were usually more influential than the Slavophiles.

Further discussion

Before proceeding to the legacy of these two main currents in modern Russia, we should first briefly follow the main trends in the development

41 Aksakov, 'Peredovye statii gazety *Molva*'.

42 Mikhail Katkov, 'Nashe varvarstvo – v nashei inostrannoi intelligentsii' [Our Barbarism Is in Our Foreign Intelligentsia], <http://dugward.ru/library/katkov/katkov_nashe_varvar.html> (Accessed 14 November 2016).

43 Ibid.

of Westernism and Slavophilism in the nineteenth and twentieth centuries.

Vladimir Solovyov at the end of the nineteenth century (i.e., half a century after Chaadaev) identified three phases in Western development:

> theocratic, represented by Roman Catholicism; humanitarian, defined theoretically as rationalism and practically as liberalism; and naturalistic, expressed in a positive natural-scientific direction of thought, on the one hand, and in the predominance of socio-economic interests, on the other.[44]

For example, Prince Gagarin, a well-known Westernizer, converted to Catholicism and became a Jesuit; the Westernizer Chernyshevsky, who was born a year before Chaadaev's letter was written, was primarily interested in socioeconomic issues; and Herzen is well known to have launched a revolutionary agitation. At the same time, there were both Anglophiles and Francophiles among the Westernizers of the nineteenth century. In addition, as already mentioned, it was the Westernizers who gravitated more toward radicalism and revolutionism.

Over time, Westernism becomes increasingly associated with the concept of Europeanism. Although there is a lot of debate about what Europeanism is, we will focus on the definition given by Yuri Lotman. In the late 1990s, Lotman wrote: 'Europeanism started from the idea that the "Russian way" is a path already traversed by "more advanced European culture".'[45] From this point of view, Russia actually appears as a backward part of the West, and needs to catch up with Western Europe. In this case simulation of Europe and imitation of its ways seem quite logical.

However, the ideas of the Slavophiles were also long-lived. At the beginning of the twentieth century, Berdyaev, in particular, alludes to them arguing that the Slavophiles are 'the flesh and blood of the Russian land, Russian history, Russian soul'.[46] Discussing the views of the Slavophiles, he

44 V. Solovyov, 'Zapadniki, Zadapnichestvo' [Westernizers, Westernism], in *Encyclopaedic Dictionary*, ed. F. A. Brockhaus and I. A. Efron (1894), Vol. 12, pp. 243–244.

45 Yuri M. Lotman, *Sovremennost mezhdu vostokom i zapadom* [Modernity between the East and the West], *Znamia* , No. 9 (1997).

46 Nikolai Berdyaev, 'Alexei Stepanovich Khomyakov', 1911, <http://predanie.ru/berdyaev-nikolay-aleksandrovich/book/69674-aleksey-stepanovich-homyakov/> (Accessed 16 November 2016).

concludes that it was the religious aspirations of the Slavophiles and their religious consciousness that could give Russia its geniuses – Dostoevsky, Tolstoy, Tyutchev. 'Slavophilism discovered something that will last forever, something important and necessary even for those who do not need and even despise the decrepit Slavophile clothes', Berdyaev wrote.[47]

Continuing the same idea in the middle of the twentieth century, the Russian philosopher Vasilii Zenkovsky distinguished as the main feature of Russian philosophy the fact that 'the moral doctrine is dominant in everything (even in abstract problems): here lies one of the most effective and creative sources of Russian philosophizing'.[48] This also conditions intense attention to the social problem.

By the same token, in 1973, Father Alexander Schmemann talked about

> a really amazing prophecy that we learn from the Russians. Dostoevsky not only predicted, but truly revealed the essence of the 'demons' that took possession of the Western soul. Khomyakov predicted the collapse of Western Christianity. Fedorov predicted and defined the essence and mechanism, the evil essence of the Western 'economy'.[49]

Contemporary discussion

If we consider the aforementioned letter of Pushkin to Chaadaev as a nucleus of the polemics between Westernizers and Slavophiles, it should be noted that it has not lost its relevance. Thus, in May 2016, Professor of History Alexei Lubkov commented on the famous film *Mirror* (1974) by Andrei Tarkovsky, where a boy reads this letter aloud:

47 Ibid.

48 Vasily Zenkovsky, *History of Russian Philosophy* (Rostov-on-Don: Phoenix, 2004), Vol. 1, pp. 18–19.

49 Alexander Schmemann, Notebook 1:28, 8 April 1973, New York, <http://memuarist.com/ru/events/25086.htm> (Accessed 19 November 2016).

> the connection between the personal and the historical vividly demonstrates one of the masterpieces of Russian cinema – the film by Andrei Tarkovsky *Mirror*. Its key episode is reading a fragment from the letter of A. Pushkin to P. Chaadaev of 19 October 1836. The letter is read by a boy – and this is also important [...] The Director put this episode in the centre of his cinematic narrative, which is very complex, but in fact very understandable for a person who views the world through the prism of poetry, of love for his fatherland, his past, himself, and his memory. What Tarkovsky tried to do in this film – which seems to be a chamber film, telling about the history of his family, his growing up, his perception of life – is of vital importance: the fact that this perception comes from love, from familiarization with the history of Russia.[50]

In Chekhov's story 'The Student', which Chekhov himself considered one of his most successful works, the protagonist says the same thing:

> 'The past [...] is linked with the present by an unbroken chain of events flowing one out of another. And it seemed to him that he had just seen both ends of that chain; that when he touched one end the other quivered'.[51]

Indeed, 'history is the connection of times. This is the thread that connects the meanings and values of previous generations with the values of future generations and makes it possible to consider us as one people at all times.'[52] This also includes, if you like, the words of Sergei Dovlatov's hero, for they are of the same root: 'Suddenly my throat contracted painfully. For the first time I was part of my unique, unprecedented country. I was entirely made of cruelty, hunger, memory, malice... Because of my tears I couldn't see for a moment'.[53]

50 Alexei Lubkov, 'Byt grazhdaninom znachit izuchat istoriiu strany' [To be a Citizen Is to Learn the History of the Country], 13 May 2016, <http://pereformat.ru/2016/05/izuchat-istoriyu/> (Accessed 22 November 2016).

51 Anton Chekhov, 'The Student', <http://www.free-short-stories.org.uk/anton-chekhov-the-student.htm> (Accessed 14 December 2021).

52 Lubkov, 'Byt grazhdaninom znachit izuchat istoriiu strany'.

53 Sergei Dovlatov, *The Zone*, trans. Anne Frydman (Berkeley: Counterpoint Press, 2012), p. 162.

Alongside this vision of Pushkin's, of Russian history in all its tragic grandeur, there is also a Westernist approach that forever tends to align with Europe as a standard to live by. The psychology of modern young Westernizers who have learned their ideas about the West from foreign trips, from visiting wonderful Viennese patisseries, French restaurants, famous theatres and museums, and, of course, shops, perceives Europe as a mystical and extraordinary place.

Thus, although the original terminology has been abolished and religion is largely forgotten, the essential meaning of these two schools – the Westernist and the Slavophile – together with their fierce polemics, do not fade. In our study of modern Russia of 2010–2020, we set out to investigate what was the balance of power in Russian society based on the results of a public opinion poll regarding Slavophile and Westernist ideas. Who are they – modern Westernizers and Slavophiles – and what are their beliefs?

Results of sociological surveys of Russian youth

As was argued in 2013 by the director of the Academy of Russian Sciences Institute of Sociology, M. Gorshkov, according to opinion polls 'the majority of Russians, one way or another, supports the idea of a "special path" of Russia's development in the modern world', although 'the understanding of this "special way" is different, and many Russian citizens have a shapeless and vague opinion on it'.[54] The author explains this primarily by dissatisfaction with the course of reforms carried out in Russia since the 1990s and the changes in the economy, culture and lifestyle that these reforms have led to. The Institute of Sociology conducted a joint study of values among young people alongside their Chinese counterparts.

54 M. K. Gorshkov, 'Modernizatsionnyi potentsial identichnosti' [Modernization Potential of Identity] (in lieu of preface), *Reforming Russia*, Annual part 12 (Moscow: The New Chronograph, Institute of Sociology of Russian Academy of Sciences, 2013), p. 6.

Almost half of the Russian respondents (48.8 percent) do not feel close to European society. This is also true in China. Young people in Russia do not support the 'Western way of development'. They are focused on the Russian way. A new, unexpected result was that distrust of the Western path is higher among people with higher levels of education. Researchers explain this by saying that educated young people understand that Western practices do not take root well on Russian soil.[55] Meanwhile, it is interesting to note that the point of view of the opposite Westernist camp rejects the idea of the distinctive Russian way of development as fiction. For example, in 2013, academician Yuri Pivovarov voiced the opinion that no special path for Russia is destined, and the Russian soul is no more mysterious than the German or the Polish.[56]

At the same time, a survey of young people in the Orel region, conducted in 2015, depicts a significantly different picture. The object of the study was the youth of the Orel region aged 15 to 29, located in Orel and other settlements of the Orel region (Livensky district, Mtsensky district and Kromsky district). A total of 404 respondents were surveyed, most of whom (36.9 percent) were aged 20 to 24. Young people were asked how they see the future development of Russia. Only 7.2 percent were supporters of 'radical market reforms and rapid rapprochement with Western countries'. The majority (32.7 percent) supported 'an independent Russian way of development of the country'; 14.2 percent believed that it is best to 'combine different ideas and avoid extremes'. Thus, according to the results of this survey, supporters of modern Slavophilism exceeded the number of modern Westernizers by almost five times. Nevertheless, it is difficult to call them reactionary-conservative. The results of the survey showed that the youth of the region is not interested in totalitarian, authoritarian government. Moreover, it values freedom more than success and other

55 Svetlana Vladimirovna Mareeva, 'Rossiiskaia molodezh: identichnosti, tsennosti i predstavleniia ob optimalnom obshchestvennom ustroistve' [Russian Youth: Identities, Values and Ideas about the Optimal Social Structure], *Reforming Russia*, Vol. 12 (2013), pp. 361–380.

56 Y. Pivovarov, Interview in *Rossiyskaia Gazeta* [Russian Newspaper], 22 January 2013, <https://rg.ru/2013/01/22/pivovarov.html> (Accessed 30 November 2016).

similar values, although the Orel region is traditionally considered a fairly conservative province.[57]

A similar picture was presented by the results of a large-scale international study of student youth, on the basis of which the head of the Russian leg of the project, A. A. Ovsiannikov, wrote an article entitled 'The New Generation: A Long Road in Search of New Ideals and Meanings of Life'.[58] In this study, students from various universities and of different academic levels were interviewed. The 2013 study sample consisted of 7,287 people, guaranteeing a sampling error of no more than 3 percent. This survey repeated a similar study from 1991, which allowed us to consider the results dynamically. Ovsiannikov emphasized a certain 'nationalism' of Russian students. In his article, he writes, in particular, that

> national distinctiveness is a phenomenon that has nothing in common with chauvinism and fascism. This is the recognition of national characteristics and national identity. If the word 'nationalism' did not have a strict political meaning, then national distinctiveness could be designated as cultural nationalism. In this sense, Russian students are nationalists, and over the past twenty years, this assessment continues to remain at a high level (for example, 51 per cent of Russian students believe that 'Russians are a great nation with a huge untapped potential'). As soon as the strength of national culture decreases, the bonds of social and moral norms are eroded, and the Demos weakens. Immediately the non-socialized forces of instinctive division of people come to the surface: they always take the form of primitive rules for distinguishing between fellow people and outsiders, friends and enemies, those who are against us and those who are with us.[59]

Thus, the conclusion of the sociological research pointed to the predominance, at least among the surveyed Russian youth, of Slavophile rather

57 See *Molodezh Orlovskoi oblasti v 2015 godu. Nauchnoe izdanie. Informatsionno-sotsiologicheskii bulleten* [The Youth of the Orel Region in 2015. Scientific Publication. The Information-Sociological Bulletin], Collective monograph (Orel: Central Russian Institute of Management, 2015).

58 A. A. Ovsiannikov, 'Novoe pokolenie: dolgaia doroga v poiskakh novykh idealov i smyslov zhizni' [The New Generation: A Long Road in Search of New Ideals and Meanings of Life], <http://jour.isras.ru/upload/journals/4/articles/3113/submission/original/3113-5752-1-SM.pdf> (Accessed 10 December 2016).

59 Ibid.

than Westernist sentiments. At the same time, the voices of modern Westernizers – as in the above example with academician Pivovarov – were no less loud and clear, even if they may be outnumbered by their opponents. In modern Russia, they tend to belong to the so-called liberal camp, while their opponents are usually called conservatives, and this confrontation has increasingly been gaining momentum in post-Soviet Russia. The situation in the Russian economy during the period under study, as we will see in the sequel, largely reflected this ideological alignment (just as sharply captured and discussed in literature as in the nineteenth century at the dawn of the Slavophile-Westernist debate).

Ways of development of the country in the context of modern Westernism and Slavophilism: Views of leading Russian economists in 2010–2020

Liberals in modern economics

Without a doubt, E. G. Yasin can be referred to as a liberal economist.[60] Moreover, he is the President of the 'Liberal Mission' foundation. Just as the Slavophiles and Westernizers of the nineteenth century differed in their attitude to the reforms of Peter I, modern economists differ in their attitude to the reforms of Yegor Gaidar.[61] Yasin considers Gaidar to be a

60 Yasin Yevgenii Grigorievich is a Russian economist, state and public figure, Minister of Economy of the Russian Federation (from 1994 to 1997), Research Director of the National Research University HSE (Higher School of Economics) and the President of the 'Liberal Mission' Foundation.

61 Yegor Timurovich Gaidar was a Russian statesman and politician, economist and a Higher Doctor of Science (Economics). He was one of the main leaders and ideologists of the economic reforms of the early 1990s in Russia. From 1991 to 1994, he held high positions in the Russian government, including that of the Prime Minister. Under Gaidar's leadership, the transition from a planned to a market economy began, prices were liberalized, the tax system was reorganized, foreign trade was liberalized and privatization was initiated.

genius. This is how he put it in an interview: 'In my mind there's an image of a genius that I made up, and he probably resembled it more than anybody else.'[62] Most of all, he admires Gaidar's determination and the agility with which Gaidar implemented the most radical reforms; in one year, according to Yasin, 'almost everything' was achieved. And this is no coincidence. Just like the Westernizers of the nineteenth century, modern liberals are prone to radicalism, to revolutionism. From the very beginning of perestroika, Yasin perceived it as a revolution: 'I'll just tell you: these events that took place in Russia were extraordinary, […] it felt like it was either now or never.'[63] The last phrase just repeats Lenin's famous 'Now or never', referring to the October Revolution of 1917. Yasin borrowed his economic views from Western economists. Here is how he recalled the time of Gaidar's reforms in an interview with Kolesnikov: 'Then I felt like a modern economist. I crammed English dictionaries, read books.'[64] It is clear that it is Western science that he considers modern and therefore was ready to conduct economic policy according to Western lines. He was very impressed with the book by Z. Brzezinski, which, in Soviet times, he read right away at the bookstore, while on a business trip to Finland.[65] Yasin affirms that he found that book credible. Even more, Yasin trusted his Polish colleagues who carried out reforms in Poland: 'the Poles were more radical. Balcerowicz and his deputy, Marek Dombrowski, were the adherents of radicalism. And we are friends with them and we were friends before.' Yasin's understanding of progress, like that of the old Westernizers, is related to material progress. It is according to this criterion that he evaluates Gaidar's reforms:

> If we ask whether Gaidar's reforms were successful or not – they were. When you go to a store, there are a lot of products there; you wish to go to a restaurant – there

62 Y. G. Yasin, Interview, 27 October 2014, Host N. A. Vinokurova, Part 2, <http://oralhistory.ru/talks/orh-1786> (Accessed 10 December 2016).

63 Ibid.

64 A. Kolesnikov, *Dialogi s Evgeniem Yasinym* [Conversations with Yevgeny Yasin] (Moscow: New Literary Observer, 2014).

65 Yasin, Interview, Part 2.

> are a lot of restaurants in Moscow; you want to start a business – there is such an opportunity. It worked![66]

Liberals and conservatives in economics also have different views regarding the famous economist and politician Sergei Glaz'ev,[67] who in his speeches and articles often refers to 'Slavophile' topics. So, the measure of economic success in Glaz'ev's understanding (at least, in his public statements intended for a wide audience) differs from Yasin's understanding. In 2016, he noted thus:

> The properties of our culture associated with the tendency of our people towards searching for meaning in life, self-realization, and that our people are not satisfied with only money-measured success, are not our shortcomings, but our advantage, according to monetarists.[68]

Yasin considers Glaz'ev to be his student but treats him with sharp criticism: 'I have a negative attitude to almost everything that he suggests'; 'He just wants us to do more, to have more order, to move quickly, he thinks it does not matter what/who is the boss and so on. He believes the state should be in charge .'[69] As a liberal economist, Yasin, in contrast to Glaz'ev, has opposed the strengthening of the role of the state in the economy.

66 Ibid.

67 Sergei Glaz'ev is a Russian economist and politician, adviser to the President of the Russian Federation on regional economic integration, member of the National Financial Council of the Bank of Russia. A Doctor of Science (Economics), professor and academician at the Russian Academy of Sciences, he was the former Minister of Foreign Economic Relations of Russia as well as deputy of the I, III and IV State Duma. He was also one of the leaders of the Rodina electoral bloc (2003–2004).

68 S. Yu. Glaz'ev, Public speech at panel discussion 'Traditsionnyie tsennosti v predprinimatelstve: itogi kruglogo stola' [Traditional Russian Values in Entrepreneurship], <http://www.pravmir.ru/traditsionnyie-tsennosti-v-predprinimatelstve-itogi-kruglogo-stola/> (Accessed 12 December 2016).

69 Y. G. Yasin, Interview, 27 October 2014.

Another prominent representative of the Western liberal trend is B. G. Saltykov,[70] who was the Minister of Science in the Gaidar government. It was he who started a large-scale reform of science. In Soviet times, Saltykov studied the American experience of science financing, in Soviet times and, after becoming a minister during perestroika, he helped to organize the Russian Foundation for Basic Research (RFBR). The scientific community reacted with approval. Further, Saltykov continued reforms in science according to the Western model:

> I will tell you right away that the first attempt to reform the Academy was not dictated by us, not by me, but by what is happening in the world. In the world, the Baltic States, Eastern Europe, Germany immediately closed their Academies of Sciences. Because they were all USSR-like in terms of organization.[71]

Saltykov was particularly sympathetic to the model of reforming science in East Germany, which was carried out after the unification of the country.[72] As a result, by 1996, the number of scientists in Russia had halved, and the reform served as a trigger for the emigration of the most powerful Russian scientists. Most scientists reproached Saltykov for the destruction of Russian science:

> And now everyone reminds me of this most famous phrase of mine in the Novosibirsk academic town, in the great hall of the Siberian Department, where 600-something people gathered. I explained our reforms and uttered a phrase that one still reproaches me about: 'Because there is too much science in Russia.'[73]

Indeed, many believe that the reforms were too radical and did more harm than good. Sergei Rogov, the director of the Institute of the USA and Canada of the Russian Academy of Sciences, wrote in 2010:

70 Boris Georgievich Saltykov was the Deputy Prime Minister and Minister of Science and Technology of Russia in the 1990s. He is at present a professor at the Higher School of Economics and President of the Polytechnic Museum.

71 B. G. Saltykov, Interview, 7 June 2012, <http://www.yeltsincentre.ru/decryption/intervyu-s-borisom-saltykovym> (Accessed 12 December 2016).

72 Ibid.

73 Ibid.

> As a result of the ill-conceived reforms in the 1990s, a significant part of the science sector was privatized and disappeared without a trace. Budget funding for research and advanced development was sharply reduced. The number of scientific researchers fell by two thirds. There was a loss of entire scientific schools. The current situation is the result of applying neoliberal economic concepts in Russia, according to which any state intervention in the economy leads to negative consequences.[74]

But Saltykov showed no regrets, as noted in his 2012 interview: 'These were the best times of my life, career, and so on. Because even the few things that were done, and the time, and the ways, and the manner of life in those years were just wonderful.' In response to reproaches for blindly following the instructions of Western experts, he said: 'Well, sure, we did invite in an expert, then another, but we still did all the work ourselves.'[75]

Conservatives in modern economics in the period under study

By 2020, modern economic conservatives did not care much about Orthodoxy; they focused more on defending traditional values and lifestyles. Issues such as social justice, attitudes toward money, commercialization of science, education, health and culture were subjects of discussion and discord. Conservatives were more interested than liberals in the role of non-economic factors in the economy. And this already determines how they envisioned the path to economic development – whether it was necessary and possible to copy Western models, and so on. One of the most radical conservatives was econophysicist D. S. Chernavsky (1926–2016).[76] He saw the reason for the socioeconomic crisis in Russia in

74 S. Rogov, 'Nevostrebovannost nauki – ugroza bezopasnosti strany' [Slack Demand for Science is a National Security Threat], *Nezavisimaia gazeta* newspaper, 8 February 2010.

75 B. G. Saltykov, Interview, 7 June 2012.

76 Dmitry Sergeevich Chernavsky was Chief Researcher of the Lebedev Physical Institute of the Russian Academy of Sciences. A Higher Doctor of Science in Physics

the fact that 'in 1991, there was an attempt to impose Western civilization on Russia',[77] which, in his opinion, does not correspond to the Russian mentality at all. Chernavsky, like the Slavophiles of the nineteenth century, paid great attention to Russian national characteristics. In his article, he provides a table showing, in his opinion, different variants of ideological preferences that determine 'belonging to a particular civilization'. It repeats the most common ideas about the difference between the West and Russia. Russian collectivism is opposed to Western individualism, and the Russian sense of justice to Western submission to any legislation. It is argued that the Russian civilization is characterized by the supremacy of public interests. Chernavsky believed that in Russia there is respect for work (including intellectual work), and in the West, the main thing is respect for money. Moreover, Chernavsky was sure that real tolerance exists in Russia, and not in the West, and that the West actually acts from the positions of superiority of some nations over others. As for the family in Russia, the state regulates family relations much less when compared with the West.[78] It is easy to see that in many respects these are the principles of the Slavophiles formulated in more modern terms: Aksakov's rejection of the superiority of one nation over another, collectivism as an expression of community, and reliance on the traditional family. Based on these principles, the author not only refuses to follow the Western path in the economic development of Russia, but in general argues for the need for a certain economic autarky in contrast to the ideas of globalization. He is not afraid that the population is not ready (even temporarily) to switch to the consumption of domestic goods that are inferior in quality to Western ones.

and Mathematics and professor, he was one of the founders of the 'econophysics' movement. He was also the winner of the TV program contest 'For the best explanation of the key questions of the structure of the world' (2004) with a prize fund of 1 million euros. The prize received was divided equally among 191 participants of the program.

77 D. S. Chernavsky, 'The Image of Russia in the Middle of the XXI Century', in *Socialno-economicheskii biulleten 2016* [Socio-Economic Bulletin 2016], ed. D. S. Chernavsky and A. V. Shcherbakov, Mendeleev Institute of Socio-Economic Forecasting (Moscow: Gryphon, 2016), pp. 34–47.

78 Ibid.

Interestingly, not only in theory but also in practice, Chernavsky demonstrated by his behavior what he defended as Russian values. In an interview for the 'Oral History' project, Chernavsky told how he won a million euros by participating in a television program about science that was attended by 200 leading Russian scientists from different fields of knowledge. The best was promised a million dollars. At the same time, since it was something like a show, it was designed to demonstrate 'how scientists will fight over a million'. After receiving a million, Chernavsky divided it equally among all participants of the program, and averred that he was sure that he did the right thing, even if it could be considered irrational:

> That million I shared, yes, I believe that I did the right thing. This raised the spirits of scientists, proved that scientists are scientists. Not all of them are dealers and businessmen... In the community called a 'scientific' one, the friendship parameter was increased. Yes, the solidarity parameter has been increased. And this is important, I believe, for the scientific community.[79]

Independently of Chernavsky, the famous mathematician Anatoly Vershik, one of the most cited Russian scientists, came up with similar ideas in connection with the Clay prize awarded for outstanding achievements in mathematics:

> Scientists who are able to solve such 'millennium problems' will do this without money. In this case, a million is an element of show business, a carrot on a string that is hung in front of your nose [...] I must say that my position has always had a lot of critics, mainly among Americans. All of these arguments I made to my friend Arthur Jaffe, a brilliant mathematician who was the Chairman of the Clay prize, established shortly before 2000. He explained to me that I didn't understand anything about American life: if a mother heard that mathematicians were given a million dollars to solve a problem, she would immediately send her son to study mathematics at university. I don't know how convincing this is, but my opinion has not changed in general.[80]

79 D. S. Chernavsky, Interview, 13 September 2012, Host Vladimir Grigorievich Budanov, Part 1, <http://oralhistory.ru/talks/orh-1454> (Accessed 18 December 2016).

80 Anatoly Vershik, 'Matematicheskiie progulki s Anatoliem Vershikom' [Mathematical Walks with Anatoly Vershik], Interview, Host Elena Kudriavtseva: <http://www.sib-science.info/ru/ras/ogoniok-estetika-v-matematike-30012017> (Accessed 26 November 2016).

And then he recalls the Russian mathematician Grigory Perelman, who rejected this award:

> Quite unexpectedly, Grisha's refusal to receive this and other awards (and he refused many awards, except for the award of our St Petersburg Mathematical Society) had a positive effect. The general audience realized that there are mathematicians who separate science from money. It is much more useful for modern society to know that than the Poincaré hypothesis.[81]

This consensus of scientists from different fields might serve as evidence that their opinions are not purely personal but reflect something cultural and ingrained in the Russian cultural consciousness – if you like, the ideas of classical Russian literature that 'the power of money' is evil.

Professor V. A. Volkonsky is even closer to the Slavophiles.[82] Volkonsky recognizes the remarkable achievements of the Western economy, and he is not against the market economy in Russia. However, he is convinced that the world of 'spirituality and meaningfulness' is no less important as a productive force than the 'material-pragmatic' world. Material values, in his understanding, are not something that makes us humans. He considers material prosperity to be unworthy of being a personal goal. In his book of 2015, he imagines the future as an era of searching for 'great meanings' and predicts 'the end of the currently dominant Western civilization'.[83] Volkonsky is an idealist, like many Slavophiles.

Professor Rimashevskaya (1932–2017)[84] did not consider herself a conservative, but she did not consider herself a liberal either: 'I'm not a liberal.

81 Ibid.

82 V. A. Volkonsky is Chief Researcher of the Institute of National Economic Forecasting of the Russian Academy of Sciences, , PhD in Physics and Mathematics, Higher Doctor of Science (Economics), professor and award winner of the competition held by the N. P. Fedorenko International Scientific Foundation for Economic Research.

83 V. A. Volkonsky, *Mnogopoliarnyi mir. Ideologiia i ekonomika. Konets dominirovaniia zapadnoy tsivilizatsii. Chto dal'she gotovit nam istoriia?* [A Multipolar World. Ideology and Economics. The End of the Dominance of Western Civilization. What Does History Have in Store for Us Next?] (Moscow: Knizhny mir [Books World], 2015), pp. 5, 12, 27.

84 Natalia Mikhailovna Rimashevskaya was a Soviet and Russian economist, corresponding member of RAS, Head of the Department of Social Sciences' Laboratory

I would like to say, I am something of a Social Democrat, or somebody like that.' Unlike Yasin or Saltykov, she spoke of Gaidar's reforms almost with horror:

> The nineties, when they dragged everything to the edge, [...] everything that was in society was either destroyed, or they divided it among themselves. And now what actually works is only what they appropriated in the early nineties. How can they explain it?

She accused young modern liberal economists of having no principles, of working solely for the sake of money: 'They are paid, and so they supply what customers expect, whereas we, in general, supply what we think is right.'[85] Rimashevskaya worked on issues related to inequality and justice, quality of life, public health as well as gender. As expected, she considered Glaz'ev to be one of the greatest economists.

Adherents of pragmatism

As our study showed, economists who are pragmatic can be both liberal and conservative to some extent. But they are not prone to radicalism. Thus, they seemed ready to use the Western experience, taking into account not only national characteristics but also the global situation in general.

Academician Polterovich can be called a modern European.[86] He has advocated Western-style reform of the Russian economy. But in his works,

of Gender Issues, Institute for Socio-Economic Studies of Population (in 1988–2004, she was Director of the institute) as well as the Chief Editor of the journal *Population*.

85 N. M. Rimashevskaya, Interview, 30 March 2013, Host N. A. Vinokurova, Part 1, <http://oralhistory.ru/talks/orh-1556> (Accessed 21 December 2016).

86 Viktor Meerovich Polterovich is an academician at the Russian Academy of Sciences, President of the New Economic Association, member of the Econometric Society (1989) and the European Academy (1992). He is also a member of the editorial

he explains the failure of Gaidar's economic reforms by the fact that the reformers did not take into account modern Russian realities.[87] For him, this constitutes a necessary condition for success.

Academician Vladimir Kvint[88] is a Westernizer and a liberal who, like Yasin, stands for reducing the role of the state in the economy. In an interview in 2015, he said: 'There will be a change in the current economic model, it does not work [...] The role of the state is too strong. [...] All these companies are state-owned'; yet, he was highly skeptical of Gaidar's fascination with Western economic theory: 'This is stupid. Pure stupidity... Those people, including Gaidar, Chubais, who led the privatization, they also deceived Yeltsin. They said, "We know where to go." And they brought the country to the edge of the abyss, into the swamp.'[89]

Academician Valery Makarov[90] approached the assessment of the economic model of Russia's development innovatively, going far beyond the

board of the *Journal of Mathematical Economics* (since 1985). In addition, he was a member of the editorial board of the journal *Econometrica* (1989–1995) and a member of the Executive Committee of the International Economic Association.

87 V. M. Polterovich, *Elementy teorii reform* [Elements of Reform Theory] (Moscow: Economics, 2007), p. 446.

88 Vladimir Lvovich Kvint, Higher Doctor of Science (Economics), is Professor of Political Economy, foreign member of the Russian Academy of Sciences and Professor of International Business at the Graduate School of Business of the American University (The American University's Kogod School of Business), Washington, D.C., since 2004. He also was Professor of Management Systems and International Business at Fordham University's Graduate School of Business, New York, from 1990 to 2004, and simultaneously from 1995 to 2000 Professor of Business Strategy at New York University's Stern School of Business. From 1989 to 1990, he was Professor of Economics Policy at the Vienna University of Economics (Vienna Economic University) in Austria.

89 V. L. Kvint, Interview, 1 June 2015, Host N. A. Vinokurova, <http://oralhistory.ru/talks/orh-1897> (Accessed 21 December 2016).

90 Valery Leonidovich Makarov, Higher Doctor of Science (Economics) is professor, academician at the Russian Academy of Sciences as well as a member of the editorial board of the journal *Economic Change and Restructuring* (United States). He was Director of the Central Economic and Mathematical Institute of the Russian Academy of Sciences (1985—2017), and one of the organizers, First Rector (1992–2004) and President (since 2004) of the Russian School of Economics as well as a

boundaries of 'conservatism' and 'liberalism'. He did not just insist on the need to take into account national traditions and use them as a competitive advantage, but rather advocated 'diversity of economies'.

> Economic science is actually very diverse due to the fact that the world is extremely diverse [...] There are, well, a billion people at most who live according to the market economy that Western economics studies. The remaining six and a half billion have completely different economic mechanisms. Diversity of economies is a blessing, not a drawback. This increases the stability of the world, preserves the uniqueness of existing civilizations in the world.[91]

Conclusion

Thus, it is obvious that by 2020 the discussion on 'Westernizers' and 'Slavophiles', while evolving, did not lose its relevance in Russia. It covered all spheres of life, including the economy, and yet stemmed from the very depths of Russian culture. For example, it is clear that the debate of modern adherents of Western and Slavophile ideas (in particular, in economics) has at its roots a discussion of the fundamental values of life, as reflected in Russian literature.

This probably explains the paradoxical fact that often the followers of these ideas (e.g., in economics) on both sides of the barricades were unfamiliar with the teachings of the initiators of Westernism and Slavophilism in Russia, but nevertheless unconsciously followed these historically set lines. In other words, the continuity of value choice seems to determine the corresponding worldview and ideology.

At the same time, it must be recognized that the relationship between Russia and the West does not cease to be a burning topic and that the civilizational differences that exist between them create a permanent

member of the Executive Committee of the International Economic Association (1995).

91 V. L. Makarov, Interview, 27 May 2015, Host N. A. Vinokurova, Part 2, <http://oralhistory.ru/>.

tension between the poles. Academician Sakharov, as is well known, like St. Augustine in his time, dreamed of a certain fusion of different civilizations, of a meeting between Russia and the West somewhere near an imaginary golden mean. However, today, in the aggravated geopolitical situation, when our differences have come to the fore and obscured what unites us, such a scenario is hard to believe. And yet diversity is necessary, as in biology where species and genes need to be diverse because the loss of even one species can have unpredictable consequences for the survival of the entire ecosystem, and genetic narrowness leads to degeneration. Hence the dialectical fusion of Westernism and Slavophilism may be the key to the healthy development of Russian society and beyond. But only insofar as these two systems of views are capable of constructive dialogue. Whether it is the case, only time will show.

Bibliography

Aksakov, K. S., 'Peredovye statii gazety *Molva*' ('Uchenie slavyanofilov') [Leading Articles of the Newspaper *Molva* (The Teaching of the Slavophiles)], <http://dugward.ru/library/aksakovy/kaksakov_peredovye.html> (Accessed 25 October 2016).

Belinsky, V. G., A letter to V.P. Botkin of 28 June 1841, in V. G. Belinsky, *Complete Collection of Essays*, 13 vols (Moscow, 1956), Vol. 12. No. 179.

Berdyaev, Nikolai, 'Alexei Stepanovich Khomyakov', 1911, <http://predanie.ru/berdyaev-nikolay-aleksandrovich/book/69674-aleksey-stepanovich-homyakov/> (Accessed 16 November 2016).

Burmeister, A. N., *Dukhovnost i prosveshchenie: u istokov russkogo samopoznaniia* [Spirituality and Enlightenment: At the Origins of Russian Self-awareness] (Tyumen: TSUABCE, 2010).

Chaadaev, Peter, *The Major Works of Peter Chaadaev*, trans. and commentary by Raymond T. McNally (London: University of Notre Dame Press, 1969).

Chaadaev, Petr, *Filosoficheskie pisma* [Philosophical Letters], <http://www.vehi.net/chaadaev/filpisma.html> (Accessed 15 October 2016).

Chekhov, Anton, 'The Student', <http://www.free-short-stories.org.uk/anton-chekhov-the-student.htm> (Accessed 14 December 2021).

Chernavsky, D. S., 'The Image of Russia in the Middle of the XXI Century', in *Socialno-economicheskii biulleten 2016* [Socio-economic Bulletin 2016], ed. D. S. Chernavsky and A. V. Shcherbakov, Mendeleev Institute of Socio-Economic Forecasting (Moscow: Gryphon, 2016), pp. 34–47.

——— Interview, 13 September 2012, Host Vladimir Grigorievich Budanov, Part 1, <http://oralhistory.ru/talks/orh-1454> (Accessed 18 December 2016).

Dovlatov, Sergei, *The Zone*, trans. Anne Frydman (Berkeley: Counterpoint Press, 2012).

Glaz'ev, S. Yu., 'Traditsionnyie tsennosti v predprinimatelstve: itogi kruglogo stola' [Traditional Russian Values in Entrepreneurship], Public Speech at Panel Discussion, <http://www.pravmir.ru/traditsionnyie-tsennosti-v-predprinimatelstve-itogi-kruglogo-stola/> (Accessed 12 December 2016).

Gogol, N. 'Spory' [Debates] (from the Letter to L***), in N. V. Gogol, *Polnoe sobranie sochinenii* (*PSS*), in 14 vols (Moscow-Leningrad: Izd-vo AN SSSR, 1952), Vol. 8, p. 262.

Gorshkov, M. K., 'Modernizatsionnyi potentsial identichnosti' [Modernization Potential of Identity] (in lieu of preface), *Reforming Russia*, Annual Part 12 (Moscow: The New Chronograph, Institute of Sociology of Russian Academy of Sciences, 2013), p. 6.

Hilarion, 'Sermon on Law and Grace', <https://azbyka.ru/slovo-o-zakone-i-blagodati-mitropolita-ilariona> (Accessed 11 November 2016).

Iskander, Fazil, 'Dumaiushchii o Rossii i amerikanets' [One Dwelling on Russia and an American], <http://www.lib.ru/FISKANDER/isk_amer.txt> (Accessed 25 October 2016).

——— 'Esse i publitsistika' [Essays and Journalism], <http://www.kulichki.com/moshkow/FISKANDER/isk_publ.txt> (Accessed 15 November 2016).

———'A poet', <http://lib.ru/FISKANDER/iskan_poet.txt_with-big-pictures.html> (Accessed 23 October 2016).

Kandinsky, V. V., *Tekst khudozhnika. Stupeni* [Artist's text: Stages] (Moscow, 1918).

Karamzina, S. N., 'Pushkin v pismakh Karamzinykh' [Pushkin in Karamzin's Family Letters], Letter 3, 15 November 1836, 1836–1837 (Moscow: Publ. Academy of Sciences USSR. Institute of Russian Literature (Pushkin House), 1960).

Katkov, Mikhail, 'Literary Review and Notes', *Russian Messenger*, Vol. 35 (October 1861), pp. 107–127, <http://dugward.ru/library/katkov/katkov_koe_chto_o_progresse.html> (Accessed 20 October 2016).

——— 'Nashe varvarstvo – v nashei inostrannoi intelligentsii' [Our Barbarism Is in Our Foreign Intelligentsia], <http://dugward.ru/library/katkov/katkov_nashe_varvar.html> (Accessed 14 November 2016).

Kireevsky, I. V., 'O kharaktere prosveshcheniia Evropy i ego otnoshenii k prosveshcheniiu Rossii' [On the Character of European Enlightenment and

Its Relation to Russian Enlightenment], Letter to E. E. Komarovsky, 1852, <http://lib.pravmir.ru/library/readbook/292> (Accessed 21 October 2016).

——— 'On the Necessity and Possibility of New Principles in Philosophy', <http://knleontiev.narod.ru/context/kireevsky1.htm> (Accessed 21 October 2016).

——— 'V otvet Alekseiu Stepanovichu Khomyakovu' [In Response to Alexei Stepanovich Khomyakov], 1839, <http://dugward.ru/library/nikolay1/kireevskiy_otvet_hom.html> (Accessed 10 November 2016).

Kolesnikov, A., *Dialogi s Evgeniem Yasinym* [Conversations with Yevgeny Yasin] (Moscow: New Literary Observer, 2014).

Kvint, V. L., Interview, 1 June 2015, Host N. A. Vinokurova, <http://oralhistory.ru/talks/orh-1897> (Accessed 21 December 2016).

Likhachev, Dmitrii, 'Religion: Russian Orthodoxy', in *The Cambridge Companion to Modern Russian Culture*, Second edition, ed. Nicholas Rzhevsky (Cambridge: Cambridge University Press, 2012)

Lotman, Y. M., 'Sovremennost mezhdu vostokom i zapadom' [Modernity between the East and the West], *Znamya* , No. 9 (1997).

Lubkov, Alexei, 'Byt grazhdaninom znachit izuchat istoriiu strany' [To Be a Citizen Is to Learn the History of the Country], 13 May 2016, <http://pereformat.ru/2016/05/izuchat-istoriyu/> (Accessed 22 November 2016).

Makarov, V. L., Interview, 27 May 2015, Host N. A. Vinokurova, Part 2, <http://oralhistory.ru/>.

Mandelshtam, Osip, 'Chaadaev', <https://rvb.ru/20vek/mandelstam/slovo_i_kultura/01text/01text/10.htm> (Accessed 25 November 2021).

Mareeva, Svetlana Vladimirovna, 'Rossiiskaia molodezh: identichnosti, tsennosti i predstavleniia ob optimalnom obshchestvennom ustroistve' [Russian Youth: Identities, Values and Ideas about the Optimal Social Structure], *Reforming Russia*, Vol. 12 (2013), pp. 361–380.

Medvedev, Aleksandr, 'Sviatoi Vlamidir i Petr Velikii: russkoe samosoznanie v poiskakh edinstva' [Saint Vladimir and Peter the Great: Russian Self-consciousness in Search of unity], in *Russkaia filosofiia: istoriia, personalii, metodologiia* [Russian Philosophy: History, Personalia, Methodology], *Collected Scientific Papers* (Tyumen: TSUABCE, 2011).

Mikhailovsky, Nikolai, cited in V. V. Zenkovsky, *Istoriia russkoi filosofii* [History of Russian Philosophy], Vol. 1, Second edition (Paris: YMCA Press, 1989).

Ovsiannikov, A. A., 'Novoe pokolenie: dolgaya doroga v poiskakh novykh idealov i smyslov zhizni' [The New Generation: A Long Road in Search of New Ideals and Meanings of Life], <http://jour.isras.ru/upload/journals/4/articles/3113/submission/original/3113-5752-1-SM.pdf> (Accessed 10 December 2016).

Peace, Richard A., *Russian Literature and the Fictionalisation of Life* (Hull: University of Hull, 1976).

Pivovarov, Y., Interview, in *Rossiyskaia Gazeta* [Russian Newspaper], 22 January 2013, <https://rg.ru/2013/01/22/pivovarov.html> (Accessed 30 November 2016).

Polterovich, V. M., *Elementy teorii reform* [Elements of Reform Theory] (Moscow: Economics, 2007).

Pushkin, A. S., Letter to P. Ya. Chaadaev, in *Collected Essays*, Vol. 10 (Moscow: Literature, 1978), pp. 285–288.

Rimashevskaya, N. M., Interview, 30 March 2013, Host N. A. Vinokurova, Part 1, <http://oralhistory.ru/talks/orh-1556> (Accessed 21 December 2016).

Rogov, S., 'Nevostrebovannost nauki – ugroza bezopasnosti strany' [Slack Demand for Science is a National Security Threat], *Nezavisimaya gazeta* newspaper, 8 February 2010.

Saltykov, B. G., Interview, 7 June 2012, <http://www.yeltsincentre.ru/decryption/intervyu-s-borisom-saltykovym> (Accessed 12 December 2016).

Schmemann, Alexander, Notebook 1:28, 8 April 1973, New York, <http://memuarist.com/ru/events/25086.htm> (Accessed 19 November 2016).

Solovyov, V., 'Zapadniki, Zadapnichestvo' [Westerners, Westernism], in *Encyclopaedic Dictionary*, ed. F. A. Brockhaus and I. A. Efron (1894), Vol. 12, pp. 243–244.

Tyutchev, Fedor, *Poems*, <http://www.ruthenia.ru/tiutcheviana/stihi/bp/291.html> (Accessed 12 November 2016).

Vershik, Anatoly, 'Matematicheskiie progulki s Anatoliiem Vershikom' [Mathematical Walks with Anatoly Vershik], Interview, Host Elena Kudryavtseva, <http://www.sib-science.info/ru/ras/ogoniok-estetika-v-matematike-30012017> (Accessed 26 November 2016).

Volkonsky, V. A., *Mnogopoliarnyi mir. Ideologiia i ekonomika. Konets dominirovaniia zapadnoi tsivilizatsii. Chto dal'she gotovit nam istoriia?* [A Multipolar World. Ideology and Economics. The End of the Dominance of Western Civilization. What Does History Have in Store for Us Next?] (Moscow: Knizhnyi mir [Books World], 2015).

Yasin, Y. G., Interview, 27 October 2014, Host N. A. Vinokurova, Part 2, <http://oralhistory.ru/talks/orh-1786> (Accessed 10 December 2016).

Yazykov, N. M., Poems: 'K Chaadaevu' [To Chaadaev], <http://www.stihi-xix-xx-vekov.ru/yaziykov115.html> (Accessed 13 October 2016).

——— Poems: 'K Nenashim' [To Strangers], <http://yazykov.lit-info.ru/yazykov/stihi/k-nenashim.htm> (Accessed 13 October 2016).

——— 'Biographical Index', http://www.hrono.ru/biograf/bio_ya/jazykov_nm02.php (Accessed 13 October 2021).

Youth of the Orel Region in 2015, *Molodezh Orlovskoi oblasti v 2015 godu. Nauchnoe izdanie. Informatsionno-sotsiologicheskii bulleten* [Youth of the Orel Region in 2015. Scientific Publication. The Information-Sociological Bulletin], Collective Monograph (Orel: Central Russian Institute of Management, 2015).

Zhukovsky, V. A., *Russkii arkhiv* (Russian Archive), No. 4 (1884), p. 453; *Russkaia starina* (Russian Antiquity) (October 1903), pp. 185–186, ed. A. N. Veselovsky and V. A. Zhukovsky (St. Petersburg, 1904), p. 395.

Translated by Nikita Khmarenko

PART II

Ways and Waves of Cultural Development in the Russian Literary Mirror

OLHA CHERVINSKA

5 Rift versus Attraction as the Receptive Motivators of Russian Culture

Any 'storytelling strategies' that emerge individually and 'generate text meanings'[1] are defined by the so-called horizon of expectation (a terminological syntagma borrowed from K. Mannheim and widely used by H.-R. Jauss and V. Iser and their school of reception aesthetics). In general, the horizon of expectation connects the topic of art perception as such with the idea of mandatory comprehension of the difference between the author's own experience and the experience of subsequent generations of his readers. Hence, there can be a great many motivations for some distortion of our perception. The *rift* paradigm has come to be employed to manage/shape our perception effectively, when referring to a wide range of arts, covering an entire culturological field. The ideal model of this paradigm can be stated as 'Guernica' by Pablo Picasso (1937), because, both at the level of design and at the level of form, here we conceive the tragic irreversibility of a once complete and beautiful urban text being shredded into dead heterogeneous fragments.

The desire to bring the rift to the level of an ontological phenomenon is quite logical, as evidenced by the branching of its modern connotations: it includes the ruptures of parts of the physical body, the breakup of human relations, the generation gap, broken pattern and so on. In this vein, reference is made to the research of Margaret Mead (1960s, with respect to the generation gap), and the work of the 1970s sociologist Diana Vaughan, psychotherapist Susan Elliott (2009) and a number of other modern psychologists. However, attempts to deduce and describe certain general states,

1 Wolfgang Iser, *Die Appellstruktur der Texte: Unbestimmtheit als Wirkungsbedingung literarischer Prosa* (Konstanz, 1970), p. 5.

stages and types of conditions that lead to a rift seem mechanistic and, in general, give unreliable results. The common thread is that all cases we are dealing with are about a split of a hitherto undivided entity, where the most important thing is to accurately determine the so-called bifurcation point and the condition preceding it, which leads to the corresponding conclusions. Rift and disintegration are not the same, because 'long-term disintegration', which leads to the irreversible collapse of a certain integrity, and 'rift', which occurs according to a different formula, are not only far from being synonymous in this sense, but they are fundamentally opposite conditions.

The key point is conceiving that the rift is associated with gravity and attraction; it comes as a consequence of gravitation, being 'secondary', and not primary in relation to it; it becomes a certain threshold, the radical completion of a certain existential. This is clearly reflected by the historical, artistic and philosophical thought of Russia, the perception of which by other cultures remains very contradictory due to numerous discrepancies in historical and cultural parameters. In particular (including gaps), the latter is well understood as an example of Zeno's ontological paradox (bootstrap paradox) about the immobility of a flying arrow resting at every moment of time, and therefore supposedly always motionless. In accordance with it and the doctrine of relativity, identical objects moving at different speeds are different for external observers, but, moreover, these objects also perceive their surroundings differently.

Thus, with regard to the Russian theme, the rift should have its own special accents. Russian culture as a whole is characterized by an extraordinary sensitivity to any kind of external influences, which can be designated through a number of certain polar conditions: for example, war or reconciliation, revolution or civil war and the like. Historical experience can confirm how radical the fluctuations in the perception of the world by Russian culture and ideas about the culture formed from the outside are. Historical periods that give rise to the rupture of conventional states have some intrinsic similarities, although these are not necessarily obvious.

Let us listen to Vasily Zen'kovsky's opinion about the eighteenth century. Calling this period the age of 'secularization', the philosopher emphasizes the rift:

> The former unity of culture is broken, creative work in the Church consciousness and outside of it goes not in a single direction, but in two different directions. This dual process, which is going on in the eighteenth century with an extraordinary, somewhat mysterious speed, may seem mysterious only at first glance; in fact, it simply reveals what has happened in the depths of Russian life for a long time (since the end of the sixteenth century and especially in the seventeenth century).[2]

Thus, starting with Peter's divide – one of the most important 'bifurcation points' of Russian history – the philosophers of the eighteenth century radically rethink the conservative tradition of their culture.

First of all, we refer to the 'Brotherhood of Learning' of Peter the Great. Feofan Prokopovich (1681–1736) was a merchant's son who became a representative of the higher clergy – an active church reformer (the introduction of a Synod instead of the abolished Patriarchate) who was somewhat cynical in achieving his goals and at the same time creatively energetic. Many people experienced his spiritual authority, including the equally dynamic and active intellectual Vasily Tatishchev (1686–1750). A participant in military campaigns, industrialist, diplomat, and founder of Russian historical scholarship, Tatishchev also founded the cities of Yekaterinburg and Perm. They are followed by Antiochus Cantemir (1708–1744), the author of brave satires on reactionaries, the apologist of 'the laws of Peter / By which we have suddenly become a new people' (Satire 2, 'To the envy and pride of the evil-minded nobles') and, of course, Mikhail Lomonosov (1711–1765). The ideas and deeds of these people provoke the emergence of a significant dilemma in the near future (Westernism or Slavophilism), and the Russian consciousness rests on this confrontation to this day. It should also be noted that each of them came out of the margins in one way or another and had considerable experience communicating with other people's environment that, I believe, prompted revisionist tendencies in their activities. Hence, the break with the conservative way of life is perceived in the eighteenth century as a kind of renewal, as a health-improving, progressive fact of culture.

The opposite motivation (as the idea of gravity, contraction, 'stitching', etc.) in the nineteenth century comes from the doctrine of the beginning of

2 Vasily Zen'kovsky, *History of Russian Philosophy* (Moscow, 2001), p. 57.

collegiality, developed by such an unusual, multitalented person as Alexei Khomyakov (1804–1860), who had an undeniable influence on many Russian philosophers – first of all, on Nikolai Berdyaev, Vasily Zen'kovsky and on the intuitionism of Nikolai Lossky, who emphasized sensual, intellectual and mystical intuition. Based on Khomyakov's philosophy, the rift is associated with freedom, while collegiality requires sacrificing it. Lossky draws our attention to the following maxim of Khomyakov: 'Rome preserved unity at the cost of freedom, and Protestants gained freedom at the cost of unity.'[3] An important role in this direction was also played by the authority of Ivan Kireevsky (1806–1856). Any future deviations of the Russian philosophical consciousness somehow tend to reach one of these extremes, and attempts to find a compromise are extremely rare.

The 'Russian Socrates' Grigory Skovoroda (1722–1794) almost always falls out of the list of Russian thinkers who took part in the stratification and adjustment of Russian social consciousness, but perhaps it is his ideas (sometimes stylistically too baroque) with regard to the rift issue that may be most remarkable. Zen'kovsky calls him 'the first philosopher in Russia in the strict sense of the word', emphasizing that 'the religious and mystical worldview of Skovoroda was embodied by him with amazing frankness in his life'. Another significant remark made by this scholar is that 'Skovoroda becomes a philosopher because his inner religious turmoil requires it – he moves from his Christian consciousness to conceiving of a man and the world.' Skovoroda's metaphysical dualism was finally expressed in his teaching 'on the inner unity of good and evil'.[4] Interpreting the philosopher's experience, Zen'kovsky emphasized that Skovoroda's anthropological position becomes the intellectual basis of his ethics, according to which,

> in the depths of each person there is a secret principle of his growth – therefore, first of all, you need to find yourself. All the sufferings and torments that a person goes through arise only from the fact that a person lives and contradicts what he was created for.[5]

3 Nikolai Lossky, *History of Russian Philosophy* (Moscow, 1991), p. 87.

4 Zenkovsky, *History of Russian Philosophy*, pp. 65; 66; 69; 76–80.

5 Ibid., p. 77.

In Skovoroda's debates with many famous researchers (in particular, with Dmitry Chizhevsky, Vladimir Ern, and Gustav Shpet), Zen'kovsky puts the final stress on the statement, which we should agree with:

> It would be historically unjust to forget that Skovoroda, breaking away from sensory being and delving into the study of the 'genuine' world, moves forward as a researcher. His bold theory that the disintegration of being into opposites (good and evil, life and death, etc.) is true only for the empirical sphere and it does not entail metaphysical dualism – in other words, that empirical antinomies are 'resolved' in the mystical sphere – all this is precisely Skovoroda's teaching, and not any peremptory statement.[6]

The distinctiveness of Skovoroda's philosophical worldview can be largely taken as essential in the process of contemplating the theme of rift by the Russian literary tradition.

In terms of 'rift poetics', certainly, one particular case is the oeuvre of Fedor Dostoevsky (1821–1881), which in its general approach is typologically close to that of G. Skovoroda. It provides a plethora of material. I will not say that the writer set himself the task of dissecting the rift as such. Nevertheless, this issue can be found in any of his novels in a variety of registers and in any combination: the gap of consciousness (*The Idiot*, 'The Dream of a Ridiculous Man'), the rupture of morality (*Demons*, 'The Dream of a Ridiculous Man'), the breakdown of public relations (*Crime and Punishment*, *Demons* and again 'The Dream of a Ridiculous Man'), fractures in family relationships and traditions (*The Adolescent*, *The Brothers Karamazov*), to name but a few. The rough outline of the problem can be rendered more precise and complete by analysis of any of the above writings to arrive at the author's invariable original anatomy of the rift.

In this case, we will mention only such a classic parabolic writing as 'The Dream of a Ridiculous Man',[7] which is important for an in-depth understanding of the literary and spiritual experience of the last period of the writer's life, and any of his later works. For example, this writing fully reflects what A. Kovacs saw in the novel *Demons*:

6 Ibid., p. 80.

7 Fedor Dostoevsky, *Complete Works*, 30 vols (Leningrad, 1983), Vol. 25.

> The ideological confrontation between Stavrogin and Tikhon reveals the metapoetics of bifurcation […] with its typical features of Dostoevsky. Firstly, the phenomenon is clearly identified as of 'internal', psychological and 'mental' nature; secondly, its catalyst role of the problems of axiological nature, establishment of moral-philosophical ideas is stressed; finally, it reveals Dostoevsky's 'literary technique' and his devices for creating a narrative of the fantastic: doppelganger – Myself, and not Myself; the oscillation between the real and the supernatural (the image of the devil); the fantastic as means of psychological and artistic realism.[8]

The semantic potential of the 'The Dream of a Ridiculous Man' is outlined by a formal and meaningful integrity: with the matrix of duality used as a parody key, and also, with the three-pointed vector of existence 'slumber – demise – rebirth'. Here, of course, one can see some kinship of the author's idea with the metaphysical symbolism of G. Skovoroda (at least, at the typological level – compare the metaphor 'the whole world is asleep' repeated many times in Skovoroda's works).

Parabolic, 'ruptured' duality is in general not only the leading compositional principle of the architectonics of this text, but it is also the dominating idea of all the text's dimensions, its main receptive key. In particular, the image of an unhappy girl triggers the entire narrative counterpoint – from the beginning to the very last phrase ('And I found that little girl … And I go! And I go!'); the universe is reflected in the parameters of two stars (our Sun-1 and Sun-2); social existence – in the images of the earthly paradise (utopia) and earthly hell (dystopia); human existence – in the parameters of two connotations (I and They) and two states (reality – dream – awakening). In fact, good and evil, heart and mind, faith and disbelief, normal and abnormal are here versions of the same consistently unfolding allegory of the rift.

In Dostoevsky, 'the Ridiculous Man' parodies himself: the 'dark and unpleasant thing' that accompanies him in his sleep is himself. From the beginning to the end of the story (in this case, these compositional elements fit into a parabolic shape), he remains a hopeless outsider, completely alien to the whole world, in his opinion – the lone owner of the truth, and this determines his essence. The main formula of his worldview is highlighted

8 Albert Kovacs, *Poetics of Dostoevsky* (Moscow, 2008), pp. 110–111.

by the opening of the text – a nine-fold repetition of the antinomy of 'I' and generalized 'They'. Alienation from people, resentment of what is in their eyes, and in his own eyes he is nothing short of a 'ridiculous man': it all delivers the hero of the parable to the power of unbridled pride. It is very important to note that in the storyteller's narrative, these two qualities – 'ridiculous' and 'proud' – are so merged that it is not clear to the reader which of them is ultimately defined as a 'terrible quality'. For Dostoevsky, the object of observation is primarily a process of consciousness, conscious being, and not the events of this character's life – almost nothing is said about them, except for references to university studies in the past, a meeting with friends, a small room on the fourth floor of a lodging house where he lives and, finally, a significant meeting with an unfortunate girl.

First of all, the process of consciousness of the so-called ridiculous man becomes the main driving force of the entire narrative. The mind is the main arena of battle, where the breaking of all ties with the world and all the character's previous self-esteem is carried out. All this is expressed painfully, to the point of exhaustion and apathy, and in many different ways depending on questions about the reality and meaning of human existence, society and the universe as a whole. Dostoevsky brilliantly reproduces how the hero's thought fatally plunges into perpetual nothingness (the syntagma 'it's all the same', repeatedly highlighted in the author's italics, is mentioned 14 times in different contexts in the first and second chapters of the text):

> the terrible misery that was growing in my soul [9]through something which was of more consequence than anything else about me: that something was the conviction that had come upon me that nothing in the world mattered [...] I suddenly felt that it was *all the same* to me whether the world existed or whether there had never been anything at all. I began to feel with all my being that there was nothing existing [...] If at least I had solved my problems! Oh, I had not settled one of them, and how many there were! But I gave up caring about anything, and all the problems disappeared.

9 Fedor Dostoevsky, 'The Dream of a Ridiculous Man', tr. by Constance Garnett. See https://www.berfrois.com/2015/05/the-dream-of-a-ridiculous-man-fyodor-dostoevsky/#:~:text=Perhaps%20it%20was%20owing%20to,nothing%20in%20the%20world%20mattered (Accessed 29 April 2023).

The fact that cannot go unnoticed is that the motif of death is represented in a very special, somewhat paradoxical way, which, I think, is easiest to perceive as ontology of the rift between the existence of 'this' world and 'that'.

In the cognitive sense, here death is presented figuratively, as a background or, more precisely, as an ordinary threshold: death is presented, first of all, as a state (a description of the grave impressions of a 'ridiculous man' who shot himself) or a certain preliminary event – for the writer, actions that happen afterward are more important. So, the thing that happened to the girl's mother (obviously it is death) is served here only as the cause of the child's horror. In his dream, it is he who commits his most terrible crime ('terrible truth'!) – he corrupts the society of hitherto sinless people. The transition to eternity is depicted in two contrasting expanded versions: as a terrible consequence of suicide or, on the contrary, as a happy ending to a sinless life. Beyond this threshold, the main event of the text takes place – the hero's contemplation of his own worth.

This parable has a deep teleological meaning since it is about the 'movement of consciousness towards the future' (according to Paul Ricoeur).[10] It can be assumed that the capstone of the full 'dream' is primarily the philosophical teleology of the author in his reflections on human nature, the integrity of which is broken by sin.

Finally, we address the poetic consciousness, which always lives in the historical and cultural text of its time and is motivated by its reception; first, we will witness the most vivid poetization of the rift in the texts of the Futurists who proclaimed 'going beyond boundaries of art' – declared a break with tradition. There are many suitable examples in their poetry. Here the rift is a stop: stop as a compositional technique with all the accompanying exuberant features. In particular, in the early 1910s, the practice of Cubo-Futurism presented itself interestingly, especially the St. Petersburg group 'Gilea' consisting of D. N. Burliuk, V. Khlebnikov, V. Mayakovsky, V. Kamensky, E. Guro, Kruchenykh and B. Livshits. Its 'ideologist' was Sergei Bobrov with his unassimilated concept of purism: at a time when

10 See, for example, Paul Ricoeur, *Memory, History, Forgetting* (Chicago: University of Chicago Press, 2004).

there was a desire to decompose the form into compositionally independent fragments, this position assumed a sensitive attention to the antiquity, the lubok, the icon and traditional poetic images of Russian culture.

Paradoxes of the rift (of consciousness) in approaching the topic can be seen in the example of the poem 'Vzorval' (Explodity) by the professional artist Alexei Kruchenykh (1886–1968). In this case, concerns about the 'structure of the word' (the similarly named collection of poems, 1922) begot a radical rift between the speech form and its meaning:

Vzorval'	[Explodity]
Ognia	[Of Fire]
Pechal'	[Sorrow]
Konia	[Of a Horse]
Rubli	[Cutting Off of Branches]
Iv	[Of Willows]
V volosakh	[In the Hair]
Div	[Of Wonders]

No doubt, in the poetry of Futurists the idea is also present at the level of a dramatic event. See, for example, an excerpt from the poem of Kruchenykh 'Uekhala' (She Left):

Like a hammer
Hit my head
A well-turned word,
Hammered in recklessly! –
Arrest! Guard!
I didn't say farewell.
In Kodzh ori! –
I run along the train tracks,
Scream and fall downwind.
All trains
Flashing by
Above the torpid bridge of the nose…

You detached from the railway station,
Obediently drooped the semaphores.
Whistled
Quivered the train,

With the throat
Piercing steely air.
[…]
And I looked funerally-dressed
[translator's note: robed in catafalque-like smart clothes]
In a tie…
And suddenly – called after:
– Halt! Seize!
–Is she gone forever?
Over the forest silhouettes are sundered.

In another of his poems ('First of May'), the rift breaks even the air: 'The air burst with joy.'

However, the topic of the rift was not only in the mind of the Futurists who radically broke everything that came to hand. The undeniable, immanent expressiveness of the rift situation could not fail to become a common note of poetry as a whole. So, we also find our own version of the rupture in the Acmeists – the famous exclamation of Osip Mandelstam to the violinist: 'Play your aorta-bursting orison'.

They swoon for long-clawed Paganini
Like gypsy mobs they swarm and prance
A Czech is sneezing sneezes, and a Pole is balling squeezes
And a Magyar's in a rowdy sort of whackadoodle dance

Hey, girl, yeah you, proud parvenu,
Whose sound is broad like Yenisei,
Consume me with your fiddle play.
You sport that Polack curled hairdo,
Like Rina Mnishek, locks astray,
Your bow's a high-strung roundelay.

Console me with Chopin the roan-hued,
Play solemn Brahms – no, hold on, lass,
Do Paris, when she sweats and goes lewd,
Carnivalistic, showing her ass,
Splash out Vienna beer, home-brewed.

Your notes should fidget, frock-coats' tails,
Danube fireworks sparking on the rails,
Bow me a waltz, say, waltz from grave to cradle
Pour revelry in spangled gleams from bacchanalian ladle.

Play your aorta-bursting orison,
With cat's head in your mouth, off-tune.
Three fiends there were, and you're the fourth one
The last berserker-fiend in bloom!

(Translated by U. R. Bowie)

Here you can observe the real 'anatomy of a receptive rift': from increasing emotional euphoria, maximum accumulation and clearly fragmented image series to the final, absolutely unreadable 'Gothic' quatrain with the significant exclamation 'play your aorta-bursting orison'. Here, the rift, as expected, is associated with a certain effort. The 'caliber' of the rift depends on the background of this rift. The rift itself is significant not only for its unpredictability but also for its backstory, which turns into poetic working material.

It is interesting that the difference between the radicalism of the Futurists and the conservatism of their more 'tranquil' contemporaries also reveals itself in the perspective of this topic. Here the rift is perceived with a different sign. As a rule, this is not a sanative bloodletting, but pain.

The rift is a poetic state that reminds us of Zeno's ontological paradox of the flying arrow. For the poet, it is divided into integral static parts. The following is fragmented: moment, feeling, state, space and finally, the text itself as such (frequent use of the figure of a *razryv/obryv* [rift], omission: [...]). A revealing remark about the function of gaps is mentioned in a critical commentary on her writings:

> In a number of poems Akhmatova maintains internal 'gaps' in the text, noting their rows of dots, leaving unfinished lines within the text (see, for example, 'The Northern Elegies' no. 3: 'In that house it was very scary to live...'). Therefore, it is often difficult to distinguish between the unfinished works, 'not fully fished out from memory' and those written consciously, those 'not fully recalled' or turned into a fragment.[11]

The most precise thing about the gap is its prehistory, the consequences of which are no longer so interesting to the poet, or rather, they go into the perspective of a different existence. Hence the desire of many poets

11 Anna Akhmatova, *Collected Writings*, 6 vols, Vol. 1: *Poems 1904–1941* (Moscow, 1998), p. 681.

to compose cycles from these prehistories is not accidental. In the works of Anna Akhmatova (1889–1966), there is a cycle, eloquently designated by her as a 'Rift'. Here, bifurcation points are designated by some 'unforgettable dates'. We find a characteristic remark about working on cycles in Lydia Chukovskaya's *Notes on Anna Akhmatova*. In the entry for 25 January, we read about a conversation with Akhmatova, and her comment on chronology: 'I'm not going to ruin my book with chronology. Even Pushkin is ruined by chronology':

> But in any case, the idea is necessary: one way or another, the pages of the book should convey the passage of time, make visible new stages, new periods of the author's creative life. Cycles? Yes, of course, cycles, but, unfortunately, Anna Andreevna is in no hurry to make them. I understand that looking back, catching the 'beginnings and ends' of relationships, breakups and comebacks, fulfilled and unfulfilled premonitions and prophecies is not an easy task. Anna Andreevna makes it slowly.[12]

Let's look at the first poem of the cycle 'Razryv' (Rift, translated here as 'Parting'):

> 1
> Not weeks, not months – years
> We spent parting. Now at last
> The chill of real freedom,
> And the gray garland above the temples.
> No more treasons, no more betrayals,
> And you won't be listening till dawn
> As the stream of evidence
> Of my perfect innocence flows on.
>
> (1940)
>
> (Translated by Judith Hemschemeyer)

What remains beyond the 'rift line', the poet does not hide. It does not disappear into nowhere; it retains its absolute significance. It proceeds to memory. In other words, it is important that everything remains as if it has already happened.

12 Lydia Chukovskaya, *The Akhmatova Journals*, Vol. 3: *1965–1966* (Moscow, 1997), p. 151.

2
And, as always happens in the days of final rupture,
The ghost of the first days knocked at our door,
And in burst the silver willow
In all its gray, branching splendor.
To us, frenzied, disdainful and bitter,
Not daring to raise our eyes from the ground,
A bird began to sing in a voice of rapture
About how much we cherished one another.

(25 September 1944)

(Translated by Judith Hemschemeyer)

Here, in the second poem of the sequence, there is great meaning in the first phrase 'as it always happens', suggesting the reading of the rift as having the ability to mystically ('ghost') restore the integrity of the past as a memory.

In the third poem, the theme of the break is designated by the first quatrain, which is a tragic image of a torn integrity (the famous Akhmatova oxymoron 'loneliness together'):

3
I drink to our ruined house,
to the dolor of my life,
to our loneliness together;
and to you I raise my glass,
to lying lips that have betrayed us,
to dead-cold, pitiless eyes,
and to the hard realities:
that the world is brutal and coarse,
that God in fact has not saved us.

(27 June 1934)

(Translated by Stanley Kunitz and Max Hayward)

The analysis of the poetics of the rift in this cycle by Akhmatova certainly requires a separate and more detailed research argumentation. I have limited myself to a very conditional outline of it. Unfortunately, in this chapter, I have to ignore another Akhmatova version of the poetics of the rift in the 'Poem without a Hero', read literally at all levels of this text, which is indicated not only by its main idea, fundamental retrospect, fragmentary composition, rhythm and so on but also by numerous authors' comments, additions, editorial changes and research observations.

Thus, a break does not in any case necessarily mean a radical destruction of integrity, because a broken integrity can, in many cases, preserve itself in fragments. This means overcoming the negative trend toward irreversible disintegration. So, for example, a rift does not mean the disappearance of integrity for the 'people' paradigm, because each individual representative of it may be able to preserve some version of the 'formula' of this integrity in any disintegration. Similarly, here, as a thematic paradox, we can recall the popular novel *The Mysterious Story of Billy Milligan* (1981), based on a real fact, about the coexistence of 24 separate personalities in one person, each of which had different kinds of enhanced abilities, but at the same time, when psychiatrists 'put together' this personal fragmentation of Milligan, his total abilities became much poorer.

At the level of fiction, such a variant, for example, is played out in the poem 'Cup'[13] by the modern Ukrainian children's writer Natalia Kukonina (winner of the Korneychuk prize in 2015):

Разбилась Чашка – как печально! –
На двадцать розовых кусков,
Она разбилась не случайно
На двадцать дочек и сынков.

Она сама так захотела –
Сползла тихонько со стола,
Отважилась и полетела –
И двадцать деток родила.

Я не расстроилась нисколько,
Я знала Чашкины мечты,
И с пола подобрав осколки,
Я посадила их в цветы.

Зарыла в землю все кусочки,
Водой обильно полила:
'Растите, дочки и сыночки!'
И целый день ждала, ждала.

13 Natalia Kukonina-Samoilenko, *Vibrani Tvori* (Chernivitsi, 2015), p. 24.

А утром стала я счастливой –
Вот здорово! Какой сюрприз!
В горшках цветочных всем на диво
РАСЦВЕЛ ФАРФОРОВЫЙ СЕРВИЗ!

Natalia Lukonina has also translated the poem into English:

The Cup smashed – swoosh! bang! (what a pity!)
Into a dozen rosy bits,
Into a pile of babes, so pretty,
It happened not by chance for kids.

She wished to have them so truly,
Slipped down the table, held her breath,
And dared flying off, and duly
To long-awaited kids gave birth.

The Cup was gone… I took it easy
I knew Her innermost thoughts,
And picked up fragments, scared and dizzy,
And buried in the flower-pots.

I poured Her kids with pure water
While chanting magic words along:
"Do grow, Sons! Arouse, Daughters!"
And all day I waited, waited …

But in the morning I was happy –
Wonderful! What a surprise!
In the pots everyone marvels,
The porcelain has flowered!

So, we can sum up all this as follows: a broken integrity can and does generate a new set of very diverse identities, which in the case of Russian literature with its two polar motivators forms the necessary horizon of expectation for our perception (without removing the acuteness of the question about the purpose of literature itself).

Bibliography

Akhmatova, Anna, *Collected Writings*, 6 vols, Vol. 1: *Poems 1904–1941* (Moscow: Ellis Lak, 1998).

——— *Poema bez geroia. Proza o poeme. Nabroski baletnogo libretto: materialy k tvorcheskoi istorii* [*Poem Without a Hero; Prose on the Poem; Sketches of a Ballet Libretto; Materials for a Creative History*], published and compiled by N. I. Kraineva (St. Petersburg: Izdatelskii Dom "Mir", 2009).

Chukovskaya, Lydia, *Zapiski ob Anne Akhmatovoi* [*Notes on Anna Akhmatova*], 3 vols, Vol. 3: *1965–1966* (Moscow: Soglasie, 1997).

Dostoevsky, Fedor, *Complete Works*, 30 vols (Leningrad: Nauka, 1983), Vol. 25.

Iser, Wolfgang, *Die Appellstruktur der Texte: Unbestimmtheit als Wirkungsbedingung literarischer Prosa* (Konstanz: Universitätsverlag, 1970).

Kovacs, Albert, *Poetika Dostoevskogo* [*Poetics of Dostoevsky*] (Moscow: Vodolei, 2008).

Kukonina-Samoilenko, Natalia, *Vibrani Tvori* [*Selected Works*] (Chernivitsi: Misto, 2015).

Lossky, Nikolai, *Istoriia russkoi filosofii* [*History of Russian Philosophy*] (Moscow: Sovetskii pisatel, 1991).

Ricoeur, Paul, *Memory, History, Forgetting* (Chicago: University of Chicago Press, 2004).

Zenkovsky, Vasili, *Istoriia russkoi filosofii* [*History of Russian Philosophy*] (Moscow: Akademicheskii proekt, 2001).

Translated by Nikita Khmarenko

SARAH OSSIPOW CHEANG

6 Marina Tsvetaeva's Poetry as an Embodiment of Russian Cultural Dialectic of Rupture and Continuity

The aim of this chapter is to read Marina Tsvetaeva's poem 'The Bolshevik' (1921) in light of the dialectic opposition between a disruptive principle and a continuous one that is at the heart of Russian culture. In this perspective, it is worth a brief reminder that, during the course of its history, Russia has been plagued by recurrent upheavals that have marked it with the stamp of instability. From Ivan the Terrible's reign (1533–1584) to the 1917 Bolshevik revolution – without forgetting the forced Westernization undertaken by Peter I (1672–1725) in the eighteenth century – Russian historical processes have rarely followed a smoothly evolutionary and progressive pattern. The sometimes-extreme violence of its history and the radicalism that characterizes those events are particularly striking, and this phenomenon often triggers an unavoidable sense of bewilderment. Thus, the definition used by Winston Churchill to characterize Russia, 'a riddle, wrapped in a mystery, inside an enigma',[1] is highly emblematic of the difficulty experienced by many outside observers in explaining its history and cultural heritage. As Geoffrey Hosking puts it, Russia's history is 'too large, too close to us, and too strange to fit into any comfortable pigeonholes'.[2] The difficulty in shedding a rational light on it through a progressive and continuous

1 Alan Conwell, 'Churchill's Definition of Russia Still Rings True' *New York Times*, 1 August 2008. <https://www.nytimes.com/2008/08/01/world/europe/01iht-letter.1.14939466.html> (Accessed 20 December 2020).

2 Geoffrey Hosking, *Russian History* (Oxford: Oxford University Press, 2012), p. xv.

narrative is not in the least surprising, and many Russian thinkers have themselves asserted that trying by means of a progressive evolutionary narrative to rationally understand their country's history in general, and cultural history in particular, is a fallacy. In this regard, it suffices to remember Fedor Tyutchev's poem 'Russia Cannot Be Understood With the Mind Alone' (1866) proclaiming the vanity and uselessness of any attempt at understanding his country by means of Cartesian categories. Rather than judging Russia for its ability to match with a set of easily understandable rules, Tyutchev asserts the necessity to have faith in it. In other words, the poet confesses to the elusiveness of Russian history. Yet the task of scholars, historians and literary critics is to try to make sense of it by highlighting the various social, political, economic and cultural factors that have contributed to such a high instability as well as by underlining the persistent and recurrent features regularly emerging in the course of Russia's history. In this context, the semiotician Mikhail Lotman's demonstration that in Russia 'the spatial parameters constitute one of the most important constants of history'[3] is particularly worth considering, since, indeed, the sheer immensity of the Russian territory makes a ubiquitous factor in its identity and greatly contributes to its complexity. According to Lotman, the constant fluctuation of the borders of Russia's territory triggers deep anxiety regarding its identity. To illustrate this long-standing anxiety, he quotes Tyutchev's poem 'Russian Geography' in which the author expresses the ungraspable nature of the seemingly limitless space of Russian territory:

> Но где предел ему? и где его границы –
> 'На север, на восток, на юг и на закат?'[4] –
>
> But where is its limit? And where are its boundaries?
> At the north, at the east, at the south or at the west? [lit. 'sunset']

3 Mikhail Lotman, 'History as Geography: In Search for Russian identity', *Sign Systems Studies* Vol. 45, Nos 3 and 4 (2017), p. 263.

4 Quoted by Lotman, 'History as Geography', p. 272. [The translation of verses from Russian is mine].

The feeling of uncertainty reflected in these lines has been exacerbated in the ensuing decades and even centuries. In this respect, Tsvetaeva's poem 'The Bolshevik' is especially relevant, since in it the immensity of the Russian space is also pivotal and links various historical periods within a single unified poetic unit that questions Russian fate and identity. Indeed, the geographical sites mentioned in the poem refer to incompatible sets of values, and this antinomy undoubtedly creates an explosive streak within the poem.

Before proceeding to a close reading of the poem, it is worth putting it in its real-life context: its date and title indicate that it was written just after the Civil War that followed the 1917 revolution. This circumstance is of paramount importance since it means that Tsvetaeva had only just witnessed the endless shifting of the front line between the communist Red Army and the anti-Bolshevik White forces. Inasmuch as her husband had voluntarily enrolled with the latter, it would have been fully understandable had Tsvetaeva irrevocably taken that side. However, Tsvetaeva was well known not only for the radicalism of her poetic style and the singularity of her creations but also for her refusal to belong to any official and well-established group, be it literary, religious or political. Thus, her refusal to merge into the anonymous mass and to follow the dogmatic rules of any given artistic school as well as the staccato-like rhythm of her poetry mark her as a representative of the disruptive streak of Russian culture. Yet, unlike the Futurist poets of the early 1920s, Tsvetaeva disrupts the classical language and literary genres without negating them altogether. As Greta Slobin puts it, Tsvetaeva was an innovator 'with an archaist bent and a passionate interest in Russian's premodern tradition'.[5] No wonder, then, that she managed to seamlessly merge a multitude of artistic tendencies into her own idiosyncratic style. Her exceptional ability to integrate the past with the present and even transcend time marks her out as an embodiment

5 Greta N. Slobin 'Language, History, Ideology: Tsvetaeva, Remizov', in *Russians Abroad: Literary and Cultural Politics of Diaspora (1919–1939)*, ed. Nancy Condee and Katerina Clark (Boston, MA: Academic Studies Press, 2013), pp. 57–73. JSTOR, <www.jstor.org/stable/j.ctt1zxsjrg.7> (Accessed 16 December 2020).

of the resilience forged over time in Russia that enabled artists to create under various oppressive regimes, be it the tsarist or Soviet censorships.

To better understand how Tsvetaeva succeeds in mingling various artistic styles and heterogeneous approaches within her writing, it is worth reading her essay 'Art in the Light of Conscience' (1932) where she asserts that the creative act realized by geniuses necessitates their disintegration to the level of the atom and that it is from the artist's resistance to this phenomenon that the new work of art arises.[6] Obviously, the disintegration mentioned by Tsvetaeva should be understood metaphorically, and it is more a psychological disintegration than a physical one. Yet, as Nina Osipova underlines, Tsvetaeva's intimate connection with an explosive principle is so pervasive in her poetry that the poet identifies her own birth with an explosion.[7] These statements leave no doubt regarding the presence of an explosive impulse, typical of Russian culture, in Tsvetaeva's poetry, and yet, at the same time, this aspect of her creation is counterbalanced by a very strong attachment to the classical and older traditional forms of literature. Thus, I propose to analyze how these two opposite principles interact in Tsvetaeva's poetry, and more particularly, in the poem 'The Bolshevik' (1921), which opens with the following lines:

От Ильменя – до вод Каспийских
Плеча рванулись в ширь.
Бьёт по щекам твоим – российский
Румянец-богатырь

From Ilmen to the Caspian waters
The shoulders rushed across the expanse.
In your cheeks – the Russian
Ruddiness-Bogatyr pulses.

6 Marina Tsvetaeva, *Polnoe sobranie poezii, prozy, dramaturgii v odnom tome* (Moskva: Alfa-Kniga, 2009), p. 838. [Translation mine].

7 Nina Osipova, *Slova i kul'tura v dialogakh serebryanogo veka* (Moskva: Stagirit, 2008), p. 206.

The real-life prototype of the lyrical hero was Boris Bessarabov (1897–1970), a young Red Guard deeply convinced by the new communist ideology, who befriended Tsvetaeva at the beginning of 1921.[8] As the poet writes in her notebook, she saw in him not only an embodiment of the radically new ideology but also features of the Old Russia, and it is precisely this apparently incompatible mix of the traditional and revolutionary that Tsvetaeva mingles in the poem. The opening line makes it very clear that the geographic factor constitutes a highly significant element in the poem. Interestingly, by delineating a geographic axis spanning from Lake Ilmen in the north-west of Russia to the Caspian in the south, Tsvetaeva hints at a whole chain of highly significant historical associations regarding the origin of the Russian state; needless to say that this topic had always been fairly controversial and even more so since the publication of Nikolai Karamzin's *History of the Russian State* highlighting 'Russia's steady advance towards the ideal of a unitary Imperial state whose greatness lay in the inherited wisdom of its Tsar and the innate obedience of its citizens'.[9] However, Karamzin's assertion that the Russian people constitutes a group willingly surrendering its freedom to a strong leader was counterbalanced by the proponents of another historical school, namely that of the Decembrists who 'stressed the rebellious and freedom-loving spirit of the Russian people and idealized the medieval republics of Novgorod and Pskov and the Cossack revolts of the seventeenth and eighteenth centuries'.[10] By writing the poem 'Generalam dvenadtsatogo goda' ('Генералам двенадцатого года'; To the Generals of 1812) in honor of the Decembrists, and another one about the rebellious Cossack leader Stenka Razin (1630–1671), Tsvetaeva made it clear that she too was particularly inspired by the historical figures fighting for freedom. Thus, in her poem 'The Bolshevik', she underlines, right from the very start, the importance of this freedom-searching streak of Russian cultural history, notably by mentioning Lake Ilmen as the starting geographical as

8 Nadezhda Kataeva-Lytkina, 'Bol'shevik i Marina Tsvetaeva: Boris Bessarabov kak lichnost' i prototip geroia stikhotvoreniia "Bol'shevik" i poemy "Egorushka", *Voprosy literatury*, Vol. 5 (1996), pp. 272–292.

9 Orlando Figes, *Natasha's Dance. A Cultural History of Russia* (London: Penguin Books, 2002), p. 134.

10 Ibid., p. 135.

well as poetical point of the poem. Indeed, situated in the north-west of Russia, the lake is located well inside the territory that used to constitute the medieval republic of Velikii Novgorod; the latter, which thrived from the thirteenth to the fifteenth centuries, is not dissociable, in the historical collective consciousness, from the birth of the Russian state, as the historian Olga Sevastyanova underlines.[11] Moreover, because of its advanced democratic institutions based on the limitations of the prince's power by means of a local assembly, the *vetche*, Velikii Novgorod became, in the Decembrists' views, an inspiring model of a fair society.[12] Undoubtedly, it is far from accidental that Tsvetaeva's veiled allusion to the idealized medieval republic of Velikii Novogorod (by association with Lake Ilmen) was uttered at the very moment of the Bolsheviks' victory. On the contrary, hinting at the legendary medieval republic at a time when Russia was becoming a totalitarian state is obviously a reminder to the reader to not forget the country's past and its potential for a fairer public life based on the idea of genuine respect for its people.

To come back to the poem, let us note that the second geographical place mentioned in its first line is the Caspian Sea. Here, it is worth recalling that the territory situated to the north of it was conquered by Ivan the Terrible in 1556. In addition, the Caspian Sea also evokes Stenka Razin's series of victories against the central imperial power during which the rebellious Cossack reached its shores. Thus, by alluding to two historical sites where the centralized imperial power fought with local rebellious forces, Tsvetaeva implicitly warns her readers about the devastating, chaotic and disruptive streak of the communist rule that had just forcibly established itself in her native country.

Furthermore, the vertical North–South axis introduced in the first line is counterbalanced in the second line by a horizontal axis alluded to by the depiction of the hero's shoulders spanning widely across the space. Here, Tsvetaeva's insistence on the enormous spatial dimensions in which the

11 Olga Sevastyanova, 'La fondation de Novogorod', in *Novogorod ou la Russie oubliée*, ed. Philippe Frison and Olga Sevastyanova (Editions Le Ver à Soie: 2015), pp. 41–44.

12 Ibid., p. 374.

action of the poem takes place is reminiscent of the observation she made in her essay 'Poet-alpinist' (1933): 'Russians, as one knows, love extended space. The spatiality of the steppe and that of the river. Its irrepressible nature and, as a result of it, its lack of form.'[13] Consequently, if one defines the cultural impulse as the desire to give a form and a meaning to the surrounding world, the Russian people, according to Tsvetaeva's statement, are prone to be attracted by a wilder principle, in which the raw energy of natural elemental forces, such as water, are not entirely tamed. In other words, the stanza refers to what the philosopher Nikolai Berdyaev (1874–1948) called 'the renascent barbarism'[14] that characterized not only the Futurist movement, for which Berdyaev coined the expression, but also the overall Russian society of the 1910s and 1920s. In the first strophe of Tsvetaeva's poem, this raw energy is expressed with the mention of the watery element, prevalent in the depiction of the geographical scenery, delimited by Lake Ilmen in the north and the Caspian in the south. This verticality brings up the idea of a flowing stream and is counterbalanced, in the second line, by the mention of the width of the territory which allows the shoulders to expand. At this stage, given the title of the poem, one expects that the shoulders are those of a Bolshevik, that is, a new man resolutely turned toward the future and a brand-new kind of society. However, instead of the latter, the reader is presented with the traditional hero (*bogatyr'*) of the traditional folk epic poetry, the *bylina*, in which the hero is known to accomplish numerous feats owing to his extraordinary strength. Interestingly, it was precisely at the time of the Novgorod's republic that the figure of the *bogatyr'* appeared in Russian culture.[15] Yet in the poem, *bogatyr'* is not qualified with the adjective (*russkii*) derived from the ancient Rus' but with a more recent qualifier, namely *rossiiskii* that, instead, refers to the Russian imperial/federal state. Thus, the expression '*rossiiskii bogatyr'*' coined by

13 Marina Tsvetaeva, *Neizdannoe. Svodnye tetradi* (Moskva: Ellis Lak, 1997), Vol. 1, p. 19.

14 Quoted in Nina Gurianova, *The Russian Futurists and Their Books*, translated from Russian by Andrew Bromfield (Moscow: Avant-garde, 1993), p. 8.

15 Sevastyanova, *Novogorod ou la Russie oubliée*, p. 64.

Tsvetaeva indicates a continuity between two seemingly incompatible historical periods.

How to interpret, then, the mention of the *bogatyr'*: is it a flattering comparison or is it an ironic statement? As will be shown, it is most likely to be both. The point to reiterate, though, is that far from being depicted as a pragmatic and realistic type, Tsvetaeva's Bolshevik is referred to as a long-passed mythical figure, typical of the *bylina*, who embodies an immense physical force, as the depiction of his shoulders' movement, from Russia's utmost north to the very south of the country, indicates. Another important point to highlight in these few lines is the hint at the fact that the *bogatyr'*s force is raw, as indicated by the mention of the violent blushing of his cheeks. Furthermore, the raw principle, in other words, the prevalence of an elemental and natural principle over a cultural one, is reinforced by the linguistic deviation from the normative language indicated by the use of the plural form *plecha* (shoulders) instead of the commonly accepted form *plechi*. In addition, the association of the hero of the poem with a wild and primitive force is also alluded to, by the omission of any individualizing features. Indeed, the hero of the poem is not designated by a proper name. This is especially telling, since the use of a proper name is precisely what enables one to become aware of one's own individuality. Moreover, proper names are of paramount importance in Tsvetaeva's poetry. Indeed, in her foreword to her collection of verses *Iz dvukh knig* (From Two Books), published in 1913, she highlights that her artistic writing is 'a poetry of proper names'.[16] In her view, the properly named lyrical hero is an individual endowed with a soul, as the foreword indicates. In fact, as the scholar Kseniya Zhogina rightly remarks, for Tsvetaeva, proper names are the personality's quintessence, and they are an essential component of the life of individuals.[17] As Zhogina underlines, 'for the poet, the ritual of naming is like an initiation from which the individual ontological aura

16 Marina Tsvetaeva, *Sobranie sochinenij v semi tomakh* (Moscow: Terra, 1997), Vol. 5/1, p. 230.

17 Kseniya B. Zhogina, '"Poetika imeni" M. I Tsvetaevoi', in *Marina Tsevaeva: Lichnye I tvorcheskie vstrechi, perevody ee sochinenii: Sbornik dokladov* (Moscow: Dom-muzei Mariny Tsvetaevoi, 2001), p. 286.

stems'.[18] A striking evidence of the link, in Tsvetaeva's poetry, between the properly named person and their endowment with a soul can be found in the poetic cycles she has dedicated to Aleksandr Blok (1880–1921) and Anna Akhmatova (1889–1966). By contrast, the lyrical hero of the poem 'The Bolshevik' is designated as a type who is not individualized but, on the contrary, generalized. The generalization of Tsvetaeva's lyrical hero is reinforced by the use of the hyphen enabling the poet to create the neologism *Ruddiness-bogatyr'* (*Rumianets-bogatyr'*). By referring to her hero as a type rather than as an individualized entity, Tsvetaeva renders him anonymous and associates him with the mass of countless other Bolsheviks. In doing so, she alludes to the dehumanizing principle at the heart of the new political regime.

Thus, the first stanza is striking in that it mixes both elements of traditional ancient literature, such as the genre of epic poetry, together with a use of language typical of the Futurist school, namely, the creation of neologisms, which was a linguistic device widely used by the latter.[19]

In the second stanza of Tsvetaeva's poem, one discovers that, unlike what happens in traditional epic poetry, the extraordinary power of the *bogatyr'* seems to be destructive rather than constructive.

> Дремучие – по всей по крепкой
> Башке – встают леса.
> А руки – лес разносят в щепки,
> Лишь за топор взялся!
>
> Thick and all around the sturdy
> Head the forests rise.
> But the hands smash them into chips,
> Had they only grabbed an axe!

The two first lines of this stanza paint a picture of a disheveled head metaphorically designated with the image of dense forests – a place typical of

18 Ibid., p. 284.

19 Elina Knorpp, 'Évolution et manifestation de la nouvelle esthétique de l'image et de la poétique de la parole dans l'avant-garde russe, exprimée dans les livres d'artistes futuristes', <http://trans.revues.org/484> (Accessed 23 April 2016).

folk poetry. The stylistic tone of the stanza is also reminiscent of traditional folk poetry in which the repetition of a preposition is fairly common.[20] Interestingly, the repetition of the preposition is also typical of traditional folk laments, as the scholar Patricia Arrant notes.[21] In the context of 'The Bolshevik', one can interpret Tsvetaeva's use of this archaism, together with the hero's readiness to use an axe, as a warning against the contemporary disregard for the beauty of the natural world.[22] This is confirmed by the fact that the hero seems willing to smash a forest at any time and without a qualm. Yet, in the third strophe, the lyrical voice expresses some ambivalent feelings toward the menacing power of the *bogatyr'*, which has already brought a glow to his face. Indeed, instead of the expected expression of fear and horror, the lyrical voice rather ironically encourages the reader to admire the hero's self-confidence:

> Два зарева глаза и щеки –
> Эх, уж и кровь добра! –
> Глядите-кось, как руки в боки,
> Встал посреди двора!

> A double glow of eyes and cheeks
> – ah, how healthy the blood is! –
> Look at him, hands at his sides
> Standing in the middle of the courtyard!

In these lines, it is hard not to notice that the colorful depiction of the Bolshevik-*bogatyr'*'s face is highly reminiscent of Malevich's supremacist manner that gives paramount importance to colors. Likewise, the first line of the stanza evokes the image of two red circles representing the hero's face. Surprisingly, the tone of the lyrical voice changes radically

20 Vladimir Propp, *Russian Folk Lyrics*, trans. and ed. Roberta Reeder (Bloomington: Indiana University Press, 1992), p. xi.

21 Patricia Arant, 'Alliteration and Repeated Prepositions in Russian Traditional Lament', in *Slavic Poetics. Essays in Honor of Kiril Taranovsky*, ed. Roman Jakobson and C. H. Van Schooneveld (Paris: Mouton, 1973), p. 1.

22 Anastasya Kostetskaya, 'Khlebnikov vs Mayakovsky: A Budletianin and a Futurist in the Mirror of Their Verbal Painting', Ph.D. Dissertation, Department of Slavic and East European Languages and Cultures, Ohio State University, p. 3.

when it describes the *bogatyr*'s face, as indicated by the modification of the enunciation: indeed, when it comes to the face, the poem is no longer written in third person but in second person. In other words, it becomes an address, first, to the readers and, second, to the eternal Russia. Even though Tsvetaeva could not have read Emmanuel Levinas's philosophical work regarding the importance and the significance of the human face in social interactions and the significance of the latter in the field of ethics,[23] which was written after her death, it appears, nevertheless, that she, too, had intuitively understood the fundamental role played by the face of the Other in human encounters. In the poem, this phenomenon manifests itself by the change of tone triggered in the lyrical voice after its observation of the Bolshevik's face, which no longer embodies an anonymous type but, on the contrary, the entire past of Russia:

Весь мир бы разгромил – да проймы
Жмут – не дают дыхнуть!
Широкой доброте разбойной
Смеясь – вверяю грудь!
И земли чуждые пытая,

– Ну какова мол новь? –
Смеюсь, – все ты же,
Русь святая,
Малиновая кровь.

He would have smashed the whole world – but his sleeves
Squeeze him at his armpits – won't let him breathe!
To the generous robbers' kindness
Laughing I entrust my breast!
And while I am testing foreign lands,

– How is the virgin soil?
I laugh – it is still you,
Holy Rus,
Crimson blood.

23 Emmanuel Levinas, *Totality and Infinity: An Essay on Exteriority*, trans. Alphonso Lingis (Pittsburgh: Duquesne University Press, 1969 [1961].

The interesting point to highlight in these lines is the sudden address from the lyrical voice to the ancient Rus' and the fact that it cannot refrain from laughing at the Bolshevik's attempt at conquering the vast world. This laughter can be variously interpreted: on the one hand, it could be an actualization of Velimir Khlebnikov's poem 'Incantation by Laughter' (1910) whereby the new society should rise from the all-pervasive laughter. On the other hand, the laughter of the lyrical voice could also refer to Tsvetaeva's poetic confession, according to which she always laughed at the wrong time,[24] which would suggest that the state of her beloved Russia is a pitiful one. This interpretation is in line with Nina Osipova's suggestion according to which the lyrical heroine's laughter indicates the presence of a carnival streak transforming it into a raw, complex, dangerous and unmanageable force that provokes an inversion of the hitherto admitted values.[25]

To conclude, it is striking that in her poem 'The Bolshevik', Tsvetaeva never employs the word 'Bolshevik' within the text of the poem, nor does she use the term 'Soviet'. I would suggest that the reason why she does not name the Soviet regime or the intrinsic connection of the hero with Soviet culture is that she does not believe that the latter is able to produce a Big-Bang-like creative explosion from which the artistic horizon will keep expanding. On the contrary, she sees it as a black hole sucking and destroying the explosive power of well-asserted individuals. Finally, even though the beginning of Tsvetaeva's poem expresses some concerns regarding the new type of society that is developing at the beginning of the 1920s, its end shows the strength of Tsvetaeva's ethical position which is, as Viktoriya Shveitser rightly remarks, her ability to not destroy 'the enemy' but, on the contrary, to show him mercy and generosity.[26] This is in line with Levinas's philosophy in which ethics always prevails over politics.

24 Tsvetaeva, *Polnoe sobranie poezii, prozy, dramaturgii v odnom tome*, p. 65.

25 Osipova, *Slova i kul'tura v dialogakh serebryanogo veka*, pp. 214–215.

26 Viktoriya Shveitser, *Marina Tsvetaeva* (Moskva: Molodaya gvardiya, 2002), p. 265.

Bibliography

Arant, Patricia, 'Alliteration and Repeated Prepositions in Russian Traditional Lament', in Slavic *Poetics. Essays in Honor of Kiril Taranovsky*, ed. Roman Jakobson and C. H. Van Schooneveld (Paris: Mouton, 1973).

Conwell, Alan, 'Churchill's Definition of Russia Still Rings True', *New York Times*, 1 August 2008, <https://www.nytimes.com/2008/08/01/world/europe/01iht-letter.1.14939466.html> (Accessed 20 December 2020).

Figes, Orlando, *Natasha's Dance. A Cultural History of Russia* (London: Penguin Books, 2002).

Gurianova, Nina, *The Russian Futurists and Their Books*, trans. Andrew Bromfield (Moscow: Avant-garde, 1993).

Hosking, Geoffrey, *Russian History* (Oxford: Oxford University Press, 2012).

Kataeva-Lytkina, Nadezhda, 'Bol'shevik i Marina Tsvetaeva: Boris Bessarabov kak lichnost' i prototip geroia stikhotvoreniia "Bol'shevik" i poemy "Egorushka"', *Voprosy literatury*, Vol. 5 (1996), pp. 272–292.

Knorpp, Elina, 'Évolution et manifestation de la nouvelle esthétique de l'image et de la poétique de la parole dans l'avant-garde russe, exprimée dans les livres d'artistes futuristes', <http://trans.revues.org/484> (Accessed 23 April 2016).

Kostetskaya, Anastasya, 'Khlebnikov vs Mayakovsky: A Budetlianin and a Futurist in the Mirror of Their Verbal Painting', Ph.D. Dissertation, Department of Slavic and East European Languages and Cultures, Ohio State University, 2010.

Levinas, Emmanuel, *Totality and Infinity: An Essay on Exteriority*, trans. Alphonso Lingis (Pittsburgh: Duquesne University Press, 1969 [1961]).

Lotman, Mikhail, 'History as Geography: In Search for Russian Identity', *Sign Systems Studies*, Vol. 45, Nos 3/4 (2017), p. 263.

Osipova, Nina, *Slova i kul'tura v dialogakh serebryanogo veka* (Moskva: Stagirit, 2008).

Propp, Vladimir, *Russian Folk Lyrics*, trans. and ed. Roberta Reeder (Bloomington, IN: Indiana University Press, 1992).

Sevastyanova, Olga, 'La fondation de Novogorod', in *Novogorod ou la Russie oubliée*, ed. Philippe Frison and Olga Sevastyanova (Editions Le Ver à Soie: 2015).

Shveitser, Viktoriya, *Marina Tsvetaeva* (Moskva: Molodaya gvardiya, 2002).

Slobin, Greta N., 'Language, History, Ideology: Tsvetaeva, Remizov', in *Russians Abroad: Literary and Cultural Politics of Diaspora (1919–1939)*, ed. Nancy Condee and Katerina Clark (Boston, MA: Academic Studies Press, 2013), pp. 57–73. *JSTOR*, <www.jstor.org/stable/j.ctt1zxsjrg.7> (Accessed 16 December 2020).

Tsvetaeva, Marina, *Neizdannoe. Svodnye tetradi* (Moscow: Ellis Lak, 1997).

—— *Polnoe sobranie poezii, prozy, dramaturgii v odnom tome* (Moscow: Alfa-Kniga, 2009).

—— *Sobranie sochinenii v semi tomakh* (Moscow: Terra, 1997).

Zhogina, Kseniya B., '"Poetika imeni" M. I Tsvetaevoi', in *Marina Tsevaeva: Lichnye I tvorcheskie vstrechi, perevody ee sochinenii: Sbornik dokladov* (Moscow: Dom-muzei Mariny Tsvetaevoi, 2001).

LARISA V. POLYAKOVA

7 Creative Personality as an Indicator and Formula for the Discontinuity/Continuity of Culture: Yevgeny Zamyatin

On the methodology of problem research

The theme of Russian cultural continuity reflects the urgent need for modern cultural studies and philosophy of culture: an ever-relevant and difficult-to-solve problem of the fate and prospects of one particular national culture. And there may be other monoethnic or heterogeneous cultural formations, besides the Russian one: the tools of analysis are exclusive, invented in antiquity, improved along with the changing epochs and remain far from ideal even to this day. It can hardly become different, because the subject of research, starting with the concept of 'culture', is not defined even at the doctrinal level within its boundaries. As a result, historically in the study of culture, many approaches, concepts, schools, theories, teachings and hypotheses, sometimes mutually exclusive, have been developed.

We do not set ourselves the task of discussing the fate of Russian culture as a whole. The question of the place of literature in the history of culture is not simple, but it is quite obvious that it is an expressive segment of culture, and it has its own laws of development and its own specifics. Russian philosophers of the end of the nineteenth and first half of the twentieth century wrote convincingly and at length about this. Some of them even thought that 'Russia has no cultural environment, no cultural middle ground, and almost no cultural tradition'.[1] But it is the study and the understanding of artistic literature, the laws of its development, that

1 N. A. Berdyaev, *O russkikh klassikakh* (Moscow: Vysshaya Shkola, 1993), p. 111.

become more of a guide in assessing cultural values and their social existence as well as in understanding cultural anthropology as a whole.

If we discuss literature and the peculiarities of its development, its 'explosions' and 'flames', and whether there is a reason to speak about the history of Russian literature as a single and whole artistic phenomenon, then it must be emphasized: due to the specific nature of the 'cryptogram' of the artistic language, it is hardly possible to write an authentic, scientific literary history: the history of the art of writing. Fiction is polymorphic and polysemantic, and by its very nature, it is doomed to debatable assessments and a priori hypothetical discussions of its history. At the same time, true artistic discovery is resilient, it does not succumb to the 'explosion' even with the ultra-precise and super-powerful 'impact' of innovators: the 'core' is not destroyed – traditions are preserved and developed, accumulated, and more than enough intelligent research has already been written about these. Try to present a literary and artistic discovery as tied up to chronology – it will not work. It is born, of course, at a certain time, but already at birth it does not belong to that particular time. The idea proposed by Claude Lévi-Strauss is clear: creators 'whether they know about it or not, but they never move along the path of creation on their own'.[2] The date of a particular discovery in literature is only a factitious chronology because it is a synthesis of previous individual and historical-literary influences. Changing current literary events are the accompaniment, the entourage of the history of literature, but not its driving force . It is the discoveries that stimulate historical and literary developments: they focus on the creative impulses, the artist's individuality, his philosophical and moral precepts as well as the challenges of the era. It is artistic discoveries that create and build, in the terminology of I. Rozanov, 'the pulse of poetic epochs'.[3]

The true creation of the art of writing cannot perish as a result of outside blows, such as social and political upheavals, it cannot die because of the very 'revolutionary consciousness' that leads the country, rewrites the past and, in all types of art, creates the illusion of a 'break'. The true

2 Claude Lévi-Strauss, *Put' masok* (Moscow: Respublika, 2000), p. 97.

3 I. N. Rozanov, *Literaturnye reputatsii* (Moscow: Nikitinskie subbotniki, 1928), pp. 5–11.

creation of the artistic language does not crumble even when it is physically destroyed, for example, by burning: in the process of its birth, it has been located in the atmosphere of national and world art as well as in the atmosphere of the fictional world already created by the author himself, and it has breathed their air, at the same time filling it with its fragrance. The law of continuity in the literary art also works in extreme situations. In the historical movement of literature, there can be no explosions with, as their consequences, 'breaks' or 'discontinuities', but only that creative European Promethean fire – the spirit that M. Voloshin had in mind in the poem 'Russia' (1924) with a very original and not indisputable view of the history of Russia – can dominate and warm the creators: the spirit of creativity, nobility, courage, talent and ingenuity, as a result of which humanity is gifted with cities, factories, books, palaces and temples. This fire is creative, constructive, sacrificial and selfless. In the historical evolution of literature, between the extreme phenomena there is always a multitude of various intermediate ones . In the history of literature, renewals are associated with artistic discoveries, and therefore it does not shudder from frequent changes; its greatness is in an epically calm movement or development. Its renewing tremors are not frequent, but very noticeable. This seismography is not destructive, but creative. Otherwise, in literature and culture in general, there can only be their final death as one of the signals of the coming apocalypse.

In the historical and literary movement, there are straight and cross paths, passes and bridges, circumferential and alternate roads, but, as a rule, there is always a high road, a path to the source, the root. And this is not the path of return, but the route of the umbilical cord. Every discovery in fiction is a step forward, not necessarily on the path of progress, but precisely a step forward in the development and, at the same time, strengthening of the root of the national art of writing. The pioneer Futurist V. Mayakovsky was well aware of it, as he sends signals of kinship to Pushkin across a century in his poem 'Jubilee'.

In the study of the highly complex morphology of the history of literature, which is always lively and mobile, and at the same time an integral and incomplete aesthetic system, there can be no simple and therefore indisputable solutions in the analysis of its individual (so to speak) ontogenesis and historical genealogy. However, the history of literature as a cultural phenomenon not only corresponds to the general law of cultural development but also confirms it: discontinuity has a relative, even visible character; continuity is absolute, universal and basic for the dynamics of movement and the accumulation of new aesthetic values.

Even earlier, N. Berdyaev actively used the metaphorical characteristics of the extreme literary and creative state of being at his seminar at the Free Academy of Spiritual Culture during the winter of 1920–1921, and then in the fundamental cycle of works on Dostoevsky with his 'vortex anthropology', 'ecstatic-fiery atmosphere', 'fiery movement in man' and 'flow of hot lava' in prose. These were often quoted by M. Voloshin and Yu. Lotman.

The philosopher compared the Russian writer's interest in man with the positions of Dante and Shakespeare, spoke of his 'contemplation of the polarity of human nature', 'an essentially different position' of his perception of man, when 'the abyss opened up in the depths of man himself, and there God and the devil, heaven and hell were again revealed', and of Dostoevsky's path to man, different from theirs, 'the path of spiritual immanence, not transcendence'. However, at the same time, Berdyaev specifically emphasized that 'this does not mean, of course, that he denied the reality of the transcendent'.[4]

Thus, in his reflections on anthroposophy and Dostoevsky's worldview, actively using, let us say, the 'apocalyptic' lexicon, the philosopher did not ascribe to works by the Russian genius ideas of 'discontinuity', 'death' or 'explosion' from the discoveries whether of Italian or English literary luminaries in particular or of world literature in general. However, it was Berdyaev who would use the term 'discontinuity' in his mid-1930s work *The Origins and Meaning of Russian Communism*. It is Berdyaev's methodology of the historical development of literature that is instructive for us.

For understanding, perhaps, the more conspicuous characteristics of the advancement of culture in time, it is verbal art with its universal tool of influence on a person – the word – that is most indicative. The art of writing allows us to speak clearly about the prerequisites; causes and laws of discontinuity/continuity; its kinds, types and character; artistic flexibility;

4 Berdyaev, *O russkikh klassikakh*, pp. 125, 126, 127, 111.

and chronological extension. In culture, and especially in fiction, as a rule, everything is personified. Culture, to a greater extent than other spheres of human activity, is subject to history and its laws, and to some extent, it forms them. This is primarily related to the question of the role of the individual in history. It is the creative individuality of the artist that is in many ways an indicator, a tool and a formula, even an emblem; according to Spengler, it is a symbol of the processes of discontinuity/continuity in culture as a whole or at a certain historical stage. It is, in addition to being an intermediate phenomenon in cultural history, the most reliable 'island of salvation' from the destruction of culture.

In order to clarify the stated postulate, we will turn to the history of Russian literature of the twentieth century and the tragic fate of Yevgeny Zamyatin (1884–1937), which is typical of the complex and ambiguous processes that took place in the culture of this period as a whole. Zamyatin's path in literature follows events that have the ability to stimulate not only the searches and solutions of artists among problems and themes but also possible processes of discontinuity in their creative activity: the First Russian Revolution (1905–1907); the First World War (1914–1918); the February and October Revolutions (1917); the Civil War (1918–1922); the strengthening of the dictate of the Bolsheviks in literary life, the resolution of the Central Committee of the RCP (b) of 1925 'On the Party's policy in the field of fictional literature' with its paragraph on the so called 'fellow-travelers' – writers who did not openly criticize the Party, but at the same time were not fully in agreement with its activity; and finally, the leading role of RAPP figures and their radical journal'Na postu' ('On Guard'), with its ideological bludgeon. The path of this writer ended with his sudden death in Paris, where he moved out of necessity, with the permission of Stalin in the fall of 1931, keeping his Soviet passport and a paid apartment in Leningrad, and in June 1934, with the active request of colleagues and, above all, M. Gorky, he was admitted in absentia to the Union of Writers of the USSR. In 1935, as part of the Soviet delegation, he took part in the Paris Anti-fascist International Congress of Writers in Defense of Culture, which was attended by 230 writers from 35 countries. Nevertheless, Zamyatin had a painful sense of being an outcast.

In the general initial assessment of the literature of the twentieth century, N. Berdyaev again sounds convincing. He called the first decades of the 'Russian cultural Renaissance' as 'one of the most refined epochs in the history of Russian culture', when there was a turn to religion and a creative rise of poetry and philosophy. At the same time, in *The Meaning of History* (the chapter 'The End of the Renaissance and the Crisis of Humanism: The Disintegration of the Human Image '), in contrast to the European Renaissance, he characterized the beginning of the twentieth century of the cultural life of Russia as the 'end of the Renaissance'.

> It was at the same time an era of the emergence of new souls, a new sensitivity … Russian souls were seized with premonitions of impending catastrophes. I was growing deeply disillusioned with the literary environment and wanted to leave it. I found Petersburg disgusting … literary sectarianism aroused protest in me.

There was 'a break with the tradition of the Enlightenment'; 'a break with the ethical tradition of literature of the nineteenth century'; and 'the social and ethical element, so strong in the nineteenth century, was weakened'. Berdyaev emphasized that there were 'toxic fumes'; 'something twofold'; 'there was no volitional choice'; 'mystical sensuality was brewing', which previously did not exist in Russia. Russian people of that time, according to him, 'lived in different floors and even in different centuries. The cultural Renaissance did not have any broad 'social radiation', and 'it lacked a moral character'. This was the era of 'great self-enrichment of souls, but also softening of souls'.[5]

Yevgeny Zamyatin came into the world of literature in this bright yet complex and contradictory literary and general cultural atmosphere. With regard to the question of discontinuity/continuity in the development of culture, for the sake of brevity and chronological order, we will briefly indicate only the main milestones in the writer's creative path, with the slow fuse of persecution that detonated his decision to leave Russia in the late 1920s.

At the end of 1905, Zamyatin was arrested and imprisoned for three months in a solitary cell in the Pre-Trial Detention House on Shpalernaya

5 N. A. Berdyaev, *Smysl istorii* (Moscow: Mysl', 1990), pp. 132–144.

Street in St. Petersburg for participating in revolutionary student demonstrations (see the story 'Odin'). In 1913, Zamyatin's novel 'A Provincial Tale' (*Uyezdnoye*)was published in the pages of the magazine *Zavety*; K. Chukovsky reported on the birth of the 'new Gogol'; and the author wrote a new story, 'In the Middle of Nowhere', which was published by the same *Zavety* magazine in 1914. This issue of the magazine was confiscated, and the editorial board headed by R. Ivanov-Razumnik and the author were brought to court for their desire to defame the army and insult the military class, and were tried for 'violating' morality. Consequently, the writer was exiled to Kem' in the north.

In 1919, he was arrested, along with A. Blok, A. Remizov and R. Ivanov-Razumnik, in a case involving left Social Revolutionaries. In 1921–1922, a reading of his 'seditious' novel *We* resulted in a series of oral presentations by the author, which would continue in the following years. In 1922, he was arrested in Petrograd as part of a group of philosophers and writers who were to be expelled from Russia. He was put in prison, where he was handed a decree of indefinite expulsion from Russia; however, as a result of a petition from writers, the expulsion was canceled. He was released from prison on his recognizance that he would not leave the country. At the end of September, he took part in seeing off a departing steamer with exiled philosophers and writers going abroad. He applied for the permission to leave , but it was refused. In 1922, the *Notes of Dreamers* published a story 'The Cave', no less seditious than the novel *We*, and in 1923, this story was published in the academic journal *The Slavonic Review* in English, translated by D. Svyatopolk-Mirsky alongside his article 'The Revival of Russian Prose', assigning Zamyatin a leading role in the domestic literary process and characterizing the story as a 'masterpiece'.

In 1924, the novel *We* was published in New York in English (translated and with a foreword by G. Zilboorg). 'Perhaps for the first time in the history of the last few decades', as this writer and psychoanalyst specifically emphasized,

> a Russian book, inspired by Russian life, written in Russia and in Russian, was published for the first time not in Russia, but abroad, and not in the language in which it was written, but translated from a foreign language, […] And this is a huge tragedy: the spiritual loneliness of the artist, who cannot turn to his people […] In

> the novel *We*, using a unique artistic method, it is shown what the tragedy of the independent spirit in modern conditions is. The conflict between the creative personality and the crowd is not exclusively a Russian problem today. It is as acute in the conditions of the Bolshevik dictatorship as in the Ford factory.[6]

Unpublished in Russia, the novel in its oral versions was highly appreciated by some of Zamyatin's contemporaries. In 1927, with the mediation of R. Jakobson, the novel appeared in the Prague newspaper *Lidove Noviny*, and there was a separate edition published in Czech. The chapters of the novel in Russian were published behind the author's back in the Prague Socialist-Revolutionary magazine *Volya Rossii* with a preamble stating that the novel was published in a reverse translation from Czech and English. And yet, it was this publication that resulted in the massive harassment of the writer in the Soviet press.

Zamyatin's play *Atilla: A Tragedy in Four Acts*, which was completed in 1928 (in three editions), was intended to be performed on the stage of the BDT (Bolshoi Drama Theatre) in Leningrad with N. Monakhov in the title role. Announced in the posters of this theatre, it never saw the light of the day during the author's lifetime – either in the printed version or in the stage version. It was published for the first time in the American *New Journal* (1950, No. 24, pp. 7–70), and in Russia 40 years later in the journal *Modern Drama* (1990, No. 1. pp. 205–227). In 1929, the French translation of *We* was published.

On 2 May 1929, the Leningrad one-day *Literature Newspaper* published an epigram by A. Bezymensky, 'A Reference to Social Eugenics', which angered Zamyatin. In protest, Zamyatin resigned from the Board of the Union of Writers, of which many of his friends were members. In August, at the dacha of M. Voloshin in Koktebel (Crimea), Zamyatin read in the *Literature Newspaper*, *Red Newspaper*, and *Komsomolskaya Pravda* of the 26 and 27 of that month, that he and B. Pilnyak, the author of the story 'Mahogany', were accused of collaborating with the foreign white emigrant press. However, despite this, in 1930, the Moscow publishing house 'Nedra'

6 G. Zilboorg, *Predislovie k pervomu izdaniiu Evgeniia Zamjatina 'My': Tekst i materialy k tvorcheskoi istorii romana*; Sost., podgot. teksta, publ., komment. i stat'i M. Yu. Lyubimovoi i Dzh. Kurtis (St. Petersburg: Mir, 2011), pp. 307, 308.

published a novel by Pilnyak about the construction of a new reservoir, *The Volga Flows into the Caspian Sea*. In September 1929, Zamyatin addressed an open letter to the editorial office of the *Literary Newspaper*, at the end of which he wrote: 'To be a member of a literary organization that at least indirectly participates in the persecution of its members – I cannot do that and this letter declares my withdrawal from the All-Russian Union of Writers'.[7] In 1929, the almanac *Land and Factory* published Zamyatin's novel *Flood*, which is far from the ordinary for Soviet literature, and the cooperative publishing house Federation published Zamyatin's collected works in four volumes. However, the novel *We* is not included in it. At the same time, performances of Zamyatin's plays were gradually banned in theatres. There had been performances staged with great success in 1925 at the Moscow Art Theatre (Moscow) and the BDT (Leningrad) based on Zamyatin's play *The Flea*, while in the Mikhailovsky Theatre (Leningrad), the tragicomedy *Society of Honorary Bell Ringers* based on the story 'The Islanders' was performed). The writer's books were withdrawn from libraries, Soviet magazines were closed for him, and his name was crossed out from the lists of editorial boards. The last work of Zamyatin published in the USSR, which did not escape the red tape of the staffers, was his preface to the play by Richard Brinsley Sheridan titled *The School for Scandal*, from the publishing house 'Academia' in 1931.

In June 1931, in a detailed 'Letter to Stalin', first printed in 1955 in *Litsa*, in a collection of his writings published by the Chekhov Publishing House in New York, Zamyatin wrote:

> Dear Iosif Vissarionovich,
>
> Sentenced to capital punishment, the author of this letter asks you to replace this measure with another […] In the Soviet code, the step below the death sentence is the eviction of the criminal from the country. If I am really a criminal and deserve punishment, I think it shouldn't be as severe as a literary death, and therefore I ask that this sentence be replaced by expulsion from the borders of the USSR – with the right for my wife to accompany me. If I am not a criminal, I ask permission to go abroad with my wife, temporarily, for at least one year, so that I can return as soon as

7 E. I. Zamyatin, *Sobranie sochinenii v 5 tomakh*; Sost., podgot. teksta i komment. St. S. Nikonenko i A. N. Tyurina (Moscow: Russkaya kniga, 2003), Vol. 2, p. 549.

> it becomes possible for us to serve big ideas in literature without pandering to small people; as soon as there is at least a partial change in the perception of the role of the artist of the word here. And this time, I am sure, is upon us, because after the successful creation of the material base, the question will inevitably arise of creating a superstructure – art and literature that would really be worthy of the revolution.[8]

With the mediation of M. Gorky in the autumn of 1931, the Zamyatins left for Paris via Riga and Berlin. In 1952, 15 years after the writer's death, the novel *We* was published in Russian by the Chekhov Publishing House in New York, 'and according to statistics in the publisher's report on 15 January 1953, the book *We* was included in the ten best-selling books'.[9] In 1958–1959, the novel appeared in various publishing houses in German, Italian, Finnish, Swedish, Norwegian, Danish and for the second time in English. In 1960, the work was included in the American *Anthology of Russian Literature of the Soviet Period*. Prof J. Curtis of the University of Oxford, in her vivid work *Studies of the Novel 'We' Abroad*, analyzes numerous foreign responses to Zamyatin and, above all, to *We* and testifies thus:

> The reviewed works of leading Western and some Russian specialists demonstrate an extraordinary variety of approaches to reading and researching the novel – from political to feminist, from Freudian to linguistic, from cultural-historical to intertextual. Not read during the author's lifetime, the novel opened up to subsequent generations all the richness of the possibilities inherent in it, it became popular with the readership in the socio-cultural situation of the first decade of the twenty-first century.[10]

In the writer's homeland, Zamyatin's works began to be published only after more than a half-century break: a volume of selected works was published in Voronezh,[11] and *We* was published in the pages of the magazine *Znamya* in 1988 (Nos 4–5).

8 Ibid., pp. 550, 553.

9 Yukio Nakano, *Istoriia izdaniia romana 'My' na russkom yazyke* (Tambov: Izd-vo TGU im. G. R. Derzhavina, 2014), pp. 208–209.

10 Julia Curtis, *Issledovaniia romana* 'My' *za rubezhom* (St. Petersburg: Mir, 2011), p. 559.

11 E. I. Zamyatin, *Povesti, Rasskazy*; Predisl. O. N. Mihailova (Voronezh: Centr.-Chernozemn. kn. izd-vo, 1986).

Tragic was not only the fate of Zamyatin, but also of his creative legacy, especially the outstanding novel *We*: even with its numerous foreign translations and editions, as a result of incessant metamorphoses owing to issues around its publication in his homeland, the sketches, notes, drafts and the manuscript itself (typewritten) of *We* were lost, not preserved even by his wife Liudmila Nikolaevna Zamyatina. It was only in the 1990s that the typewritten manuscript with notes by the writer's wife were discovered by J. Curtis in the American archive, as reported by the English researcher in the publication *Eugene Zamyatin, 'We': Text and Materials for the Creative History of the Novel.*[12]

As we can see, external factors affected not only Zamyatin's state of mind but also his creativity and output, and they became a heavy cross to carry through his entire creative path from its very beginning to its completion. Finally, the posthumous conspiracy of silence at home lasted for more than half a century. All this could be enough to ensure in the creative evolution of the artist as a whole or at some stage in the chain, a 'break', a violation, a destruction of the interconnectedness, of the system of individual artistic explorations, decisions, and national historical and cultural integrity. However, this did not happen; despite the obstacles and challenges, Zamyatin – as an artist, thinker and psychologist; novelist working in a variety of genres; playwright and screenwriter; publicist; literary critic and literary theorist; literary and public figure – has always kept up his creative energy and activity as well as his brilliant creative dynamics. And prolific results were his reward: his literary authority and prestige have strengthened over the years; his artistic discoveries, have been appreciated not only by admirers of Zamyatin's talent but also by students and successors, eventually transforming into traditions that have influenced not only Russian but also foreign writers. The strong will provided by the artist's individuality worked ('I am a stiff and self-willed person. So I will remain'),[13] as well as the power of his bright and prolific creativity, the ability to attract the attention of contemporaries and interest descendants, the intellectual capital

12 Curtis, *Issledovaniyia*, p. 499.

13 E. I. Zamyatin, 'Pis'ma E. I. Zamyatina raznym adresatam', *Novy mir*, No. 10 (1996), p. 143.

of the writer. All these factors contributed to Zamyatin overcoming the prevailing circumstances through preservation of the vitality of his literary art and his salvational ability to self-purify by not allowing anything to interfere with the normal creative process, and resisting to having to make significant changes to his artistic plans and their implementation. Let us call this ability of the creative organism a phenomenon of natural, non-violent individual-creative absorption, which also communicates impulses of continuity and development to the historical and cultural movement.

Reaction of the world outlook as a force of creative resistance

It is clearly not fair to represent the situation in Zamyatin's creative life as bleak among his contemporaries in Russia: Chukovsky's words about the birth of the 'new Gogol' in connection with the story 'Uyezdnoye' have already been quoted; Zamyatin was supported by M. Gorky (although the latter did not accept some of his works), A. Remizov, B. Eikhenbaum, V. Shklovsky, Ya. Brown, K. Fedin, Yu. Annenkov, B. Kustodiev and others. In 'Essay on the History of Modern Russian Literature', V. E. Yevgeniev-Maximov reported on Zamyatin's students and wrote:

> No matter how one treats the ideological side of Zamyatin's works of recent years, it cannot be denied that his artistic talent is in full bloom, thanks to which Zamyatin has had and continues to have a strong influence on the artistic life of our time.[14]

Russian emigrants spoke particularly highly of the writer's works. In 1926, in his article 'On the Current State of Russian Literature', D. Svyatopolk-Mirsky predicted: 'If we had an Academy, no one would be more worthy to enter it than Anna Akhmatova, Yevgeny Zamyatin and Vladislav Khodasevich'.[15]

14 V. E. Yevgeniev-Maximov, *Ocherk noveishei russkoi literatury: etiudy i kharakteristiki; Izd. chetvertoe* (Moscow: Gos. izdat., 1927), p. 262.

15 D. P. Svyatopolk-Mirsky, *O nyneshnem sostoyanii russkoi literatury; Blagonamerennyi* (Brussels, 1926), Kn.1. Janv.– févr., p. 92.

Foreign figures, including artists who worked in the same vein as the author of *We* (Aldous Huxley and later George Orwell), expressed their interest in his work. A. Werth, a well-known English journalist and author of several books about the USSR who interviewed Yevgeny Zamyatin in 1932 in France, noted thus:

> Yevgeny Zamyatin is one of the most significant names of modern Russian literature [...] The quantity of his 'literary output' is small, but it is all of the finest quality. As a stylist, he is one of the recognized masters of Russian literature, with a whole constellation of students.[16]

In 1934, the correspondent of the Paris edition of *Comoedia*, Frédéric Pottecher, who visited the seriously ill Zamyatin in Paris, felt it necessary to emphasize: 'Some of the stories of his that were published in our magazines are real masterpieces'; he is 'one of the most interesting personalities of modern Russian literature'; he is 'a skilled satirist, gifted with subtle humour and often crazy gaiety'; he has a 'subtle scientific mind'; and in his works there is 'high-quality humour'.[17] In one of his works, L. Geller gives an assessment of Zamyatin by the French Slavist Jacques Catto: 'Jacques Catto quite accurately defined the situation, calling Zamyatin a living geometric center of all the literary possibilities of his time'.[18] And L. Geller himself is greatly appreciative of Zamyatin: he 'passed the most difficult test of strength', and 'this test is passed by genuinely great writers – classical ones'.[19] These are only few of the numerous examples that characterise Zamyatin. And after the death of the writer, his name did not leave the pages of the foreign press. It was a way of preserving the continuity of the artist's classical heritage.

16 A. Vert, *Literatura v sovetskoi Rossii: Interv'iu s Evgeniem Zamyatinym; Zamyatin, E.I. 'Ya boyus'* (Moscow: Nasledie, 1999), p. 263.

17 Frédéric Pottecher, *Comoedia*, 29 July 1936.

18 L. Geller *Utopiia v zerkale gematrii, ili ezotericheskii modernizm E. Zamyatina; E.I. Zamyatin: pro et contra*, Antologiia Sost. O. V. Bogdanova, M. Yu. Liubimova (St. Petersburg: NP; 'MOPO Apostol'skii gorod – Nevskaya perspektiva', 2014), p. 265.

19 L. Geller, *Novoe o Zamyatine* [New about Zamyatin] Sb. statei pod red. L. Gellera (Moscow: Izd-vo MIK, 1997), p. 4.

A different situation – deafening silence – developed in Zamyatin's homeland, Russia. However, this does not in any way indicate that the name of this outstanding creator has disappeared into oblivion: his works were read primarily in the literary circles. The literary school he left behind persevered on, and its traditions continue to flourish in Russian literature, which became the subject of research in the doctoral dissertation of E. Boroda, 'Artistic Discoveries of E. I. Zamyatin in the Context of Russian Literature Search in the Second Half of the Twentieth and Early Twenty-First Centuries (2011) and in her monograph *Russian Fiction as a Realization of the Aesthetic Resource of Russian Literature of the Twentieth Century: The Strugatsky Brothers and Yevgeny Zamyatin* (2007). Works of E. Boroda on the fundamental conceptual views of Zamyatin studies on the problem of Zamyatin traditions in modern Russian literature are the first of their kind. Here the writer's artistic discoveries are considered as an inexhaustible artistic and philosophical source of modern Russian prose from the second half of the twentieth century to recent years. In the view of the researcher, there is not only the prose of the brothers A. and B. Strugatsky ('Noon, 22nd Century', 'The Final Circle of Paradise', 'Invasion from Mars', 'The Kid from Hell', 'The Doomed City', 'The Inhabited Island'), but also of I. Efremov ('The Bull's Hour', 'Razor Blade'), V. Makanin ('Manhole', 'Baize-Covered Table with Decanter'), V. Voinovich ('Moscow – 2042'), V. Pelevin ('Hermit and Sixfinger', 'Omon Ra', 'Yellow Arrow', essay 'Zombification'), P. Krusanov ('Bom-Bom', 'American Hole', 'Angel Bite'), and other brilliant prose writers.

'Zamyatin had a significant influence on the contemporary literary process', writes E. Boroda:

> His role for posterity was no less large-scale. And the best proof of this is not even the triumphant return of the writer to his homeland, not the grandiose demand for his creative heritage at the peak of interest in 'returned' literature and so-called anti-totalitarian prose. It is much more convincing that Zamyatin's artistic discoveries, his ideas, theories, and forecasts are confirmed and proved timely in the absence of the author, at a time when his name seemed to be forgotten. The demand for artistic discoveries in themselves, not supported by the magic of the name – is the best proof of the depth and accuracy of these discoveries.[20]

20 E. V. Boroda, *Otechestvennaia fantastika kak realizaciia esteticheskogo resursa russkoi literatury nachala XX veka: brat'ia Strugatskie i Evgeny Zamyatin* (Tambov: Izd-vo Pershina R. V., 2007), pp. 7–8.

Today, not only abroad, but also in Russia, multivolume sets of Zamyatin's works as well as books about him are published.

In the complex and contradictory picture of the literary life of the twentieth century, the brilliant figure of Zamyatin stands out as an artist whose work seems to have reflected all the vicissitudes of national life and the most characteristic artistic searches not only in the segment of his creative path but also in the future. For the art of the twentieth century, Zamyatin is an artist whose work is largely iconic, unifying and quintessential. His personality, creative behavior and peculiarities in prose, drama, journalism, criticism and theory are so unique and yet so typical of Russian literature, not only in the first third of the century but throughout, that turning to the legacy and creative biography of this writer gives us the key to having a balanced view of the entire literary process of the century.

The man of the first third of the twentieth century, depicted by Zamyatin, is a pronounced national character, woven from screaming contradictions of spirit and behavior and tormented by 'hate-love'. 'If, along with the sharpness and sophistication of the European, Sologub assimilated the mechanical, desolate soul of the European', Zamyatin said in 1924 in a speech at the gala evening at the Aleksandrinsky Theatre dedicated to the anniversary of Fedor Sologub,

> then he would not be the Sologub that is so close to us. But under the strict, restraint European dress, Sologub retained an unrestrained Russian soul. This white love that demands everything or nothing, this absurd, incurable, beautiful disease – not only Sologub's disease, not only Don Quixote's disease, not only Blok's (Blok died of this very disease) – this is our Russian disease, morbus rossica. This is precisely the disease that affects the best part of our intelligentsia – and, fortunately, it will remain so, no matter how it is treated. Fortunately, because a country in which there are no longer irreconcilable, eternally dissatisfied, always restless romantics, in which there are only healthy Sancho Panzas and Chichikovs – sooner or later is doomed to snore under the quilt of philistinism. The Russian disease could have been born only in the vast expanse of the Russian steppes, where it feels as if the Scythians, who did not know any power, any settlement, rode only recently. Despite all his Europeanism, Sologub comes from the Russian steppes, in spirit – he is a Russian writer much more than many of his contemporaries, than, for example, Balmont or Bryusov. The cruel time will erase many, but Sologub will remain in Russian literature.[21]

21 Zamyatin, *Sobranie sochinenii v 5 tomakh*, Vol. 3, p. 29.

Zamyatin did not call the article 'F. Sologub', which would be in line with other literary portraits that made up the collection *Litsa* (Faces) (first published posthumously by the Chekhov Publishing House in America in 1955). In the manuscript, the speech was called '*Morbus Rossica*' (Russian Disease), and the first magazine publication of it was entitled 'White Love'(1925). The author thus emphasized the special typicality of the character of the author of 'The Little Demon' and 'The Created Legend' for the Russian person. Undoubtedly, it was not only Zamyatin's pneumatology, but also, metaphorically speaking, it was the way in which he tried on himself (and above all himself!) the clothes of a special cut.

Throughout the century, the image of man Zamyatin created by his life and legacy, taught moral lessons, without which our understanding of the ontological upheavals of Russian life is not complete. A great lesson, a magnetic attraction of thought, is felt today in the whole 'Zamyatin literary space': the history of the creation and publication of his works, their perception by the reader, the creation of literary theories based on his own perceptions, the preservation of professional and human dignity in the conditions, of 'literary death', as he put it himself in his letter to Stalin. The '*morbus rossica*' proved to be a panacea and bearing support.

The lessons of Zamyatin's fate, his writing practice, as modern Zamyatin studies show, are still not easily grasped today. The politicization of the creative heritage of the author of *We* in the spirit of assessments of the 1920s is not only preserved in some works but often remains the starting point in writing a literary and critical portrait of the writer.[22]

Yevgeny Zamyatin passed through the historical 'reefs' of the first third of the twentieth century. However, as an artist he was formed in many respects not so much under their influence as in spite of them. He had to constantly correlate his ontological ideas that were forming and eventually becoming more complex with the changing realities of life itself, with the processes of 'discontinuity of culture' namely as elements of how the world

22 L. V. Polyakova., *Sovremennye otsenki tvorcheskogo naslediya E. Zamyatina, tendentsii podkhodov* (St. Petersburg: RHGA, 2015), pp. 418–459.

is contemplated.[23] He had to formulate his ideas using clear constructions of theoretical propositions that generalize his own artistic practice in different periods of creativity. Of the numerous examples, I will name only a few, but it seems that they are milestones in his creative path.

Having grown up in a priest's family in a provincial town in the Tambov region and having started his career in literature mainly with the artistic analysis of the Russian provinces in the novel 'A Provincial Tale' as a Realist, a 'new Gogol' Zamyatin felt the need to comprehend the methodology of this whole artistic school, in which A. Remizov, M. Prishvin, S. Sergeev-Tsensky, A. Tolstoy, V. Rozanov, V. Shishkov, S. Yesenin, N. Klyuev, S. Gorodetsky and others worked at that time. It is known that Zamyatin perceived his own work as part of a certain system of Russian literary discoveries. He was to combine these discoveries into one strand and call it Neorealism, formulate the main features and principles, and specify 'I also belong to the same trend'.[24] This was the real manifesto of a writer expressing his intention to produce serious and promising work in literature, to choose his own creative path.

However, as it quickly became clear, the creative path of the writer never had a restrictive boundary: Zamyatin's array of creative quests and discoveries always amazed his contemporaries. At the same time, what was also surprising was the unity and integrity in this diversity, the constant interest in the life of his compatriots and the everyday problems of creativity. This is also typical of the 1914 novella *A Godforsaken Hole*, the publication of which angered the St. Petersburg Committee for Press Affairs and resulted in the seizure of the story in addition to the arrest of its author and the editorial board of the journal *Zavety*.

On the pages of the Russian press, *A Godforsaken Hole* was to appear for the second time in the early 1920s, and literary critics would immediately react sharply. One of the first assessments, which was largely shared in the

23 P. A. Florensky, Vvedenie k dissertatsii 'Ideia preryvnosti kak element mirosozertsaniia' [Introduction to the dissertation 'The Idea of Discontinuity as an Element of World-Contemplation'], *Istoriko-matematicheskie issledovaniia* 30 (Moscow: Nauka, 1986), pp. 159–164.

24 E. I. Zamyatin, *Sochineniia* (Moscow: Kniga, 1988), p. 132.

following years as well, was given by A. K. Voronsky. In the article titled 'Eugene Zamyatin', he particularly emphasized the lyricism of Zamyatin's prose as 'special', 'authentic, high and touching' and 'feminine'. At the same time, a well-known critic perceived the work as a 'political satire'. In the spirit of official censorship, he also appreciated the officers depicted in the story: '*The Duel* by Aleksandr Kuprin pales before the picture of moral rot and decay drawn by the writer: cesspools in the back yard'.[25]

Everything – the plot, its dynamics, the figurative structure, the author's assessment, the general pathos of the work – is determined by the role of three characters: Nikolai Petrovich Schmit, his wife Marusia and Andrei Ivanych Polovets. They make up a kind of love triangle, although not in the classic intensely dramatic manner. It is in them that the type of Russian character is embodied, which has been written about more than once by representatives of world and Russian philosophy, to which musicians, painters and writers have sought analogies in their 'crescendos' and 'pianissimos', watercolors and pastels, hymns and elegies.

> Russian plains, as well as Russian ravines, are symbols of the Russian soul [...] The soul spreads out over an endless plain, goes into endless distances [...] It cannot live in boundaries and forms [...] this soul is directed towards the finite and the ultimate [...] This is an apocalyptic soul in its basic mood and aspiration [...] It is not turned into a fortress, like the soul of a European man [...] It has a penchant for wandering through the endless plains of the Russian land. The lack of form, the weakness of discipline leads to the fact that the Russian person does not have a real instinct for self-preservation, he easily destroys himself, burns himself, is dispersed in space.[26]

It is these self-incinerating features , is it not, that have been spotted and depicted by Zamyatin in the character traits of his favorite heroes? And it is difficult to name another work of this artist in which with such a force of expressiveness such realities of a national character would be conveyed, which army life in a godforsaken hole only aggravated.

In a word, the subject of satirical ridicule and exposure in the story is clearly marked and significant: it is the very Russian reality of the 1910s

25 A. K. Voronsky, *Izbrannye stat'i o literature* (Moscow, 1982), pp. 123, 122.

26 Berdyaev, *O russkikh klassikakh*, pp. 186–188.

that gave rise to the element of the mundane, of the humdrum everyday life – the life of the backwoods in the literature of that period.

However, the main component, the leitmotif of the author's moods and the pathos of the entire narrative of *A Godforsaken Hole* remains not an exposure, not a satire, but a dramatically intense empathy for the characters, beautiful and strong in their passions . It seems that the whole story was written by Zamyatin to tell us about these provincial people, who are so rebellious, pure, with a mad hurricane of feelings that they express in their own way, always different from the generally accepted, philistine ideas about human duty and attachments.

Zamyatin's heroes did not become happy, but, with their purity of morals, mutual relations, ability and readiness for love, they resisted the sucking swamp. And it is not their fault that they did not win. Zamyatin's *A Godforsaken Hole* is full of the 'great' love of the author for his compatriots, as in Andrei Ivanych's love for Marusya, and the great compassion for them, which was naturally perceived as the author's protest against social conditions that humiliate human and national dignity. Naturally, as a consequence, both the book and its author were penalized.

In 1913–1914, the four-volume *Works* of Bernhard Kellermann was translated from German and published by the Prometheus Publishing House. The response of Zamyatin – the author of 'A Provincial Tale ' – was instant (*Monthly Magazine*, 1914, No. 5). It was one of the early literary-critical works of the artist, who later wrote a lot not only about Russian but also about English, French and other national literatures. In the review of the *Works* of the German classic, a certain selectivity of the reviewer draws attention to itself: first of all, and most of all, he is interested in the novel *In the Tunnel* (this is how the title of *Der Tunnel* was translated). Almost the entire analysis of the *Works* is tied by Zamyatin to this work. And not by accident. The novel shocked the Russian artist, and against the background of the previous works of the 'gentle', 'melodious' and 'subtle' Kellermann, it was perceived as strange and unexpected: roar and whirlwind; the mad dance of life; the deathly pale, tired people of the *Tunnel* (Zamyatin preferred this exact name of the work); a drilling machine in the underground depths, 'in the heat of hell'; an ominous picture of human madness, from which the 'gold kings' extract millions of profits. The first person who was ground down by the drilling machine of technological progress turned out to be Allan – the 'machine god', the creator of the idea of a tunnel under the ocean between America and Europe: 'work and work, the tunnel does not wait, money does not wait, interest does not wait', 'the tunnel possessed Allan like a demon'. The reviewer was then captivated by this fantastic plot, which is only rarely mentioned by researchers without any analysis of the text. However, it is possible that even then the young writer, admiring the novel, set himself a number of questions that would worry him in the years that followed, and in the script 'Gunton's Dungeon', the last work written but not published in Russia, Zamyatin was to practically establish many analogies not only with his own works, but also with the novel written by the German writer.[27] The symbols of the cave, with its gradually narrowing space; the lamp, the only source of light (as well as heat), which is gradually fading and disappearing, which suspends the hero on the precipice of life and death; the confrontation in the plotline; the very theme of the 'dungeon' – all of these are not only transformed in *We*, but also enter Zamyatin's work as the defining coordinates of his aesthetics.

The novel caused a violent reaction but received not only devastating but also positive – even enthusiastic – reviews at home and abroad; however, its evaluation by the literary officials was sharply negative. The eight-point response to Zamyatin's letter to *Literaturnaya Gazeta* – 'From the Editorial Office' – read as follows:

1. E. Zamyatin has written an outrageous parody of communism.
2. This parody was rejected by the Soviet press.
3. E. Zamyatin sent his parody *We* abroad.
4. The Social Revolutionaries were delighted with Zamyatin's parody, having printed it in the *Will of Russia*.
5. Since *We* was written, and since *We* was printed abroad, no special changes for the better have occurred in the work of E. Zamyatin.
6. All the White Guard newspapers are trying hard to shield and protect E. Zamyatin.

27 See the screenplay 'Gunton's Dungeon' with the Introduction by R. Goldt in *Novoe o Zamyatine*, ed. by L. Geller (1997), pp. 147–175.

7. The General Meeting of the VSP (All-Russian Union of Writers) members in Leningrad joined the resolution of the Moscow writers and stated that he did not renounce this parody of his.
8. E. Zamyatin, despite all that has happened, hides behind considerations of chronology and refuses to talk in essence about the writer's work and politics.[28]

Such an 'interpretation' of the novel did not correspond in any way to the series of Zamyatin's works published before the release of *We*, which were in some way preparing the reader for the perception of the complex and controversial text, or to the real content of the novel itself, or to the assessments by many famous Russian and foreign literary figures. This meant that the author was forced to decipher the code of his idea and to formulate his authorial position. In 1921, when the novel was almost completed, Zamyatin wrote about his guesses and insights to Yu. Annenkov:

> Technology is all-powerful, all-blessed. There will be a time when everything is only organization and expediency, when man and nature will turn into a formula, into a keyboard … The men are oiled, polished, and become clock-work , like a six-wheeled hero of the train Timetable. Deviation from the norms is called insanity … And then – from the most delicious latrines everybody will run under the unorganized and inappropriate bushes.

This letter to Annenkov, as is well known, is rated as 'the shortest comic synopsis of the novel *We*'.[29] In an article with an epigraph from *We* – 'About literature, revolution, entropy and so on' – Zamyatin wrote:

> Live literature lives not by yesterday's time, and not by today's, but by tomorrow's. This is a sailor sent up to the mast, where he can see the sinking ships, see the icebergs and the maelstroms, which are not yet visible from the deck … A sailor on the mast is needed in a storm. Now there's a storm, a distress signal coming from different sides.[30]

28 Zamyatin, *Sobranie sochinenie v 5 tomakh*, Vol. 2, pp. 588–589.

29 Yu. P. Annenkov, *Yevgeny Zamyatin* [Vospominaniia], *Literaturnaia ucheba*, No. 5 (1989), pp. 118–119.

30 Zamyatin, *Sobranie sochinenii v 5 tomakh*, Vol. 3, p. 175.

The homogenization of humanity, the general technocratization and mechanization of life, the strength and power of the world's Benefactors – these are the dangers that Zamyatin saw from his writer's mast earlier than other artists did and, relying on the experience of his predecessors, signalled in his work. He warned against a borderline situation, a moment of the deepest human upheavals, and his work sounds today like a tragic symphony of prognostic historiosophical ideas of the writer, psychologist and philosopher.

It is as if the author's own recognition of *We* has not been read: 'the novel *We* is a protest against the impasse in which European-American civilization rests, erasing, mechanizing and motorizing man';[31] it is as if the author's explanation, made in 1932 in Paris in an interview with Frédéric Lefèvre for the magazine *Les Nouvelles Litteraires*, was not heard: Zamyatin said at the time,

> Myopic reviewers saw in this thing no more than a political pamphlet. This, of course, is not true: this novel is a signal about the danger that threatens man, humanity, from the excessive power of machines and the power of the state – no matter what state it is. The Americans, who a few years ago wrote a great deal about the New York edition of my novel, saw in it a reflection of their Fordism, not without a reason. It is very curious that in his latest novel, the famous English fiction writer Huxley develops almost the same ideas and plot positions that are given in *We*. The coincidence, of course, is accidental, but such a coincidence indicates that these ideas are all around us, in the pre-storm air that we breathe.[32]

In the spirit of the worst criticism of the 1920s, the politicized approach of modern criticism to Zamyatin's novel, I think, is the least consistent not only with the statements of the author himself, but also with the objective content of the work. If it were otherwise, the novel, translated into many languages of the world, simply would not be able to survive, drained of blood, cut off from the roots, from the motherland, from national traditions. Modern literary critics cite the facts of Huxley's admission that the first impetus for writing *Brave New World* (1932) was his reading of Zamyatin's novel. They talk about connections of *We* with works of Ray

31 Zamyatin, *Sochineniia*, p. 540.
32 Ibid.

Bradbury, George Orwell and other science-fiction writers of the twentieth century.

'Zamyatin took the place of not only a classic, but also the founder of literature that castigates technocrats with their rationalistic obsession, describing the hell that will reign on earth "when the last hour of nature strikes"', A. Zverev has written. This researcher quotes the Canadian critic Northrop Frye who stated more than 20 years ago that Zamyatin created 'utopian satire … sui generis'. It has become 'a product of the modern technological society, in which the feeling is growing that everything in the world is destined for the same fate and there is nowhere to hide from it'.[33]

The modern reader's interest in the novel is not accidental. The awakening of the self-consciousness of the individual, the understanding of the catastrophism of society, where the individual is oppressed, 'destroyed', the awareness of the ruinous processes of the universalization of ideas and faith, the rationalization of culture and art, and the whole complex of processes leading to the collapse of humanism – this is the pathos of our current reality. And Zamyatin's novel works for us; it terrifies us with the images of the possible future, which are depicted by the artist in a pointedly grotesque, mercilessly cruel logical and artistic conclusion: robots who have lost their souls and spirits, forcibly deprived of the ability and need to think, make decisions, create, remember – figures like the *mankurt*, soulless slaves in the Sarozek legend used by Chingiz Aitmatov in the novel *Buranny Polustanok* (The Day Lasts More Than a Hundred Years). With this appeal to man, Zamyatin's work reaches the spiritual coordinates of great Russian literature with its universal responsiveness and turns first of all to the traditions of Dostoevsky: namely, to his search for the solution to the eternal insoluble contradictions, collisions and conflicts between the individual and society, freedom and bread, freedom and happiness, hatred and love, and the moment and eternity.

Perhaps the novel will most vividly resonate in Zamyatin's own work – this must be mentioned because this internal resonance is of a specific nature – in 'A Story about the Most Important Thing' (1923), in

33 A. Zverev, 'Kogda prob'et poslednii chas prirody…' (Antiutopiya XX veka) *Voprosy literatury*, 1989 No. 1, p. 36.

its unthinkably absurd intersection of separate worlds. First, the world of the lilac bush: eternal, vast and inexplicable with the yellow-pink worm Rhopalocera. The second is the transparent world of iron and the blue sky-bridge over the river, on different banks of which there are the Soviet peasants of Oryol, and the enemy, motley peasants of Kelbuy; they solve their difficult tasks during the period of requisitioning of farm produce (*prodrazverstka*). The third world is cosmic: 'an invisible dark star is rushing towards the Earth from the infinities', which is capable of burning everything to ashes upon its impact on the Earth. In this intersection, these worlds have entered the worlds of the heroes of the story, Kukoverov, Talia and Dorda. Two forces compete with each other: the kite, which 'turns its head to the right and left on its armless shoulders' while hunting for its prey, and the Mother, who gives life and is concerned with giving people air. Here the influence of the poem 'The Kite' by the beloved and highly revered Blok seems indisputable, in which

> with a huge, incendiary force – like the rays of the sun through a biconvex glass – the best of what is in us, Russians, was refracted ... In Blok, we love the best that is in us. In us it burns as a spark, but in him there was a flame; for some it's only a hindrance, it gives them burns, but for him - it burned him down.[34]

However, the creative fates of Zamyatin and Blok were similar, and their creative finale also became significant – work on Scythian problems and on the theme 'East and West': a small poem by Blok 'Scythians' (1918) and Zamyatin's unfinished final novel *The Scourge of God* (*Scythians*). Is there any pattern here? The nature of the creative heritage of these two artists helps to answer the question. Both writers were arrested together in February 1919 in the case of the left Social Revolutionaries; they knew each other well, worked together on the editorial board of *World Literature* and collaborated on the 'Section of Historical Paintings' organized by Gorky at the Petrograd Theatre Department (1919–1921) in order to dramatize world history. And although they had differing views about the 'forces of nature' as an ontological category (Zamyatin) and 'the forces of nature ... both in the sense of nature and in the sense of unbridled human essence'

34 Zamyatin, *Sobranie sochinenii*, Vol. 4, p. 332.

(Blok), they were brought together by their shared feelings toward Russia and their service to the country. In 1927, the Russian philosopher G. P. Fedotov was to write his most interesting literary and philosophical 'commentary experience' to Blok's poetic cycle 'On the Kulikovo Field', and at the very beginning of his research, he would specify that all of Blok's works

> can be perceived as the movement of several basic symbols (perhaps even *a symbol*), which outgrow the plane of art. The symbols of Blok are rooted in the very depths of his personality, and by their unfolding they determine his life and even his death. They have a tragic meaning for him.

Fedotov elaborated:

> However, not only for him. Some of them are no less important to all of us. This is, first of all, the symbol of Russia … The most stable national characteristics have to be revised, rebuilt, because we are dealing with a moving object, with a changing image. The self-consciousness of people directly coincides with its actualization. A new feat, a new sacrifice – and a new sin – entail a new attitude of national consciousness.[35]

In 1932, in a well-known interview with Frédéric Lefebvre for the magazine *Les Nouvelles Litteraires*, Zamyatin explained why the historical novel, with material based on the play *Attila*, held appeal for him:

> If I am interested in this topic, which seems to be nowhere near us, it is only because I believe that we live in an age close to the era of Attila. As then, our time is defined by great wars and social catastrophes. Perhaps tomorrow we will also witness the death of a very high culture that is already on the decline. In addition, let me remind you that the state of Attila stretched from the Volga to the Danube, and that the main forces of his troops were Slavic and Germanic tribes.[36]

By the time this interview was published, Zamyatin had already written three editions of the Scythian play *Atilla: A Tragedy in Four Acts.* He went through a fruitless ordeal with its publication and production in the theatre and actively, as far as his physical strength permitted, created the epic canvas *Scythians*, finally written, only partially, in the form of a small

35 G. P. Fedotov, 'Na pole Kulikovom: Sovremennye zapiski', *Obshhestvenno-politicheskii zhurnal*, Vol. 32 (Paris, 1927), p. 417.

36 Zamyatin, *Sochineniia*, p. 549.

novel *The Scourge of God* about the childhood of Attila, the king of the Huns. For 20 years, since the beginning of 1918 when he wrote the polemical article 'Are They Really the Scythians?', he had been intensely studying the history of Scythia, its role in the final collapse of the Roman Empire and the place of the Slavic peoples, primarily the Russian. Without an opportunity to highlight Zamyatin's position, I will briefly describe only his approach to Attila, in connection with the analysis of which, during the difficulties with the production of the play at the Bolshoi Drama Theatre in Leningrad, he specifically explained:

> The trial of history over Attila took place … the verdict was passed … Attila and the Huns are barbarians, destroyers, villains. The same villains were recently Pugachev, Razin … I was interested in the task of changing the established view of the Huns and Attila – a much larger figure. Such a revision of the old historical concepts is now natural and appropriate and there are grounds for it.[37]

There were indeed reasons for considering Attila as a 'much larger' figure: by the time the writer began his work on the topic of the Hunnish king and the Scythians, Zamyatin's cycle concept of historical development had already advanced on the basis of the theory of entropy and heresy developed by him (see, for example, 'Conversations of a Heretic'), which in some way anticipated the ethnological teaching of L. N. Gumilev on passionarity. However, no less productive and interesting for the reader was Zamyatin's assessment of the 'much larger figure' of Attila as well as the original attitude of the author, which we read in the text of the novel and, as it were, between the lines, to the metaphorical title of the novel *The Scourge of God*, which was traditionally read in a literal sense. This is how it turned out, for example, with N. Y. Danilevsky: on the basis of his concept of local 'cultural and historical types' (civilizations), he spoke of 12 groups. In addition to positive types, the author of the historical and philosophical essay 'Russia and Europe: A View on the Cultural and Political

37 I. E. Erykalova, 'K istorii sozdaniya p'esy E. I. Zamyatina *Atilla*', in *Tvorcheskoe nasledie Evgeniya Zamyatina: vzglyad iz segodnia*. Scientific reports, papers, features, notes, theses, in 14 books; under the supervision of L. V. Polyakova (Tambov: Tambov State University, 1997), Vol. 3; p. 146.

Relations of the Slavic World to the Germanic-Roman world' (published in the magazine *Zarya* in 1869–1871; a separate edition was first published in 1871) singled out entire peoples – 'the scourges of God' – who were destined to play a negative role in history by speeding up the death of civilizations which were on the road to perdition (e.g., according to Danilevsky, such a negative role was played by the Huns, Mongols and Turks).

Twelve years after *Attila*, living far from his homeland and experiencing not just discomfort but obvious long-term despondency because of this , Zamyatin was tackling the general questions of life, which were dictated to him by the time of the Scythian movement and the fate of Attila the king of the Huns. Of course, in the writer's artistic consciousness there is indisputably a correlation of the epochs of the Huns, the 'Scythians' of the fifth century, and the first decades of the twentieth century. But could it be that we are being tendentious, and, at that, not only in the interpretation of the historical concept but also in general in the assessment of the historiosophical ideas of the writer at the end of his creative life, during his work on the novel *The Scourge of God* (*Scythians*)? To justify our stance, it is important to take *time* into account, not only as the change of epochs in Russia and in the world, but also as a long-lasting ontological factor that forms and therefore determines physical, intellectual, psychological and mental, social, cultural and other norms for a person. It easily destroys them as an obvious inevitability, breaking or creating a person as a special microcosm, and together with it marking the boundaries of the emergence and death of epochs. Referring to the events of the fifth century, to the life of specific ethnic groups and their specific representatives, Zamyatin deduced a moral and philosophical formula for the dependence of the human lot on the actions of a person or of all humankind, on the peculiarities of their path to Calvary. Zamyatin, in general, fascinated by the historical Attila, 'Attila Ivanovich', could not have set out to write a farewell novel and make it – a literary and artistic 'scourge', a particularly painful 'whip' for the Huns and their tsar – a kind of ethnic scaffold. On the contrary, the author's plan was to create an epic tragedy.

The 'Scourge of God' is a reference point for the reader as well as a reference point for one of the artistic meanings of the work and obviously the main one: namely, a reference to the biblical story of the betrayal of Jesus

Christ by Judas and the consequences of this betrayal. The plot is based on the Agony of Christ, connected with the events that brought Christ both physical and spiritual suffering in the last days and hours of his earthly life. A special place in the Agony of Christ is occupied by the events that occurred after the Last Supper and in a certain sequence: arrest, trial, flagellation and execution. Among these Passions of the Lord, as we can see, is the scourge, the punishment with the blows of the whip. The scourge is one of the tools – one of the instruments of the Agony of Christ (the theme of the attributes pertaining to the Agony of Christ in Zamyatin's novel still awaits its researcher and is reflected in objects, animals, relics, gestures, facial expressions, etc.). According to the Gospel (John 19:1), after a discussion with Christ in the praetorium, the procurator Pontius Pilate orders him to be scourged. Flagellation – abuse – crowning with a crown of thorns; then the road to Calvary with a heavy cross in his hands, the place of shameful execution by crucifixion; climbing the hill; tearing off clothes; a demonstrative crucifixion at the same time as the killing of two robbers; and a tablet 'The King of the Jews'. On Friday at 3 p.m. Jesus says, 'Father! Into Your hands I commit My spirit.' Longinus (a soldier) strikes Christ in the rib with a spear, and the blood of Jesus is spattered. This is followed by his removal from the cross. They wrap Jesus in a shroud with myrrh and aloe and place him in a coffin in a niche in the mountain. But there is a great earthquake, for an angel from heaven has rolled away a stone from the door of the tomb, and is sitting on it, and tells the weeping women that Christ has risen. The resurrection from the dead takes place at the cost of huge sacrifices as a result of a great catastrophe and is set against its background.

Perhaps the most interesting modern understanding, which contains the contradictory and at the same time surprisingly harmonious complexity of the biblical plot, corresponds to the view, feeling, spiritual and soul state of Zamyatin during his work on the theme of Attila at the time of writing his farewell novel 'The Scourge of God' and which we hear today in the reflection of Pope Francis before reading the Christian prayer 'Angel of the Lord'.

> Jesus never hits. He cleanses with tenderness, with mercy, with love. Mercy is His way of putting things in order. May each of us allow the Lord to come in with His

> mercy – not with a whip, no, with His mercy – to bring order to our hearts. The scourge of Jesus for us is His mercy. Let's open the doors for Him to clean up a little ... anyone is a child of God.[38]

Maybe in *The Scourge of God* this metaphor has a more generalized, even global meaning, which is not only connected with Attila: almost every character in the novel, every participant in the Roman-Byzantine-Hun tragic action, feels the need for Him to come and 'clean up a little'. After all, it is no accident that Zamyatin called this published part of the epic *Scythians*, already carefully spelled out in the expanded plan, not *Atilla*, as it was in the play, but *The Scourge of God*.

But anyway, I believe that Zamyatin's historiosophical concept, laid down by him in the final novel *The Scourge of God*, hastily written first as parts of the epic, is overshadowed by the personal experience, Zamyatin's personal Calvary. It is no accident that in the novel, in the published part of it, this phrase is not personified; moreover, it is absent entirely. The author himself needed the purifying merciful Scourge of God.

In the process of completing *The Scourge of God* and anticipating that it might not take place, Zamyatin, thinking about the closed circle of historical existence and the existence of an individual, relentlessly returned to his childhood, to his parental home in Lebedyan, to the world of the rule of Orthodox traditions and to a life in accordance with their spiritual and moral commandments, and to the world created by his father Ivan Dmitrievich, the 'Pokrov father', the priest of the Church of the Intercession of the Blessed Virgin. And, probably, the novelist would rather agree with L. N. Gumilev regarding his opinion of Attila and his interpretation of the assignment of the metaphorical anthroponym 'the scourge of God' to him rather than with the numerous interpretations of it as a symbol, a sign of unacceptable behavior worthy of the inevitability of punishment, punishment of this heroic Hun.

Gumilev, the author of *The History of the Hunnu People*, wrote:

> Calling Attila 'the scourge of God' is not justified at all.– Of course, he was a strong-willed, intelligent and talented person, but so squeezed by the ethnic situation that

38 Radio Vatikana, *Sibirskaia katolicheskaia gazeta*, 2015, 10 marta.

> for the sake of saving himself and his people, he was forced to go with the flow. The Huns in Pannonia were surrounded on all sides by hostile subjects, so they were led by the majority, who did not like them. On the Catalaunian field, Aetius' advance was held back not by the allies of the Huns, but by their mighty men who died on the battlefield. In Italy, many Huns died of an epidemic in an unaccustomed climate. There was no one to make up for the losses, because the Akatsirs of the Northern Black Sea region were unreliable.[39]

The Scourge of God is a concentrated artistic generalization, the seed of Zamyatin's philosophy and aesthetics, which has yet to be sprouted in the study of his creative heritage.

The historiosophy of *Scythia*, comprehended and developed by Zamyatin throughout almost all of his creative life, can be considered in some way to concentrate many of Zamyatin's world-modeling guesses and reveal the features of his classical aesthetics. The writer's commitment to this problem testified to the constancy of his interests and preferences, to the possibilities and scope of the historical-genetic, sociohistorical material chosen for understanding, to the difficulties and issues of artistic comprehension of the contradictions determined both historically and geographically, and of patterns of Russian life and the peculiarities of the national character. Zamyatin did not blindly reject Western achievements, but throughout his career tried to 'integrate' the specifics of the Russian character and Russian history within the parameters of both Western and Eastern civilizations.

Conclusion

Thomas Mann liked to repeat Goethe's words: 'An artist must have an origin, must know where he came from.'[40] Yevgeny Zamyatin had it and never forgot about it. The sense of Russia, its history and national

39 L. N. Gumilev, *Istoriia naroda khunnu* (Moscow: Institut DI–DIK, 1998), <http://www.litmir.co/br/?b=11329&p=4> (Accessed 22 December 2016).

40 Thomas Mann, *Put' na volshebnuiu goru* (Moscow: Vagrius, 2008), p. 48.

specifics never left him. It is a visible, easily discernible feature of the work and personality of this writer. It was the feeling of the homeland that prevented Zamyatin from finding comfort and pleasure in his foreign life. This feeling determined both the way of behavior and the so-called neutrality, or rather, the sense of national dignity in his writings . And this is not a political position of the artist, but rather a mental, personal and deeply moral one. The never-disappearing feeling of his native land prompted his Zamyatinian 'Scythianism' and predetermined a position of compromise in the polemics of 'Westerners' and 'Slavophiles'.

In the essay 'About My Wives, About Icebreakers and About Russia', first published in French under the title 'Brise-glaces' (Icebreakers)[41] Zamyatin wrote:

> The Russian man must have needed especially strong ribs and especially thick skin, so as not to be crushed by the weight of the unprecedented burden that history has thrown on his shoulders. And especially strong ribs – 'frames', especially thick steel skin, double sides, double bottom – are needed for an icebreaker to withstand a single battle with ice, so as not to be crushed by the ice fields that have squeezed it in their grip. But one massive strength for this would still be not enough: you need a special cunning evasiveness, similar to the Russian 'savvy'. Like Ivanushka the fool in Russian fairy tales, the icebreaker only pretends to be clumsy, and if you pull it out of the water, if you look at it in the dock – you will see that the outline of its steel body is rounder, more feminine than many other ships. In cross-section, the icebreaker looks like an egg – and it is as impossible to crush it as an egg with your hand. It endures such blows, it comes out of such alterations intact and only slightly dented, which would sink any other, more spoiled, more beautifully dressed, more European ship.[42]

Zamyatin always lived with this feeling of Russia. It created a sense of attachment to his native land, formed the personality of the writer, developed his creative personality, provided the intellectual support with which the creator is able to withstand global irritants of the epoch. At the same time, it determined the direction of the artist's creative path and

41 E. I. Zamyatin, 'Brise-glaces', in *Marianne* (Paris) (4 January 1933); in Russian: *Bridges* (Munich) No. 9 (1962), pp. 21–25.

42 Zamyatin, *Sobranie sochinenii v 5 tomakh*, Vol. 4, pp, 348, 351.

its duration in time and stimulated tragic plotlines with their, as a rule, bitterly ironic resolution.

Zamyatin's creative destiny makes it possible to clearly differentiate and formulate the driving potencies of the process of cultural discontinuity/continuity, to analyze its causes and features and to see factors that are objective (history, its components) and subjective (the author's view, the personality of the creator). And it is the subjective, individual-creative determinants that are defining. They not only show the strength of resistance to historically evolving circumstances and situations but also concentrate the characteristics of both the artist's own work and the whole historical and literary stage. P. Florensky was accurate when he called one of his earliest works exactly this: 'The idea of discontinuity as an element of world-contemplation.'[43] Not a worldview, not a world-attitude, not a world perception, but a world-contemplation, with its focus on personal epistemology, a sensory attitude to the comprehension of the world, on the Ego, individual assessment and psychophysical perception of what is happening and, in the end, to a large extent, on the subjective perception of life phenomena and their assessment. And this attitude to the world is primarily a characteristic of the creators of cultural values.

The artificially organized, half a century long, violent historical-literary 'break' in the chain entitled 'the artist and Russian literature of the 1930s to late 1980s', even though it did affect the creative fate of Zamyatin, was unable either to form a real 'break' or to provide at least the appearance of 'discontinuity' in the dynamics of the life of the writer's heritage and the history of the national literature that he represents. Russian classical literature of the twentieth century, born in the cataclysms and the atmosphere of paradoxes of sociopolitical confrontation, found special natural ways to sustain itself through interaction with other creators and even continents. In conditions no less tragic than the beginning of the century, with the dominance of now unstoppable and yet biased literary-critical assessments and hypotheses, the previously 'restrained' classical heritage now provides grounds for reevaluation of many existing, to some extent established, historical and literary ideas about the creative contribution of

43 Florensky, 'The Idea of Discontinuity as an Element of World-Contemplation'.

each great artist as well as about the features and ways of Russian literature throughout the century as an entire and unceasing phenomenon of national culture with its own laws of movement. And this is the way to save it from total oblivion, from death. The demand for cultural phenomena is due to the historically changing needs of human life. Culture not only has its own laws of birth, development and conservation of energy but also of being in demand. This is not a process of resuscitation, but of actualization. The processes of discontinuity occur not so much in culture, but in the life of society and of man with changing epistemological, gnoseological possibilities of the latter. Sometimes though they are taken for the phenomena of culture as such, but this is only an illusion.

Bibliography

Annenkov, Yu. P., *Yevgeny Zamyatin* [Vospominaniia], *Literaturnaia ucheba*, No. 5 (1989).

Berdyaev, N. A., *O russkikh klassikakh* (Moscow: Vysshaya Shkola, 1993).

——— *Smysl istorii* (Moscow: Mysl', 1990).

Boroda, E. V., 'Khudozhestvennye otkrytiia E. I. Zamyatina v kontekste poiskov russkoi literatury vtoroi poloviny XX – nachala XXI vekov', Doctoral dissertation Tambov: Derzhavin Tambov State University, 2011.

——— *Otechestvennaia fantastika kak realizaciia esteticheskogo resursa russkoi literatury nachala XX veka: brat'ia Strugatskie i Evgeny Zamyatin* (Tambov: Izd-vo Pershina R.V., 2007).

Curtis, John, *Issledovaniia romana 'My' za rubezhom: Evgeny Zamyatin, 'My'; Tekst i materialy k tvorcheskoi istorii romana*; Sost., podgot. teksta, publ., komment. i stat'i M. Yu. Lyubimovoi i Dzh. Kurtis (St. Petersburg: Mir, 2011).

Erykalova, I. E., 'K istorii sozdaniia p'esy E. I. Zamyatina Atilla', in *Tvorcheskoe nasledie Evgeniya Zamyatina: vzgliad iz segodnia*. Scientific reports, papers, features, notes, theses in 14 books under the supervision of L. V. Polyakova (Tambov: Tambov State University, 1997).

Fedotov, G. P., 'Na pole Kulikovom: Sovremennye zapiski', *Obshchestvenno-politicheskii zhurnal*, Vol. 32 (1927).

Florensky, P. A., Vvedenie k dissertatsii 'Ideia preryvnosti kak element mirosozertsaniia' [Introduction to the Dissertation 'The Idea of Discontinuity as an Element of World-Contemplation'], *Istoriko-matematicheskie issledovaniia 30* (Moscow: Nauka, 1986), pp. 159–164.

Geller L., *Novoe o Zamyatine*; Sb. statei pod red. L. Gellera (Moscow: Izd-vo MIK, 1997).

——— *Utopiia v zerkale gematrii, ili ezotericheskii modernizm E. Zamyatina; E.I. Zamyatin: pro et contra. Lichnost' i tvorchestvo Evgeniya Zamyatina v otsenke otechestvennykh i zarubezhnykh issledovatelei*; Antologiia Sost. O. V. Bogdanova, M. Yu. Liubimova, Vstup.st.: E. B. Skorospelova, Nauchn. red. T. T. Davydova, L. V. Polyakova (St. Petersburg: NP 'MOPO Apostol'skii gorod – Nevskaia perspektiva', 2014).

Gumilev, L. N., *Istoriia naroda khunnu*; Sost. i obshh. red.: A. I. Kurkcha: V 2-kh kn. Kn. 1 (Moscow: Institut DI–DIK, 1998), <http://www.litmir.co/br/?b=11329&p=4> (Accessed 22 December 2016).

Levi-Strauss, Claude, *Put' masok* (Moscow: Respublika, 2000).

Lossky, V. N., and L. A. Uspensky, *Smysl ikon* (Moscow: Yeksmo; Pravoslavnyi Svyato-Tikhonovskii gumanitarnyi universitet, 2012).

Mann, T., *Put' na igoru* (Moscow: Vagrius, 2008).

Nakano,Yukio. *Istoriia izdaniia romana 'My' na russkom yazyke: po arkhivnym materialam Gleba Struve, Mihaila Karpovicha, i Izdatel'stva imeni Chekhova*; Literaturovedenie na sovremennom etape: Teoriia. Istoriia literatury; Tvorcheskie individual'nosti; Po materialam mezhdunarodnogo kongressa literaturovedov, 1–4 October 2014 g.: V 2-kh kn. Kniga pervaia, Otv. red. i sost. L. V. Polyakova (Tambov: Izd-vo TGU im. G. R. Derzhavina, 2014).

Polyakova, L. V., *Sovremennye otsenki tvorcheskogo naslediia E. Zamyatina, tendentsii podkhodov: polemika; E. I. Zamyatin: Lichnost' i tvorchestvo pisatelia v otsenkakh otechestvennykh i zarubezhnykh issledovatelei*, Sb. st. Sost. O. V. Bogdanova (St. Petersburg: RHGA, 2015).

Pottecher, Frédéric, *Comoedia*, 29 July 1936.

Radio Vatikana, *Sibirskaia katolicheskaia gazeta*, 10 March 2015.

Rozanov, I. N., *Literaturnye reputatsii* (Moscow: Nikitinskie subbotniki, 1928).

Svyatopolk-Mirsky, D. P., *O nyneshnem sostoianii russkoi literatury; Blagonamerennyi* (Brussels: A. E. Izmaylov, 1926) Kn.1. Janv.– févr.

Vert, A., *Literatura v sovetskoi Rossii: Interv'iu s Evgeniem Zamyatinym; Zamyatin, E.I. 'Ya boyus'*; Sost. i komment A. Yu. Galushkina (Moscow: Nasledie, 1999).

Voronsky, A. K., *Izbrannye stat'i o literature* (Moscow, Khudozhestvennaya literatura, 1982).

Yevgeniev-Makximov, V. E., *Ocherk noveishei russkoi literatury: etiudy i kharakteristiki*; Izd. chetvertoe (Moscow: Gos. izdat., 1927).

Zamyatin, Yevgeny, 'Brise-glaces', *Marianne* (Paris), 4 January 1933; in Russian: *Bridges* (Munich) No. 9 (1962), pp. 21–25.

—— *'My': Tekst i materialy k tvorcheskoi istorii romana*; Sost., podgot. teksta, publ., komment. i stat'i M. Ju. Lyubimovoi i Dzh. Kurtis (St. Petersburg: Izd. dom 'Mir#', 2011).

—— 'Pis'ma E. I. Zamyatina raznym adresatam', ed. T. T. Davydova i A. N. Tyurina; Introduction and commentary by T. T. Davydova, *Novy mir*, No. 10 (1996), p. 143.

—— *Povesti, Rasskazy*; Predisl. O. N. Mihailova (Voronezh: Centr.-Chernozemn. kn. izd-vo, 1986).

—— *Sobranie sochinenii v 5 tomakh*; Sost., podgot. teksta i komment. St. S. Nikonenko and A. N. Tyurina (Moscow: Russkaya kniga, 2003).

—— *Sochineniia*; Sost. T. V. Gromova, M. O. Chudakova; Avtor St. M. O. Chudakova; komment. E. Barabanova (Moscow: Kniga, 1988).

—— 'Sovremennaia russkaia literatura', *Lit. ucheba*, No. 5 (1988).

—— *We*, Authorised Translation from the Russian by Gregory Zilboorg (New York: E. P. Dutton, 1924).

Zil'boorg, G., *Predislovie k pervomu izdaniiu Evgeny Zamyatin 'My': Tekst i materialy k tvorcheskoi istorii romana*; Sost., podgot. teksta, publ., komment. i stat'i M. Yu. Lyubimovoi i Dzh. Kurtis (St. Petersburg: Izd. dom 'Mir#', 2011).

Zverev, A., 'Kogda prob'et poslednii chas prirody…' (Antiutopiia XX veka) *Voprosy literatury*, No. 1 (1989).

Translated by Nikita Khmarenko

ELENA TCHOUGOUNOVA-PAULSON

8 'Ah, they'll be driven off to the steppes, my Harlequins…': Pnin the Wanderer as an Incarnation of Russian *Fin de Siècle* Culture Abroad

There is no error more absurd, and yet more rooted in the heart of man, than the belief that his sufferings will promote his spiritual safety.[1]

Writing about Nabokov is easy and hard at the same time (Nabokov himself would definitely make a subtle joke about all the possible impediments regarding this situation). On the one hand, he is a vivid example of a standard, showing 'how a genius in exile would find his way to success (both in literary and mundane worlds) despite all the obstacles, some of which were mind-boggling enough on their own', but on the other, is he not that type of person with whom you would never imagine associating yourself no matter how hard you tried? Both perceptions of him seem to be valid in one way or another, but there is one thing that could potentially link them together: the path Nabokov chose and how he did it.

As an inseparable part of the first crumbling, then fading and finally vanishing world of Russian gentry, the Old World (*Старый Міръ*, *Stary Mir*) with its idle tea parties and long walks around the once grand and slightly shabby estates (*усадьбы*, *usad'by*) somewhere in rural Russia, Nabokov had never reshaped himself according to the demands of the new world he unwittingly found himself in, being thrown out of what was once his country and what then became something completely different and alien to him. A resident of Berlin, a student at Trinity College,

1 Charles Robert Maturin, *Melmoth the Wanderer* (London: R. Bentley, 1892), Vol. 2, p. 123.

Cambridge, a lecturer at Cornell, a Montreux local – he was unequivocally Russian par excellence, with all the benefits and burdens this conferred on him (and the burdens unquestionably prevailed). That is why the *ostranenie* (defamiliarization) phenomenon in his writings is so uncanny and so mesmerizing: he reinvents his Russianness every time he writes, and the Russia of his imaginarium is always semi-*terra incognita* (Zembla, Estoty). And in this sense, based upon recollection and relinquishing, *Pnin* as a novel is a perfect example of this reinvention. Indeed, in it, as in a droplet of water, one can see the interplay of the old and the new or, more precisely, how the cultural offshoots of the Old World find their way in the new one. In other words, it reveals how culture perpetuates itself, surviving and perishing at the same time. Pnin is a mini-saga whose main plot concerns an individual with the overwhelming burden of the (crumbling) Old World on his shoulders, who is wandering around the new lands, recollecting – and reinventing – himself altogether, and rebuilding those parts of the fallen universe into something unquestionably new.

Pnin was the fourth novel, which some critics call 'an early campus novel',[2] written by Vladimir Nabokov in English in 1957, alongside *The Real Life of Sebastian Knight* (1940), *Bend Sinister* (1947) and, of course, *Lolita* (1954). The publishing history of *Pnin* is as intricate and full of confusion as the main character, Professor of Russian Literature Timofey Pavlovich Pnin, is himself. Nabokov started to work on the text of *Pnin* when he was already writing *Lolita*: as the author said once, *Pnin* was a 'brief, sunny escape' from 'Lolita's intolerable spell'.[3] Literary critic David Lodge mentioned, in his review *Exiles in a Small World*, that

> in the summer of 1953, when (on sabbatical leave from Cornell) he was drawing at last towards the end of this novel, Nabokov wrote a short story called 'Pnin', about

2 David Lodge, 'Exiles in a Small World', *The Guardian*, Saturday, 8 May 2004, <http://www.theguardian.com/books/2004/may/08/classics.vladimirnabokov> (Accessed 16 May 2021).

3 Aleksandar Hemon, 'Fiction Podcast: Aleksandar Hemon Reads Vladimir Nabokov', *New Yorker*, 1 December 2014, <http://www.newyorker.com/books/page-turner/fiction-podcast-aleksandar-hemon-reads-vladimir-nabokov> (Accessed 15 February 2021).

> the comical misadventures of an expatriate Russian professor on his way to deliver a lecture to a women's club in a small American town. He created the new character partly as a relief from the dark obsessive world of Humbert Humbert.[4]

At first, *Pnin* was just a collection of essays that Nabokov published 'more than fifty times in the pages of the New Yorker',[5] and consisted of the separate chapters 'Pnin's Day', 'Pnin', 'Victor Meets Pnin' and 'Pnin Gives a Party'. From the very beginning, 'Pnin's Day' was portrayed as

> a day in the life of the Russian professor, Pnin, at an American college. He has had trouble finding suitable living quarters but now he enjoys living in a rented room in the Clements' house. Prof. and Mrs. Clements are visiting their daughter in the West. Pnin goes to his classes, and when they are thru he sits in his favorite spot in the library doing research for the 'Petite Histoire' of Russian culture he is writing. In the evening he sees some Chaplin movies which he does not understand, and then some films made in Russia in the late forties, which brings tears of homesickness to his eyes. He goes to bed but is awakened by the returning Clements family, the daughter almost rushes into his room.[6]

Eventually, Nabokov turned this fragment into chapter three of his novel: the structure of *Pnin* was changed, and the author decided to not kill his character at the very end of the novel.

It is curious that *Pnin* is Nabokov's thirteenth novel, which makes it somehow significant: an unlucky number for a work describing the unlucky (not to mention miserable) life of a Russian émigré in the United States, Professor Pnin, and his life full of struggles, misunderstandings, absent-mindedness and sudden obstacles. No wonder that at first Nabokov was going to name the novel *My Poor Pnin*; however, later he changed its title reducing it just to the name of the character.

4 Lodge, 'Exiles in a Small World'.

5 Jon Michaud, 'Eighty-Five from the Archive: Vladimir Nabokov', *New Yorker*, 26 February 2010, <http://www.newyorker.com/books/double-take/eighty-five-from-the-archive-vladimir-nabokov> (Accessed 25 April 2021).

6 Vladimir Nabokov, 'Pnin's Day', *New Yorker*, 23 April 1955, <http://www.newyorker.com/magazine/1955/04/23/pnins-day> (Accessed 6 May 2021).

So, what is still so special about Pnin as a character and, generally, *Pnin* as a novel? And could Pnin's life, its ups and downs, its adventurous (or rather mis-adventurous) core be somehow compared with the real (non-literary) average experience of the modern Russian immigrant – educated, neurotic, often depressed (or maybe not) and lonely – who is about to start everything (literally, everything: speaking a new language, getting a new job, making a variety of relationships with people) from scratch?

As it turns out, Pnin is indeed a peculiar character. In Nabokov studies, it is a common view to see him as a Quixotic maverick: for example, Stephen Casmier in his article 'A Speck of Coal Dust: Vladimir Nabokov's Pnin and the Possibility of Translation' notes thus:

> It is fairly common knowledge that Vladimir Nabokov hatched the idea for the novel that became *Pnin* (1957) while teaching *Don Quixote* to students at Harvard in 1951. In his *Lectures on Don Quixote* (posthumously published in 1983), Nabokov puzzles over questions concerning the fidelity of the author to his creations and the translation and appropriation of these creations over time by the reading public. Something about *Don Quixote* and its eponymous character, Nabokov observes, remains irreducible and immutable as they withstand centuries of translation and uncountable 'multiplications'. In *Don Quixote*, he says, we 'are confronted by an interesting phenomenon: a literary hero losing gradually contact with the book that bore him; leaving his fatherland, leaving his creator's desk and roaming space after roaming Spain. In result, Don Quixote is greater today than he was in Cervantes's womb. He has ridden for three hundred and fifty years through the jungles and tundras of human thought – and he has gained in vitality and stature' (p. 112). In *Pnin*, Nabokov engenders such a figure. This novel offers us a reading of *Don Quixote* that includes a theory of translation that responds to our poststructuralist, postmodern world where everything is secondary, constructed, and inauthentic and all efforts at faithful translation are at best quixotic. Through its cavalier play with ontological and epistemological boundaries – recreating author as character while invoking physical suffering and the immutable tragedy of the Holocaust – Nabokov creates a character who also 'leaves his creator's desk' despite attempts by the narrative to capture, limit, translate, ridicule, and appropriate him.[7]

Another Nabokov researcher, Brian Boyd, also describes Pnin as

7 Stephen Casmier, 'A Speck of Coal Dust: Vladimir Nabokov's Pnin and the Possibility of Translation', *Nabokov Studies*, Vol. 8 (2004), pp. 71–86.

> Nabokov's reply to Cervantes. It is no accident that the book's risible name, that 'preposterous little explosion', almost spells 'pain'. Pnin has become as much a source of mirth on the Waindell campus as the Knight of the Mournful Countenance once was in old Castile. [...] He has a complex inner existence Don Quixote is never allowed, and his pain suddenly matters. Mistake-prone Pnin comes to sum up all human mishaps and misfortunes, the strange blend of comedy and tragedy in all human life.[8]

Pnin's attitude, to face all difficulties not exactly fearlessly but openly, indeed reminds us of Cervantes's iconic character, but still not quite: Pnin as a personality is not imaginary in the way he functions, because it is exactly what each of us, the readers of the novel, could imagine for ourselves, as if we were not good enough for the current (and tough) circumstances. But the main thing is that Pnin, with 'his memory, with all the lights on and all the masks of the mind a-miming, toward the days of his fervid and receptive youth (in a brilliant cosmos that seemed all the fresher for having been abolished by one blow of history)'[9] is a figure from the past – from a time that can be considered as not exactly suitable for modern life, mobile and energetic (remember, the plot is set in the 1940s). Pnin's youth is the Russian Silver Age, *fin de siècle* era, to which he definitely belonged:

> Pnin came from a respectable, fairly well-to-do, St Petersburg family. His father, Dr Pavel Pnin, an eye specialist of considerable repute, had once had the honour of treating Leo Tolstoy for a case of conjunctivitis. Timofey's mother, a frail, nervous little person with a waspy waist and bobbed hair, was the daughter of the once famous revolutionary Umov (rhymes with 'zoom off') and of a German lady from Riga.[10]

And this narrative Nabokov recreates in chapter five, jokingly putting his own name among the Russian émigré authors:

> This was the first time Pnin was coming to The Pines but I had been there before. Émigré Russians – liberals and intellectuals who had left Russia around 1920 – could be found swarming all over the place. You would find them in every patch of speckled shade, sitting on rustic benches and discussing émigré writers – Bunin,

8 Brian Boyd, *Nabokov: The American Years* (Princeton, NJ: Princeton University Press, 1991), p. 272.

9 Vladimir Nabokov, *Pnin* (New York: Doubleday, 1957), p. 12.

10 Ibid., p. 29.

> Aldanov, Sirin; lying suspended in hammocks, with the Sunday issue of a Russian-language newspaper over their faces in traditional defence against flies; sipping tea with jam on the veranda; walking in the woods and wondering about the edibility of local toadstools [...]
>
> Pnin and Chateau, both born in the late nineties of the nineteenth century, were comparative youngsters.[11]

In this sense, Pnin's queerness, awkwardness, nervousness and timidity become clearer: he belongs to an era when being eccentric was part of the lifestyle – let us recall the literary movements of that period (*fin de siècle*) and, especially, Russian Symbolism. The *Philosophy of All-Unity* and the conception of the *Eternal Feminine* (also *das Ewig-Weibliche*) created by Vladimir Solovyov and his understanding of the role of the symbol in art were the theoretical basis and semantic impulse of Russian Symbolism, which defined its main tasks as cultural inclusiveness, synthesis of arts, integration of actual reality and personal spiritual experience. Russian Symbolists worked on renewal of genres, introduced new principles of making poetry and reformed art and theatre. In theoretical Symbolist works, new non-classical models of the universe with recurrent time were created. This gave an opportunity to recreate the distinctive features of ancient eras and different types of thinking. Somehow, a new type of personality was also created: a sensitive, intellectual man whose life was dedicated to the arts and academic research. The October Revolution became a critical point for such people, noble and relatively wealthy: people like young Pnin – and the young Nabokov as well. Their immaturity, sensitivity and utter impracticality were life-threatening for many of them. Paradoxically, however, this type of individuality, which might have been totally exterminated, survived – primarily, outside post-revolutionary Russia. Were they the same? Was Pnin the same? No, they – and he – were not: going through tragic ordeals (departure from his native country, endless wanderings and the death of his first love, Mira, the daughter of Professor Belochkin, at Buchenwald), Pnin was transformed into a sufferer, but still, an odd one. He is a miserable *harlequinesque* hero (Nabokov describes Pnin

11 Ibid., p. 88.

as a person with *spindly legs*) who failed almost everywhere. He turned into a character who could be compared with many classical examples of weird and lonely strangers, such as the already-mentioned Don Quixote or the already-quoted Melmoth the Wanderer. Pnin is tongueless (his English is broken and limited), which also could be regarded as a sign of despair – but a funny one. As Nabokov always does with his favorite characters, Pnin's hopelessness looks – and feels – carnivalesque. Let us hear one of the best-known fragments of the novel that describes Pnin's futile linguistic attitudes:

> The organs concerned with the production of English speech sounds are the larynx, the velum, the lips, the tongue (that punchinello in the troupe), and last, but not least, the lower jaw; mainly upon the jaw's overenergetic and somewhat ruminant motion did Pnin rely when translating in class passages in the Russian grammar or some poem by Pushkin. If Pnin's Russian was music, his English was murder. He had enormous difficulty ('dzeefeecooltsee', in Pninian English) with depalatization, never managing to remove the extra Russian moisture from 't's and 'd's before the vowels he so quaintly softened. His explosive 'hat' ('I never go in a hat, even in winter') differed from the common American pronunciation of the adjective 'hot' (typical of Waindell townspeople, for example) only by its briefer duration, and thus sounded very much like the German verb 'hat' (has). Long 'o's with him inevitably became short ones, his 'no' acquiring for the nonce the rounded orifice of a British or Bostonian 'o' in 'not', and this was accentuated by his Russian trick of duplicating the simple negative. ('May I give you a lift, Mr. Pnin?' 'No-no, I have only two paces from here.') He did not possess (nor was he aware of this lack) any long 'oo'; all he could muster when called upon to utter 'noon' was the lax 'o' sound of the German 'nun' ('I have no classes in afternun on Tuesday. Today is Tuesday.')[12]

This dark and witty humor, however, makes Pnin neither weak nor unpleasant: this is a quirk Nabokov creates on purpose. Pnin is strange, but not ominous, unlike Nabokov's other character Humbert Humbert. This is why it is hard to disagree with the description of the novel made by Charles Poore in the *New York Times* that

> it is also an original, heartbreakingly funny book. Then Edmund Wilson weighs in with the thought that Mr. Nabokov's writing is something like Kafka, something

12 Ibid., p. 34.

> like Proust, and 'probably something like Gogol'. No one, so far, has brought up a comparison with Chekhov, but I imagine this will come.

Mr. Nabokov writes with a remarkable blend of realism and fantasy and the ranging humor of delightedly observed eccentricities in everyone, himself included. Telling the story of Pnin, he digresses – if anything can be called a digression in this hilarious triumph of free association – to matter-of-fact sketches about his own and Pnin's adventures that seem so romantic in Pnin's eyes. The faithless lady who married Pnin before going on to other liaisons and marriages has a history that only Mr. Nabokov can finally untangle. Meantime, the bumbling, jubilant, humble and arrogant Pnin marches onward, if not always upward, with the arts.

> *Pnin*, as a novel, belongs to the looking-glass literature by émigrés about other émigrés in their infinitely compartmented exile. Luckily, it is not written for them alone. We can all share its universal aspects of the human comedy. [13]

Pnin's shout in chapter two (after his ex-wife Liza's visit) '*I haf nofing left, nofing, nofing!*'[14] could portray not only his physical and psychological instability but also more generally his unreadiness to face the new – obscure and dramatic – future. The audience feels sympathy for Pnin and at the same time laughs at him. Pnin's misery, expressed in this dramatic and comic way, reminds us of Holy Fools (*юродивые*, *yurodivye*) and their sufferings (Maturin, who wrote about his Wanderer, Melmoth, once said that 'It is actually possible to become amateurs in suffering'[15]): they also had nothing – and their impersonation was also as eccentric as you only can imagine.

Pnin is one of the few novels in which Nabokov explicitly demonstrates his concern for the main character: neither with Humbert Humbert nor with Professor Kinbote from *Pale Fire* does he do this. It is conceivable that, in this sense, Pnin is a creature in transition between the vile and seductive Humbert Humbert and the megalomaniac Professor Kinbote. As

13 Charles Poore, 'Books of the Times', *New York Times*, 7 March 1957.

14 Nabokov, *Pnin*, p. 32.

15 Maturin, *Melmoth the Wanderer*, p. 311.

Professor Gennady Barabtarlo, the translator of *Pnin* into Russian, pointed out (and we agree with him completely),

> Pnin has always had a gam of admirers who delight in the hilarious aspect of the book and regard it as poignant yet 'warm', even though they may be indifferent to other books by the same author. Seventy-seven reviews appeared in English alone during the first six months since its separate publication in 1957, most of them momentary, but, in general, Pnin has fallen under somewhat less vigorous study than Nabokov's other English novels, perhaps because of its seemingly (but deceptively) straight sailing.
>
> Placed chronologically between Humbert and Kinbote, and in sharp contraposition to both, Professor Pnin has little command of the English idiom, and his verbal gawkiness, combined with a bent for divagations, spins fabulously amusing situations.[16]

Pnin's finale looks like an Eternal Recurrence encrypted into the looped plot: Pnin has left his college for something obscure, and the chairman of the department where Pnin worked has started telling his story to the narrator. Does it mean that Nabokov is ready to kill off his professor? We doubt it. Although the author did say in chapter one that

> some people – and I am one of them – hate happy ends. We feel cheated. Harm is the norm. Doom should not jam. The avalanche stopping in its tracks a few feet above the cowering village behaves not only unnaturally but unethically.[17]

More likely, he prepares Pnin for another adventure, or another wandering, that might be more fortunate and courageous, as he does it with his Harlequins in the poem of the same name:

> Ах, угонят их в степь, Арлекинов моих.
> В буераки, к чужим атаманам!
> Геометрию их, Венецию их
> Назовут шутовством и обманом.

16 Gennady Barabtarlo, 'A Resolved Discord (Pnin)' *Aerial View: Essays on Nabokov's Art and Metaphysics* (New York: Peter Lang, 1993), <https://www.libraries.psu.edu/nabokov/barab21.htm#FOOT0>) (Accessed 20 March 2021).

17 Nabokov, *Pnin*, p. 25.

Ah, they'll be driven off to the steppes, my Harlequins.
Into the gullies, to other people's chieftains!
Their geometry, their Venice
Will be called buffoonery and deceit.[18]

Maybe we all – we, who live so far from Russia – also will face it. Who knows? Let us see.

Conclusion

We completely understand that ours is one of many attempts to explore what is behind the title and the plot of this most *fin de siècle* novel by Nabokov.[19] Its modernist/émigré performativity puts *Pnin* in a special place among Nabokov's works: first, because *Pnin*, despite a fairly straightforward narrative, is still a tricky story with layers of flashbacks, the unfolding of which is a non-trivial task (Nabokov never ceases to amaze his reader in this sense), and second, because *Pnin* is perhaps one of the best (if not *the* best) intimate portrayals of the complex metaphysics of the first wave of Russian emigration. In other words, Nabokov's Pnin is the epitome of a Russian émigré who left his *Oekumene* (i.e., pre-revolutionary Russia) in order to preserve its enduring value in his most precious, long-lasting memories, which can be quite challenging. Reading about his hardships and failures gives the audience a glimpse of the transformative idea of *aerial toll houses*, or *mitarstva*. This term came from Eastern Orthodox exegetics, and it means a long and complicated journey by a soul that has left a body, to Heaven or otherwise. Pnin as a forlorn figure without the

18 Vladimir Nabokov, *Smotri na Arelkinov!* (Moscow: Azbuka-Klassika, 2010).

19 For everyone who is interested in recent sources about Nabokov, we would recommend, for example: *Vladimir Nabokov in Context*, ed. David M. Bethea and Siggy Frank (Cambridge: Cambridge University Press, 2020); *Insomniac Dreams: Experiments with Time by Vladimir Nabokov*, ed. Gennady Barabtarlo (Princeton: Princeton University Press, 2017) and *The Garland Companion to Vladimir Nabokov*, ed. Vladimir E. Aleksandrov (London: Routledge, 2014).

help of comforting delusions who, despite all the ordeals, perseveres in upholding his magnanimity, is another way of thinking that his wanderings, making a full circle in the novel, would find closure one day. And it gives us hope: after losing everything – and everyone – from that tremendous abandoned universe, the Russian Atlantis, Pnin the Wanderer continues to move on, to progress, to reestablish himself, evolving into a new character, whose driving force will never cease, because historical continuity is fair and knows better.

Bibliography

Barabtarlo, Gennady, 'A Resolved Discord (Pnin)', in *Aerial View: Essays on Nabokov's Art and Metaphysics* (New York: Peter Lang, 1993).

Boyd, Brian, *Nabokov: The American Years* (Princeton, NJ: Princeton University Press, 1991).

Casmier, Stephen, 'A Speck of Coal Dust: Vladimir Nabokov's Pnin and the Possibility of Translation', *Nabokov Studies*, Vol. 8 (2004), pp. 71–86.

The Garland Companion to Vladimir Nabokov, ed. Vladimir E. Aleksandrov (London: Routledge, 2014).

Hemon, Aleksandar, 'Fiction Podcast: Aleksandar Hemon Reads Vladimir Nabokov', *New Yorker*, 1 December 2014, <http://www.newyorker.com/books/page-turner/fiction-podcast-aleksandar-hemon-reads-vladimir-nabokov> (Accessed 15 February 2023). *Insomniac Dreams: Experiments with Time by Vladimir Nabokov*, ed. Gennady Barabtarlo (Princeton, NJ: Princeton University Press, 2017).

Lodge, David, 'Exiles in a Small World', *The Guardian*, Saturday, 8 May 2004, <http://www.theguardian.com/books/2004/may/08/classics.vladimirnabokov> (Accessed 9 March 2023).

Maturin, Charles Robert, *Melmoth the Wanderer* (London: R. Bentley, 1892).

Michaud, Jon, 'Eighty-Five from the Archive: Vladimir Nabokov', *New Yorker*, 26 February 2010, <http://www.newyorker.com/books/double-take/eighty-five-from-the-archive-vladimir-nabokov> (Accessed 9 March 2023).

Nabokov, Vladimir, *Pnin* (New York: Doubleday, 1957).

——— 'Pnin's Day', *New Yorker*, 23 April 1955, <http://www.newyorker.com/magazine/1955/04/23/pnins-day> (Accessed 16 March 2023).

——— *Smotri na Arelkinov!* (Moscow: Azbuka-Klassika, 2010).
Poore, Charles, 'Books of the Times', *New York Times*, 7 March 1957.
Vladimir Nabokov in Context, ed. David M. Bethea and Siggy Frank (Cambridge: Cambridge University Press, 2020).

ELENA V. GLUKHOVA

9 Cultural Transfer and Continuity: Gothic in the Russian 'Estate Text'

In this chapter, we would like to consider the adaptation and assimilation mechanism of Western European Gothic-related literature plots, characters and themes that are borrowed by Russian culture. The problem of Gothic style in Russian literature is quite extensive and has repeatedly become the subject of modern research. We believe that it is reasonable to take heed of the formation and subsequent change of the Gothic tradition in Russian culture based on the Russian estate text. According to the French scholar Michel Espagne, who proposed the term 'cultural transfer', in the process of transferring from one cultural situation to another, any object falls into a different context and acquires a new meaning. From this point of view, cultural exchange is not a circulation of objects and ideas as they are, but rather their unceasing reinterpretation, reconsideration and re-denotation.

The Russian estate, as a semiotic phenomenon, is unique. On the one hand, this phenomenon is unparalleled; on the other hand, it undoubtedly exists within the framework of the Western European tradition. So, the architecture of the city and of the country noble estate from the end of the eighteenth century follows French classicism – both strictly in architectural execution and in interior design. After the French regular garden of the Versailles type, the Russian estate borrows the tradition of the English landscape garden.

It is safe to say that the Russian estate bears the imprint of the culture of a particular era – in architecture, interior design, composition of colors to be used in the garden and the like. Instead of strict adherence to the classical canon – with the English landscape garden or a garden and park ensemble in the French manner – a variety of architectural styles dictated by the taste of the landowner is used. So, this is how estates in the Art Nouveau style (especially the city mansion) appear, peacefully coexisting with Russian pseudo-archaic and Western European neo-Gothic styles. In turn, similar trends are observed in literature: the Russian estate text reflects the peculiarities of the literary trends of the nineteenth to early twentieth centuries, which consistently answered the problems of Classicism and then the Romantic style, Realism and Modernism in the broad sense. Simultaneously with the emergence of the Gothic style in architecture, at the end of the eighteenth century in England and Germany, the 'Gothic' novel also gained more and more popularity. Horace Walpole's novel *The Castle of Otranto* (1764) became a model of the Gothic canon in literature, marking the beginning of a series of imitations. It should be noted that in addition to the actual literary influence, Walpole's Strawberry Hill estate was a kind of architectural model for copying the Gothic style; the writer himself designed it using elements of medieval castle architecture (fancy turrets, lancet windows), thereby establishing the neo-Gothic style of the English estate.

Russian literary Gothic follows its own path in the development of the Western European canon by creating its own national version.[1] In the era of Modernism, mystical, esoteric and 'diabolical' motifs and plots, equally typical for both Symbolism and Gothic narrative, go beyond literature into the field of life-building (cf., for example, the novel *The Fiery Angel* by V. Ya. Bryusov and his mystical life-building constructions with Andrei Bely and Nina Petrovskaya).[2] A vivid example of this is the biography of the writer Leonid Andreev, whose artistic method is not usually considered as inheriting the principles of literary Gothic; nevertheless, his stories 'Red Laugh', 'He: An Unknown's Story' and 'The Abyss', which belong rather to the field of poetics of supernatural horror,[3] fulfill the Gothic discourse

1 S. V. Khachaturov, 'Gothic Taste', in *Russian Fiction of the Eighteenth Century* (Moscow: Progress-traditsiya, 1999).

2 On Gothic tradition in the novel by V. Ya. Bryusov, see the article by V. Ya. Malkina, 'Gothic Tradition and the Historical Novel: "The Fiery Angel" by V. Ya. Bryusov', in *The Gothic Tradition in Russian Culture* (Moscow: RSUH, 2008), pp. 250–266.

3 For contemporaries writing about the poetics of fear and of horror in Leonid Andreev's work, see G. N. Boyeva, 'The Poetics of Horror in the Works of

as a 'memory of the genre'. In 1908, Andreev built a dacha estate called 'White Night' (formerly called 'Villa Advance') in Vimmelsuu (Finland). Externally, the house resembled an English cottage, made in the style of 'northern Art Nouveau': built of huge logs, partially faced with red brick, with numerous chimneys and a tiled roof; 'the inhabitants of the local villages called it Pirulinna, which means 'devil's castle' in Finnish.[4]

The interior of Andreev's dacha estate was deliberately decorated in a medieval style: in the study, there is a marble fireplace and a high carved wooden chair, made according to the sketches of the writer. A huge oak table, rough-hewn benches and a dark-wood stool on a wolfskin rug near the fireplace also give the impression of a medieval Gothic setting. The low ceiling, whitewashed, with tarred rafters and the walls decorated with wainscot wood paneling, hung with copies of the gloomy allegorical paintings of Goya, were created by the owner of the estate – all this was supposed to evoke the atmosphere of a medieval castle. According to the memoirs of Andreev's contemporary S. G. Kara-Murza:

> In this large, uncomfortable office, the owner himself was eerie, and when he wrote his terrible things at night, L. N. was afraid to be alone, and his wife sat with him all night without sleep, wrapped in a warm foulard.[5]

The Russian estate literary topos is flexible and multifaceted; depending on the intention of the narrator, it carefully nurtures the heartwarming national patriarchal paradise of the noble abode. Then, on the contrary, the

---

Leonid Andreev: The Receptive Aspect', Scholarly Notes of Petrozavodsk State University: Philological Sciences, Vol. 2, No. 3 (May 2015), pp. 66–70 and S. Rolet, 'Fear in the Works of Leonid Andreev', in *Semiotics of Fear*, ed. Nora Buks and Francis Kont (Moscow: Russian Institute 'Europe', 2005), pp. 168–171. However, on the memory of the Gothic novel genre in Andreev's poetics, no particular research was discovered.

4 G. N. Boyeva 'On the House as a Life-Building Practice of Modernity: A House of Leonid Andreev on the Black River', *Press and Word of St Petersburg* (St. Petersburg: Petersburg Reads, 2012), part 1: *Bookwork: Cultural Studies; A Collection of Research Papers*, St. Petersburg: SPSUITD, 2013), p. 184.

5 A. L. Sobolev, 'From the Memoirs of S.G. Kara-Murza: 1, *Literature Fact*, No. 5 (2017), p. 84.

dying and abandoned world of the dilapidated estate becomes overgrown with negative connotations, contributing to the expansion of the Gothic narrative. Assimilating with Russian realities, the Western European Gothic castle is replaced by the topos of a Russian estate. The chronotope of the estate space has a special status of time span, establishing the connection between real and historical time; the estate in Russian culture has the ontological status of a life cycle, where the space–time relations are organized differently rather than in conventionally combinatorial models, being essentially a heterotopia.

A significant part of the modern research literature is devoted to the analysis of works of Russian classical prose with the Gothic tradition: 'The Island of Bornholm' (1793) by N. M. Karamzin, 'The Castle of Wenden' (1821) by A. A. Bestuzhev-Marlinsky and 'The Kiev Witches' (1833) by O. M. Somov; the plots and motifs of Gothic prose are traced in the texts of A. S. Pushkin, M. Yu. Lermontov, I. S. Turgenev, F. M. Dostoevsky and L. N. Tolstoy.[6] To a much lesser extent, this phenomenon is studied in the literature of Modernism of the late nineteenth to the early twentieth century. Some works are devoted to the short story 'The Black Monk' by A. P. Chekhov,[7] stories by I. Bunin[8] and novels by F. Sologub.[9] The literary

6 From a variety of research works on this issue, one may note the collection *The Gothic Tradition in Russian Literature*, introduced by N. D. Tamarchenko (Moscow: RSUH Centre, 2008).

7 A. Komaromi, 'An Unknown Force: Gothic Realism in Chekhov's *The Black Monk*', in *The Gothic-Fantastic in Nineteenth-Century Russian Literature* (Amsterdam; Atlanta, 1999), pp. 257–276; A. Guirivenko, 'Literary Archetypes of the Monk in Chekhov's Prose', in *Young Researchers* 3 (Moscow, 1998), pp. 70–74; N. A. Shipachyova, 'The Mystic and Enigmatic in A. P. Chekhov's Story "The Black Monk"', in *Works of A.P. Chekhov: Poetics, Origins, Influence* (Taganrog, 2000), pp. 117–124.

8 O. G. Talalayeva, 'I. A. Bunin's Prose and Gothic Tradition in Russian Literature', *Tambov State University Review*, Vol. 7, No. 99 (2011), pp. 165–171.

9 M. A. Lvova, 'On the Composition of *The Created Legend* by F. Sologub: The Issue of Alchemic Reminiscence in Novel Structure Organization', *Yaroslavl Pedagogical Bulletin*, No. 1 (2001), <http://vestnik.yspu.org/?page=2000_4> (Accessed 1 October 2020); J. Syta, 'Chronotope and Gothic Tradition in the Symbolic Novels of F. Sologub: Between Condition and Lifetime', *Uzhorod National University Herald: Philology Series*, Vol. 2, No. 38 (2017), pp. 61–65.

process of the turn of the century brings significant changes to the genre structure; there is also a reinterpretation of the boundaries of the Gothic canon. First of all, this was due to the rejection of the mandatory novel structure. With regard to an aspect that thrills us, this process is also typical for the literature of the nineteenth century – small prose forms are more easily adapted to the reader, demonstrating the forms of the Gothic in the small genres of the novella and short story, where the action and plot differ in the brevity and concentration of the series of events. See, for example, 'The Ring' (1831) by E. A. Boratynsky; 'The Sylph' (1837) and 'Cosmorama' (1840) by V. Odoevsky; 'The Ghoul' (1841), 'The Family of the Vourdalak' (1839) and 'Meeting in Three Hundred Years' (1839) by A. K. Tolstoy.[10]

Since we use the term 'Gothic literary canon', we should explain its meaning. Modern researchers[11] understand it as a special set of factors that refer to plot and composition. If there are several characteristics found together in the text, we can say that a Gothic narrative is present: a specific chronotope; a distinctive introduction, referring to the Middle Ages; exotic places (a castle, an abandoned house, a gloomy estate); a terrible mystery, as a plot-forming event; the participation of supernatural forces in the development of the plot; a focus on authenticity; distinctive female images (female vampire, witch, lamia, succubus, sylph); the motif of selling the soul to the devil; the motifs of fear, horror; the irrational.

A. K. Tolstoy's story 'The Ghoul' (1841) and the continuing parts of the trilogy 'The Family of the Vourdalak' and 'The Meeting in Three Hundred Years' are a rather rare phenomenon of concentrated factors of Gothic narrative in Russian literature of the mid-nineteenth century: there is a terrible family secret, a vampire ball and the secret of a portrait of a beautiful stranger. In 1890, the novel was republished with a preface by the philosopher and poet V. S. Solovyov, in which he described the story as 'a

10 M. P. Odessky, 'Vampires in the Early Prose of A. K. Tolstoy: Experience of Creating Plot Topic', *Literature Questions*, No. 6 (2010), pp. 207–241.

11 V. Ya. Malkina, and A. A. Polyakova, 'The "Canon" of the Gothic Novel and Its Types', in *The Gothic Tradition in Russian Literature* (Moscow: RSUH, 2008), pp. 15–32.

surprisingly complex fantastic pattern on the canvas of ordinary reality'.[12] The plot of the story of A. K. Tolstoy's 'The Ghoul' was inspired by the novel 'The Vampyre' (1819) by the English writer John William Polidori, which was published in Russian translation in Moscow in 1828. Within the plot of Tolstoy's story, three independent plotlines can be distinguished, where the main characters are representatives of different generations of the Ostrovich family: the Marfa–Ambrose plotline, the Praskovya Andreevna–Pietro d'Urgina plotline and the Dasha–Runevsky plotline. These plotlines represent the story of the curse of the old Hungarian Ostrovich family. The lack of an objective assessment of the narrative offers the reader a choice among three points of view: the first, all the events that occur with the hero can be explained logically (Vladimir); the second, unquestionable trust in the unreal (Rybarenko); the third, genuine existence of supernatural forces cannot be established in a single way (Runevsky). The plot-forming significance of the story is played by the topos of an old Russian estate, built according to the project of an unknown Italian architect, while the artistic space of the estate is organized according to fantastic canons. An old Italian palazzo is a clear parallel to it.

Consistent with the narrative logic, we turn to a number of Gothic stories, the action of which takes place in a noble estate. It can be assumed that the narrative of mystical events with the main characters represented by witches and vampires in the literature of the last third of the nineteenth century disseminated widely in popular literature dominates the genre of 'tabloid novel'. For example, the little-known novel by Viktor Pribytkov, editor and publisher of the first pre-revolutionary Russian spiritualist magazine *Rebus*, titled 'The Legend of an Ancient Baron's Castle: Neither a Fairy Tale, nor a Fact' (1883)[13] started the 'estate' Gothic of Russian Modernism. The novel is set in an old Baltic estate, which hides the bloody secret of the Baltic baron family of von F. The narrative was based on the

12 V. S. Solovyov, 'A preface to "The Ghoul" by the count A.K.', in *Collected Essays of Vladimir Sergeevich Solovyov*, ed. S. M. Solovyov and E. L. Radlov (St. Petersburg: Prosveshcheniye, 1899), Vol. 9 (1897–1900), p. 377.

13 V. A. Pribytkov, *The Legend of an Ancient Baron's Castle: Neither a Fairy Tale, nor a Fact* (St. Petersburg: V. Demakov, for *Rebus*, 1883).

turn-of-the-century craze for spiritualistic séances, spirit apparitions and mediumistic revelations.

When investigating A. K. Tolstoy's stories or a novel by Pribytkov, we find explicit references to a Western European Gothic modus of Russian estate culture. On the one hand, there's an estate designed by an Italian architect, and on the other, there's a castle of an Ostsee baron in the Baltic region. However, in most cases, actions take place in a Russian traditional estate. The Russian estate or Gothic castle constitutes a distinctive kind of meta-hero of the Gothic narrative, while together with them are all the realia of the usual estate toponymics: the country house with its yard services, its garden, an avenue and a pond. In the plot of A. P. Chekhov's story 'The Black Monk', the Gothic narrative[14] is revealed not only in the motif of the ever-wandering mysterious black monk who appears to magister Kovrin, but also in the gloomy realities of the ancestral estate of landowner Pesotsky, with whom the story begins:

> Pesotsky had an immense house with columns and lions, off which the stucco was peeling, and with a footman in swallow-tails at the entrance. The old park, laid out in the English style, gloomy and severe, stretched for almost three-quarters of a mile to the river, and there ended in a steep, precipitous clay bank, where pines grew with bare roots that looked like shaggy paws; the water shone below with an unfriendly gleam, and the peewits flew up with a plaintive cry, and there one always felt that one must sit down and write a ballad.[15]

Thus, the architecture of the Pesotsky estate indirectly refers to the tradition of the English Gothic novel. No less significant are the decorations of the huge estate orchard. At night, Kovrin meets Tanya in the garden; at the same time, the surrounding landscape does not create a romantic mood, but it heightens a sense of vague anxiety, a premonition of impending events, a story about the hero's insanity:

14 For detailed research of Gothic motives in 'The Black Monk', see Lvova, 'On the Composition of *The Created Legend*'.

15 A. P. Chekhov, 'The Black Monk', in *Complete Essays and Letters in 30 Volumes: Essays* (Moscow: Nauka, 1986), Vol. 8. The English translation: https://www.ibiblio.org/eldritch/ac/blackmonk.htm (Accessed 1 May 2023).

> In the big orchard [...] a thick, black, acrid smoke was creeping over the ground and, curling around the trees, was saving those thousands from the frost. Here the trees were arranged as on a chessboard, in straight and regular rows like ranks of soldiers, and this severe pedantic regularity, and the fact that all the trees were of the same size, and had tops and trunks all exactly alike, made them look monotonous and even dreary.[16]

The appearance of the mysterious black monk to Kovrin against the background of the estate landscape foreshadows sad events in the life of the whole family. After marrying Tanya and moving to the city, Kovrin renounces the ideal of a landowner's life with its continuous peasantry and becomes the cause of the death of both the orchard and landowner Pesotsky, whose fate is closely connected with the estate – 'My father is just dead. I owe that to you, for you have killed him. Our garden is being ruined; strangers are managing it already – that is, the very thing is happening that poor father dreaded', Tanya writes in her last letter to Kovrin.[17] In Chekhov's story, the Gothic canon is presented in an extremely adapted form, revealed indirectly, but what is important is that it is presented in the context of the Russian estate text.

In the Russian tradition, Western European Gothic motifs are replaced by themes and images of national folklore. For example, in the story 'The Witch' by Z. N. Gippius (1897), folklore and mythological image are closely connected with the Romantic tradition of Russian Gothic (N. V. Gogol's narrative 'May Night, or The Drowned Maiden', O. M. Somov's 'Kiev Witches'), while the plot conflict is solved in a Modernist manner. The plot begins with the arrival at an estate of a mysterious French governess, exhausted by unknown events of Madame Linot's personal life, always black-clad, while her servant Marfushka who sympathizes with her is a dreamy girl, overcome by visions of a witch's flight, for whom a dream is an escape from the boring everyday life:

> She was staring right into a dark corner, and unintentionally imagined the blue moonlit vast, free, chainless, with no land under her feet, a full yellow moon close

16 Ibid.

17 Ibid.

> by, huge as a mill wheel [...] And the wind is whistling in her ears from fast flight [...] Can she do that [...]?[18]

In the story by Gippius, the theme of the presence of supernatural forces that manifest themselves in the world of the estate life is emphasized by the deliberately mysterious description of the estate lake; the lake water acts as the sign of a twofold world, a gate into another space, organized according to the irrational laws of folklore and mythology universals. Lake, pond and water serve as a place of mystical connection with another reality; water, as a reflection of the heavenly abyss, is a mirror reflecting the entrance to another, supernatural world. Marfushka stares into the depths of the lake, trying to see there 'a strand of green hair or even a pale hand of a mermaid at least'. The image of the mermaid, as a harbinger of the imminent death of the heroine, is symbolically emphasized by the long greenish dress presented to her by the governess, which was worn by her deceased daughter. This dress becomes a tangible sign of connection with the other world, foreshadows the death of the governess and then of Marfushka, who, one night, while secretly trying on a mermaid outfit, feels the mysterious coolness of its greenish fabric and, feeling the irresistible call for freedom, escapes through the window to the lake. She imagines in the pool that the world under her feet is overturned into the glassy blackness of the water's surface. The ending of the story is symbolic – Marfushka jumps down into the water, but it seems to her that she soars up to the crescent moon, thereby realizing one of D. S. Merezhkovsky's favorite Gnostic formulas: 'The sky is up – the sky is down'. The image of a mysterious French governess whose former life can only be guessed and of the mystical death of the heroine against the scenery of the estate in the story of Gippius fits perfectly into the Russian version of the Gothic canon.

The plot of the novel about vampires is the basis of the storyline of Ye. A. Nagrodskaya's 'Motherly Love' (1914).[19] S. Shargorodsky, in the preface

18 Z. N. Gippius, 'The Witch', in *Mirrors: A Second Book of Stories* (St. Petersburg: Navji chary, 2002), p. 132.

19 Ye. Nagrodskaya, 'Motherly Love', in *A Visitress with Red Lips: Russian Vampire Prose from the Nineteenth to the Second Half of the Twentieth Century*, edited, preface and commentaries by S. Shargorodsky (n. p., Salamandra P. V. V., 2018), Vol. 1, <https://www.litmir.me/br/?b=606321&p=1>

to his collection of 'vampire' prose of Russian Modernism compiled by him, noted: 'The pre-revolutionary years were marked by the appearance of numerous vampiric works – writing about vampires and ghouls there are F. Sologub, G. Chulkov, A. Remizov, E. Nagrodskaya, A. Amfiteatrov, S. Auslender and others, not to mention the most prominent Symbolist poets like A. Blok and K. Balmont.'[20] The action of Nagrodskaya's story takes place in an old, cold, gloomy Baltic estate near Revel in the winter season: 'a rather high building, two stories, under a high tiled roof. Its walls were devoid of any architectural decoration, except for the coat of arms of the Grabenhof barons, above the gate.' The plot of the story is quite traditional: a young governess is hired for the little daughter of the owner of the estate, a baroness with a self-explanatory surname Grabenhof.[21] The little girl is a hideous pale freak with thin spider legs, a vampire who feeds on blood of the governesses invited to her, and if they are not around, then the blood of her own mother. The story has a happy ending – the heroine manages to avoid a tragic death – but the ending is didactic: too much maternal love is a pathological and fatal phenomenon.

The motifs of the Gothic story about vampires can also be traced in several stories of the Symbolist writer Georgy Chulkov: 'Midnight Light' (1904), 'The Ghoul' (1909), 'The Dead Groom' (1911) and 'Sister' (1909). The poetics of Chulkov's early stories fit into the problems of Symbolist prose in general – full of typical motifs of a mysterious connection with the supernatural world and death as a liberation from the shackles of boring everyday life. The heroines of his stories are pale, emaciated women with red lips, terminally ill, or with a secret. According to Hansen-Loewe: 'In decadence, the femme-fatale often turns out to be a vampire [...] The malevolent lover appears in the image of a vampire or a vamp woman (femme fatale).'[22] While in Chulkov's story 'The Ghoul' vampirism rather acts as a sexual metaphor, the story 'The Sister' quite fits into the poetics of the Gothic novel of mystery.

---

20 Ibid., p. 11.

21 From the German *graben* – to dig.

22 Aage A. Hansen-Löve, *Russian Symbolism: The System of Poetic Motives in Early Symbolism* (St. Petersburg: Akademichesky Project, 1999), p. 237.

The space–time organization of the Gothic novel is known to be built in a special way:

> In the chronotope of the Gothic novel, the main thing is the connection of periods, the present (in relation to the reader's reality, it is historical past) with the past of the characters (mainly the ancestral past, the past of family traditions) [...] This determines the choice of location (castle, abbey, etc.).[23]

The chronotope of Chulkov's story 'The Sister' is organized according to the laws of the Gothic novel space. The scene of the action is a country house where the interiors are in the style of an old castle: 'From everything seeped the spirit of antiquity, oblivion [...] in the bedroom, the study, the library and the corner room, the furniture was of a special type, apparently created by a modern artist on samples from the Middle Ages.'[24] The selection of books in the estate library refers to the Catholic mysticism of the Middle Ages and the French Enlightenment:

> Along with the French freethinkers of the eighteenth century, you could find St Augustine and 'The Little Flowers' of Francis of Assisi and, along with the great German metaphysicians, such mystics as Swedenborg. In a special department were kept the works of high poets of antiquity, the Middle Ages and our days.[25]

Another motif is the sinful passion that the hero feels for his own sister, and this feeling is not accidental: in a letter left by the deceased aunt, the mystery of the characters is clarified, an unknown chain of laws that determined their relationship in the present. In the last incarnation, the sister was the bride of the hero-narrator, and therefore in the next life, the balance would be restored, and she would again become his bride. The story has a number of other 'Gothic' motifs and plot moves: the early death of the beautiful heroine (the motif of a 'dead bride'), the appearance of the deceased aunt to the hero, the revealing of the mystical secret of the close emotional connection between brother and sister. All these signs suggest that in Chulkov's story, the estate topos turns out to be a

23 Malkina and Polyakova, 'The "Canon" of the Gothic Novel and Its Types', p. 31.

24 G. I. Chulkov, *Stories Book 1* (St. Petersburg, 1909).

25 Ibid.

necessary part of the Gothic narrative, somehow located on the border of two worlds – the world of the past and the present, connecting the world of supernatural forces and reality.

The estate narrative of Russian Symbolism is characterized by a keen interest in folklore heritage, the peculiarities of folk speech and the desire to build a neo-mythological reality. Turgenev's hero, the *raznochinets* (non-aristocratic intellectual), is replaced by an intellectual nobleman, who heads the revolutionary agitation against the tsarist regime. This trend in the estate text of the turn of the nineteenth to the beginning of the twentieth century noticeably rises under the influence of Dostoevsky's novel *Demons*, which for decades has set a strong bond between the revolution and the devilry plots. The estate text of Russian Symbolism reinterprets this idea, and the Russian revolution experience will be reinterpreted in a mystical and religious way ('The Silver Dove' by Andrei Bely, *The Created Legend* by F. Sologub, *Roman the Tsar* by Z. Gippius). This trend was started by F. Sologub's novel *The Created Legend*, which largely determined the key topic of the Symbolists' estate text, focusing on solving the peculiarities of the interaction between the leftward sentiments of the enlightened nobility and the revolutionary agitation in the masses. One of the features of the novel is the distinctive interconnection of the theme of the revolutionary enlightenment of the masses and the establishment of a community of new people in the estate[26] with mystical and occult motifs in the image of the main character of the novel, the teacher and poet Trirodov, who at the same time represents the type of a Freemason-educator of the eighteenth century – a mystic, a sorcerer, an alchemist. It was Sologub's novel that influenced the peculiarities of the plot and the system of characters in Bely's story 'The Silver Dove' and the novel by Gippius titled *Roman the Tsar*. And if Gippius modeled the Symbolist idea of a popular religious revolution that united social and religious ideals, then Andrei Bely proposed a model of a new community based on unconventional revolutionary religiosity – namely, the spiritual Khlysty community, which the intellectual nobleman Peter Daryalsky, overcome by revolutionary sentiments

26 Trirodov's estate is a prototype of infant communities for neglected children that were created on the basis of forfeit estates in the pre-revolutionary times.

and mystical searches for a spiritual path, tries to enter. According to the researcher Syta, 'Sologub introduces elements of the knight's novel, the Gothic novel, the melodrama and the detective story into the narrative.'[27]

The critic A. Izmailov has argued that, in Sologub's novel, 'sober reality' was mixed with 'the purest fantasy, the techniques of the naturalistic school – with pure decadence'.[28] Indeed, *The Created Legend* is a novel that models the neo-mythological discourse of a specifically Symbolist narrative with a rich imagery rooted in Russian folklore. So, in the first published version, the novel had the name 'Navi charms' – from the dialect 'navi' – witchcraft, mortal, dead. The spatial model of the novel, especially the first part of it, 'Drops of Blood', is constructed in a special way. The novel takes place between two significant topos – a provincial town and the elemental forces – which is represented by two estates located not far from each other. One of the estates, 'Rameyevskaya', belongs to the landowner Rameyev, and the other is 'Prosyany Polyany', which is recently acquired from him by the chemistry teacher Trirodov, who organizes a children's educational community program there. While the landscape of the Rameyevskaya estate corresponds to the traditional estate space, an estate on a hill and a garden descending to the river, a birch grove behind the house and a lime avenue, the structure of the Trirodov estate is organized differently. It is a complex architectural complex designed based on a Masonic plan:[29] the entrance is a network of mazes with gates and fences; the house is surrounded not by a park, but by forest glades, groves and ponds, which symbolize the untouched elemental forces of virgin nature. The laws and regulations established in the Trirodov children's colony follow the idea of the Rousseauist education of a new person, based on freedom of behavior and expression, and detachment from the generally accepted social attitudes that bind the true nature of a person. Children

27 Syta, 'Chronotope and Gothic Tradition in Symbolic Novels of F. Sologub'.

28 Ayaks Izmaylov, 'Dym i pepel' [Smoke and Ashes], *Birzhevye Vedomosti*, No. 13175 (3 October 1912), p. 5.

29 V. A. Lyotin, and N. N. Lyotina, 'Grounds for Research in the Typology, Structure-Function, Semantics-Symbolism of the Russian estate, from the Seventeenth to the Beginning of the Twentieth Century', *Yaroslavl Pedagogical Bulletin*, Vol. I, No. 4 (2011), pp. 279–284.

and teachers go without shoes, wear short clothes and swim naked in the local lakes, without feeling ashamed, as if they were a part of nature. This detachment from the outside world models another space of the estate that is inhabited by folklore and mythological creatures: a mermaid Zoi (a creature of lower Slavic mythology, personifying the forest spirit) appears on a stone near the lake and calls out from the forest, while *zhirovik* and *lesovik* (folklore creatures *pudge* and *silvan*) wander around the neighborhood. This world is contrasted with the space of a provincial city, filled with infernal evil spirits and imps that arise from gray dust. The motif of the evil sun in the novel, as in Sologub's early work, is associated with a number of mythological images: the sun is an evil dragon, or a fiery serpent that mercilessly burns all living things. The image of the sun and its demonic incarnations – the Dragon and the Serpent – are part of the central image of evil in the writer's individual mythology.[30]

The nature kindred of Trirodov's commune pushes the boundaries of the usual idea of life and death, the finiteness of human existence, and the space in the estate loses its tridimensionality, gaining the ability to contract and expand – inside one space you can find another. From an external perspective, it is motivated by Trirodov's profession: he is a chemistry teacher, and by his preoccupation, he is an alchemist who can raise the dead. The 'quiet' children in his homestead are resurrected boys who died prematurely by violent death – beings belonging to the world of angels rather than demons. These creatures have a protective function; they are disembodied and able to be in different places at the same time. The mysterious disappearance of one of the characters, Dmitry Matov, who was transformed into a cube by alchemical manipulations, is connected with Trirodov's chemical experiments.[31] The idea of substance transformation, the transition of the corporeal into the ethereal and vice versa as well as the acquisition of a body by the beings of the ethereal world are all found

30 L. I. Sobolev, 'About Fedor Sologub and His Novel', in F. Sologub, *Created Legend*, ed. with an afterword by L. I. Sobolev; commentaries by A. L. Sobolev (Moscow: Fiction, 1991), Vol. 2 pp. 260–279.

31 For more details on alchemy motives in the novel, see Lvova, 'On the Composition of *The Created Legend* by F. Sologub'.

in Masonic searches. In addition, Trirodov's room resembles an alchemist's laboratory; the objects of his study are also significant. For example, in the mirror, which unexpectedly has magical properties, the Rameyev sisters see themselves as decrepit old women, and then regain their youth. The meaning of the mirror, as is well-known, plays a significant role in the mythopoetics of Russian Symbolism, being a sign of the twofold world: the intermediary between the real world and the supernatural world. However, in Gothic tradition, reflections have a significant meaning (the vampire, as it is known, is not reflected in the mirror). In a commentary on the novel, A. L. Sobolev noted that Trirodov's mirror resembles the one made by the devil, in which 'the good and the beautiful was twisted and belittled to the utmost; on the contrary, the bad and the ugly became more noticeable and even uglier'.[32]

The Masonic and alchemical plots in the context of the estate text of Russian Modernism find their continuation in Kuprin's novel *The Star of Solomon* (1917). The story is based on the Faust plot of the hero's trial by the devil. The trickster plot unfolds according to the laws of a fantastic narrative. The morning visit of Mr. Toffel[33] to minor official Ivan Tsvet and the incredible events that follow form the plotline: the hero receives an unexpected inheritance, goes on a trip to the old estate of his late uncle and in the end finds a completely logical explanation – all this was just a dream for the hero. The spatial composition is distributed between two significant loci: the old estate and the city. A trip to the estate by train is a 'round trip', according to the fairy tale categories, but at the same time it is the crossing of a mystical border, because the logic of the narration of events in the uncle's estate is subordinated to the logic of a fantastic narrative. Aleksandr Kuprin, who himself underwent Masonic initiation, relies on the plot of the legend about the Temple of Solomon, which is devoted

32 F. Sologub, The Created Legend, ed. with an afterword by L. I. Sobolev; commentaries by A. L. Sobolev (Moscow: Fiction, 1991).

33 It should be noted that there is a tangible correlation with Dostoevsky's novel *Demons* when an imp visits Ivan Karamazov. In Dostoevsky's text, just as in Kuprin's, there is an explanation for this event: whereas Karamazov is chased in his morbid hallucinations, Ivan Tsvet sleeps with a hangover after boozing with friends the previous day. Moreover, the characters have the same name.

to the theme of searching for and reclaiming the 'lost word by a Mason'.[34] At the same time, Tsvet, who loves to solve riddles and has inherited loads of intricate cards with letters, manages to arrange them in the correct order, placing them inside the 'star of Solomon'; the word is found, but until it is pronounced, Mr. Meph Is Toffeles is in his service. Thus, the lost word turns out to be a spell of demonic power and not a true Masonic incantation.

A typical description of the old estate of Uncle Tsvet, where everything fell into disrepair and only his Mason uncle's room, the office of the philosopher and alchemist, remained intact, reads as follows:

> it looked like a rare amateur library, and the office of a draftsman, and the laboratory of an alchemist, and the workshop of a blacksmith. Most of all, there was a gaping, black-mouthed, overhanging forge, built of massive, sooty brick; beside it, on the side, on a stand, were placed inflating double bellows. One round tripod table was covered with retorts, flasks, stoppers, crucibles, beakers, thermometers, scales of all sorts, and many other instruments, the meaning and purpose of which I could not comprehend.[35]

It should be noted that the mysterious events in the estate associated with the alchemical and Masonic tradition in Russian literature of the nineteenth century have at least two prototypes: E. Baratynsky's story 'The Ring'[36] and 'The Sylph' by V. Odoevsky.[37]

In Baratynsky's story, the mysterious landowner Opalsky lives like a hermit in a remote estate outbuilding and, at first glance, is a traveler through time and epochs ('Opalsky repented of terrible crimes, of witchcraft; he

34 A. A. Shyuneyko, and O. V. Chibisova, 'Word Semantics and Pragmatics in Masonic Tradition', *Bulletin of Kemerovo State University,* Vol. 21, No. 3 (2019), pp. 869–880.

35 Aleksandr Kuprin, 'The Star of Solomon', in *Collected Essays* (Moscow: Literature, 1958), Vol. 5, pp. 432–527.

36 Ye. A. Baratisnky, 'The Ring', in *White Apparition: Russian Gothic* (St. Petersburg: Azbuka-klassika, 2007), pp. 169–183.

37 V. F. Odoevsky, 'The Sylph', in *White Apparition: Russian Gothic* (St. Petersburg: Azbuka-Klassika, 2007), pp. 206–232. The following research work is devoted to V. F. Odoevsky's heritage in the context of Russian Gothic: N. J. Cornwell, 'Vladimir Odoevsky and the Russian Gothic', in *Vladimir Odoevsky and Romantic Poetics: Collected Essays* (Oxford, 1998), pp. 145–156.

confessed that he was 450 years old, that this long life was given to him as a punishment and it is not known when his rest will come').[38] He is a slave of the magic ring, a cabalistic talisman. Opalsky's office is filled with mysterious artifacts that resemble an alchemy laboratory: 'Well-known skeletons stood in the corners, the walls were hung with bunches of dried herbs and roots, bottles and cans of various infusions stood on the windows'.[39] At the same time, according to the logic of the Gothic narrative, the mysterious plot at the end of the story receives a simple explanation: the hero is mentally ill and, thus, the mysterious events of his life acquire a realistic motivation.

The official's visit to his uncle's estate is extremely reminiscent of the plot of Odoevsky's story. In Odoevsky's story, the hero inherits an estate with an outbuilding where his uncle's old library is housed; once he finds an old grimoire in his uncle's library, he starts nurturing a fairy-tale creature, a Sylph, in a vessel with water. As in many works written in a Gothic manner, the events in the story have a double motivation and are explained by the illness of the hero and a temporary dementia – just as in Kuprin's story, the events turn out to be only a hangover dream of the main character.

The Gothic mode of Russian estate text is preserved both in emigrant literature – for example, the novel in essays by S. R. Mintslov titled *After Dead Souls* (1922) and Aleksandr Belinsky's novella *The Secret of the Old Estate (Juniper Bush)* (1926) – and in the literature of the Soviet period, where this theme is transformed in genre terms and takes the form of a children's detective story – such as the novel by A. N. Rybakov *The Bronze Bird* (1956).

The theme of the dying noble estate, an ancient family curse that weighs on the passing era of noble nests, continued in the Russian prose of the emigrant period. Writer and bibliophile Sergei Mintslov's novel *After Dead Souls*, as the name implies, became a kind of rewriting and reinterpretation of the plot of N. V. Gogol's *Dead Souls*. The events in the story are constructed around a trip in search of estate libraries and rare books in the landowners' estates of central Russia at the beginning of the twentieth century. The narrative is presented by a consistent chain of fairly real travel

38 Ibid.
39 Ibid.

essays; at the same time, notes of mysterious events and realities are inserted into the outline of the narrative, forcing the reader to include them in the context of the Gothic tradition. We are talking about the motifs of desolation and destruction of the estate life, and this process began long before the culture of the landowner's habitat was destroyed in post-revolutionary Russia. One of the essays is devoted to a trip to an abandoned estate that has fallen into disrepair. The Gothic plot is revealed in the story that an old housekeeper tells of a series of deaths of the former owners of the estate who died one after another under strange circumstances. In addition, the mystical essence of the old estate is manifested in the mysterious echo of chilling sounds and creaks of the old forgotten house.

In a broader sense, the phenomenon of the Russian landowner's estate can also be considered from the philosophical point of view as heterotopia, an exceptional place that reproduced itself for almost 150 years of pre-revolutionary Russia. Among the features of the Russian estate one can name a different time duration, focused on the repeatable seasonal peasant cycle, with a typical complex of stable patterns of lifestyle and household behavior. The structure of the estate world is beyond the usual cultural binary oppositions such as 'city–village' or 'urban environment–rural life'. In the tradition of Russian literature of the nineteenth century, the estate is not just a setting for the events that take place, but rather one where the action is localized in a different space–time continuum. It is no accident that the most significant events in the lives of heroes take place in the noble estate (Pushkin's *The Captain's Daughter*, Gogol's *Dead Souls*, Turgenev's *Fathers and Sons*, Chekhov's *The Cherry Orchard*). Starting with the literature of Classicism, several stable narrative models are assigned to the 'estate topos': at the turn of the eighteenth to nineteenth centuries, this is epistolary literature and memoirs (historical notes of A. T. Bolotov, which he writes in his village, after retiring), a ladies' album, an elegy and a poem (e.g., the works of A. S. Pushkin of the period of 'Boldino Autumn'). It is no accident that at the beginning of the twentieth century the semiosphere of the Russian estate is the 'endlessly lasting eighteenth century', with its collection of book rarities, and artistic and cultural artifacts of the age of Classicism and Enlightenment. Hence the special property of the world of the Russian estate – it served as a repository of intellectual and cultural memory, as every landowner's house necessarily had a library, filled with books and art objects. 'Nests of gentlefolk' often served as museum repositories – and, as you know, heterotopias are characterized by the accumulation of time. It can be noted that one of the first post-revolutionary decrees of the People's Commissariat of Education concerned the nationalization of cultural values, and the first expeditions to save the heritage went to Russian estates – for national antiquities, art objects, books and the like. One step remained from the accumulation of national and cultural memory to its destruction; the phenomenon of the destruction of the estate life was marked by A. P. Chekhov in the drama *The Cherry Orchard*. After the revolution, radical changes took place: the landowner's estate was destroyed as a historical fact, but symbolically this meant the destruction of the national cultural memory. At the same time, the most important signs of homestead heterotopia are preserved: first of all, it is the memory of the place, the memory of the 'estate locus' and its geopoetics.

Gothic challenges in connection with the estate text were not developed in Soviet times, and in genre terms, they were transformed into a children's detective story in Anatoly Rybakov's novel *The Bronze Bird* (1956). The historical background of the book is the first years of the Soviet Republic, famine and devastation, the Civil War and the organization of colonies for the homeless in former landowners' estates. A group of children reveals the secret of the bronze statue of a bird that was in the landowner's house, and the murder mystery exposes the former Count Karagaev.

The idea of 'memory of a place', the memory of the locus of a noble estate, is the basis of the recently published novel by Russian literary critic and writer Aleksandr Sobolev titled *Griffins Guard the Lyre* (2020). In Sobolev's novel, the estate locus of the forgotten and destroyed estate is reproduced, not in real but in literary terms – thus, the continuity of the tradition of estate text for two centuries closes up. The estate locus in question is related to the work of another writer Alexei Skaldin,[40] whose novel *The Wanderings and Adventures of Nikodim the Elder* (1917) – known only to a select group of specialists – remained without the attention of

40 Alexei Skaldin, *The Wanderings and Adventures of Nikodim the Elder* (Petrograd: Felana, 1917).

modern critics and, in the Soviet era, was firmly forgotten. Skaldin's novel can be considered as one of the precursor texts on which Sobolev's novel is based: for example, both main characters have the bizarre and rare name Nikodim; in Skaldin's novel, the hero is looking for his mother, while in Sobolev's novel, the hero is looking for his father. In the former, the action takes place mainly in an estate with an unusual architectural design – it has an extension, a tower. It can be noted that the main character of Sobolev's novel is given the task of discovering the ruins of an old estate with a tower and something suggests that he is looking for the same estate from Skaldin's novel: 'to find the ruins of a former house, and among the ruins it was necessary to identify the ruins of the tower, since the customer, who was in an unclear relationship with the deceased owner, was interested in it. This tower, or rather what was left of it, had to be carefully captured.'[41] We assume that in the novel *Griffins Guard the Lyre* the technique of 'completing' someone else's text is used: it is, in its own way, a conceivable continuation of it. As in the post-revolutionary reality of Soviet Russia, where noble estates were destroyed and their owners either left their abodes or were subjected to violence, so in Sobolev's novel, where a different course of historical time is modeled, the popular consciousness is invariably barbarically destructive and insidious – local residents do not admit to looting the estate even a few decades later, assuring the newcomer that there was no estate at all:

> The mysterious estate behind Shestopalikha still existed and was definitely destroyed and looted: the practical peasant mind liked to find a use for ownerless excesses in the economy, and with special zeal tried to achieve a passing humiliation of things – to use, for example, a carved mahogany cane with fine filigree work as a poker.[42]

The historical time in the novel is verified but unrecognizable: it is set in Russia in the mid 50s of the last century. However, the historical canvas is bizarrely turned inside out – this is the conditional, imagined country: Russia in which the Bolsheviks did not win during the 1917 troubles but, on the contrary, became exiles. This is a narrative of a historically conventional

41 A. L. Sobolev, *Griffins Guard the Lyre* (St. Petersburg: Ivan Limbakh, 2020).
42 Ibid., p. 429.

flow of time in which the era of Modernist culture of the Silver Age did not disappear, but naturally became part of the everyday reality of the urban intellectual space, instead of the socialist reality. The gap between the city and the village has widened, and the mystical life of the village, which is closely connected with the Khlysty rituals, is still far removed from the idea of the city dweller. The plotlines of the novel – the presence of the protagonist at a social event in an old city mansion, a mysterious murder in a dacha, the subsequent chain of strange events that forces the main character to hastily flee to a remote village where the inhabitants practice whiplash rituals, the hero being part of the ritual of exorcism, his subsequent imprisonment in a village building, the motive for finding his father, whom he has never seen – generally create recognizable features of the detective genre in a Gothic mode. The sought-for ruined estate is located near the village of Shestopalikha, meaning 'six fingers' – a popular sign that its owner is familiar with evil spirits. The main character observes in the village church the ritual of exorcising a woman possessed by a demon, and in the vicinity, there were many women possessed by demons.

It should be noted that both novels, from 1917 and 2020 are in principle incomplete: this effect of broken storylines implies continuation, further completion and creative reinterpretation of artistic reality through the novel's interaction with the reader.

The cultural transfer of Western European Gothic into Russian estate text is achieved through the emphasis on Russian life realities, one of which remains intact. It is the old noble estate modus that appears to be the meta-hero of the narrative. One of the key requirements for successful employment of Russian estate Gothic is the mystery modus. In regard to attributes of Russian Gothic, it is the interior of the estate: a library that consists of a set of books of esoteric content and ancient manuscripts – objects of the former owner's research. Strangely, estate Gothic undergoes a transformation during two centuries: it becomes enriched with folklore realities and is sought by nobility esoterics, following the distinctive character of the Russian psychological novel on the one hand and literature trends of the century on the other. From Romanticism to Symbolism, through plots of mass literature about vampires and ghosts to the children's detective stories of Soviet times, it finally transforms into the contemporary metahistorical novel.

Bibliography

Baratisnky, Ye. A., 'The Ring', in *White Apparition: Russian Gothic* (St. Petersburg: Azbuka-klassika, 2007), pp. 169–183.

Boyeva, G. N., 'On the House as a Life-Building Practice of Modernity: A House of Leonid Andreev on the Black River', in *Press and Word of St Petersburg* (Petersburg Reads 2012), Part 1: *Bookwork: Cultural Studies; A Collection of Research Papers* (St. Petersburg: SPSUITD, 2013), p. 184.

—— 'The Poetics of Horror in the Works of Leonid Andreev: The Receptive Aspect', *Scholarly Notes of Petrozavodsk State University: Philological Sciences*, Vol. 2, No. 3 (May 2015), pp. 66–70.

Chekhov, A. P., 'The Black Monk', in *Complete Essays and Letters in 30 Volumes: Essays* (Moscow: Nauka, 1986), Vol. 8.

Chulkov, G. I., *Stories*, Book 1 (St. Petersburg, 1909).

Cornwell, N. J., 'Vladimir Odoevsky and the Russian Gothic', in *Vladimir Odoevsky and Romantic Poetics: Collected Essays* (Oxford: Berghahn Books, 1998), pp. 145–156.

Gippius, Z. N., 'The Witch', in *Mirrors: A Second Book of Stories* (St. Petersburg: Navji Chary, 2002).

The Gothic Tradition in Russian Literature, intro. N. D. Tamarchenko (Moscow: RSUH Centre, 2008).

Guirivenko, A., 'Literary Archetypes of the Monk in Chekhov's Prose', in *Young Researchers* 3 (Moscow, 1998), pp. 70–74.

Hansen-Löve, Aage A., *Russian Symbolism: The System of Poetic Motives in Early Symbolism* (St. Petersburg: Akademichesky Project, 1999).

Izmaylov, A. (Ayaks), 'Dym i pepel' [Smoke and Ashes], *Birzhevye Vedomosti*, No. 13175 (3 October 1912), p. 5.

Khachaturov, S. V., *'Gothic Taste' in Russian Fiction of the Eighteenth Century* (Moscow: Progress-traditsiya, 1999).

Komaromi, A., 'An Unknown Force: Gothic Realism in Chekhov's *The Black Monk*', in *The Gothic-Fantastic in Nineteenth-Century Russian Literature* (Amsterdam Amsterdam-Atlanta, GA, 1999), pp. 257–276.

Kuprin, A. N., 'The Star of Solomon', in *Collected Essays*, (Moscow: Literature, 1958), Vol. 5, pp. 432–527.

Lvova, M. A., 'On the Composition of *The Created Legend* by F. Sologub: The Issue of Alchemic Reminiscence in Novel Structure Organization', *Yaroslavl Pedagogical Bulletin*, No. 1 (2001), <http://vestnik.yspu.org/?page=2000_4> (Accessed 1 October 2020).

Lyotin, V. A., and N. N. Lyotina, 'Grounds for Research in the Typology, Structure-Function, Semantics-Symbolism of the Russian Estate, from the Seventeenth to the Beginning of the Twentieth Century', *Yaroslavl Pedagogical Bulletin* , Vol. 1, No. 4 (2011), pp. 279–284.

Malkina, V. Ya, 'Gothic Tradition and the Historical Novel: "The Fiery Angel" by V. Ya. Bryusov', in *The Gothic Tradition in Russian Culture* (Moscow: RSUH, 2008), pp. 250–266.

——— and A. A. Polyakova, 'The "Canon" of the Gothic Novel and Its Types', in *The Gothic Tradition in Russian Literature* (Moscow: RSUH, 2008), pp. 15–32.

Mirror: Reflection Semiotics. Works on Semiotic Systems 22, Research Notes of the University of Tartu, No. 831, 1988.

Nagrodskaya, Ye, 'Motherly Love', in *A Visitress with Red Lips: Russian Vampire Prose from the Nineteenth to the Second Half of the Twentieth Century*, Vol. 1, ed., preface and commentaries by S. Shargorodsky (n.p.: Salamandra P. V. V., 2018), <https://www.litmir.me/br/?b=606321&p=1>.

Odessky, M. P., 'Vampires in the Early Prose of A. K. Tolstoy: Experience of Creating Plot Topic', *Literature Questions*, No. 6 (2010), pp. 207–241.

Odoevsky, V. F., 'The Sylph', in *White Apparition: Russian Gothic* (St. Petersburg: Azbuka-Klassika, 2007), pp. 206–232.

Pribytkov, V. A., *The Legend of an Ancient Baron's Castle: Neither a Fairy Tale, nor a Fact* (St. Petersburg: V. Demakov, for *Rebus*, 1883).

Rolet, S., 'Fear in the Works of Leonid Andreev', in *Semiotics of Fear*, ed. Nora Books and Francis Kont (Moscow: Russian Institute 'Europe', 2005), pp. 168–171.

Shipachyova, N. A., 'The Mystic and Enigmatic A. P. Chekhov's Story "The Black Monk", in *Works of A.P. Chekhov: Poetics, Origins, Influence* (Taganrog, Sphinx, 2000), pp. 117–124.

Shyuneyko, A. A., and O. V. Chibisova, 'Word Semantics and Pragmatics in Masonic Tradition', *Bulletin of Kemerovo State University*, Vol. 21, No. 3 (2019), pp. 869–880.

Skaldin, Alexei, *The Wanderings and Adventures of Nikodim the Elder* (Petrograd: Felana, 1917).

Sobolev, A. L. 'From the Memoirs of S.G. Kara-Murza: 1', *Literature Fact*, No. 5 (2017), p. 84.

——— *Griffins Guard the Lyre* (St. Petersburg: Ivan Limbakh, 2020).

Sobolev, L. I., 'About Fedor Sologub and His Novel', in F. Sologub, *The Created Legend*, ed. with an afterword by L. I. Sobolev; commentaries by A. L. Sobolev (Moscow: Fiction, 1991), Vol. 2, pp. 260–279.

Sologub, F., *The Created Legend*, ed. with commentaries by A. L. Sobolev (Moscow: Fiction, 1991).

Solovyov, V. S., 'A Preface to "The Ghoul" by the Count A.K.', in *Collected Essays of Vladimir Sergeevich Solovyov* (1897–1900), ed. S. M. Solovyov and E. L. Radlov (St. Petersburg: Prosveshcheniye, 1899), Vol. 9, p. 377.

Syta, J., 'Chronotope and Gothic Tradition in the Symbolic Novels of F. Sologub: Between Condition and Lifetime', *Uzhorod National University Herald: Philology Series*, Vol. 2, No. 38 (2017), pp. 61–65.

Talalayeva, O. G., 'I. A. Bunin's Prose and Gothic Tradition in Russian Literature', *Tambov State University Review*, Vol. 7, No. 99 (2011), pp. 165–171.

Translated by Nikita Khmarenko

VLADIMIR GOLSTEIN

10 Continuities and Discontinuities of Russian Culture through the Prism of Turgenev's *Fathers and Sons*

Turgenev's novel *Fathers and Sons* opens on a particular date, 20 May 1859, as the very first sentence of the novel announces, making the conflict between generations, which the novel explores, both time- and place-specific. The death of Nicholas I and the ensuing Great Reforms left a clear mark on the make-up of the conflict; yet Turgenev also approaches this conflict *sub specie aeternitatis*, so to speak: juxtaposing the contemporary and concrete with the recurrent and general. The two opposing generations of the 1840s and the 1860s are viewed against the background of unique and recurrent, disruptive and continuous. The presence of Nikolai Kirsanov and Fenechka's baby son – technically Arkady's brother but belonging to the subsequent generation by age – reminds the sons that they will soon be cast in the role of fathers, with all the ensuing tensions. A short span of human life is measured against the eternal cycle of nature.

Turgenev would not be the master that he was had he not approached his characters as well as their predicaments and conflicts from this broad perspective. Recall, for example, a little vignette in which Kirsanov, having been accused by his son Arkady of falling behind the times, remembers how he himself had mounted a similar accusation against his own mother (*PSS*, VIII, 248).[1]

1 All references to Turgenev are from *Polnoe sobranie sochinenii i pisem v 28 tomakh* (hereafter *PSS* in text), ed. M. P. Alexeev et al. (Leningrad: Nauka, 1961–1968). The volume and page number are given in parenthesis following the quotation itself.

Dmitry Merezhkovsky, a great admirer of Turgenev's double vision, made the following evaluation of Turgenev's ability to embrace different perspectives:

> Turgenev, they say, is outmoded. The two gigantic caryatids of Russian literature – Tolstoy and Dostoevsky – really have overshadowed Turgenev for us. Forever? For long? Are we not fated to return to him through them? In Russia, in a land of every sort of maximalism, revolutionary and religious, a land of self-immolations, a land of the most frenzied excesses, Turgenev – after Pushkin – is almost the sole genius of measure and, therefore, a genius of culture. For what is culture if not the measuring, the accumulation and preservation of values? In that sense Turgenev, as opposed to our great creators and destroyers Tolstoy and Dostoevsky, is our only guardian, our only conservative, and like any true conservative, is at the same time a liberal. [2]

Merezhkovsky defines culture in a way that is directly connected with the theme of generational conflict. For him, 'culture is measuring, the accumulation and preservation of values'. In their rebellion against the old, the young specifically refuse to accumulate and preserve what has been accomplished before. Culture is directly related to the continuity of values and attitudes transmitted from one generation to another. Classifying Turgenev along with Pushkin among the founding fathers of Russian culture, Merezhkovsky places him within the camp of those who prefer evolution to a radical break with the tradition.

Equally intriguing is the very concept of return, which Merezhkovsky articulates in connection with Turgenev's cultural role. Having traveled in the company of maximalists and destroyers such as Tolstoy or Dostoevsky, Russian culture has to return to Turgenev, who is presented as the catalyst for such a return. The figure of the Prodigal Son, which plays a central role in Turgenev's novel,[3] clearly left its mark upon Merezhkovsky's own thinking.

I also indicate in parenthesis when the quotation is from Turgenev's letters. All translations are my own, unless otherwise indicated.

2 D. S. Merezhkovsky, *Vechnye sputniki* (Moscow: Nauka, 2007), p. 692.

3 For the discussion of how the parable functions in the unfolding of the novel's plot, see Harold K. Schefski, 'The Parable of the Prodigal Son and Turgenev's Fathers and Sons', in *Ivan Turgenev: Bloom's Modern Critical Views*, ed. Harold Bloom (Philadelphia: Chelsea House Publishers, 2003), pp. 85–96.

Turgenev's Arkady Kirsanov, we recall, having traveled in the company of 'a great destroyer', Bazarov, has eventually returned in order to embrace the world of his father Nikolai Kirsanov, a modest and decent landowner.

Turgenev highlights the parable of the Prodigal Son, as he describes the meeting between Nikolai and Arkady Kirsanov, in which the father goes out of his way to welcome his returning son: ' "Arkasha, Arkasha", screamed Kirsanov, and ran and waved his hands ... A few moments later his lips were kissing the dusty, suntanned, and beardless cheek of a young graduate' (*PSS*, VIII, 199). Biblical parable narrates a similar story: 'But when he [the son] was yet a great way off, his father saw him, and had compassion and ran, and fell on his neck and kissed him' (Luke 15:20). Herzen recognized this dimension of Turgenev's Symbolism when he observed a propos the young radicals: 'Bazarovs are our prodigal children.'[4]

The fate of two friends, Arkady Kirsanov and Yevgeny Bazarov, returning home from their studies, acquire a particular poignancy when viewed from the perspective of this parable. At the opening of the novel, Arkady returns home only externally, remaining as he is under the profound influence of Bazarov. By the end of the novel, however, he returns inwardly as well. Bazarov, on the contrary, even though he dies on his father's estate, never really returns home: nihilism and discontinuity remain his to the end. It is highly symbolic that when Bazarov, after his duel with Pavel Kirsanov, is forced to go home, he phrases his decision to Arkady in the following terms: 'Well, I was heading to my ancestors [*nu-s, vot ia i otpravilsia k'otsam*] and stopped here on my way' (*PSS*, VIII, 370). The combination of the verb *otpravit'sia* with the strange plural *k otsam* instead of either *k otsu* or *k roditeliam* implies a Russian version of the Latin expression *ad patres* (*otpravitsia k praotsam* – to die, to head for one's ancestors); Bazarov's father, in fact, uses the original form of this expression *ad patres* (*PSS*, VIII, 314). On a subconscious level, Bazarov views his return to his parents as self-annihilation and death.

So, while both friends end up in the houses of their parents, in one case this return is symbolized by a continuation of life and cultural legacy,

4 A. I. Herzen, 'Eshshe raz Bazarov. Pis'mo vtoroe', in *Sobranie sochinenii v 30 tomakh* (Moscow: Nauka, 1960), Vol. 20–21, p. 346.

while in the other by death. What is the reason behind such different fates? Is Bazarov's premature death caused by his failure to adjust, to mature and to grow into the new responsibilities of fatherhood? Or is there more to Bazarov than just a maladjusted romantic rebel incapable of embracing the rituals of ordinary civilized life?[5]

Turgenev – as he contrasts Bazarov's blatant individualism against communal commitments of Arkady – examines his own youthful fascination with Lermontov-like rebellion, radical individualism and rupture, comparing it with the sober, measured and tradition-focused outlook of Pushkin. Incidentally, it is precisely the Russian public return to Pushkin that Turgenev highlighted in his 1880 speech at the opening of Pushkin's monument in Moscow (*PSS*, XV, 75). Similar to Arkady Kirsanov, Turgenev chooses the continuity of tradition over the discontinuity of rebellion.

On the philosophical plane of the novel, Pushkin embodies the wisdom of interaction and interdependence of nature, time, family and generations. The return to Pushkin became for Turgenev – long before Merezhkovsky – the measure of one's willingness and readiness to accept one's place within the chain of being, within the cultural tradition of the fathers. Conversely, every new rebellious generation in Russia, as it proclaims its liberation from tradition, embraces 'discontinuity' by discarding Pushkin 'from the ship of modernity' (cf. the famous slogan of the Futurists).

Due to his own intellectual trajectory and the vagaries of Russian cultural development, Pushkin became a cultural founding father, and therefore inscribed into the culture, tradition and world of the fathers. It is hardly surprising, therefore, that various generational rebels have turned him into the caryatid of the old regime that had to be challenged, undermined, if not destroyed outright.

While the younger generations included Pushkin among the fathers from whom they declared their independence, the 'fathers' rushed to enlist

5 The latter view has become rather popular, articulated by the studies of Gary Saul Morson, 'Genre and Hero/Fathers and Sons: Intergeneric Dialogues, Generic Refugees and the Hidden Prosaic', in *Literature Culture and Society of Modern Age*, ed. Edward J. Brown, Stanford Slavic Studies 4 (1991), pp. 336–381; and Jane T. Costlow, *Worlds within Words* (Princeton: Princeton University Press, 1990).

Pushkin to their camp, as was beautifully illustrated in an anecdote recorded by Vladimir Mayakovsky. When he, along with other Futurists, arrived at some provincial town to give their performance, the chief of police warned them, 'to attack neither Pushkin nor other superiors' (*i drugikh nachal'nikov*).[6]

*****

As Turgenev's first narrative effort, entitled *Two Generations* (1848), testifies, the interaction of generations had interested him from the start. This interest remained in its latency, however, until Turgenev's firsthand experience with the young Turks who took over *Sovremenik* (The Contemporary), a magazine that played a fundamental role in shaping the generational conflict of the 1860s and beyond. In his presentation of new men, Turgenev responded to the dramatic changes experienced by Russia in the 1860s. Bazarov's and Arkady's rejection of their cultural heritage is a defining feature of the process that the sociologist Lewis Feuer called 'de-authorization', and that he viewed as central to any generational conflict.[7] For Feuer, the fathers' loss of authority is tied to their involvement in the discredited and no longer acceptable power structure. It is this loss of authority, the moral bankruptcy of the Old Regime resulting in the Crimean War fiasco, which the novel skillfully explores, providing an excellent picture of the loss of authority experienced by the older generation of landowners and their political and spiritual leaders.

By the time of the Great Reforms, the world of 'gentry nests' began to crumble, and so did the political and cultural authority of the gentry elite that had governed the country so far. Even the peasants seem to be aware of this fact, as one peasant's mockery of none other than Bazarov reveals. Having been asked by Bazarov to elucidate the concept of commune (*mir*), the peasant replies

6 Vladimir Mayakovsky, *Polnoe sobranie sochinenii v trinadtsati tomakh* (Moscow: Khudozhestvennaia literatura, 1955), Vol. 1, p. 22.

7 Lewis S. Feuer, *The Conflict of Generations: The Character and Significance of Student Movements* (New York: Basic Books, 1969), pp. 150–61 in particular.

> in a kind of patriarchal, good natured sing-song: 'and as against ours, that is to say, the *mir*, we know there is the master's will; because you are our fathers. And the stricter the master's rule, the better for the peasant.' (*PSS*, VIII, 384)

Yet, when Bazarov leaves, the same peasant dismisses Bazarov 'with a certain scornful gruffness' as he comments: 'of course, he is a master (*barin*); what does he understand?' (*PSS*, VIII, 384). In other words, while Bazarov views the older generation as 'useless aristocrats', for the peasants, Bazarov automatically becomes that part of the 'father-class' (cf. 'you are our fathers') which, in the time of crisis, is viewed as a nuisance that might be humored, but otherwise dismissed or ignored.

Turgenev had his own experience with the young rebels whose features he incorporated into the novel when he began to write for *Sovremenik*. The magazine had reached a new height of popularity under the leadership of Nikolai Nekrasov who, by the late 1850s, began to side with the young and radical authors such as Chernyshevsky and Dobroliubov, surrendering to them a key role in all editorial decisions. This shift in power did not sit well with the older and more established authors, offended as they were by Chernyshevsky's doctrinaire opinions and the free hand that he enjoyed in running the magazine from 1854 onward. Eventually, the older authors abandoned the journal altogether: Tolstoy in 1858, Grigorovich in 1859 and Turgenev in 1860.

While for Tolstoy Chernyshevsky's self-righteousness was itself a sufficient reason to leave the magazine, the more liberal and tolerant Turgenev stayed with the journal for another three years. Turgenev witnessed the ascent of Nikolai Dobroliubov, whose brusque manners and arrogance could not help but insult the older generation. According to Chernyshevsky's memoirs, Turgenev was eager to talk with Dobroliubov and to build bridges. Dobroliubov, however, did his best to avoid these conversations until the point he declared to Turgenev: 'I am bored when I am talking to you. Let's stop it once and for all.'[8]

8 S. Reiser, ed., *N. A. Dobroliubov v vospominaniakh sovremennikov* (Moscow: Khodozhestvennaia literature, 1986), p. 154.

It is worth stressing that among the most contentious issues that split even progressive authors who gathered around *Sovremenik* was the attack on Pushkin generated by polemics focusing on the social value of art. Neither Pushkin's respect for history and tradition nor his aesthetic principles could appeal to the radicals who explicitly rejected both aesthetics and history.

Scandalized by the Young Turks' hostility toward culture in general, and Pushkin in particular, Turgenev could not embrace the new radicalism, as much as he tried. His skepticism and irony toward the young are revealed, in fact, on the very first page of *Fathers and Sons*. The first 'new man' whom we encounter on the first page of the novel is presented in a highly ironic manner. I refer to the description of Kirsanov's servant, Peter, 'about whom everything – the turquoise ring in his ear, coiffured multicolored hair, soft movements, in a word, everything – proclaimed him to be a man of the new improved generation' (*PSS*, VIII, 195).

The simplistic dichotomies as well as the categorical rejection of the world of the fathers by the radicals have clearly left a mark on Turgenev and his presentation of Bazarov, who dismisses the older generation with the following observation: 'your father is a nice fellow, but he is already retired and done for … He reads Pushkin' (*PSS*, VIII, 238).

Turgenev's novel proved to be very popular with the Russian public. This popularity among the ordinary readers, however, did not in itself guarantee success with the critics. In fact, the appeal of Dobroliubov – the subject of Turgenev's fictional interrogation – was such that even the liberal-minded friends of Turgenev were more than ready to support Dobroliubov, rather than the more measured views of Turgenev. In the eyes of his critics, Turgenev was not sufficiently subservient to their extreme positions and arrogant behavior. Thus, when *Fathers and Sons* was published, Marko Vovchok (Maria Markovich, a close personal friend of Turgenev who translated Maria's work from Ukrainian into Russian), chastised Turgenev for daring to lampoon and malign Dobroliubov in the figure of Bazarov, perceived by the majority of young radicals to be a negative and repulsive figure.[9]

9 Nikolai Chernyshevsky, 'Vospominania ob otnoshenii Turgeneva k Dobroliubovu', in Chernyshevsky, *Polnoe sobranie sochinenii v 15-ti tomakh* (1939–53), Vol. 1, p. 737.

It should be stressed, however, that Turgenev's Bazarov is a far more intriguing, radical and nihilistic figure than was Dobroliubov. Judging by Dobroliubov's diaries, his true literary incarnation is Dostoevsky's Underground Man, rather than the strong and independent Bazarov. Indeed, most of his diary entries reveal a combination of a sharp mind, weak will and an uncanny oscillation between self-pity, self-aggrandizement and social anxiety.[10]

In one of his letters to Herzen, Turgenev calls Bazarov 'a wolf' (*PSS*, Pis'ma, IV, 383), claiming that 'it would have been easy to portray him as ideal; to portray him as a wolf and yet to justify him was difficult' (*PSS*, Pis'ma, IV, 383). In a letter to Sluchevsky, Turgenev again refers to Bazarov as 'wolf' (*PSS*, Pis'ma, IV, 381). Turgenev's persistent comparison implies not only Bazarov's strong and predatory nature, but also his inability to settle down, to be domesticated, the inability stressed by the Russian proverb: 'skol'ko volka ne kormi, on vse v les smotrit' (no matter how much you feed a wolf, it still looks toward the forest).

The text of the novel is rather explicit in its use of this Russian proverb. Katya acknowledges the wolf-like aspect of Bazarov when she calls Arkady and herself 'domesticated, tamed' (*ruchnyie*) as opposed to the 'predatory' (*khishchnyi*) Bazarov. In his final nightmare, Bazarov keeps returning to the image of a forest, as if suggesting his natural habitat: 'There is a forest here' he mumbles, before bidding Odintsova his final goodbye, and then mentions the dogs that pursue him in his nightmare (*PSS*, VIII, 396).

As opposed to his young opponents, Turgenev was well aware that destruction or violence once started could not be contained. As he put it in his famous essay 'Hamlet and Don Quixote':

> But in negation as in fire, there is a destructive force – and how is one to confine this force within boundaries, how is one to point out just where it should stop, when that which it should destroy and that which it should spare are often melded and linked inseparably. (*PSS*, VIII, 183)

10 Cf. T. I. Pecherskaia, 'Dnevniki Dobroliubova', in *Raznochintsy shestidesiatykh godov XIX veka: Fenomen samosoznaniia v aspekte filologicheskoi germenevtiki* (Novosibirsk, 1999), pp. 61–95.

The red dogs that haunt Bazarov before his death might very well refer to that destructive fire that now consumes Bazarov himself. In fact, Bazarov is associated with fire from the start, as shown in one of his earliest remarks of the novel when he requests matches from Arkady.

Bazarov's equation between his return to the ancestral home and failure is shared at one point by Arkady, who views his marriage to Katya and return to his father as some sort of surrender. Yet while Arkady's apparent defeat transforms into victory, Bazarov's ambitions, energy and power do not quite mesh with the life of a country doctor in some obscure village. Nor do they fit in any other place, since, no matter where he finds himself, he manages to create situations that make his stay unbearable, be it falling in love with Odintsova at her estate or dueling with Pavel Kirsanov at Kirsanov's estate. What is it that makes Bazarov turn away from home, from the world of his fathers, and why does he eventually become such a powerful cultural symbol of self-assertion and the rejection of the old? In Turgenev's depiction, Bazarov's motives for the radical break with the world of his fathers go beyond purely generational; they are also ideological, social and temperamental. Furthermore, Bazarov's rebellion, his rejection of any connection – not just to the past, but also to the present and the future – contains a strong existential component, and this makes him special among the gallery of various angry young men of Russian culture.

The radical generation entering the scene in the 1860s, while boasting Bazarov's youthful intensity, mannerisms and some of his outlandish opinions, had a much more narrow scope of questioning and negation. Resembling Bazarov only superficially, they seemed to embrace Dobroliubov's dogmatic rejection of the past, his call for immediate action (*delo*) and the newly emerged doctrine of 'serving the people', which they followed with almost religious fever. Dobroliubov's authority had been catapulted into the stratosphere by his death at the age of 26, which immediately cast him in the roles of martyr and prophet.

As far as the radical camp was concerned, Turgenev's presentation of the radical Bazarov proved inadequate. Bazarov's consistent nihilism and skepticism failed to satisfy young idealists. According to Kropotkin's *Memoirs*, the young felt frustrated with

> the merely negative attitude of Turgenev's hero. Nihilism [...] was but a first step toward a higher type of men and women who [...] live for a great cause. In the nihilists of Chernyshevsky [...] they saw better portraits of themselves.[11]

This greater cause – for the young idealistic radicals of the period – was the desire to 'serve the people', the cause that Bazarov subjects to the same questioning as numerous other 'causes'.

Bazarov was too complex, and his embrace of discontinuity was too thorough for the radical intelligentsia to digest. Both in their tastes, ideology, and their actions, the radical generation of the 1860s was much closer to Bazarov's parodies in the novel, Sitknikov and Kukshina, or to their equally shallow if more solemn versions of 'new men' crafted by Chernyshevsky in his celebrated novel *What's to Be Done* (1863).

The new generation of Russians was rather antithetical to Turgenev's ideals of moderation and harmony. They preferred a bitter generational war to the mutual understanding and compromise. Turgenev bent over backward to understand and articulate the unique and valuable features of each generation, yet this evenhandedness itself was counted against him. According to Turgenev's own 'Apropos Fathers and Sons' one angry reader accused him of negating the values of each generation: 'Neither Fathers nor sons, that is the real title of your novel, and you yourself are a nihilist' (*PSS*, XIV, 103).

The radical generation of the 1860s preferred a less nuanced and highly partisan attitude toward the generational conflict of the day, as exemplified by the short 1862 poem entitled 'Otsam' (To the Fathers), published by Ivan Goltz-Miller in the radical newspaper *Russkoe slovo* (Russian Word).[12]

> You are the shadows of the past,
> Our souls are striving for the future.
> You are scared of your deathbed visions,
> We are waiting for the dawn of a new day.
> You are suffering under the burden of old tales

11 P. A. Kropotkin, *Vospominania. Zapiski revolutsionera* (*Memoirs of a Revolutionist*) (St. Petersburg: Izdatel Gennady Markelov, 2018).

12 Quoted in A. Egolin, *Osvoboditel'nye i patrioticheskie idei russkoi literatury XIX veka* (Moscow: Sovetskii Pisatel', 1946), p. 192.

And of the dirt that accumulated through centuries...
You have only one road: repentance;
Your strength is in the power of prayers.
Work and struggle is our calling,
And we are ready for the future struggles.
We are strong in our faith in people,
Strong in our sacred yearning for truth
Strong since the deadly hand of century's rust
Hasn't touched us yet.
It is unclear who will win in our struggle;
But we are the enemies, and at the hour of perdition
Don't expect any mercy from us,
Nor will we ask for any mercy from you.

This bombastic poem, in which an individual speaker hides behind the group and rejects the older generation as if they were bitter enemies, sounds as if either Sitnikov or Kukshina composed it. Even a consistently witty and independent Dmitry Minaev, a poet far more sophisticated than Goltz-Miller, failed to register Bazarov's remarkable personality. In one of his poetic responses to Turgenev's novel, a poem entitled 'Fathers or Children?' (1862), Minaev asserted that Turgenev glorified the mannered aristocrat Pavel Kirsanov while deliberately belittling Bazarov:

Hero can be recognized by his features,
But this gloomy nihilist,
With his medicine and his lancet
Shows no signs of heroism. [13]

Individualism, Pechorin and youthful rebellion

While radical publications like *Sovremenik* or *Iskra* dismissed Bazarov as a hostile caricature intended to lampoon the reigning orthodoxies and

13 *Poety 'Iskry': V dvukh tomakh*, ed. I. G. Iampolsky (Leningrad: Sovetskii Pisatel' 1987), Vol. II, pp. 43–45.

personalities of the period, Turgenev's novel did provoke one extremely insightful response from the young radical critic Dmitry Pisarev. Two of his essays, 'Bazarov' (1862) and 'Realists' (1864), recognized that Bazarov is a peculiar type of personality, 'realist' or 'empiricist', as Pisarev described him. For Pisarev, Bazarov cuts a far more radical, nihilistic and complex figure than Dobroliubov's new men.

An individualistic loner, Pisarev died too young to have his ideas fully integrated into Russian consciousness. His unorthodox writings, inspired by Bazarov's example, strove to articulate an independent mode of behavior based on individualistic values. And as was the case with Bazarov, Pisarev's project proved too paradoxical for his audience, dependent as they were on groupthink, following the more accessible intellectual attitudes of the period.

In his reevaluation of values, Bazarov not only questions beliefs and attitudes of older generations, but he also questions himself along with such sacred cows of Russian radicalism as the idea of serving the people, that is, the peasants. In a highly dramatic gesture, Turgenev allows Bazarov to pronounce the following sacrilegious statement: 'I've conceived a hatred for the poorest peasant – Philip or Sidor – those for whom I am expected to kill myself and who won't even thank me for it … besides, what the hell do I need his thanks for? So, he'll be living in a solid hut, while I'm pushing up burdock: and so what?' (*PSS*, VIII, 325).

Bazarov's rebellion made him stand out among his generation of angry young men in search of some shared utopian goal. Musing on Hamlet, a clear predecessor of Bazarov as far as Turgenev is concerned, Turgenev observes: 'Doubting everything, Hamlet, of course, does not spare himself; his mind is too developed to be satisfied with what it finds' (*PSS*, VIII, 176). Similar to Turgenev's Hamlet, Bazarov does not spare himself either. Dostoevsky immediately recognized Bazarov as 'a person full of anxiety and yearning', while observing that 'anxiety has always been a sign of a great heart'.[14] Bazarov's 'anxious heart' is the heart that challenges and questions

14 Fedor Dostoevsky, 'Zimnie zametki o letnikh vpechatleniiakh', in *Polnoe sobranie sochinenii v 30 tomakh* (1972–80), Vol. 5, p. 59.

itself. In the novel, Bazarov formulates it this way: 'once you start mowing, be ready to cut your own feet' (*PSS*, VIII, 325).

Bazarov's strong, predatory personality, along with his nihilism, points to an important yet frequently understated movement – individualism – itself an ideology made popular by the generation of fathers and their embrace of Romanticism.[15] Bazarov is an individualist and megalomaniac, and, in that, he is not that different from Pavel Kirsanov, with whom he ends up having a duel. Bazarov rejects the world of the fathers not necessarily for ideological reasons (both Pavel and Bazarov are individualists), but also owing to his almost compulsive need to assert himself by rejecting others. Clearly such a multifaceted personality as Bazarov complicates Turgenev's presentation of the generational conflict, but it also points to his deep understanding that no ideological conflict can be reduced simply to a clash of political or social causes. One's personality and individual quirks remain relevant, if not defining, in one's choice of conduct or ideology. While these personal traits might complicate the neat schemas of social science, they reveal Turgenev's nuanced understanding of social and cultural phenomena. As a great novelist, Turgenev presents social conflicts of the period through the paradoxes and complexities of the human personality.

I, therefore, attribute to Turgenev the discovery of an important paradigm, further developed by Dostoevsky and Bely. As they rebel against the world and traditions of their fathers, each new generation of youth is drawn to a leader, to a person whose commitment to individualism, nihilism and rebellion makes him exhibit the features of a self-assertive Romantic hero. Within Russian cultural tradition, the best embodiment of such a Romantic rebel was Lermontov's Pechorin.[16] Those who eventually decide

15 In my study of Lermontov, I examined in great detail not only Lermontov's contribution to and dependence on individualism, but also a complex and contradictory reception-history that individualism encountered in Russia. See Vladimir Golstein, *Lermontov's Narratives of Heroism* (Evanston: Northwestern University Press, 1998), pp. 1–27.

16 While Turgenev's indebtedness to Romanticism in general and Lermontov in particular have been discussed in criticism (see, for example, David Lowe, *Turgenev's* Fathers and Sons [Ardis, 1983], pp. 65–70, 114–121), the relevance of individualism for both authors remains unexplored.

to return to the world of their fathers, however, part their ways with Byronic rebels and maximalists and embrace the path suggested by the 'Russian genius of measure and culture', Pushkin. Such a hero is Turgenev's Arkady Kirsanov. In other words, the opposition between Pushkin and Lermontov becomes more than the question of poetic preference. It reveals, ultimately, one's attitude toward cultural continuity and tradition.

Continuing the line of reasoning worked out by Turgenev, Dostoevsky – in his celebrated Pushkin speech – also connects Russian development with Pushkin's trajectory: an initial fascination with Byronic rebellion followed by overcoming of pride and self-centeredness symbolized by the return to the community and its values.[17] The group of young terrorists in Dostoevsky's *The Demons* are all drawn to Stavrogin – a demonic, Pechorin-like character to whom they assign the role of their spiritual leader. Likewise, Raskolnikov emulates the Napoleonic superman only to return to the spiritual values of common Russians. Similar is the trajectory of Nikolai Ableukhov in Bely's *Petersburg*.

In his perceptive analysis of Turgenev's novel, N. N. Strakhov zeroed in on those aspects of Bazarov's character that connect him to Romantic individualists:

> Bazarov is the first strong character, the first whole character to appear in Russian literature from the sphere of so-called educated society. Whoever fails to value that, whoever fails to understand the importance of that phenomenon, had best not judge our literature.[18]

Strakhov goes on to describe Bazarov in the following terms: 'Apparently Bazarov is a proud man, terribly egoistical and offending others by his egoism. But the reader makes his peace with that pride because simultaneously Bazarov lacks all smugness and self-satisfaction; pride brings him no joy.'[19] Strakhov's observation on the Byronic underpinnings of Bazarov finds its counterpart in Dostoevsky, who allows Stepan Trofimovich

17 See Dostoevsky, 'Pushkin', *PSS*, XXVI: 139.

18 N. N. Strakhov, 'Fathers and Sons'. In Turgenev, Ivan, *Fathers and Sons*, Second edition, ed. Ralph E. Matlaw (New York: Norton 1989), pp. 219–220.

19 Ibid., p. 224.

Verkhovensky to characterize Bazarov as 'a vague mixture of Nozdrev with Byron'.[20] One can wonder as to why both Strakhov and Dostoevsky point to Byron, while glossing over Bazarov's immediate predecessor in Russian literature – an assertive and individualistic Pechorin. Perhaps it was easier for them to imagine that such an individualistic and aggressive character was a purely Western product.

Turgenev did not have to be so blinded by Byron and his rebels. He was well aware of his own indebtedness to Lermontov and of his struggle to outgrow it. In a letter to his publisher, Katkov, Turgenev calls Bazarov 'a hero of our time', thus merging his and Lermontov's protagonists together, explaining that

> perhaps my view of Russia is more misanthropic than you suppose: In my eyes, Bazarov is really a hero of our time. 'What a hero and what a time', you will say … But that is the way it is. (*PSS*, Pis'ma, IV, 303)

In his artistic rendering of a new man, Turgenev connects Bazarov to his intellectual and literary source, namely, the Romantic rebel Pechorin, thus highlighting Bazarov's indebtedness to the ideology and practice of individualism, the movement that embraces autonomy, self-reliance, and independence from the culture of fathers.

In his youth, Turgenev felt the strong influence of Lermontov. Not only Turgenev's poetry, but also his early prose such as 'Andrei Kolosov', 'The Duelist' and 'Three Portraits', testify to the overwhelming impact of Lermontov and his dashing hero. Apollon Grigoriev recognized Turgenev's indebtedness to Lermontov immediately, calling Turgenev 'a talented poet of Lermontov's school', while adding that 'Turgenev started from the very extremes of that movement which we inherited from Lermontov'.[21]

In crafting his nihilist Bazarov, a character strong enough to reject any external pressures or ties, Turgenev was bound to return to the only heroic rebellious character of the Russian literary tradition – Pechorin. In doing so, Turgenev also revisited and relived his own infatuation with Lermontov.

20 Fedor Dostoevsky, *PSS*, X: 171.

21 A. A. Grigoriev, 'I. S. Turgenev i ego deiatel'nost'', in *Sochineniia Apollona Grigorieva* (St. Petersburg: Tovarishchestvo 'Obshchestvennaia pol'za', 1876), p. 311.

Turgenev presents Bazarov as skeptical, yet strong and assertive – a combination that characterized Lermontov's Pechorin as well. Lacking any ideal or belief, Pechorin remains confident and energetic despite his skepticism and nihilism:

> I like to have doubts about everything: this inclination of mind does not impinge upon resoluteness of character. On the contrary, as far as I am concerned, I always advance with greater courage when I do not know what awaits me.[22]

In his 1869 recollection of his two encounters with Lermontov, Turgenev singles out the presence of force, power and demonism in Lermontov's appearance, the same features that would later resurface in the presentation of Bazarov:

> Lermontov's appearance had something sinister and tragic, his dark face exuded some shimmering and threatening force … and passion … His whole figure, short and bow-legged, produced an unpleasant sensation, but the power that he had was recognized by anyone. It is known that to some degree he depicted himself in Pechorin. (*PSS*, XIV, 80)

Summarizing Lermontov's artistic achievement, Turgenev highlights the strength of Lermontov's personality: 'the strength of the independent, critical, protesting personality rebelled against falsehood and banality' (*PSS*, XIV, 40). For Turgenev, Lermontov embodies a 'protesting force', the image to which he frequently returns in his writings. In his essay on the writers of the first half of the nineteenth century, Turgenev once again refers to Lermontov as the emblem of a force that he defines as 'sinister, tragic, and dark' (*PSS*, XIV, 80).

Bazarov's individualism explains the hostility he provoked in both radical and conservative camps. Russian ideologues (conservative and radical alike) were inherently suspicious of any independent, self-reliant person. Both camps of Russian theoreticians embraced what Louis Dumont calls a 'holistic worldview', that is, an outlook that privileges the collective, be it patriarchal *sobornost* or progressive commune. Strong, independent

22 M. Yu. Lermontov, *A Hero of our Time*, in *PSS* in 5 vols, Vol. 5: *Prose Works and Letters* (Moscow: Academia, 1937 [1935–1937]), pp. 185–321; p. 192.

characters, such as Pechorin or Bazarov, were bound to be criticized and rejected by both sides.[23] A radical critic of the 1860s, M. A. Antonovich is a case in point. His vicious review of *Fathers and Sons* published by *Sovremenik*, under the title 'Asmodeus of Our Time', borrows heavily (both in its title and imagery) from the novel by the conservative V. I. Askochensky, who parodied Lermontov's *Hero of Our Time* in the 1840s.

While individualism tends to be criticized in Russia, its core values lie at the heart of two cardinal ideals of modernity: equality and liberty.[24] Furthermore, diverse doctrines of individualism appeal to such values as 'respect for human dignity, autonomy, privacy and self- development'.[25] Formed at the time of Romanticism, Turgenev was clearly attracted to the explosive combination of revolt, demonism, nihilism and individualism that Romanticism ushered in. In his famous letter to Pauline Viardot, Turgenev confesses: 'I prefer Satan, I prefer Prometheus, that type of revolt and individuality. I might be an atom, but I am my own man, I want truth and not salvation' (*PSS*, Pis'ma, I, 279).

Turgenev's agnosticism, skepticism and insistence on the paramount importance of freedom and independence of thought hardly need articulation. Yet he was also aware that consistent individualism, pride and ambition are ultimately destructive and self-destructive. Approaching life as a process of overcoming one's egoism for the sake of others, Turgenev maintained at one point,

> Bazarovs are not needed now. For current social activity neither special talents nor even special intelligence is needed – nothing big, overpowering, over individualistic [...] One must know how to sacrifice oneself without any ado; one must know how to humble oneself and not to abhor petty, insignificant, even lowly work [...] What could be simpler, for example, than to teach a peasant to read, to help him, to organize hospitals, etc.? Does one need talent and even education to do that? Only

23 In his study of individualism, French sociologist Louis Dumont juxtaposes the concept of individualism with that of 'holism', which he defines as 'an ideology that valorizes the social whole and neglects or subordinates the human individual'. Louis Dumont, *Essay on Individualism: Modern Ideology in an Anthropological Perspective* (Chicago: Chicago University Press, 1986), p. 279.

24 Steven Lukes, *Individualism* (Oxford: Basil Blackwell, 1973), pp. 125–145.

25 Ibid., p. 125.

> the heart is necessary, the ability to sacrifice one's egoism … a feeling of duty, the sense of patriotism in the most profound dimension of the term – that's all that's necessary. (*PSS*, Pis'ma, X, 295)

The function of a group, be it a family, a team, a party or a country, requires certain sacrifices on the part of its members – sacrifices that Bazarov is incapable of undertaking.

Turgenev is fully aware of the limits and tragic implications of consistent individualism. The novel's individualists seem to be lonely, fruitless and cut off from life (the name Odintsova – from Russian 'one' [*odin*] – is very suggestive in this respect), while the very first line that Bazarov pronounces in the novel intimates that consistent individualism is itself an oxymoron. Questioned about his name, Bazarov replies: 'Yevgeny Vassiliev'. The old-fashioned form of the Russian patronymic that Bazarov chooses (Vassiliev) literally means 'belonging to Vassily', that is, to his father; it immediately points to the link, to the continuity between fathers and children. Here we have the title of the novel replayed: fathers and children are interconnected; human beings are not alone, nor are they self-begotten: they are characterized both by their personal and their father's name.

No matter how hard Bazarov tries to be his own man and to attack family ties and feelings, he is bound to fail; it is hardly surprising that Turgenev invokes the concept of tragedy when he describes his hero. In his letter to Sluchevsky, Turgenev insists: 'The qualities assigned to him are not accidental. I wanted to present him as a tragic figure – without any tenderness. He is honest, straightforward, and a democrat to his fingertips' (*PSS*, Pis'ma, IV, 379).

The individualist's primary function is to branch away from the family, from the proscriptions and prescriptions of the older generations. It is thus hardly surprising that, in their depiction of heroic individualists, both Byron and Lermontov either chose orphans for their protagonists or simply ignored their family ties, thus avoiding the situations that might have presented their heroes in less flattering circumstances.

Even though he never married and had to deal with rather selfish and self-centered parents, Turgenev nevertheless recognized the importance of family and the mutual recognition and sacrifice upon which a family is built. After the marriage of his friend Annenkov, Turgenev writes to him:

> This event, so unexpected at one time, seems to me absolutely natural and necessary, and the more I think about it, the more joyful and beautiful your future life appears to me. Thank God! The man has made his nest, he has entered a harbor – thus, not all of us are lost!' (*PSS*, Pis'ma, IV, 187)

It is hardly a coincidence that the novel's self-reliant, strong and individualistic characters, such as Pavel Kirsanov, Odintsova or Bazarov, remain lonely and barren, preferring instead relationships based on rivalry. Bazarov's individualism and strength, while important for some other spheres, prove to be inadequate for the task of creating and maintaining family life as well as the life of culture, all of which rely on compromise and sacrifice for the sake of continuity.

Lermontov, we recall, faults his heroic individualists such as Arbenin, Pechorin or Demon both for their destructive violence and their ethical and aesthetic bareness. Following Lermontov, Turgenev questions the very ability of individualist heroes to function within a complex social and cultural framework, a network of mutual obligations and creative reworking of tradition. Turgenev stresses the artistic and cultural fruitlessness of Bazarov's type of nihilism and individualism.[26]

But before we dismiss Bazarov as a force that disrupts natural flow, cultural tradition and family dynamics, we should pay him his dues and appreciate him within the larger context of Russia's cultural situation. Turgenev himself wanted his readers to recognize and come to terms with Bazarov's heroism:

> Bazarov nonetheless overwhelms all the novel's other characters ... If the reader does not grow to love Bazarov, with all his coarseness, heartlessness, pitiless dryness, and sharpness – if he doesn't grow to love him, I repeat – then I am at fault and did not achieve my goal. (*PSS*, Pis'ma, IV, 379)

Bazarov's ambivalent strength, his energy coupled with his propensity toward disruption and destruction, became commonplace for all the future sons in their need to articulate their nihilistic and individualistic dogmas, while stressing their strength as the proof of their superiority.

26 See the discussion of Lermontov's criticism of his own heroes in Golstein, *Lermontov's Narratives of Heroism*, pp. 186–191.

One may recall the braggadocio of the Futurists, or the assertions of strength and nihilism by the characters of Gorky, Babel or Olesha (helped as they were by a new spin on the concept provided to them by one such belated Romantic nihilist Nietzsche).

Turgenev's ambivalence vis-à-vis Bazarov's owes much to Turgenev's complex attitude toward force (*sila*), independence and other individualistic attributes. Since the time of Milton, if not earlier, these attributes were associated with the demonic and therefore questioned if not condemned outright. During the period of Romanticism, however, they became the subject of reevaluation, if not praise. Turgenev, as he himself grew parallel to Romanticism, could not possibly miss that shift.

Turgenev explored the affinity between individualism, strength and (demonic) nihilism in his other writings as well. Thus, in his essay 'Hamlet and Don Quixote', written while composing the novel, Turgenev observes: 'Hamlets are preoccupied with themselves, hence they are lonely and fruitless [...] they leave no trace behind themselves, except the trace of their personality' (*PSS*, VIII, 178). Yet Turgenev also sees in Hamlet a centripetal force, which is as necessary for the development of humanity as that of the centrifugal force of Don Quixote, the force oriented toward other people.

Turgenev's novel is dedicated to the memory of Belinsky, one of the first Russian champions of an autonomous personality and individualism.[27] Turgenev clearly shared his illustrious contemporary's embrace of individualism and Romanticism. In his 1845 review of Vronchenko's translation of *Faust*, he provides the following description of a Romantic hero:

27 Belinsky, after he entered his post-Hegelian phase, asserted in his letter to V. P. Botkin that 'the human personality [*chelovecheskaia lichnost*] is now more sacred to me than history, more sacred than society, more sacred than mankind. This is the idea and the thought of our age!' (V. G. Belinsky, *Sobranie sochinenii v 9 tomakh* [Moscow: Khudozhestvennaia Literatura, 1978] Vol. 9, p. 403) (emphasis in the original). On the impact of Belinsky's individualism upon Turgenev, see A. I. Batiuto, *Tvorchestvo I. S. Turgeneva i kritiko-estetitechskaia mysl' ego vremeni* (Leningrad: Nauka, 1990), pp. 213–217.

> He becomes the center of the world around him; he [...] does not obey anyone, he forces everything to obey himself [...] he is a romantic, yet romanticism is no more than the apotheosis of personality. He is willing to discuss society, social questions, science; but society, like science, exists for him – not he for them. (*PSS*, I, 220)

Bazarov's militant self-centeredness is tied to his courageous embrace of existentialism:

> The narrow space I occupy is so tiny compared to the rest of the universe, where I am not present, and where nobody cares about me [...] Yet in this atom [...] blood circulates, a brain functions and desires. How unbearable. What nonsense. (*PSS*, VIII, 323)

Following Turgenev's lead, Shelgunov described Bazarov's nihilism as

> a healthy phenomenon, at its foundation lies the feeling of dignity and independence, the feeling of standing firmly on one's feet. It is the same feeling that makes Americans look straight into the eyes of any earthly and even unearthly power.[28]

Shelgunov articulates here Bazarov's feature highlighted by Turgenev himself, that he is 'a democrat to his fingernails' (*PSS*, Pis'ma, IV, 379).

Before he returns to his father, Arkady travels in the company of Bazarov. Individualism has to be experienced and outgrown, rather than simply discarded. A successful and meaningful return to the world of fathers starts with leaving, with breaking away from fathers and the embrace of individualistic values. True continuity is achieved only by overcoming discontinuity.

Bazarov and Pushkin

Turgenev was so disturbed by the hostile reception of his novel that he felt obliged to defend his masterpiece in an essay entitled 'Apropos Fathers

28 N. V. Shelgunov 'Liudi sorokovykh i shestidesiatykh godov', in I. S. Roman, *Turgeneva 'Otsy i deti' v russkoi kritike*, ed. I. N. Sukhikh (Leningrad: Leningradskii universitet, 1986), p. 293.

and Sons' published in 1869. He concludes this essay with the following rather unexpected plea directed toward the younger generation: 'And my request consists of the following: guard our language, our splendid Russian language, transmitted to us by our predecessors, at whose head Pushkin again shines' (*PSS*, XIV, 109). This appeal seems to be totally out of place in an article that focuses on ideological battles and is therefore all the more significant. It is equally significant that Turgenev places it at the very end of his essay. Seemingly disappointed in his hope of establishing a genuine dialogue with the younger generation, Turgenev nevertheless feels obliged once again to highlight the obvious and fundamental link that connects generations, namely, language and culture. It is this medium that links us to our predecessors, and the person who perfected this medium for Russians was, of course, Pushkin.

The image of Pushkin hovers over Turgenev's novel, skillfully uniting its diverse aspects. While his last appearance occurs in the final paragraph of the novel with a reference to 'indifferent nature', a term taken from Pushkin's profound lyrical meditation on the passing of generations 'Brozhu li ia vdol' ulitz shumnykh' (When I Wander Through the Noisy Streets, 1829), the poet makes his first appearance at the end of the third chapter. This appearance is highly emblematic and deserves further exploration. Impressed by the beautiful spring day, the old Kirsanov recites to his son a line from Pushkin's *Eugene Onegin*. The reciting of this line, which comments on the passage of seasons and generations, is interrupted by Bazarov, who asks for a match to light up his pipe. While father and son find a common language through the poetry of Pushkin, Bazarov interrupts, introducing the destructive element of fire and precluding the communication between the father and son and, more emblematically, between respective generations and Pushkin.

Pushkin's next appearance occurs in the tenth chapter of the novel, in which Arkady replaces Pushkin's narrative poem *The Gypsies*, which his father was reading, with a book of materialist philosophy. Needless to say, Pushkin's Byronic poem not only foreshadows the tragic love of both Pavel and Bazarov, it also points to the inevitable predicament of a strong individualistic personality like Bazarov. The rebellious Aleko escapes from European civilization only to discover that he does not really fit in with the Gypsy life either. The Old Gypsy, the father of the girl murdered by Aleko in a fit of jealousy, explains to him that their decision to exile him is motivated by the fact that 'you want freedom only for yourself': a description that summarizes Bazarov as well. The poem, therefore, contains a warning that neither Bazarov nor his loyal pupil Arkady is willing to listen or contemplate. One dismisses Pushkin at one's own peril – this seems to be Turgenev's suggestion.

Pushkin reappears in one of the longest chapters in the novel (chapter twenty-one) in which the two friends, Bazarov and Arkady, discuss various existential questions while resting on a haystack at Bazarov's little estate. As he converses with Arkady, Bazarov first admits his total lack of knowledge about his grandfather and then articulates his insight that any ideology is useless since one acts solely on the basis of one's sensations and desires (an observation that impressed Pisarev). Bazarov then decides to make further fun of Pushkin by attributing to him some militaristic verses along with the following almost Kharmsian line: 'nature inspires in us the silence of a dream' (*PSS*, VIII, 325). Eventually, Bazarov insults Arkady's relatives, practically provoking a physical fight with Arkady. The two friends are saved from this embarrassing episode by the appearance of Bazarov's father.

Bazarov's aggressive and provocative behavior as well as his preposterous jokes at the expense of Pushkin indicate that he has indeed reached the end of his tether as he breaks all possible connections to his fellow human beings. Bazarov's abuse of Pushkin is not only symptomatic, but it is also emblematic. On the one hand, Bazarov tries to camouflage his aggressiveness by attributing the lines of bombastic militarism to Pushkin, while on the other, his remark on nature deliberately perverts Pushkin's insights into the importance of natural rhythms and the human need to understand and accommodate them. As he mocks and dismisses Pushkin, Bazarov makes his alienation from his culture, his parents and his best friend explicit.

It is worth stressing that when Bazarov leaves his heartbroken parents, his father comforts himself and his wife with reference to the natural rhythms dismissed by Bazarov yet glorified by Pushkin. Bazarov Senior compares himself and his wife to two mushrooms growing on a tree stump while likening their son to a falcon. It is nature's complex, frequently contradictory, processes that give Bazarov's parents the strength to confront their loss. The young nihilist, however, refuses to understand this wisdom.

Turgenev, of course, buries Bazarov by giving the last words exactly to nature and Pushkin, as the novel concludes with a reference to 'indifferent nature' (*ravnodyshnaia priroda*), a quotation from Pushkin's 'When I Wander Along the Noisy Streets', the poem that juxtaposes individual ambitions with the cycle of natural rhythms and generations: 'And let the young life play by the entrance to my grave, and let the indifferent nature flaunt its eternal beauty.' Pushkin's acceptance of nature's beauty and wisdom, regardless of individual decline and death, is contrasted with Bazarov's futile and unwise self-aggrandizement.

In fact, the joke at the expense of Bazarov's failure to comprehend Pushkin and his relevance goes even further, since in his challenge to death – to typhus, to be precise – Bazarov echoes the plight of another glorious individualist and the champion of fighting for the sake of fighting: Pushkin's Walsingham. As he mocks Pushkin during his confrontation with Arkady, Bazarov claims that every page of Pushkin features an assertion: 'to the battle, to the battle [*na boi*], for the honor of Russia' (*PSS*, VIII, 326). Pushkin, of course, never wrote such lines, yet Bazarov's parody invokes Walsingham's embrace of 'battle' (*boi*): 'there is intoxication in battle'. Turgenev draws a curious parallel between Bazarov and Walsingham, enabling us to interpret the demise of Bazarov against the background of Walsingham's futile rebellion.

Turgenev, as a great artist and psychologist, shows that Bazarov's collapse took root from within. In order to pursue one's individualistic ambitions, to stand alone while rejecting all forms of authority, duty and obligation, one has to know that one is right. Yet Bazarov is being slowly robbed of his self-righteousness. He is left in a fix: to pursue his scientific experiments, which are becoming increasingly mechanical and myopic, or to harness his ambitions and begin following in his father's footsteps. This proves equally difficult. Bazarov's own father compares him to Napoleon, while Bazarov views himself as a Promethean figure, hardly fitted to be part of the family cycle and settle for the job of a country doctor. Hence, his half-conscious suicide. Bazarov's return to the house of his father is accompanied by his loss of direction. Bazarov's rejection of art, religion, beauty, family and traditions leaves him exposed and vulnerable: he has nothing to fall back onto. In his profound poem 'Two Feelings are Miraculously Dear To Us' ('Dva chuvstva divno blizki nam', 1830), Pushkin points to the only source that guarantees one's strength and self-reliance. He calls it 'love for the native abode and for one's ancestors' graves'. Paradoxically, it is the link to the world of the fathers that enables one to weather ruptures and discontinuities. The failure to connect to the world of his ancestors – to embrace the set of values embodied by his family and culture – eventually saps the strength out of Turgenev's rebellious character. For Pushkin, the guarantee of one's self-reliance and strength lie not in rebellion, but in the interaction with one's family, ancestors and history.

Bazarov, on the contrary, insists on breaking ties with his ancestral home; he admits to living at his parents' house for only two years, while wandering for the rest of his life. Nor does he remember or care much about his ancestors or parents. For Bazarov, the past is irrelevant. He dismisses it as 'Romanticism'. As he puts it on one occasion, 'why should I be dependent on time, let the time depend on me' (*PSS*, VIII, 226).

Throughout the novel, Bazarov appears to be attacking, mocking or rejecting Pushkin. The presence of Pushkin at key moments in Turgenev's novel highlights, however, the inadequacy of Bazarov's outlook, as measured against both nature and culture. Bazarov's fighting for fighting's sake puts him beyond the cycle of sons and fathers, beyond civilization and culture, beyond life itself.

Pavel Kirsanov recognizes 'satanic pride' in Bazarov. The key attribute of satanic rebellion is the rejection of God's role as a creator, a universal maker, a father.[29] In Milton's *Paradise Lost*, Satan insists on being 'self-begotten'. Bazarov, of course, has parents; Turgenev, however, has envisioned him as existing outside of the usual dynamics of fathers and children. In a letter to Sluchevsky, Turgenev acknowledges that Bazarov appeared to him

29 Turgenev's next novel, *The Smoke*, contains his bitter attack, and dismissal, of the so-called *samorodki* – literally, 'self-begotten' – the name applied to the young radicals, who claim to make great discoveries in art and science relying only on themselves.

as 'the figure […] half grown from the ground […] some sort of strange counterpart to Pugachev' (*PSS*, Pis'ma, IV, 381).

Bazarov's death points to Turgenev's profound understanding of the very nature of generational conflicts. All rebels start by denying their ties to their real and metaphorical fathers. Yet, after experiencing the excesses of rebellion and destruction, his wisest characters return to measure, culture and civilization, serving life and nature rather than their own self-centered pursuits. They embrace continuity.

Bibliography

Batiuto, A. I., *Tvorchestvo I. S. Turgeneva i kritiko-estetitechskaia mysl' ego vremeni* (Leningrad: Nauka, 1990).

Belinsky, V. G., *Sobranie sochinenii v 9 tomakh* (Moscow: Khudozhestvennaia Literatura, 1978).

Chernyshevsky, Nikolai, *Polnoe sobranie sochinenii v 15-ti tomakh* (Moscow: Goslitizdat, 1939–1953).

Costlow, Jane T., *Worlds within Words* (Princeton: Princeton University Press, 1990).

Dostoevsky, Fedor, 'Zimnie zametki o letnikh vpechatleniiakh', in *Polnoe sobranie sochinenii v 30 tomakh*, ed. V. G. Bazanov et al. (Leningrad: Nauka, 1972–1980).

Dumont, Louis, *Essay on Individualism: Modern Ideology in an Anthropological Perspective* (Chicago: Chicago University Press, 1986).

Egolin, A., *Osvoboditel'nye i patrioticheskie idei russkoi literatury XIX veka* (Moscow: Sovetskii Pisatel', 1946).

Feuer, Lewis S., *The Conflict of Generations: The Character and Significance of Student Movements* (New York: Basic Books, 1969).

Golstein, Vladimir, *Lermontov's Narratives of Heroism* (Evanston: Northwestern University Press, 1998).

Grigoriev, A. A., 'I. S. Turgenev i ego deiatel'nost'', in *Sochineniia Apollona Grigorieva* (St. Petersburg: Tovarishchestvo 'Obshchestvennaia pol'za', 1876).

Herzen, A. I., 'Eshshe raz Bazarov. Pis'mo vtoroe', in *Sobranie sochinenii v 30 tomakh* (Moscow: Nauka, 1960).

Kropotkin, P. A., *Vospominania. Zapiski revolutsionera* [Memoirs of a Revolutionist] (St. Petersburg: Izdatel Gennady Markelov, 2018).

Lermontov, M. Yu., *A Hero of our Time*, in *Polnoe sobranie sochinenii i pisem v 28 tomakh* (*PSS*) in 5 vols, Vol. 5: *Prose Works and Letters* (1937) (Moscow: Academia, 1935–1937), pp. 185–321.

Lowe, David, *Turgenev's Fathers and Sons* (New York: Ardis, 1983).

Lukes, Steven, *Individualism* (Oxford: Basil Blackwell, 1973).

Mayakovsky, Vladimir, *Polnoe sobranie sochinenii v trinadtsati tomakh* (Moscow: Khudozhestvennaia literatura, 1955), Vol. 1.

Merezhkovsky, D. S., *Vechnye sputniki* (Moscow: Nauka, 2007).

Morson, Gary Saul, 'Genre and Hero/Fathers and Sons: Intergeneric Dialogues, Generic Refugees and the Hidden Prosaic', in *Literature Culture and Society of Modern Age*, ed. Edward J. Brown, *Stanford Slavic Studies* 4 (Palo Alto, CA: Dept. of Slavic Languages and Literatures, Stanford University, 1991), pp. 336–381.

N. A. Dobroliubov v vospominaniakh sovremennikov, ed. S. Reiser (Moscow: Khodozhestvennaia Literatura 1986), p. 154.

Pecherskaia, T. I., *Raznochintsy shestidesiatykh godov XIX veka: Fenomen samosoznaniia v aspekte filologicheskoi germenevtiki* (Novosibirsk: Institut filologii RAN, 1999), pp. 61–95.

Poety 'Iskry': V dvukh tomakh, ed. I. G. Iampolsky (Leningrad: Sovetskii Pisatel', 1987).

Schefski, Harold K., 'The Parable of the Prodigal Son and Turgenev's Fathers and Sons', in *Ivan Turgenev: Bloom's Modern Critical Views*, ed. Harold Bloom (Philadelphia: Chelsea House Publishers, 2003), pp. 85–96.

Strakhov, N. N., 'Fathers and Sons', in Ivan Turgenev, *Fathers and Sons*, Second edition, ed. Ralph E. Matlaw (New York: Norton, 1989), pp. 219–220.

Turgenev, Ivan Sergeevich, *Polnoe sobranie sochinenii i pisem v 28 tomakh* (*PSS*), ed. M. P. Alexeev et al. (Leningrad: Nauka, 1961–1968).

PART III

From Literature to Performing Arts: Shifts of Cultural Paradigm

GALIMA LUKINA

11 The Problem of Continuity in S. I. Taneev's Views on the Future of Russian Music

Introduction

Where is humankind heading – toward destruction or a new stage of development? At this moment, we find ourselves at a point marking a civilization shift, which is accelerating due to the rapid development of a technology-based society. The gap between the present and the past, the modern and the traditional, is widening.

Is it possible to ensure continuity despite the vortexes of history that carry away the past experience of building a cultural dialogue?

Unfortunately, the predictions made by the American scientist Samuel P. Huntington about the intensified dispute between civilizational attitudes in the world have proved correct. Nevertheless, a human being is not a slave of history, but its participant. An example of this is Sergei I. Taneev (1856–1915), an outstanding Russian composer, scientist and teacher with a personality of considerable stature. It is only now that his uniqueness and the important role he played in the history of Russian music are being recognized.

Together with P. I. Tchaikovsky, his teacher, Taneev was the head of the Moscow school of composition. Among his students were S. V. Rachmaninoff, A. N. Scriabin, R. M. Glière, N. K. Medtner, A. D. Kastalsky, A. V. Nikolsky, S. N. Vasilenko, A. N. Aleksandrov, A. V. Stanchinsky, A. S. Arensky and S. S. Prokofiev. Taneev was instrumental in the establishment of the People's Conservatory in Moscow (1906–1916). Studying Taneev's notes, letters, diaries and theoretical works;

listening to the intonations of his cantatas *St John of Damascus* and *At the Reading of a Psalm*; the choral cycle to the lyrics by Ya. P. Polonsky; instrumental and vocal compositions; and the *Oresteia* trilogy, one becomes increasingly convinced of the rare integrity in all aspects of his work as well as his pedagogical, scientific and social activity.

Why is research into Taneev's work so important today for people of a different mentality? The reason is that the main theme of his creative legacy is world unity in the highest aspirations of the human spirit. Was Taneev himself aware of this great purpose? Not only did he know about it, but most importantly, he lived for it. Such was the heartfelt message of his entire life and work.

How much Taneev worshipped Tchaikovsky, and how much he appreciated all his remarks! Taking this fact into account, it is incredible that he argued with Tchaikovsky defending his main idea – his vision of the evolution of Russian and world culture that he wanted to be a party to.[1] Like M.I. Glinka, Taneev believed that contemporary Russian culture had not reached its 'full and complete development',[2] and he focused on searching for the roots of high art. Taneev was striving toward the spiritual ideals of Russian music in its unity with the Western musical experience, combining the lofty past with the future. He was convinced that the prominence of future art depended on the artist's efforts. What a strong spiritual message! A deep yearning for the unity of secular and church music shaped Taneev's idea of creating an Orthodox cantata. It was when he presented the cantata *St John of Damascus* – his first opus (undoubtedly a masterpiece!) – that Tchaikovsky recognized the importance of the way Taneev had chosen. Its essence can be found in Taneev's epistolary legacy, including his earliest notes entitled 'What should Russian composers do?'

1 See S. I. Taneev's Correspondence with P. I. Tchaikovsky (1880–1881) in *P. I. Tchaikovsky, S. I. Taneev. The Letters*, under the editorship of V. A. Zhdanov (Moscow: Goskul'tprosvetizdat, 1951). All further references to Taneev's correspondence with Tchaikovsky refer to this source.

2 *S. I. Taneev's Correspondence with P. I. Tchaikovsky*, under the editorship of V. A. Zhdanov (Moscow, 1951), p. 58.

('From a Memorable Notebook', 1875, 1877, 1879)[3], letters to Tchaikovsky and aesthetic notes dating back to the 1895–1896 period.[4] Taneev's global vision of the evolution of Russian music could possibly be compared to the concept of history of Russian culture as a whole developed by many Russian philosophers and writers of the second half of the nineteenth and early twentieth century, namely, the representatives of the epoch known as 'Cultural Renaissance of Russia'.

Referring to Sergei Taneev's writings, we shall focus on the main ideas concerning the subject matter indicated in the title of this chapter.

Spiritual crisis of European culture

Like many Russian thinkers of that time, Taneev was observing the cultural transformation of spiritual values. According to him, the focus on creative activity and life was shifting from 'high human aspirations' to material comfort. He noticed the connection between such a life-philosophy and the changes taking place in contemporary music of the time, and he criticized composers' rejection of the tonal system, long form and, in general, the achievements of the classical legacy. In his opinion, the symptoms of the disease of the spirit appeared first in Western European culture and, consequently, in music: 'Its classical age has passed, it is leaning towards mannerism and triviality' (Taneev's letter to Tchaikovsky, 6 August 1880).[5]

3 'S. I. Taneev Notebook 1875–1879', Archive of the Tchaikovsky State House-Museum, S. I. Taneev's Museum Fund, B 4, No. 20.

4 Presumably, these records date back to the period of most regular communication between S. I. Taneev and L. N. Tolstoy. The reason to refer to the dates mentioned is that it was during this time that L. N. Tolstoy was working on *What Is Art?* and shared his thoughts with the composer. The records show Taneev's intention to present his own artistic concept and to document his own idea of a perfect work of art.

5 *S. I. Taneev's Correspondence with P. I. Tchaikovsky*, p. 50.

Discussing trends in the work of some contemporary Western European composers in a letter to Tchaikovsky dated 17 December 1910, Taneev raised the following questions: 'Why is the desire for novelty limited to two areas – harmony and instrumentation? Why is there nothing new and noticeable about counterpoint? Why, on the contrary, is it falling into decay compared to before? Why is the potential of forms not unveiled? Why are the very forms becoming shorter and decaying?'[6]

Taneev comprehended the evolution of Russian music comparing it with that of Europe: 'Music in Europe is diminishing. There is nothing to match high aspirations. Contemporary European music perfectly displays the character of its creators: sophisticated, elegant, somewhat weak, accustomed to or striving for a comfortable life, and enjoying zest. The people, the music… However, it is important to be accurate in statements: it is not right to say that such is our time and such is our music. Western music is experiencing such a time – that would be more precise. But do not apply this to us' (Taneev's letter to Tchaikovsky, 6 August 1880).[7]

Taneev's arguments send us back to the dispute between Slavophiles and Westernizers about Russia's relation to the West, the opportunities and ways of manifesting the national character in art, the theory of historical-cultural types by N. Ya. Danilevsky and V. S. Solovyov's Russian idea.

One of the first in Russian literature to address the subject of critique of Western culture in a systematic form was V. F. Odoyevsky (in the 1830s). In the words of Faust, the protagonist of 'Russian Nights', Odoyevsky expressed the idea of the decay of the West, of the internal disintegration of its former strength:

> We venture to say something which will perhaps seem strange to many people today, but in time will become all too plain: the West is perishing. So now the salvation of Europe is possible only if a new nation with fresh energies enters the historical scene.

According to Odoyevsky, it was the Russian people: 'We, Russians, must not merely save the body of Europe; we must also save its soul, for it

6 Ibid.

7 Ibid.

is a question of the internal transformation of the very foundations of Western culture' – says Faust.[8]

The topic of the crisis of Western civilization, culture, philosophy and the search for new ways of development is a recurring issue for Russian thought at the turn of the century. It was especially relevant in the 1870s, largely owing to the work of V. S. Solovyov.

Taneev's view coincides with the culturological theories of many philosophers of the second half of the nineteenth century who drew attention to the decay of the very idea of personality. In the 1880s, K. N. Leont'ev wrote that in decaying Europe, people are besotted with 'progress', outwardly attractive technical advancements and material benefits that in essence are aimed at quickly equaling, mixing and merging everyone into godless and impersonal 'average bourgeois', 'the ideal and the instrument of ultimate destruction'.[9]

In Western European culture, the national in human existence was gradually suppressed by the social, and, as stated by P. E. Astafiev,[10] the idea of a nation was being replaced by that of a 'society'.[11] Against this background formed by the mid-nineteenth century, Russian culture clearly defined its own position: the preference for ideas, images and music material with a pronounced national character. It was to exactly the idea of national character that many representatives of nineteenth-century art devoted effort, Taneev included.

8 V. F. Odoyevsky, 'Russian Nights' (novel), <http://az.lib.ru/o/odoewskij_w_f/text_0020.shtml>

9 K. N. Leont'ev, 'Vostok, Rossiia i slavianstvo' [The East, Russia and Slavdom], <https://azbyka.ru/otechnik/Konstantin_Leontev/vostok-rossija-i-slavjanstvo/>

10 Pyotr Astafiev (1846–1893) is a Russian philosopher, psychologist and legal expert. In his philosophical works, he developed the concept of the relationship between faith and knowledge of the Eastern Church Fathers.

11 P. E. Astafiev, 'The Religious "Renewal" of Our Days' (1891), in *Faith and Knowledge in the Unity of the Worldview* (Moscow, 1893), pp. 1–53, pp. 17–18.

Sergei Taneev: 'What should Russian composers do?'

Taneev's first opinion regarding the future of Russian art can be found in his famous notes entitled 'What Should Russian Composers Do?' Here, Taneev critically evaluated the course taken by his compatriot composers:

> Russian musicians are learning Western music and encounter ready-made musical forms. They either create European-style compositions, or try to squeeze the Russian song into European forms, neglecting the fact that they are not organically connected. The form of any composition is closely related to the material it is based on [...] European forms are alien to us, we do not have the forms of our own. (February 1879)[12]

In one of the letters to Tchaikovsky in 1880, Taneev voiced the problem of the future of Russian music again:

> We are groping in the dark. This is absolutely true about what we call the Russian style, Russian harmony. The best evidence of this is that in the textbook on harmony written by our first composer, there is not a word about these harmonic progressions which bring special charm and bear the imprint of a Russian character. Is this not evidence that this style has not been clearly defined and developed into a harmonious system, similar to the Western one? Indeed, we are groping in the dark.

Taneev analyzed the history of the establishment of European forms and formulated his own vision of the development path that Russian composers should follow:

> No form has been established accidentally; they all necessarily followed from the previous ones. Therefore, the foundation for European music is folk songs and church melodies. They have been processed for several centuries, which has resulted in establishing Western European forms. Thus, these folk melodies gave rise (*in potentia*) to all contemporary European music. It was only necessary to apply a human thought to them, so that they turn into lavish forms [...]

12 S. I. Taneev, 'From a Memorable Notebook 1875, 1877, 1879', in *History of Russian Music in Research and Materials: Sergei Ivanovich Taneev; Personality, Creativity and Documents of His Life, on the 10th Anniversary of His Death 1915–1925*, 2 vols, ed. K. A. Kuznetsov (Moscow: Music Sector of Gosizdat, 1925), pp. 73–77; p. 74.

> The objective of every Russian musician is to contribute to the creation of national music. The history of Western music demonstrates what should be done to reach it: namely, apply thinking to the Russian song, as it has been done to the Western song; and we will have national music.[13]

Taneev directed his compatriots toward not imitation of European culture, but 'creation of national music' and 'clarification of the Russian character'. He wrote to Tchaikovsky:

> We can feel this Russian character; it injects new life into your compositions and those of Glinka. My idea is that the Russian colouring in music will get more and more pronounced with time, thus developing into a style significantly different from that of Europe.[14]

Taneev's reflections on the future of Russian music developed into the idea of a genre that would continue the Russian tradition of choral singing. In a letter to Ya. P. Polonsky, he wrote: 'As the basis [...] for the cantata I would like to take ancient melodies of our Church and therefore create an Orthodox cantata' [underlined by Taneev].[15] This idea was further implemented in the scores *St John of Damascus* and *At the Reading of a Psalm*.

For Taneev, it was of the utmost importance to preserve the spiritual and genetic code of Russian culture, which originated from church culture. According to V. V. Medushevsky, the difference between secular serious music and church music is that 'the divine grace of church music transforms and creates, while that of secular can only encourage'.[16] Taneev seems to remind us of these origins of music. He thoroughly studied hooked notation, the eight church modes and the general theory and history of

13 Ibid.

14 *S. I. Taneev's Correspondence with P. I. Tchaikovsky*, p. 58.

15 N. S. Ganenko, 'S.I. Taneyev on spiritual music (in letters to Ya. P. Polonsky)' in *Old Russian lyric poetry: Based on conference materials "Brazhnikovsky Readings - 2002"* (St. Petersburg: St. Petersburg (Leningrad) Conservatoire named after N. A. Rimsky-Korsakov, 2004), pp. 292-299. P. 294.

16 V. V. Medushevsky, 'Tainstvennye energii muzyki' ('Mysterious energies of music'), *Music Academy*, No. 3, 1992, pp. 54–58. P. 55.

Russian church singing; transcribed chants; and participated in Orthodox choral events. All these testify to Taneev's deep involvement in the establishment of the so-called New Direction in sacred music at the turn of the twentieth century. Through his selfless devotion, Taneev preserved and strengthened the ethos of Russian culture in order to keep art connected with its innermost spiritual source – namely, the creativity of the Russian people. It was clear to him that in challenging times only a single organic intonation system would stand out, led by traditional principles: Russian music experience and mentality.

Meanwhile, Taneev was not the only one to be genuinely interested in the topic of originality of Russian art and the preservation of its national character. The prominent figure of that time was V. V. Stasov, the art critic and renowned ideologist of the Balakirev circle. In his work *Twenty-Five Years of Russian Art* (1882–1883), Stasov wrote:

> The distinguishing feature of the Russian School is its constant search for national character. This began with Glinka and has continued until the present time. Such a desire is nowhere to be found in any other European school.[17]

Specific features of Taneev's interpretation of national character can be comprehended through its comparison with V. V. Stasov's theory.

S. I. Taneev and V. V. Stasov: Understanding national character in art

Despite the marked ideological difference between the Moscow school of composition and the Balakirev circle, both S. I. Taneev and V. V. Stasov had a similar interpretation of the creative goal of Russian composers: namely, strengthening the national identity that contributed to

17 V. V. Stasov, 'Twenty-Five years of Russian Art', in *History of Aesthetics*, ed. M. F. Ovsiannikov (Moscow: Iskusstvo, 1969), Vol. 4, pp. 653–658; p. 657.

the development of the Russian style in music. However, there are two different methodologies for creating national character.

Thus, Stasov believed that for the new Russian School 'recognized authorities [...] do not exist';[18] moreover, 'the artist has neither the right nor the opportunity to represent the centuries which he himself has not lived in and does not know from life'.[19] According to Stasov's theory, the second key feature of the Russian style besides national character is realism based on 'denial of ideality'.[20] Such understanding of realism is partly due to the fact that Russian philosophical and aesthetic thought is continuously influenced by the atheistic materialism of the 'Sixtiers' and the ideas of the 'critical movement' of N. G. Chernyshevsky. But in Taneev's aesthetic concept, these influences cannot be heard. Taneev establishes spiritual realism – realism in its highest sense. For Taneev, art is a 'spiritual activity [...] uniting people by means of love, not violence, and providing the sense and joy of unity or suffering from separation anxiety' and 'reality is not what happens, but what takes place in the artist's soul'.[21]

The key aspects of Taneev's concept of national character in Russian music are as follows:

> Firstly, Taneev is not referring to reproducing what is immediately seen in Russian life or quoting musical folk tunes.

Taneev considered that the Russian national character in an artist grows gradually; an artist acquires a national temperament, being naturally impressed by the land, the people and the surrounding world. Here is an abstract from Taneev's letter to Tchaikovsky dated 18 August 1880:

18 Ibid.

19 Ibid., pp. 655–656.

20 Ibid., p. 654.

21 S. I. Taneev, various extracts and notes on philosophy. Archive of the Tchaikovsky State House-Museum: S. I. Taneev's Museum Fund, 3, Nos 40 and 41 (pp. 1–5). For more details, see G. U. Lukina, *S. I. Taneev's Works in Relation with the Russian Spiritual Tradition* (Moscow: Compositor, 2015).

> the fact that you were born in Russia, heard the songs, lived among the nature that influenced the temperament of the Russian people – these and many other reasons make your music often have a special, different from European, character.[22]

This discussion is very close to A. S. Khomyakov's view: 'The artist does not create on their own; it is the spiritual power of the nation in the artist that creates.'[23] A similar statement can be found in the works of Taneev's contemporary, the Russian philosopher S. N. Bulgakov: 'Nationality is identified in the intuitive experiencing of reality [...] The national spirit is not limited to any of its demonstrations, does not fuse with them, does not stiffen in them.'[24] In other words, the national spirit is a living and creative element, which is related to the soul gravitating toward the source of eternal life and salvation.

Unlike Stasov with his materialistic understanding of realism, Taneev believed that 'without a conscientious and sincere attitude to the spiritual side of one's nature, a person cannot become either moral or happy' (Letter to Yu. I. Sabaneeva dated 1897).[25] For Taneev, the primary indicator of the Russian national character was 'the highest human aspirations'.[26] Therefore, according to him, the main value criterion of Russian art is ethos – that is, orientation toward the 'inner person'.

Secondly, for Taneev, national character was the main dimension in a composer's self-comprehension. He was looking for Russian patterns and signs of what 'thinking the Russian way' implied.

The main goal for Taneev in his experimental creative work with folk songs was not so much to accurately preserve the original melodic source in his interpretation, but to develop creative sensitivity to folk traits and folk musical language in such manifestations as fluctuating structure,

22 *P. I. Tchaikovsky and S. I. Taneev's Letters,* ed. M. I. Tchaikovsky (Moscow: P. Jurgenson, 1916), p. 148.

23 A. S. Khomyakov, 'On the Possibility of Russian School of Art' (1847), in *Collected Works* (Moscow, 1861), Vol. 4, p. 414.

24 S. N. Bulgakov, *Two Cities: Research of the Nature of Public Ideals* (Moscow, 1911), Vol. 2, p. 284.

25 S. I. Taneev, *Materials and Documents,* Vol. 1: *Correspondence and Memoirs* (Moscow, 1952), p. 311.

26 From Taneev's letter to Tchaikovsky, 6 August 1880.

asymmetrical phrase construction, absence of theatrical thematic contrasts, amplitude and freedom of melodic development, and chanting of words (this refers to melodious lyrical songs). Taneev felt that melodiousness was an important distinguishing feature of Russian thinking. In a letter to Tchaikovsky, Taneev mentioned that 'Russian melodies must be placed in the foundation of music education' (18 September 1880).[27] The gradual introduction of national melodic material into the musical consciousness of composers, from Taneev's perspective, could contribute to the emergence of the Russian style.

Thirdly, in Taneev's aesthetic concept, unlike that of Stasov, a necessity was continuity between the work of Russian composers and all that was valuable in European music. Composers' attention to the treasures of the European past was declared to be 'the direct way forward'.

According to Taneev, 'the age-old wisdom of European musicians' was necessary to find what is best for Russian art. Though he studied European music, he had no intention of copying it, nor did he ever dream of becoming a European composer. In other words, he revered Western classical music for the sake of the prosperous development of Russian music.

Understanding pedagogical activity as transferring knowledge received from previous generations, Taneev relied on the knowledge acquired from the great teachers – from medieval singers and Dutch polyphonists to Tchaikovsky. N. K. Medtner mentioned this in his book *The Muse and the Fashion*: 'The past teachers of musical theory, in teaching us the laws of our art (with the aid of rules), passed on to us a kind of testament of the former great musicians'.[28] Many of the prominent representatives of the Russian school of composers, performers and scientists, being Taneev's students, followed the principles of the 'World Teacher' (as defined by A. K. Glazunov).

27 *S. I. Taneev's Correspondence with P. I. Tchaikovsky*, p. 58.

28 N. Medtner, *The Muse and the Fashion; Being a Defence of the Foundations of the Art of Music* (Paris: YMCA Press, 1978), p. 63.

The two roads or 'Russian synthesis'

Performing one of fundamental tasks of Russian musical art, that is, searching for ways to save music from 'the decay of musical form' and the 'degeneration of the structure of individual parts and the depression of the general composition',[29] Taneev developed a concept according to which Russian composers can

> on the one hand, contribute to the growth of the European tree, but on the other hand, cultivate our own crops [...] Glinka followed both of these ways [...] My idea is that, over time, Russian features in music will acquire their specific character, which will contribute to the development of a unique style, distinctly different from the European one. (Taneev's letter to Tchaikovsky, 18 August 1880)[30]

At a first glance, there is a certain contradiction: on the one hand, Taneev criticized Russians 'composing in the European style', while, on the other, he said they 'should learn from the Europeans'. In fact, in Taneev's opinion, the distinguishing characteristic of the Russian style should be a harmonious combination of Russian and European principles, possible, for example, in the form of a 'Russian fugue' or an 'Orthodox cantata'.

In his day, M. I. Glinka strained after 'espousing the western fugue with the norms of our music' (letter to K. A. Bulgakov in November 1856).[31] Then it was Taneev who encouraged his compatriots:

> We shall start with basic counterpoint forms, and further move on to more complex ones, develop the form of a Russian fugue, and then complex instrumental forms. It took the Europeans several centuries, but in our case the time shall be considerably reduced. We know the way, we know our goal, and we can easily turn to the European experience. Let us learn from the experience of the early contrapuntists and take on

29 S. I. Taneev, *Convertible Counterpoint in the Strict Style*, ed. S. S. Bogatyriov (Moscow, 1959), p. 10. Taneev writes about these changes in many of his works, including in his letters to Tchaikovsky (August 1880); in a diary entry (15 March 1896); in a letter to N. N. Amani (8 November 1903); and in the Introduction to *Convertible Counterpoint in the Strict Style*.

30 *S. I. Taneev's Correspondence with P. I. Tchaikovsky*, p. 58.

31 M. I. Glinka, Letter to K. A. Bulgakov, *Russian Archive*, 1869, No. 12, p. 280.

> a difficult but glorious task. Who knows, maybe we will leave new forms, new music to the generations to come.[32]

Taneev considered himself to be as good as a successor of the work started by Glinka who put together a 'program' for creating national music.

Characterizing Russian classical culture, the contemporary philosopher S. S. Horujy noted that in the nineteenth century the need to 'bring together all the components of a patchwork culture'[33] was recognized. 'The task of Russian synthesis was to successfully transform the alien into one's own, the borrowed and patchwork into the organic and creative'. Undoubtedly, this task is fully consistent with the one set for the Russian composers by Taneev. The latter explains Taneev's desire to comprehend the basics of medieval monody, counterpoint, Bach's polyphony, the music of Mozart and Beethoven as well as the history of church singing. He aimed at finding a solid foundation for the universal experience of intonation construction for Russian music.

Taneev's 'immersion into the depths of history' in the context of the dynamic culture of the time may seem paradoxical, but only at first glance. Unlike many artists of the Silver Age, not being afraid to seem 'old-fashioned', he turned to well-known forms that seemed 'obsolete' at the turn of the twentieth century but revealed some universal principles that ensure the continuous development of culture.

'Non-modernity' as a property of Taneev's muse expresses the composer's exceptional responsiveness to the Eternal. The most important indicator of art for the composer was 'the highest aspirations of a person'. In a letter to A. S. Arensky, Taneev wrote:

> The goal [of creativity] is to rise above what people consider important and essential and what is actually insignificant and vulgar, to know and create the truly great, truly beautiful. Achieving this goal is the perfect happiness available to man. [34]

32 Taneev, 'From a Memorable Notebook 1875, 1877, 1879', p. 74.

33 S. S. Horujy, 'Slavophiles, Westernizers, and the Birth of Russian Philosophical Humanism', in *A History of Russian Philosophy 1830–1930: Faith, Reason, and the Defense of Human Dignity* (Cambridge: Cambridge University Press, 2010).

34 Taneev, *Materials and Documents*, p. 96.

Conclusion

L. L. Sabaneev described the historical significance of the figure of S. I. Taneev in the following way:

> We have come to a point when all values get re-evaluated [...] the achievements that were worshipped before are becoming obsolete with a breakneck speed. What was new yesterday has today become old, dull and ordinary. Music, like some sport, has turned into a race and is developing in an unknown direction with constant acceleration [...]. Wise man Taneev appears to be right again, his attitude to eternal beauty is again justified [...] the musical community is again longing for beautiful sound forms. [35]

It has been almost a hundred years since Sabaneev expressed this idea, but the thirst for the beauty of music, and of art in general, as well as for the beauty of ideas and meanings is even more intense now.

Many of the issues raised by Taneev continue to be relevant today: for example, the situation of an uncertain future, existential isolation and the lack of a large-scale reality due to technical and information dependence.

Therefore, let us follow Taneev's wisdom, which implies salvation of a person through preservation of traditions and transfer of artistic achievements across generations owing to which deep transcendental connection of cultural experience is translated through time.

Bibliography

Astafiev, P. E., 'Religious "Renewal" of Our Days' (1891), in *Faith and Knowledge in the Unity of the Worldview* (Moscow, University printing house, 1893), pp. 1–53.

Bulgakov, S. N., *Two Cities: Research of the Nature of Public Ideals* (Moscow, Tovarishchestvo tipografii A.I.Mamontova, 1911), vol. 2, p. 313.

35 L. L. Sabaneev, *Memories of Taneev* (Moscow: Classic-21, 2003), p. 38.

Glinka, M. I., Letter to K. A. Bulgakov, *Russian Archive*, No. 12 (1869), p. 280.
Khomyakov, A. S., 'On the Possibility of Russian School of Art' (1847), in *Collected Works* (Moscow, 1861), Vol. 4.
Lukina, G. U., *S. I. Taneev's Works in Relation with the Russian Spiritual Tradition* (Moscow: Compositor, Compositor, 2015), p. 364.
Medtner, N., *The Muse and the Fashion; Being a Defence of the Foundations of the Art of Music* (Paris: YMCA Press, 1978), p. 156.
Sabaneev, L. L., *Memories of Taneev* (Moscow: Classic-21, 2003), p. 196.
Stasov, V. V., 'Twenty-Five Years of Russian Art', in *History of Aesthetics*, ed. M. F. Ovsiannikov (Moscow: Iskusstvo, 1969), Vol. 4, pp. 653–658.
Taneev S. I., *Convertible Counterpoint in the Strict Style*, ed. S. S. Bogatyriov (Moscow, Gosmuzizdatel'stvo, 1959), p. 383.
——— 'From a Memorable Notebook 1875, 1877, 1879', in *History of Russian Music in Research and Materials: Sergei Ivanovich Taneev; Personality, Creativity and Documents of His Life, on the 10th Anniversary of His Death 1915–1925* , ed. K. A. Kuznetsov, 2 vols (Moscow: Music Sector of Gosizdat, 1925), pp. 73–77.
——— *Materials and Documents*, Vol. 1: *Correspondence and Memoirs*, ed. K. A. Kuznetsov, V.A. Kiselev, T.N. Livanova, V.V. Protopopov (Moscow, Izdatel'stvo akademii nauk SSSR, 1952), vol. 1, p. 356.
——— Notebook 1875–1879. Archive of the Tchaikovsky State House-Museum, S. I. Taneev's Museum Fund, B 4, No. 20.
——— *S. I. Taneev's Correspondence with P. I. Tchaikovsky*, ed. V. A. Zhdanov (Moscow, Goskul'tprosvetizdat, 1951), p. 557.
———Various Extracts and Notes on Philosophy. Archive of the Tchaikovsky State House-Museum. S. I. Taneev's Museum Fund, B 3, Nos 40 and 41, pp. 1–5.
Tchaikovsky, P. I., *P. I. Tchaikovsky and S. I. Taneev's Letters* ed. M. I. Tchaikovsky (Moscow: P. Jurgenson, 1916), p. 188.

Translated by Natalia Dezhina

ELENA ARTAMONOVA

12 Silver Age Aesthetics versus New Conceptions of Soviet Time in Music: Continuity or Discontinuity with the Past?

Our listening habits are firmly rooted in our upbringing, our inner circle and surroundings that form our interests, likes and dislikes. We associate the idea of a national character with folklore and authenticity of traditions, in which art is recognizable and, therefore, appeals to its people. The newborn world of socialism in 1917 wanted to break with tradition and find complete freedom of expression for artistic personality. It sought to revolutionize the world and discover new horizons. In order to achieve these goals, the new Socialist state needed new music, literature and art created by faithful citizens. This formal renunciation of everything connected to the past laid foundations for the appearance of new tendencies and experiments in music, which, in the words of Nikolai Roslavets, one of the most unconventional composers of the avant-garde, 'dreamt of new unheard worlds of sound'.[1] Did composers really break with tradition or skillfully adjust and modify their language according to the requirements of the new musical era? The aim of this chapter is to find out how far and why these concepts found their continuation and modification in Soviet times. The under-researched

1 Nikolai Andreevich Roslavets, 'N.A. Roslavets o sebe i svoyom tvorchestve' [Nikolai Roslavets on Himself and His Creativity], *Sovremennaia muzyka*, No. 5 (14 January 1924), p. 133. Russian avant-garde artists of this period (1890s to early 1930s) strove for radical innovations and experimentations in art, music and culture by pushing artistic and social boundaries of tradition and the norm. All quotations from Russian sources and texts cited in this chapter have been translated by the author, Elena Artamonova.

writing of Alexei Losev on music will also be discussed. The analysis in this chapter relies heavily on unpublished and little-researched materials from the archives in Moscow.

Writing about the production of *Boris Godunov* in 1913, the music critic Viacheslav Karatygin emphasized the following:

> Tradition is a faceless arithmetical average of different performances of a certain work by various talented artists. Its honesty rests in the fact that distinguished talents took part in its creation. Its deceit is that it is an average proportional, uncoloured, bloodless and faceless object. Abandon its deceit without forgetting about its honesty and breathe new life and power into tradition. Do not break ties with what it has of true honesty. Impart this honesty to a new light that is shining with the fire of your talent.[2]

Issues of spiritual and artistic unity as well as efforts to strengthen the force of spirit by discovering sacred sides of other worlds occupied the thoughts of young Russian intellectuals at the turn of the twentieth century. This period is regarded as the 'Silver Age' of Russian culture owing to the emergence of a highly gifted generation of musicians, writers and painters. The inner world of an artist of the Silver Age was intensely engaged with questions of life and death. They were the staples of internal existence and, therefore, the reality coexisted with people's dreams and images.

The ideas of one of the most distinguished Russian philosophers and philologists of the twentieth century Alexei Fedorovich Losev (1893–1988) were on the cusp of the Silver Age and the avant-garde cultures. They had an immense impact on the musical language of the time:

> A musician is so intoxicated with his inner depths of thought standing at the edge of a deep abyss of the cosmos, of irrational images of mysteries and discoveries, and

2 Viacheslav Karatygin, 'Muzykal'naia drama. O postanovke Borisa Godunova' [Musical Drama. On the Production of Boris Godunov], *Apollon*, No. 8 (1913), p. 68. Quoted in *Iz istorii muzykal'noi zhizni Rossii. XIX–XX veka* [From the History of Musical Life in Russia in the Nineteenth-Twentieth Centuries], ed. E. K. Kulova (Moscow: MGK, 1992), p. 79.

> he is so much absorbed in the magical world of sounds that he carelessly observes catastrophes happening in real life.[3]

This was a certain cause for an alliance with the new Soviet power. Many philosophical works of Losev were published in the twentieth century, but his short stories and novels were discovered only shortly after his death by his second wife in the drawers of his working desk at his home in Moscow. His understanding of music and its content as well as the issue of the correlation and dissimilarity between music and human life are the key subjects of these works. Akin to the conception of one's own exploration through cognition, for Losev 'cognition is the creation, feast and symphony of life itself'.[4] Consequently, one should interpret creativity in music as a method of cognition and the means of getting to the inner meaning of existence.

This subject matter of affinity between the elements of existence and creativity in music, as a method of cognition and as a synthesis of all mortal beauty and inventiveness in the world, traditionally associated with the pre-Revolutionary Silver Age aesthetic, was also expressed by the avant-garde composers, including Arseny Avraamov, Nikolai Roslavets and Arthur Lourié. Thus, Arseny Avraamov (1886–1944), the Commissar of Arts of the Soviet Republic, an academic of the GAHN[5] and the creator of the ultra-chromatic 48-tone microtonal system called 'The Universal System

3 Alexei Losev, *Ia soslan v XX vek* [I Am Sent to the Twentieth Century] (Moscow: Vremia, 2002), Vol. 1, p. 126. More than 800 pieces of Losev's work were written on different subjects in aesthetics and dialectics, ancient and Christian philosophies as well as on myth, logic and name. Losev gained professional degrees in philosophy, classical philology and music as well as in mathematics. However, the basis of his ideas was not only the result of remarkable formal intellect and erudition. The perception of unity, first introduced by the philosopher Vladimir Solovyov (1853–1900), made a great impact on Russian writers, musicians and philosophers, and guided and directed the philosophical views of Losev.

4 Losev, *Ia soslan v XX vek*, Vol. 1, p. 180.

5 GAHN is the abbreviation for the State Academy of Arts Science. It was founded in 1921 in Moscow in order to pursue detailed scientific research into issues of art and culture, including a synthesis of the arts. It had the following three departments: physics/mathematics, philosophy and sociology.

of Tones', who is better known for his *Simfoniia gudkov* (Symphony of Factory Sirens, 1922), also tried to combine the epistemology of life with creativity. He interpreted creativity as love, art, religion, science, philosophy and revolution, and as a synthesis of all mortal beauty and inventiveness in the world. In August 1923, Avraamov called these six powerful 'Virgin-Leaders' (gurus) as the 'six great creative powers force Mankind towards the boundless steppes of the Future on their way from epistemology to creativity in life.'[6] However, he admitted that these powers were opponents who fight with each other. Avraamov even compared these antagonists with the legend of the construction of the Tower of Babel as they failed despite their individual strengths. He acknowledged that this failure was the ominous paradox of the present Soviet time. Avraamov believed that the unity of these powers through revolutionary actions would bring 'the Great Kingdom of Harmony', which would direct humankind to breath-taking prospects of creativity.

Striving for independence and the value of one's own experience and evaluation based on personal wisdom as the means of creative perfection, while retaining the favor of the authorities of the past, occupied young intellectuals at the turn of the century. This viewpoint also correlated with the position of the new Soviet authorities that publicly denied the value of the achievements of ancestors. Thus, Avraamov commented that, in his view, the contribution of Johann Sebastian Bach led to chronic stagnation in music:

> In 20–30 years, the great legacy of Bach will become a part of ancient legend … It is enough that we have already lost two hundred years of logical evolution in arts. We will answer with our counterrevolution to the revolution of Bach regardless of the many sacrifices this would bring to the altar of our future.[7]

6 Arseny Avraamov, 'Revtraktat o NOVMUZERE "bez predkov" SSSR 6-oi god I-go veka' [Revolutionary Treatise on New Music 'Without Ancestors' in the USSR of the Sixth Year of the First Century]. Quoted in Sergei Rumianzev, *Ars novyi, ili dela i prikliucheniia bezustal'nogo kazaka Arseniia Avraamova* [New Arts or Activities and Adventures of the Tireless Cossack Arseny Avraamov] (Moscow: Deka-VC), p. 60.

7 Arseny Avraamov, 'Griadushchaia muzykal'naia nauka i novaia era istorii muzyki' [The Future Science of Music and the New Era of Music History], *Muzykal'nyi*

This approach in turn links with the idea of the Silver Age aesthetic in which the means of comprehension was not simply an intellectual process but a heroic deed of life, which became a destiny for only a few. 'The definition of understanding means for one to experience, renovate and rise above the renovated, and then to be transformed into the raison d'être or in other words into existence.'[8] These dreams of idealistic ethics proved to be unattainable outside their philosophical, literary and artistic contexts, but astonishingly they correlated with Bolshevik ideas to create a new world with a newly transformed man. The only difference was that the Bolsheviks wanted to involve all masses in this process of reformation of minds, whereas the Silver Age aesthetic was almost exclusively targeted at intellectuals.

Throughout the first years after the Socialist Revolution of 1917 and especially after the end of the Civil War, there was a general atmosphere of euphoria. It was the time of outstanding human endeavor to build and construct a new society with equal rights for all. 'This life is given only once! And you must live through it in such a way that you do not torment yourself about years spent aimlessly and that you do not feel devoured by disgrace for the despicable past!'[9] This quotation was an aphorism of the time given in the powerful message of Pavel Korchagin, a young worker who was severely disabled because of his wounds during the Russian Civil War and faced the rest of his life as an invalid. Despite his physical immobility, he found the strength of soul to live and create. At the end of the twentieth century, his words were turned into farce when the belief in an imaginary perfect world where everyone is happy proved to be a communist utopia with no connection to reality. However, the implication of this declaration, given in a plain language by a worker with an unrefined background, bears a similar message to the philosophy of Losev on the exploration of yourself and cognition as the ways of perfection and creation.

---

sovremennik, No. 2 (1916). Quoted in Rumianzev, *Ars novyi, ili dela i prikliucheniia bezustal'nogo kazaka Arseniia Avraamova*, p. 193.

8 Losev, *Ia soslan v XX vek*, Vol. 1, p. 287.

9 Nikolai Ostrovsky, *Kak zakalialas' stal'* [How the Steel Was Tempered], <https://librebook.me/kak_zakalialas_stal/vol2/3> (Accessed 14 February 2021).

This striking resemblance between the ideologies of the classes in Russian society was the main reason why many scholars, writers, composers and musicians initially supported the Socialist Revolution or at least maintained political neutrality, despite the unprecedented scale of brutality of that time.

This perception of unity as the means of coexistence was first introduced by the Russian philosopher Vladimir Solovyov in 1877: 'The subject of mystical philosophy is neither the world of phenomena that reflects our senses nor the world of ideas that form our thoughts. It is the reality of the life of mortals in their inner existence.'[10] Existence and life are the elements of universal essence/being. The significance of Losev's writing as an adherent of Vladimir Solovyov's philosophy rests not only in his generation's intellectual conceptions of aesthetic value, but also in its vivid portrayal of living in Russia during the pre- and post-revolutionary periods. His symbolic interpretation of real events is a literary reflection of the thoughts and insights into the lives of the most talented musicians and performers that were the cream of the crop of the musical field of the time.[11] This life with its vileness and loathsomeness creates the unmanageable insanity of a man and his music because any music contains the image of a continuously changing existence or life. However, it is not entirely a material image. Thus, in the novel *Tchaikovsky Trio*[12] the music of Scriabin, first, carries away the main character Vershinin to the boudoir of a lady-pianist that he has fallen in love with and then the tunes of Scriabin's *Poem of Ecstasy* cause the appearance of the witches' orgy in his mind. Finally, the image

10 Vladimir Solovyov, 'Filosofskie nachala tsel'nogo znaniia' [The Philosophical Principles of Integral Knowledge]. Quoted in Alexei Losev, *Vladimir Solovyov* (Moscow: Molodaia gvardiia, 2009), p. 107.

11 Losev denied any personifications in his prose. He showed the first draft of his novel 'Zhenshchina myslitel' [Woman as a Thinker] to Maria Yudina, a leading pianist and a family friend of Losev. However, she interpreted the main character as a characterization of her life and beliefs. Their friendship was ruined forever despite the depth of influence and correlation of Losev's philosophy with Yudina's principles in music. It was the first and only attempt of Losev to share his literary works with his friends.

12 Alexei Losev, 'Trio Tchaikovskogo' [Tchaikovsky's Trio], in Losev, *Ia soslan v XX vek*, Vol. 1, pp. 106–230.

of Michelangelo's fresco 'The Creation of Adam' represents an acute sense of foreboding 'of an invincible sea of the fierce battles of life' and with the sounds of bells in the finale of the *Poem of Ecstasy*, the whole world of Vershinin is destroyed by the bombing that begins the First World War.

These mystical images and the consequent effect of Scriabin's music in this work are symbolic. The appearance of a fresco by Michelangelo is a reminder of the true Creator of the world and the word of God. In the words of Losev, the music of Mozart, Beethoven and Wagner was a genuine creation of the Western European individualistic culture when man started to idealize his limited world as opposed to the one of God. This influence spread, and Scriabin, in turn, followed this path in search of his own Absolute. These beliefs of Scriabin were enriched with a characteristic Russian element of mysticism. The attempt to bring harmony to the material and spiritual senses influenced his language, and it inspired further innovations in music led by his contemporaries and followers, including Roslavets.

Nikolai Andreevich Roslavets (1880–1944) was one of the most intriguing representatives of the group of composers that later in the twentieth century was given the name of 'Russian Avant-garde Composers' or 'Modernists'. The invention of Roslavets called 'The New System of Organised Sounds' received special attention among his contemporaries. Today, a century later, it still generates exceptional interest in this most unconventional composer and man of many contradictions. For some critics, Roslavets revolutionized the world of music, but others regarded him only as a radical manufacturer. In the words of Roslavets himself, he wanted to break with tradition and his compositional language was destined to open new horizons in music. 'In spring 1913', he wrote, 'I started to unravel the mystery. Towards 1919, I finally found my individual technique, which gave me complete freedom of expression for my artistic personality.'[13]

Roslavets felt that he had to cut his ties with everything he was taught at the Moscow Conservatoire, which one would have thought gave him all the musical knowledge and skills needed for a professional existence. Roslavets considered these skills too conventional and banal. They were not

13 Roslavets, 'N. A. Roslavets o sebe i svoyom tvorchestve', p. 134.

appropriate for his ideas of musical expression and for the representation of his inner ego, which 'dreamt of new unheard worlds of sound'.[14] He admitted that he was unsatisfied with this 'anarchy' in musical creation and strove for new ideas and greater efficiency. Many critics labeled this desire as eccentric. Perhaps Roslavets's missionary zeal and patriotic fervor, and unpredictable turn of phrase, with which he declared himself a classicist and at the same time denied any possibility of applying 'the classical system' in music, played a negative role and tarnished his image.

> This means that Roslavets is a crazy person and an extreme individualist. It seems as if I do not write anything, do not read anything, as if I have discharged myself from everything and have gone nowhere. I am a classicist, who has studied the art of our time. I do not tear flesh from flesh, bone from bone in musical culture. I conquered everything and I declare that I do not break any ties with the development of the art of music. Through my students and through their students I would like to launch a new system of organised sounds. It would replace the classical system, to which there would be no return. In this system a man would feel as Beethoven did when he created his masterworks. I managed to find this triad.[15]

His formal renunciation of everything connected to the past and to tradition, his rejection of musical conventions and the creation of new musical conceptions helped establish the reputation of Roslavets as a radical and something of an eccentric.

Did he really break with tradition or create his new musical idiom based on the discoveries of past generations? Toward the middle of the 1920s, his compositional style, meticulously perfected from 1913 and endorsed by the great number of successful public performances, had reached its peak. In January 1927, Roslavets wrote the following about his system: 'Up until now I have not made any public speeches but kept checking it as a laboratory scientist for many years.'[16] A brief overview of the musical language, form and timbre palette of Roslavets during this period of his creation

14 Ibid., p. 133.

15 Nikolai Roslavets, Lecture, 17 January 1927, Manuscript. Housed in RGALI (Russian State Archive for Literature and Art, Moscow), Fund 2659 (Nikolai Andreevich Roslavets), List 1, Folder 72.

16 Ibid.

should answer the above query. In order to avoid any comparisons with or replications of existing analyses, one should take a lesser-researched composition, preferably using a manuscript. Roslavets's 'Sonata for Viola and Piano' (1926) should be a perfect example of such work.[17]

The composer entrusted the viola with a beautiful, placid and transparent theme in *piano* dynamic that remains unchanged for the first page of the piano score. The piano part accompanies the viola voice with ascending legato passages in semiquavers grouped in two sets of triplets. Their roots are based on a combination of series of chords changed between C and F. Each chord has six notes, which may be expanded in octaves or repeated within both instrumental parts. This description of chords corresponds to the one by Roslavets in his unpublished lecture written for the Igor Stravinsky Musical-Vocal Courses in Moscow on 17 January 1927. He declared that the central six-tone harmony of his new system is *Sintet'akkord* (a Synthetic Chord).

> I think you would have an ecstatic experience if you would explore the notes and discover that this is a six-note chord that is built up in thirds or in fourths. It has a romantic character and I called it a Synthetic Chord since it has all chords found by musical civilization during its evolution.[18]

The thesis of his unpublished lecture 'The New System of Organised Sounds', which he wrote for the Stravinsky Courses on 3 December 1926, contains certain details that prove the assumption that the relationship of these opening chords or series is similar to a tonic and subdominant. Roslavets specified the following:

> This synthetic chord must replace the 'main triad' of Classicism. A simple repositioning of this chord a perfect fifth up or down brings a formula similar to the classical

17 This sonata was included in his list of works completed by hand in the early 1940s. The precise date of this list is unknown. Nikolai Roslavets, 'Spisok muzykal'nykh proizvedenii N. A. Roslavtsa' [List of Musical Works by Nikolai Roslavets], Manuscript. Housed in RGALI, Fund 2659, List 1, Folder 100. Nikolai Roslavets, 'Sonata for Viola and Piano', 1926, Manuscript. Housed in RGALI, Fund 2659, List 1, Folder 31.

18 Roslavets, Lecture, 17 January 1927.

> tonality of T-D-S [Tonic-Subdominant-Dominant]. Synthetic Chords are destined to take on not only the external role of colourful and sonorous tools in the structure of a composition, but also the internal role and to be a substitute for a tonality.[19]

The initial relation of notes within the synthetic chord moved on to relate the keys of the structural parts in the Sonata. The recurrence of this 'triad' performs the role of a traditional tonic and a substitute for tonal relations. Therefore, the harmonic layout in this sonata is a pure example of the composer's application of his compositional method with hidden links to traditional functional harmony.

Roslavets did retain some conventional features in this work but modified his approach and language. It is a one-movement sonata written in sonata form with some elements of the language of Late Romanticism. The composer preserves the illusion of a certain tonal association[20] between different synthetic harmonies despite the fact that the music is clearly atonal. However, this atonality has very interesting links with traditional tonal relations. The keys of the main and second subject in the exposition follow the traditional rules of sonata form. They are, in the terminology of functional harmony, a 'tonic', C, and a 'relative major', E flat. The most important feature of sonata form is that these themes reappear in the recapitulation in the 'tonic' key, C. It is a sonata, because of its title, key relations and reasonably standard format of sections.[21] The position of a new episode (C) after reasonably traditional development and recapitulation sections, its radical transformation, first, from a contrast theme to one distantly related to the main subject and then to the modified main subject in the coda is a pure invention of Roslavets.

The form of this sonata is a monocycle. It is rather static and circular/spiral than temporal because of the reappearance and exact duplication of

19 Nikolai Roslavets, Abstract of a Lecture, Manuscript. Housed in RGALI, Fund 2659, List 1, Folder 72, Bullet point 16.

20 The phrase 'tonal association' means that either or both vertical and melodic lines have preserved certain elements of a tonal center/basis.

21 One can describe this form as AB (Exposition) – Development – C – AB (Recapitulation) – C with Coda. A and B stand for the main and second subjects.

themes/sections. In the words of Karol Berger, it is a cycle not an arrow.[22] However, one may emphasize that it also has the features of a linear model of time. It also becomes an arrow because of the new episode (C) and its unpredictable metamorphosis into a theme, which acquires some elements of the main subject. According to the philosophy of Losev, the formation of any musical work has three stages. First, the music is always a formation; second, this formation is felt through the diversity of its types; and finally, this diversity forms an integrated development.

> A musical composition consists of many sounds. They create an impression of unity, and simplicity, and at the same time of something flowing and shapeless. This unity travels and, thus, amalgamates everything and brings flowing unification in many features.[23]

Similarly, the harmonic language of this sonata is based on synthetic chords that operate and transform according to 'The System of Organised Sounds'. Therefore, this diversity of chords is not chaotic but organized. This formation of chords travels and creates a sense of unity within the sections. This amalgamation is hidden beneath the surface of this dense piece of writing that concurrently produces the impression of something indistinct and cohesive. Only a close analysis can reveal the tonal and diatonic relations that unify all segments of its harmony.

Scriabin had a rather methodical and mathematical approach to his compositions:

> I always accept that mathematics should play a bigger role in a composition. It happens that sometimes I need to have a full calculation when I compose: the calculation of a form and of a modal plan. These features cannot be incidental otherwise there will be no crystal form.[24]

22 Detlef Gojowy, *Neue sowjetische Musik der 20er Jahre/Novaia sovetskaia muzyka 20-kh godov* [New Soviet Music of the Twentieth Century], trans. Natalia Vlasova (Moscow: Kompozitor, 2006), p. 267.

23 Alexei Losev, *Muzyka kak predmet logiki* [Music as the Means of Logic] (Moscow: Gosudarstvennoe izdatel'stvo, 1927), p. 23.

24 Leonid Sabaneev, *Vospominaniia o Scriabine* [Memoirs About Scriabin] (Moscow: Gosudarstvennoe izdatel'stvo muzykal'nyi sektor, 1925), p. 57.

Roslavets showed a similar approach to the form and language in his manuscript by calculating bars, copying certain fragments of the existing musical material and maintaining tonal relations throughout his sonata.[25] What made Roslavets calculate the structure of this work apart from his effort to create a 'crystal form'? Analytical and rational approaches become characteristic of the time. In the words of one of the leaders of Russian Futurism, the artist Pavel Filonov, 'creation is an organisational factor that transforms the intellect of an artist into divine power'.[26] It is not without reason that Roslavets's contemporaries called him a scientist, a researcher or a manufacturer of some kind. 'He does not call himself a composer, but an organizer of sounds. Classification, logical endurance and steely determination to keep up his creative ideas are the major peculiarities of the musical portrayal of Roslavets.'[27] However, Roslavets denied the existence of any external inspirations for his music. 'I know that creative art is not some mystical trance or divine discovery, but rather a moment of highest exertion of the human intellect, as it strives to transform the unconscious into a form of consciousness.'[28] Did he implement this in his timbre palette?

The first impression of the main subject of the Viola Sonata (1926) bears a striking resemblance to Impressionism. The central aspect of Impressionistic style is the usage of color and sound instead of a detailed outline in order to create effects of feeling.[29] Roslavets denied any presence

25 The manuscript of this sonata has composer's signs such as ticks, stars, rectangles and crosses in bars 2, 12, 25, 52, 116, 130 and 154, with which Roslavets indicated points of transposition and repetition.

26 Pavel Filonov, 'Zhivopis' i grafika. Katalog vystavki' [Drawings and Graphics. Catalogue of an Exhibition] (Leningrad: Iskusstvo, 1988), pp. 107–108. Quoted in *Iz istorii muzykal'noi zhizni Rossii. XIX-XX veka*, p. 130.

27 Yevgeny Braudo, 'Nikolai Roslavets. Organizator zvukov' [Nikolai Roslavets. An Organizer of Sounds], *Vestnik rabotnikov iskusstv* (1925), Vol. 2, p. 14.

28 Roslavets, 'N.A. Roslavets o sebe i svoyom tvorchestve', p. 136.

29 *The Oxford Concise Dictionary of Music* provides a similar description: 'It was applied by musicians to the music of Debussy and his imitators because they interpret their subject in a similar Impressionistic manner, conveying the moods and emotions aroused by the subject rather than a detailed tone picture' (Oxford: Oxford University Press, 2004), p. 356.

of feelings in his music. However, the manuscript of this Viola Sonata has the following markings: *espressivo*, *dolce* and *cantabile e molto espressive*, which directly refer to a portrayal of a musical mood and aura. The soft pastels and tender melody of the main subject instantly remind one of Debussy and the French Impressionists with their diverse palette of sounds, colors and light. Similar attributes characterize the musical language of Schoenberg and Webern. A new linear style needed new timbres and sound colors, which expanded performers' horizons.

It is also intriguing to recall that Roslavets was a fine artist. Some recently published documents from the archives of Kazimir Severinovich Malevich (1879–1935), an artist and the founder of the group 'Supremus' and of Suprematism (one of the most radical movements in fine arts of the pre-revolutionary period), shed light on Roslavets's youth.[30] Malevich's father worked at the same railway office administration as Roslavets's father, at first in Konotop and then in Kursk, and the young Kazimir and Nikolai became friends. In 1930, Kazimir Malevich remembered the following:

> I acted in the field of arts, but I had a friend, who is now well-known as a composer across the whole musical world, Nikolai Roslavets. He acted in the field of music. He was the only friend that I met in Konotop.[31] In Kursk, my life was tirelessly devoted to drawing and Kolia[32] Roslavets developed his work in the field of music. He founded a big Ukrainian choir and then an orchestra. The aim of this choir and orchestra was not to perform in churches, but to sing only for the Art itself.[33]

30 Kazimir Malevich, 'Konotop'. Quoted in Aleksandra Shatskikh, *Kazimir Malevich i obshchestvo Supremus* [Kazimir Malevich and the Supremus Society] (Moscow: Tri kvadrata, 2009), p. 204.

31 Kazimir Malevich, 'Glavy iz avtobiografii khudozhnika' [Chapters from the Autobiography of an Artist]. Quoted in Nikolai Khardzhiev, *Stat'i ob avangarde v dvukh tomakh. Arkhiv russkogo avangarda* [Articles on the Avant-garde in Two Volumes. The Archive of the Russian Avant-garde] (Moscow: RA, 1997), Vol. 1, p. 120.

32 Kolia is a diminutive form of the name Nikolai.

33 Malevich, 'Konotop'.

A sketch of a picture 'Portrait of Roslavets: A Song to the Blue Clouds' by Kazimir Malevich dated circa 1907 has survived and is held in Amsterdam, at the Stedelijk Museum.[34] It depicts a violinist who is playing and looking toward the countryside with trees and bushes painted and structured in geometrical abstract patterns.

Roslavets continued this theme of incorporating music and nature in his own paintings and music. Three of his watercolors have survived and are held at the RGALI, Moscow. One of them is especially stunning. It was completed in 1910 and has the signature of Roslavets in the corner.[35] It is hard to believe that Roslavets, with his analytical mind, chose scenic beauty as the subject matter of his work. Its landscape around a lake has a wonderful palette of colors depicting trees, bushes, grass and the sky. The artist used tiny, graceful strokes of paint to produce their detailed reflection in the water. This technique of painting bears a striking resemblance to the elegance of harmonic language, the exquisiteness of rhythmical approach and the immaculate precision of form in the Viola Sonata. The possibility of transpositions of synthetic chords brings elegance to the language. Roslavets achieved this elegance through the resourceful management of synthetic chords according to their place within the form. His knowledge of timbres is conducive to the formation of contrasts and transformations of themes. Roslavets showed a similar approach in this painting by creating pure images of the countryside as well as their reflection and shades. The range of the artist's palette widened to include plain and neutral in combination with vibrant and deep colors. Roslavets's methodical mind took careful and effective control of all segments of the picture. However, this painting most certainly engenders feelings of beauty, excitement and splendor: another remarkable contradiction between the words and the work of its master.

Some musicologists, including Detlef Gojowy, noticed a certain tendency among Russian composers such as Roslavets, Protopopov, Anatoly

34 Kazimir Malevich, 'Eskiz k portretu Roslavtsa: Pesn' golubym oblakam', paper, pencil, 11x12.3 cm, in Shatskikh, *Kazimir Malevich i obshchestvo Supremus*.

35 Nikolai Roslavets, 'Peizazhi' [Landscapes], Manuscript. Housed in RGALI, Fund 2659, List 1, Folder 80, Item 2.

Aleksandrov as well as Medtner to write one-movement sonatas.[36] This practice was influenced by Aleksandr Scriabin, who preferred this form for his sonatas from 1907. What attracted Roslavets and other composers of his time to a one-movement sonata form? The model of the sonata continued to inspire composers as an effective form for a musical argument, though the term 'sonata form' became rather rhetorical due to all the alterations and modifications to its structure and rudiments. The far-reaching radical innovations in the musical language of the avant-garde movement needed to regain a formal balance between the new and old. The application of a traditional form was a disingenuous strategy aimed at equilibrium and a smoother transition toward the unknown. Besides, it served as an ideal basis for further experimentation within a static/circular setting with the aim of achieving an intensity of contrasts of musical development within this minuscule structure. This impermanent form compared to a conventional sonata offered diverse compositional, harmonic, instrumental and textural approaches that all worked for the same purpose. This was a missionary endeavor. Roslavets faced the challenge by initiating skillful textural, instrumental and timbre maneuverings in addition to his elegant and methodical work with synthetic chords.

The philosopher Pavel Florensky characterized this propensity in music using the word *prostranstvennost* (expansiveness): 'Certainly, music and poetry have extreme freedom in organizing space. They can and do create spaces that are so different … Music uses material less connected to outer necessity and even more conformable to any manipulations of a creative power.'[37] By 1920s, Roslavets moved away from vocal genres, in particular, his beloved romances and the poetry of leading poets of the Silver Age, including Igor Severianin, Aleksandr Blok, Zinaida Gippius and Fedor Sologub. Apart from their bourgeois content unwelcomed by the Soviet

36 Karol Berger, *Time's Arrow and the Advent of Musical Modernity* (Cambridge, MA: Harvard University Press, 2005), p. 12.

37 Pavel Florensky, *Sochineniia* [Works] (Moscow: Mysl', 1994), pp. 61–63. Quoted in *Russkaia muzyka i XX vek: russkoe muzykal'noe iskusstvo v istorii khudozhestvennoi kul'tury XX veka* [Russian Music and the Twentieth Century: The Art of Russian Music in the History of Art Culture of the Twentieth Century], ed. Mark Aranovsky (Moscow: Gosudarstvennyi institut iskusstvoznaniia, 1997), p. 495.

authorities, such texts limited Roslavets's capacity for *prostranstvennost'*, while instrumental genres opened new artistic dimensions. Moreover, a one-movement sonata corresponded well to the fundamental principle of the avant-garde to be organized, formatted and, at the same time, sensitive to modifications of space or form. The basis of this principle and others of the time were not only the result of a remarkable formal intellect and erudition but also the 'fruits of the labors' and evolution of previous generations of writers, musicians and philosophers. Their legacy guided and directed new ideas as well as modified and reshaped conceptions that had a great impact on the Russian cultural heritage of this period.

Bibliography

Avraamov, Arseny, 'Griadushchaia muzykal'naia nauka i novaia era istorii muzyki' [The Future Science of Music and the New Era of Music History], *Muzykal'nyi sovremennik*, No. 2 (1916).

——'Revtraktat o NOVMUZERE "bez predkov" SSSR 6-oi god I-go veka' [Revolutionary Treatise on New Music 'Without Ancestors' in the USSR of the Sixth Year of the First Century].

Berger, Karol, *Time's Arrow and the Advent of Musical Modernity* (Cambridge, MA: Harvard University Press, 2005).

Braudo, Yevgeny, 'Nikolai Roslavets. Organizator zvukov' [Nikolai Roslavets. An Organizer of Sounds], Vestnik rabotnikov iskusstv, Vol. 2 (1925).

Filonov, Pavel, *Zhivopis' i grafika. Katalog vystavki* [Drawings and Graphics. Catalogue of an Exhibition] (Leningrad: Iskusstvo, 1988).

Florensky, Pavel, *Sochineniia* [Works] (Moscow: Mysl', 1994).

Gojowy, Detlef, *Neue sowjetische Musik der 20er Jahre/Novaia sovetskaia muzyka 20-kh godov* [New Soviet Music of the Twentieth Century], trans. Natalia Vlasova (Moscow: Kompozitor, 2006).

Iz istorii muzykal'noi zhizni Rossii. XIX–XX veka [From the History of Musical Life in Russia in the Nineteenth–Twentieth Centuries], ed. E. K. Kulova (Moscow: MGK, 1992).

Karatygin, Viacheslav, 'Muzykal'naia drama. O postanovke Borisa Godunova' [Musical Drama. On the Production of Boris Godunov], *Apollon*, No. 8 (1913), p. 68.

Khardzhiev, Nikolai, *Stat'i ob avangarde v dvukh tomakh. Arkhiv russkogo avangarda* [Articles on the Avant-garde in Two Volumes. The Archive of the Russian Avant-garde] (Moscow: RA, 1997).

Losev, Alexei, *Ia soslan v XX vek* [I Am Sent to the Twentieth Century] (Moscow: Vremia, 2002) Vol. 1, p. 126.

—— *Muzyka kak predmet logiki* [Music as the Means of Logic] (Moscow: Gosudarstvennoe izdatel'stvo, 1927),

——'Trio Tchaikovskogo' [Tchaikovsky's Trio] in Alexei Losev, *Ia soslan v XX vek* (Moscow: Vremia, 2002), Vol. 1, pp. 106–230.

—— *Vladimir Solovyov* (Moscow: Molodaia gvardiia, 2009).

Malevich, Kazimir, 'Glavy iz avtobiografii khudozhnika' [Chapters from the Autobiography of an Artist], quoted in Nikolai Khardzhiev, *Stat'i ob avangarde v dvukh tomakh. Arkhiv russkogo avangarda* [Articles on the Avant-garde in Two Volumes. The Archive of the Russian Avant-garde] (Moscow: RA, 1997), Vol. 1, p. 120.

—— 'Konotop', quoted in Aleksandra Shatskikh, *Kazimir Malevich i obshchestvo Supremus* [Kazimir Malevich and the Supremus Society] (Moscow: Tri kvadrata, 2009).

Ostrovsky, Nikolai, *Kak zakalialas' stal'* [How the Steel Was Tempered], <https://librebook.me/kak_zakalialas_stal/vol2/3> (Accessed 14 February 2021).

The Oxford Concise Dictionary of Music (Oxford: Oxford University Press, 2004).

Roslavets, Nikolai Andreevich, Abstract of a Lecture, Manuscript. Housed in Russian State Archive for Literature and Art, Moscow (hereafter RGALI), Fund 2659, List 1, Folder 72, Bullet point 16.

——Lecture, 17 January 1927, Manuscript. Housed in RGALI, Fund 2659 (Nikolai Andreevich Roslavets), List 1, Folder 72.

—— 'N.A. Roslavets o sebe i svoyom tvorchestve' [Nikolai Roslavets on Himself and His Creativity], *Sovremennaia muzyka*, No. 5 (14 January 1924).

—— 'Peizazhi' [Landscapes], Manuscript. Housed in RGALI, Fund 2659, List 1, Folder 80, Item 2.

—— 'Sonata for Viola and Piano', 1926, Manuscript. Housed in RGALI, Fund 2659, List 1, Folder 31.

—— 'Spisok muzykal'nykh proizvedenii N. A. Roslavtsa' [List of Musical Works by Nikolai Roslavets], Manuscript. Housed in RGALI, Fund 2659, List 1, Folder 100.

Rumianzev, Sergei, *Ars novyi, ili dela i prikliucheniia bezustal'nogo kazaka Arseniia Avraamova* [New Arts or Activities and Adventures of the Tireless Cossack Arseny Avraamov] (Moscow: Deka-VC, 2007), p. 60.

Russkaia muzyka i XX vek: russkoe muzykal'noe iskusstvo v istorii khudozhestvennoi kul'tury XX veka [Russian Music and the Twentieth Century: The Art of Russian Music in the History of Art Culture of the Twentieth Century], ed. Mark Aranovsky (Moscow: Gosudarstvennyi institut iskusstvoznaniia, 1997).

Sabaneev, Leonid, *Vospominaniia o Scriabine* [Memoirs About Scriabin] (Moscow: Gosudarstvennoe izdatel'stvo muzykal'nyi sektor, 1925).

Shatskikh, Aleksandra, *Kazimir Malevich i obshchestvo Supremus* [Kazimir Malevich and the Supremus Society] (Moscow: Tri kvadrata, 2009).

Solovyov, Vladimir, 'Filosofskie nachala tsel'nogo znaniia' [The Philosophical Principles of Integral Knowledge], quoted in Alexei Losev, *Vladimir Solovyov* (Moscow: Molodaia gvardiia, 2009), p. 107.

NATALIA SKOROKHOD

13 The Old Roots of the New Era: From Leonid Andreev to Sergei Eisenstein, the Unknown Connection

Introduction

The Soviet avant-garde of the 1920s was for a long time strongly associated with denying the heritage of Russian culture: meaning not only the classic period but also the Silver Age. However, nowadays this idea seems irrelevant since art history increasingly refers to materials and facts that show us the continuity and inheritance between the various artistic movements of these periods. Today there is no doubt that the political and social revolution, which interrupted the natural development of the art of the Silver Age, in fact, could not protect artists from the influence of certain previously created ideas and works.

This chapter is one more contribution to the discussion about how Silver Age and Soviet avant-garde are interrelated and torn apart at the same time. Our goal is to focus on the influence of Leonid Andreev's play *Tsar Golod* (King Hunger, 1907) on the plot and the poetics of Sergei Eisenstein's film *Stachka* (The Strike, 1925) as far as this topic is still unexplored: the connection between these two artworks has been discussed neither in theatre history nor in film studies. The theory of a possible impact of Andreev's unknown play on Eisenstein's famous film was first articulated by Vladimir Zabrodin (1942–2018) at the All-Russian Transdisciplinary Conference 'Sergei Eisenstein: pro et contra' (2013). He discussed blind spots in Eisenstein studies and, among other things, mentioned the idea and the plot of Eisenstein's first full-length film, *Stachka*. My subsequent explorations and archival research have affirmed my theories and revealed plenty of unexpected and crucial findings .

The Silver Age and the Russian avant-garde

It is clear that the principles of revolutionary theatre were aimed at solving the tasks of the new political and social way of thinking. Tasks of that kind had to promote a renovation of the theatre art in an ethical and aesthetic sense, which meant new styles in combination with propaganda of revolutionary ideas. However, theorists of new art and particularly P. Kerzhentsev (1881–1940), who published a manifesto of revolutionary theatre,[1] 'pursued the traditions of Russian pre-revolutionary aesthetics (Leo Tolstoy) and found a reinforcement in spiritual quests (at any level) of the revolutionary epoch' as described in the research studies of the St. Petersburg dramatic theorist Professor G. Titova (1936–2019).[2] The author of *Creative Theatre and the Theatre of Constructivism* emphasized that concepts that were rather useful for theories and experiences of the early Soviet period refer to or directly quote ideas of the Symbolists: for instance, Vladimir Solovyov's 'theatre of Sobornost' (*Sobornost* means 'a spiritual community of many people living together'); a statement about 'religious status as a weapon in the liberation of all humanity' by Andrei Bely; Leo Tolstoy's book *What Is Art?*; and Richard Wagner's essay 'Art and Revolution'.[3]

There is also a theory about the 'epic foundation of creativity' in the principles of proletarian (working-class) culture (Proletkult)[4] as was rightly pointed out by theorist of literature V. Golovchiner (1953) of Tomsk in

1 P. Kerzhentsev, *Tvorcheskii teatr* [Creative Theatre] (Moscow, Petrograd: GosIsd, 1918).

2 G. Titova, *Tvorcheskii teatr i teatralnyi konstructivizm* [Creative Theatre and Theatre Constructivism] (St. Petersburg: SPB-GATI, 1995), p. 48.

3 Ibid., pp. 45–47.

4 The government organization that united and supported any art initiatives as workshops and ateliers in terms of Soviet cultural education (*Kultprosvet*).

her research. In her opinion, it is connected 'with the representation of the world as a "co-existence", as an equality (identity) of facts and phenomena, and its congruence with unified and permanent, "native" (G. Gachev), "substantial" (G. Hegel) and universal rules'.[5] Galina Titova also found the origin of this tendency in the Silver Age: 'The actuality of epic tendency in art seems truly appropriate and especially significant due to the genuine interest of Russian philosophy in "Sobornost" and "common cause"'.[6]

The ideas specified in Kerzhentsev's book do not seem utopian these days. Ideologists of Proletkult, while thinking globally about new forms of staging, predicted various concepts that are perfectly relevant for the modern theatre. For instance, they promoted an idea about visiting theatre being directly involved in performances that absolutely reflect the main idea of participatory theatre. However, the 'creative theatre' did not establish a definite aesthetics after the revolution, but its experiences became extremely productive for the creation of outstanding theatre attainment in the middle and the second part of the 1920s. Galina Titova described the debates between the ideologist of Proletkult V. Kerzhentsev and V. Meyerhold (1874–1940) about public participation in performances and pointed out that even though Meyerhold partly transferred the action into the auditorium while staging *Zaria* (The Dawn, 1920),[7] he definitely did not break the theatrical borders:

> There is a distinct line between Meyerhold and Kerzhentsev. For the Proletkult 'left opposition' (Pavel Markov's term) who didn't deny the importance of Meyerhold and his artworks, he still was a director who didn't tear the bourgeois theatre apart instead of creating the new proletarian or workers' and peasants' theatre.[8]

Meyerhold was really interested in the 'Performance-Rally' concept, but it was just one of the steps in the transition to the 'theatre of

5 V. Golovchiner, *Epicheskaia drama v russkoi literature XX veka* [Epic Drama in Russian Literature of Twentieth Century] (Tomsk: University of Tomsk, 2007), p. 17.

6 Ibid., p. 86.

7 The First Theatre of the RSFSR. Dir. V. Meyerhold and V. Bebutov.

8 Ibid., quoting P. Markov, *O teatre* [About Theatre], 4 vols (Moscow: Iskusstvo, 1976), Vol. 3, p. 437.

Constructivism' in terms of which there were such masterpieces of theatre art as *Velikodushnyi Rogonosets* (The Magnanimous Cuckold, 1922) and *Les* (The Forest, 1924). The creative energy of the director was concentrated here on the individual method of making a performance: it was a step back from the 'common cause' as a theatre concept.

The famous production by Meyerhold of Gogol's *Revizor* (The Government Inspector, 1926) was not accepted by his colleagues from the Left Front of the Arts (LEF) at all: theatre director Igor Terentiev wrote about this performance 'Spoiled cold dinner of "miriskussniki"' (members of Mir Iskusstva [the World of Art] community in the Silver Age). Moreover, in his view, it canceled out all Meyerhold's post-revolutionary works: '*Revizor* is an ugly collection of all types of cultural atavism.'[9]

Eisenstein and Proletkult

Sergei Eisenstein (1898–1948) belonged to the second generation of professional directors and was one of Meyerhold's directing students.[10] He liked to repeat that it was the October events that helped him – at that time he was a student of the Institution of Civil Engineers – to connect his life with art.

Eisenstein began his creative career in the Moscow department of Proletkult, and soon he was known as an insolent and scandalous theatre designer and director. It is crucial to highlight that *Stachka* is both biographically and creatively a point of intersection between Eisenstein the stage director and designer and Eisenstein the filmmaker. Almost all of his previous cinematographic experiences were connected with a theatre work: for example, *Dnevnik Glumova* (Glumov's Diary, 1923) or the documentary montage *Teksty Chuzhogo* (The Stranger's Stories, 1924) for the

9 Markov, *O teatre*, Vol. 3, pp. 333, 335.

10 Studying at the High Courses for Film Directors – GVYRM, then GVYTM (V. Meyerhold run a workshop for the directors there in 1921–1923) – and working in Proletkult at the same time.

Tretyakov play *Slyshish' Moskva?* (Can You Hear, Moscow?). Moreover, the first full-length movie was made in close collaboration between First Film Studios and Proletkult – almost the full cast of the First Workers' Theatre actors played in his famous *Mudrets* (Enough Stupidity in Every Wise Man, 1923) by Ostrovsky. In the credits, the scriptwriter is given as Proletkult, but later the group of authors was presented as 'Script by S. Eisenstein in collaboration with G. Aleksandrov, V. Pletnev and I. Kravchunovsky'.[11] It is worth noting Valerian Pletnev's name there – playwright and ideologist of Proletarian culture.

The director and teacher Valentin Tikhonovich, who was close to high-level people in the Proletkult, invited the 23-year-old Eisenstein to make a spectacle based on Andreev's *Tsar Golod* in the theatrical season of 1920–1921. The performance was planned as a massive project generously funded by the government. The opening night was to take place in the Central Proletkult Arena in Moscow on 1 October 1921. Tikhonovich, who should have been the director of *Tsar Golod*, apparently communicated with Eisenstein quite often, and there is an intriguing verbal portrait of the future cinematographic genius:

> An artist of great culture and erudition, a thoroughgoing 'Zapadnik' (Westernizer), [...] shaped by his artistic work with 'dead material', and moreover, in the boom of analytic postimpressionism movements in art, he came into theatre as a constructivist and impressionist.[12]

Indeed, correspondence between young Eisenstein and his mother during his military years in the Red Army (1918–1920) and the years of his directing career beginning in Moscow proves that all of this became his 'universities': the former engineering student eagerly acquired knowledge in any field of the history of arts, including dramaturgy. Working on any play, he always tried to learn as much as possible about the author

11 I. Akseinov, *Is tvorcheskogo nalsediia* [From the Creative Heritage], 2 vols (Moscow: Iskusstvo, 2008), Vol. 1, p. 428.

12 V. Tikhonovich, *50 let v teatre i okolo teatra* [50 Years in and around the Theatre], 2 vols (Moscow: Nautchnaia biblioteka STD. Otdel rukopisei [Scientific Library of Russian Theatre Union. Department of Manuscripts], 1950), Vol. 1, p. 210.

and his other works, which turned him into a constant researcher in the field of drama.

There could be a reasonable question here: why was a play by a modernist writer (one of the most performed playwrights of the Silver Age, Leonid Andreev [1873–1919]) in the proletarian theatre repertoire? And that too, *Tsar Golod*, a dramaturgical parable based on so-called 'dead art'? It was observed that the heads of Proletkult did not cope with the ideology and practice balance; they were pretty consistent in their criticism but not in the creation of new theatre artworks. It was also obvious that there is a contradiction between the hypothetical need for renovation of the repertoire and permanent use of 'old' plays, whether they are Shakespeare's or Ostrovsky's. The favorite practice of Proletkult ideologists was making and updating the list of old classic literature that could be 'right' or 'wrong' for the new period of time. I suppose that one of the consequences of such 'revisions' is the appearance of *Tsar Golod* in the creative plans of Tikhonovich, although, not so long ago, *Tsar Golod* had in fact been strictly prohibited by the tsarist censorship. Acquaintance with the play and sketch work for the performance that finally had never been stage were both factors that had a great impact on Eisenstein at the beginning of his film career.

The Russian revolution as material for art research

Both Andreev's play and Eisenstein's film are dedicated to a particular occurrence, namely the disappointing results of the first Russian revolution in 1905: *Tsar Golod* describes the riot of starving working-class people, while *Stachka* shows the rebellion of oppressed workers. *Stachka* was dedicated to the twentieth anniversary of the events of 1905, celebrating the conditions of the victory of the working class who as a matter of fact lost in that first step of rebellion. The film was a commissioned work, as were all of Eisenstein's future films.

By contrast, Andreev wrote a play about the first Russian revolution because of his own wish and intention, not a government contract: Andreev was a real witness of those occurrences, and also, he was truly sympathetic to members of the Socialist Revolutionary Party (the SRs or Esers). It is well known that the writer spoke at meetings in 1905; moreover, his house was a secret place for 'left' forbidden political parties. Andreev was even arrested once for his participation in prohibited activities but was soon released on bail. The first Russian revolution and an overwhelming desire to speak his mind inspired Andreev – at that time only a popular fiction writer – to write plays. He wrote his first two plays, *K Zvezdam* (To the Stars, 1905) and *Savva* (1906), literally on the heels of revolutionary events. *Tsar Golod* came later, in 1907. This text was created in conditions of Andreev's theatre glory and as a continuation of the dramatic cycle *Bog, Chelovek i Diavol* (God, Man and Devil) – the plays that, in the opinion of the writer, were 'of a truly new form', 'without realism or symbolism'.[13]

Zhizn' Cheloveka (The Life of Man, 1906) that opened this cycle was rather popular in Russia; it was staged by Stanislavsky and Meyerhold in the same year of 1907. Andreev promised his new play to the Komissarzhevskaia Theatre, but the strict censorship during those periods made *Tsar Golod* unavailable for the stage. However, it was only prohibited from being staged: the play was published in 1908 by the Shipovnik (Rosehip) publishing house, where Andreev was the editor-in-chief, as a separate book with illustrations by Eugene Lanceray (a member of Mir Iskusstva [World of Art]).

Leonid Andreev sympathized with the rebellious workers and strongly supported the February Revolution. But he abhorred the Bolsheviks, and, therefore, right after the October Revolution (24 October 1917), he left his apartment in Petrograd and went to his villa in Vammelsuu (now the municipal settlement Serovo on the Karelian Isthmus). Finland separated from Russia very soon, and Andreev suddenly found himself in emigration, but his life there was not long – he died from a stroke in September 1919.

Many of Andreev's plays are popular and successful nowadays, but the fate of *Tsar Golod* was different. Ironically, up until quite recently,[14] it

13 Gorky, Maxim, and Leonid Andreev, *Gorky i Leonid Andreev: Neizdannaia perepiska* [Gorky and Leonid Andreev: Unpublished Correspondence] (Moscow: Nauka, 1965), p. 300.

14 Several episodes of *Tsar Golod* were used in the dramatic composition of *Gubernator* (The Governor, based on Leonid Andreev's short stories) by Andrei Moguchy at the Bolshoi Drama Theatre (St. Petersburg) in 2017.

was produced just once, at the Proletkult Arena in Moscow in 1921. The censorship gave no opportunity to put the work on again (this topic will be properly discussed later). However, the work on the play continued for three months, during which Eisenstein made sketches of decorations and costumes. Four years later, he made his first own full-length film *Stachka*.

The point of intersection between Andreev and Eisenstein

Once more, here is the historical sequence of the events under discussion:

> 1908: the publication of *Tsar Golod* by Leonid Andreev, illustrated by Yevgenii Lanceray (the play was forbidden for staging by the tsarist censorship)

Figure 13.1 Ev. Lansere. Illustrations to the first publication of *Tsar Golod* by Leonod Andreev, 1908 [L. Andreev, *Tsar Golod. Predstavlenie v pyati aktakh s prologom* (Performance in Five Parts with Prologue) (Moscow: Shipovnik, 1908), frontispiece (woodcut)]. Copyright: Public domain.

1921: *Tsar Golod* was prepared for staging in the Proletkult theatre under the direction of Valentin Tikhonovich, designer Sergei Eisenstein (the premiere was forbidden by the Soviet censorship)

Figure 13.2 Eisenstein. Pencil sketches for *Tsar Golod* costumes for the performance by Valentin Tikhonovich, 1921 [Russian State Archive of Literature and Art (RGALY). Fond 1923, Inventory list 1, Storage unit 723, Picture 21]. Copyright: Public domain.

1925: *Stachka* – the premiere of the film, directed by Sergei Eisenstein, script by S. Eisenstein in collaboration with G. Aleksandrov, V. Pletnev and I. Kravchunovsky.

Figure 13.3 Frame from *Stachka*, film by S. Eisenstein, USSR, 1924 [State Russian Film Archive (Gosfil'mofond)]. Copyright: Public domain.

There are not many mentions of *Tsar Golod* in Eisenstein's archive, which is because it was not being staged. We have three quotes from his letters: '*Tsar Golod*, probably, will be very exciting' wrote Eisenstein to his mother on 26 July 1921.[15] But after a month, on 20 August 1921, he changed his mind:

> There are real complications with *Tsar Golod*: they are afraid of its ideological side because of real hunger now. Apparently, 90% that it will be abandoned. My work in these two months will be paid, sure, but it would be so disappointing – seems the show has every chance to be a hit and to make some serious money.[16]

It is well known that in the autumn of 1921 there was real hunger in territories under the control of Bolsheviks – the Volga region, Kazakhstan and the Urals; it seems that in these conditions there was no possibility that the Proletkult committee would allow the staging of this play, and therefore rehearsals were not even started.

15 Tikhonovich, *50 let v teatre i okolo teatra*, p. 99.

16 Ibid., p. 101.

The third piece of evidence belongs to the beginning of the 1930s: 'You were the real witness of how I pushed directors to move forward in the right direction both in the *Meksikanets* [The Mexican] and *Tsar Golod* cases', wrote Eisenstein to his friend the actor Maxim Shtraukh from Mexico.[17]

It is indeed lucky that most of Eisenstein's pencil sketches for the play are held at RGALI, the Russian State Archive of Literature and Art, and several gouache sketches can be found in the archives of the A. A. Bakhrushin State Central Theatre Museum. In the catalogue of sketches at RGALI, the first date is 7 May while the last is in July; in the Bakhrushin Museum, 2 August. According to these dates and mentions in these archive documents, Eisenstein worked on Andreev's play for at least the whole of May and two summer months. He was interested in *Tsar Golod* both as a painter and a director; he was thoroughly acquainted with this material and his ideas were not just about the scenography, but he had also distinct directing plans for the play. It is logical to assume that plenty of his unrealized ideas in 1921 were most likely used by him in future works. In terms of that, it is interesting to note Sergei Yutkevich's recollections about working with Eisenstein during the staging of *Macbeth*:

> A very attentive researcher of Eisenstein's works looking at sketches for *Macbeth* can clearly see how consistently Eisenstein developed a system of images that excited his fantasy. The helmets of Scottish soldiers are easily recognizable: they are almost like the 'dog-knights' in *Aleksandr Nevsky* (the film itself was made a quarter-century later).[18]

So, we can make an assumption that Leonid Andreev's *Tsar Golod*, with its grotesque characters, atmosphere of total aggression causing anxiety and sorrow at the same time, and even the plot of the play, were the sources that inspired Sergei Eisenstein to create his film about the first Russian revolution of 1905, *Stachka*.

Of course, this needs to be proved. At first sight, it is hard to find any connection between these three pieces of art: the modernist play by

17 *Eisenstein v vospominaniiakh sovremennikov* [Eisenstein in Contemporaries' Memories] (Moscow: Iskusstvo, 1974), p. 78.

18 Ibid., p. 111.

Andreev with its allegorical figures, the grotesque Futuristic sketches by Eisenstein and the film *Stachka* that reproduces the events of the first Russian revolution in an almost realistic way. And do not forget that the film was created in the silent movie age, while the plays of Leonid Andreev were always overcrowded with text, conversations and remarks. But in comparing the plot and characters of the movie with those of the play, we discover many interesting coincidences.

An impact of Expressionism

Leonid Andreev was proud that *Tsar Golod* did not reflect any personal story but the story of hungry people that were brutally repressed. The plot is based on the actions of different classes (represented by different choirs): the Rich, the Poor, the Criminals and so on. The author made a point that the play, being a part of the dramatic cycle *Bog, Chelovek i Diavol*, lay somewhere in between 'Realism and Symbolism', and that the cycle suggested some kind of new, hitherto unknown scenic approach. The first play of the cycle, *Zhizn Cheloveka* (The Life of Man), written in 1905, became a remarkable event for Russian theatre. It was staged in 1907–1908 by K. Stanislavsky in Moscow and by V. Meyerhold in St. Petersburg as well. Bad luck with *Tsar Golod* did not stop Andreev from believing firmly in a new theatre aesthetic, and he wrote the next play of the cycle, *Anathema*, in 1909. The play, staged by V. Nemirovich-Danchenko in the Moscow Arts Theatre, had great success and many references in the contemporary press.

Though Leonid Andreev did not name the movement that laid the foundation for his dramatic cycle, shortly it finally did get a name. In general, 'Expressionism' developed in Germany from the beginning of the twentieth century, not so much as the style matrix, but rather as a massive aesthetic movement. First, the term 'Expressionism' appeared owing to G. Walden, one of the first theorists and main promoters of this movement. It is well known that Western theorists looking for the origin of this movement supposed that one of the first writer-forerunner was Fedor Dostoevsky. But now, in the Russian theory of literature, Leonid Andreev is considered an author whose works show real tendencies of Expressionism that were not mentioned by his contemporaries. The idea about the point of intersection between Andreev's prose and Expressionism first appeared in Russian discourse in the 1920s. Nowadays there is plenty of research[19] published about the roots of Expressionism in the works of Andreev. Among such short stories as 'Stena' (The Wall, 1901) and 'Krasny Smekh' (The Red Laugh, 1904) and the previously mentioned dramatic cycle, *Tsar Golod* is a literary work that obviously shows these Expressionist motifs.

It is common knowledge that Russian Expressionism was not a formed movement although its features can be found in artworks of many outstanding artists of the 1910s and 1920s, including Eisenstein. In the introduction of the recently published book *Soviet Expressionism: From Caligari to Stalin*, one of its co-authors Oleg Kovalov wrote: 'The Expressionism of *The Cabinet of Dr Caligari* was planned and conceptual while Expressionism in Russian cinema was considerably spontaneous and unconscious.'[20] Other authors writing about Russian Expressionism insisted on 'unconsciousness' and 'latency': 'Yes, there was no Expressionism in Russia, but at the same time there was. And it was everywhere. Both in Symbolism and Futurism.'[21] Sergei Eisenstein often spoke critically[22] about movies made in the Expressionist aesthetic, but he did not escape the influence of this

19 See, among others, N. Filonenko, 'Stanovleniie i razvitiie poetiki ekspressionizma v tvochestve L.N. Andreeva 1898–1908' [Formation and Development of Expressionism Poetics in the Works of L. N. Andreeva 1898–1908, Ph.D. dissertation, Lipetsk, 2003; M. Shestakova, 'Razvitiie ekspressionisticheskikh tendentsii v romani- stike L.N. Andreeva' [Development of Expressionistic Tendencies in Leonid Andreev's novels], *Vestnik SAMGu*, Vol. 112, No. 1 (2014), pp. 146–152; Y. Lakhno, 'Dramaturgiia L. Andreeva v interpretatsii issledovatelei kontsa XIX – nachala XX veka' [The Dramaturgy of L. Andreev in the Interpretation of Researchers of the Late XX–Early XXI Century] *Vestnik Cheliabinskogo gosudarstvennogo universiteta*, Vol. 245, No. 16 (2014), pp. 66–69.

20 O. Kovalov, Y. Margolit and M. Kireeva, *Sovetskii ekspressionizm: Ot Kaligari do Stalina* [Soviet Expressionism: From Caligari to Stalin] (St. Petersburg: Poriadok Slov, 2019), p. 26.

21 N. Khrenov, 'Vozvrashchaias' k ekspressionizmu: Ekspressionizm i russkaia kul'tura' [Back to Expressionism: Expressionism and Russian Culture], *Kul'tura i iskusstvo*, Vol. 15, No. 3 (2013), pp. 328–343, 340.

22 S. Eisenstein, 'Dikkens, Griffit i my' [Dickens, Griffith and we], in *Izbrannyie proizvedeniia* (1968), Vol. 5, pp. 129–180.

huge movement on his own. In the previously mentioned book *Soviet Expressionism*, there is an analysis of two of Eisenstein's films: *Stachka* and *Ivan Grozny* (Ivan the Terrible). The author of these chapters, Oleg Kovalov, wrote about the second part of *Ivan Grozny* (1948) comparing the director's experience with the 'style icons':

> Nikolai Cherkasov brilliantly provides flash-like mood changes of his character who has just one goal: to pressure the will of the person, to make him the servant… of the fear […] The obtrusive theme of screen Expressionism where maniacs and tyrants who rule the world looking like a nightmare – the screen emphasizes it with the angular and deformed decorations like paintings by insane people. And Ivan the Terrible in the Eisenstein movie is perfectly suited to this row of gloomy characters.[23]

Eisenstein was quite acquainted with the German cinema of Lang, Murnau and Wiene. Moreover, his 'eccentric' poetics and 'montage of attractions' were truly relevant to the Expressionist aesthetic. In *Stachka*, O. Kovalov detects 'traces' of the Fritz Lang movie *Doktor Mabuse, der Spieler* (Dr. Mabuse the Gambler, 1922).[24]

> When the sleek face of the full-fed 'bourgeois' from *Stachka* layers over the image of the office where the workers fussily run backwards and forwards – it is easy to remember the arrogant face of Mabuse which layers over the wide shot of the exchange house hall … But it's just the superficial, too obvious and probably unconscious impact: Mabuse, the generator and the king of chaos, left in *Stachka* a more significant 'trace'.[25]

The author considers that the art fixation of provocations and provocateurs (what became 'an engine of modern politics') is the most vital element that unites Lang and Eisenstein films. However, I will try to prove that it is Andreev's play that had a real impact on *Stachka*.

Furthermore, it is significant that it was Eisenstein who connected Andreev's plays with Expressionism in the early 1930s. He also worked on a textbook about directing, and in the chapter about 'Dvizhenie

23 Kovalov, Margolit and Kireeva, *Sovetskii ekspressionizm*, p. 327.

24 Before the first showing, S. Eisenstein and E. Shub tried to remount the film to make it 'ideologically true'; however, they did not succeed.

25 Ibid., p. 43.

stilei' (Moving of Styles), he created a bright image of German-Austrian Expressionism. There is an analysis of Russian Theatre Expressionism in that text: on the décor for a production of Oscar Wilde's *Salome* in 1908 by N. Evreinov and N. Kalmakov, Eisenstein made a note in brackets about Andreev: 'Well known features of modern playwriting, for instance, Andreev's plays, didn't ever connect with Expressionism which is well spread in Europe and having Munch as its one of the first representatives.'[26] I believe *Tsar Golod* has a strong association with Munch's *Scream*.

Plot

There is much in common between the plot of *Tsar Golod* and *Stachka*. Neither of them shows us the story of a particular person. It is well known that in the 1920s Eisenstein believed strongly that the plot based on an individual intrigue was the relic of an outdated bourgeois art. Viktor Shklovsky wrote about *Stachka*, 'The plot of the film consists of interactions of the different kinds of masses.'[27]

We can also indicate that both plots – of the play and of the film – are divided into six parts. Table 13.1 displays a structural comparison (T1).

So, it is obvious that the plot of the play and the plot of the film as well are based on the same action sequence:

1. a call for a revolt
2. the insurrection
3. the betrayal
4. the provocation
5. the execution of the rebels

26 Eisenstein, *Izbrannyie proizvedeniia*, Vol. 6, p. 68.

27 V. Shklovsky, *Ikh nastoiashchee* [Their Present-Day] (Moscow: Kinopechat, 1927), p. 25.

Table 13.1.

	Tzar Golod	*Stachkas*
1	King Hunger swears his allegiance to the hungry people.	A worker commits suicide after being accused of stealing without any proof.
2	King Hunger incites workers to revolt.	The worker activists are calling for a strike.
3	King Hunger provokes a riot among the hungry criminals.	The factory owners call for the Secret Police. The Secret Service employs criminals for a provocation.
4	The trial of the hungry poor.	The meeting of the manufacturers. They reject all of the workers' demands.
5	The rebellion of the hungry people and the betrayal of King Hunger.	The unceasing strike and the betrayal of the worker activist.
6	The defeat of the hungry people and the horror of the winners.	The provocation by criminals. The workers are shot by the officers of the law.

For the Proletkult theatre, the use of choruses was a very important means of expression, so, on this count, Sergei Eisenstein was influenced by the Proletkult ideology. We can also see four social groups that are exactly the same: the rich, the poor, the state repression machine, and the criminals.

Of course, the composition and visual expression are different: Andreev had to picture the actions of each social group within one act and location, while Eisenstein used his outstanding parallel and associative montage. The other point of difference is that Andreev tends to show only the result or the starting point of the event, while Eisenstein follows its course from the beginning to the end.

Locations and characters

Let us compare the two pieces. This is how the first act of *Tsar Golod* begins:

> When the curtain rises, the deep red and black interior of the factory appears before one's eyes. Red fire, crimson light from the forge, red hot iron liquid, hot drops and the shadows of people that hammer on and band together pieces of steel.[28]

And this is the piece from the prologue of *Stachka* that actually retells the plot, using movie expression language:

> Crossfading. A working plant. A far distance shot. A look above [...] Sprays of red hot steel, poured into a furnace [...] Small splashes fading in [...] Sweaty faces of the steel melters. A close-up shot. Closer up [...] A furnace, filled with molten steel, during the molding process.[29]

Figure 13.4 'Factory'. Frame from *Stachka*, film by S. Eisenstein, USSR, 1924 [State Russian Film Archive (Gosfil'mofond)]. Copyright: Public domain.

28 L. Andreev, *Dramaticheskiie proizvedeniia* [Dramatic Works], 2 vols (Leningrad: Iskusstvo, 1989), Vol. 1, p. 327.

29 S. Eisenstein, *Izbrannyie proizvedeniia* [Selected Works], 6 vols (Moscow: Iskusstvo, 1968), Vol. 6, p. 38.

Despite the fact that later Eisenstein had to change the type of the factory and not show the foundry, we know that *Stachka* begins with distant shots of the factory and its interior.[30]

The images of workers in *Stachka* and the characters' sketches for *Tsar Golod* are fundamentally different. It is obvious that Eisenstein followed Andreev's detailed stage directions in making the costumes for workers, and not the remarks only, but the lines as well. For instance, the creation of the image of the character, described in the play as 'the third worker – a dry, colourless man, sodden with acids, who lived a long life, with the ingrained paint all over him'. Looking at page two, we can see that the lines of the workers are literally used by Eisenstein in his sketch: 'The iron hammer flattens me. It crushes the blood out of my veins, it fractures my bones, it makes me flat as sheet iron.'[31]

Figure 13.5 Eisenstein. Pencil sketches for the 'Three Workers' costumes for the performance by Valentin Tikhonovich, 1921 [Russian State Archive of Literature and Art (RGALY). Fond 1923, Inventory list 1, Storage unit 723, Picture 4]. Copyright: Public domain.

30 Ibid., p. 1.
31 Ibid., p. 2.

In the play, there are three workers, presented by Andreev in the first act as the leading characters of the chorus: the First, who looks stronger than Hercules, the Second, a young boy poet and the Third, whom we have already described as an aged working man.[32] In *Stachka*, we also find three workers standing out from the workers' mass.[33] We can see the Young Worker, the Old one and the Worker-Ideologist, who is no doubt a member of the Workers' Party (which means he is stronger than Hercules). Even if in the film there is no direct use of the images of the play, we can see the signs of the indirect influence.

Figure 13.6 'Three Workers'. Frame from *Stachka*, film by S. Eisenstein, USSR, 1924 [State Russian Film Archive (Gosfil'mofond)]. Copyright: Public domain.

32 Ibid., p. 3.
33 Ibid., p. 4.

However, in creating the world of the exploiters – the factory owners, the police and its secret service agents as well – Sergei Eisenstein was close to the direct reproduction of the eccentric sketches of the play characters he made. For instance, everybody remembers how grotesque were the provocateurs' images: foxes, owls, monkeys and a bulldog that transform into the shots where actors repeat animals' grimaces.[34]

Figure 13.7 'Grotesque Characters'. Frames from *Stachka*, film by S. Eisenstein, USSR, 1924 [State Russian Film Archive (Gosfil'mofond)]. Copyright: Public domain.

34 Ibid., p. 5. The Monkey and the Bulldog were the nicknames of the agents in *Stachka*.

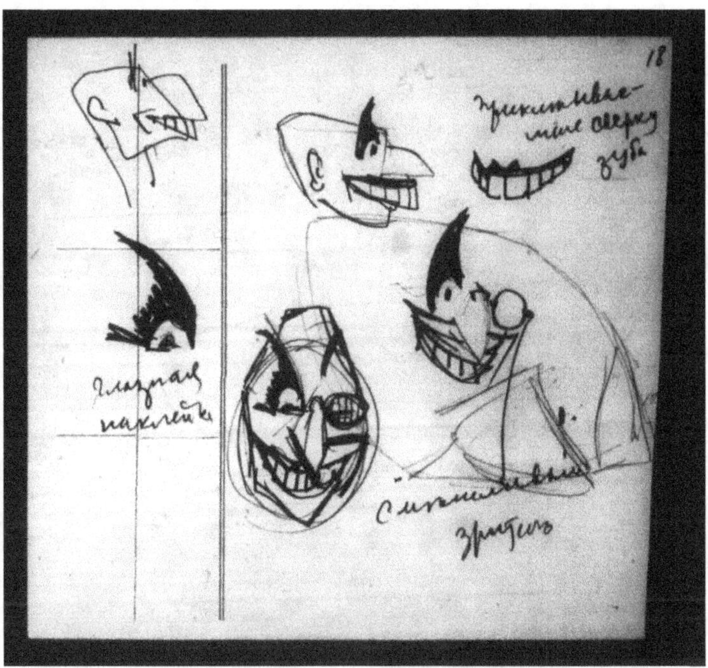

Figure 13.8 Eisenstein. Pencil sketches for make-up for the performance by Valentin Tikhonovich, 1921 [Russian State Archive of Literature and Art (RGALY). Fond 1923, Inventory list 1, Storage unit 723, Picture 18]. Copyright: Public domain.

It is widely assumed that in *Stachka* Eisenstein started to use so-called zoomorphism as the aesthetic principle, and further he repeated it – although not literally – in *October* (Kerensky – peacock), *Old and New* (rich farmers – pigs) and so on. But now we can affirm that he originally used these means of expression while making sketches for *Tsar Golod*. It is obvious that during his work on the design of the third act, where the Rich watch the trial process like a show, Eisenstein saw animal, bird and insect images everywhere: in costumes, curtains, dresses, make-up, hairstyles, shapes of drapery and dishes;[35] the sketches of the lawyer's costume and make-up; the motifs of the birds; the sketches of the dishes for the third

35 Ibid., pp. 6–8.

Figure 13.9 Eisenstein. Pencil sketches for the 'Engineer' costume for the performance by Valentin Tikhonovich, 1921 [Russian State Archive of Literature and Art (RGALY). Fond 1923, Inventory list 1, Storage unit 723, Picture 26]. Copyright: Public domain.

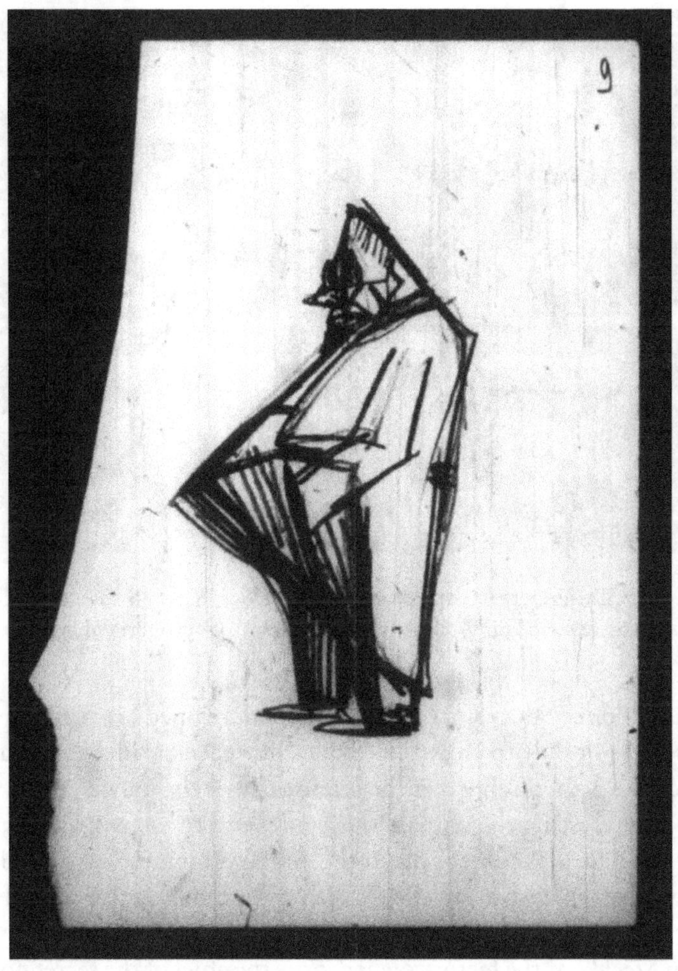

Figure 13.10 Eisenstein. Pencil sketches for the 'Engineer' costume for the performance by Valentin Tikhonovich, 1921 [Russian State Archive of Literature and Art (RGALY). Fond 1923, Inventory list 1, Storage unit 723, Picture 9]. Copyright: Public domain.

Figure 13.11 'The Factory Owner'. Frames from *Stachka*, film by S. Eisenstein, USSR, 1924 [State Russian Film Archive (Gosfil'mofond)]. Copyright: Public domain.

act. It is important that in *Stachka* Eisenstein developed his 'zoomorphism' and used it not only to create grotesque and eccentric images but also to produce the pathetic effects at the intense end of the movie.[36]

It is interesting to compare the figures of the repressive apparatus. The only villain in Andreev's play is the military Engineer, who applies the latest weapon against the rebels. We can meet the Engineer several times in Eisenstein's sketches. And we can find a character looking almost the same in *Stachka* as the factory owner[37] or as the chief of the secret police.[38] We can also feel a similar atmosphere in the sketches of the make-up for the play and in the screenshots of the satirical characters.[39]

36 Ibid., p. 9.
37 Ibid., p. 11.
38 Ibid., p. 12.
39 Ibid., p. 10.

Provocation

One of the outstanding storylines in *Stachka* is connected with the favorite image of Expressionists – the lumpenproletariat. In the film, the secret agent of the tsarist police instigates criminals – so-called 'king pins' – to set on fire a winehouse in a work settlement to provoke the police and to justify the violent subjection of the rebels. This plot device is the direct repetition of the second act of Andreev's play with the only difference being that *Tsar Golod* came to the lumpens himself. He had a specific suggestion for burglars, prostitutes and procurers, the true 'kids of Tsar Golod': to carry weight with the rebellion of workers. Here we can see the fire motif, which Eisenstein would use later in *Stachka*:

> That's the rebel! What a bloody lark!– Ho-ho-ho! – Get the matches!
>
> – Matches are cheap! […] Fire!
> – Up with the light! Ho-ho-ho![40]

Here we can note more connections between the two pieces.

So, in his search for a scenography idea Sergei Eisenstein made several sketches for the second act of the play. While working on it he relied on Andreev's remark about the second act environment: 'We can see the basement of the building […] the corners of the room are full with old useless things: an empty barrel without hoops, some boards, a wooden box, etc.'[41] And on page 30 we can see that a barrel becomes the compositional center of the sketch. We meet the same attention for barrels in other drafts. And it is natural to suppose that 'the barrels graveyard' (Kadushkin's cemetery) that became the highlight of *Stachka* – the most recognizable feature and a signature of the film – is linked to Eisenstein's work on the scenery of *Tsar Golod*.[42]

40 Andreev, *Dramaticheskiie proizvedeniia*, Vol. 1, p. 298.

41 Ibid., p. 260.

42 Eisenstein, *Izbranniie proizvedeniia*, Vol. 6, p. 14.

Figure 13.12 Eisenstein. Pencil sketches for Act 2 for the performance by Valentin Tikhonovich, 1921 [Russian State Archive of Literature and Art (RGALY). Fond 1923, Inventory list 1, Storage unit 723, Picture 26]. Copyright: Public domain.

Working on Andreev's second act, Eisenstein created not only the costumes but also all the characters, which later became the base for the characters of *Stachka*. For instance, we can assume that the leader of the rebels became the prototype of the future 'King', played by Boris Yurtsev.[43] Of course, his image is not the same; the director took the idea of costume for the episode – half-length pants and a jacket. But the leading woman rebel was adapted to *Stachka* as she was – to become the 'Queen of Thieves', played by the brilliant Judith Glizer.[44]

43 Ibid., p. 15.
44 Ibid., p. 16.

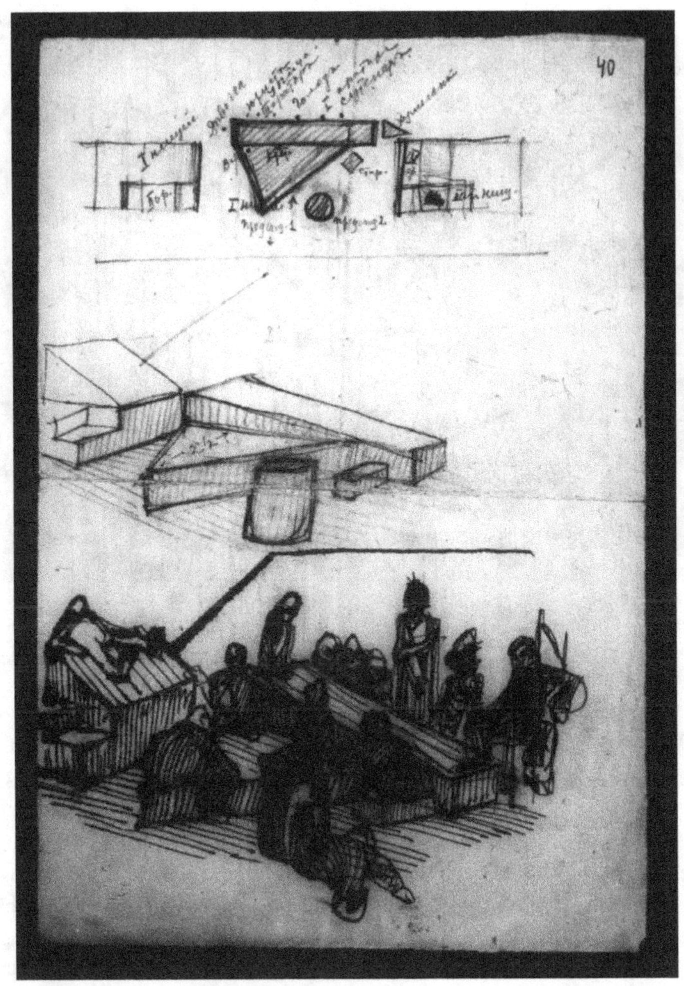

Figure 13.13 Eisenstein. Pencil sketches for Act 2 for the performance by Valentin Tikhonovich, 1921 [Russian State Archive of Literature and Art (RGALY). Fond 1923, Inventory list 1, Storage unit 723, Picture 26]. Copyright: Public domain.

Figure 13.14 'Kadushkino kladbishche'. Frame from *Stachka*, film by S. Eisenstein, USSR, 1924 [State Russian Film Archive (Gosfil'mofond)]. Copyright: Public domain.

O. Kovalov supposes that Eisenstein was inspired by Dr. Mabuse and the character of Glizer while creating these episodes:

> Wishing to fire up the lower classes to a street rebellion, Mabuse appears like an indestructible leader 'à la russe': blacked boots, *kosovorotka* (blouse with collar fastening at side) with a belt, an excited gaze under the peaked cap slightly covering his ears, and moreover his charismatic speeches at the meeting making the crowd rage. The insane gaze of Mabuse among people in that crowd strongly refers to that fury with burning eyes and enraged howl: 'Cr-rush…!', played by Judith Glizer in *Stachka*.[45]

45 Kovalov, Margolit and Kireeva, *Sovetskii ekspressionizm*, p. 45.

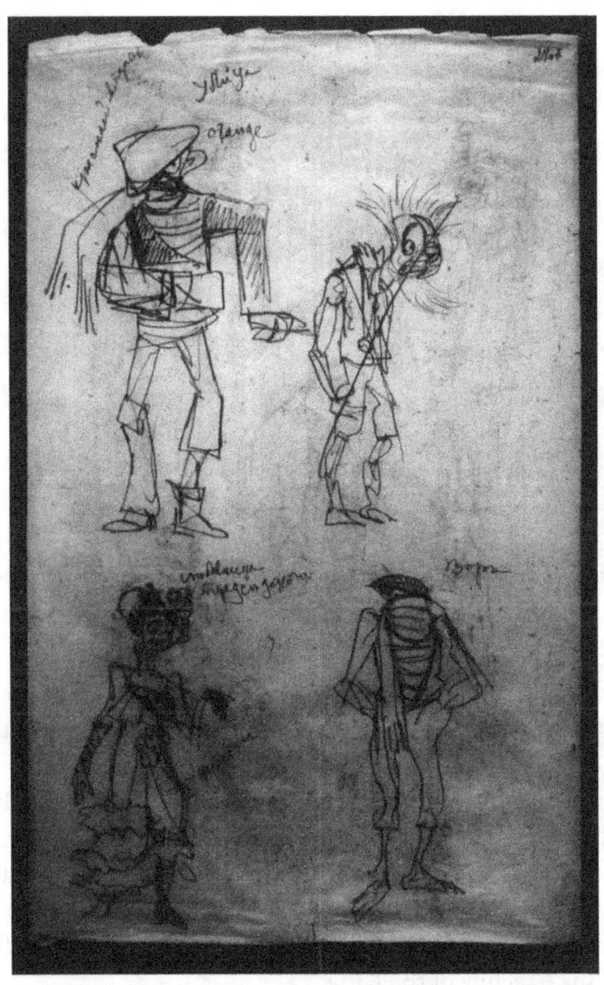

Figure 13.15 Eisenstein. Pencil sketches for 'The Chairman Favorite' for the performance by Valentin Tikhonovich, 1921 [Russian State Archive of Literature and Art (RGALY). Fond 1923, Inventory list 1, Storage unit 723, Picture 27-g]. Copyright: Public domain.

Figure 13.16 'Judith Glizer as Queen of Thieves'. Frame from *Stachka*, film by S. Eisenstein, USSR, 1924 [State Russian Film Archive (Gosfil'mofond)]. Copyright: Public domain.

So, this kind of comparison supported the idea that Eisenstein's and Andreev's creative explorations were both based on the artistic movement called Expressionism. Here is one more example. As we know, Expressionist painters were attracted to human pathologies. One figure is compulsively repeated in Eisenstein's sketches – a small barrel-shaped guy, and there is a signature 'Idiot', made by Eisenstein in one of these pictures. But there was none like him in Andreev's text; this man was created by Eisenstein himself.[46] And we can see him in *Stachka* as a halfling with a barrel – 'the Pageboy of the King'.[47]

46 Eisenstein, *Izbrannyie proizvedeniia*, Vol. 6, p. 17.

47 Ibid., p. 18.

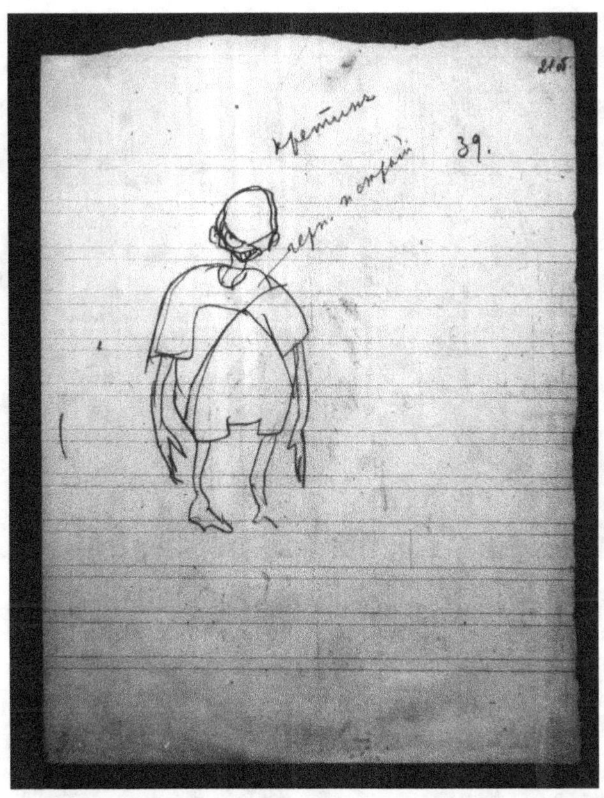

Figure 13.17 Eisenstein. Pencil sketches for 'Idiot' for the performance by Valentin Tikhonovich, 1921 [Russian State Archive of Literature and Art (RGALY). Fond 1923, Inventory list 1, Storage unit 723, Picture 39]. Copyright: Public domain.

Figure 13.18 Eisenstein. Pencil sketches for a variation of 'Idiot' for the performance by Valentin Tikhonovich, 1921 [Russian State Archive of Literature and Art (RGALY). Fond 1923, Inventory list 1, Storage unit 723, Picture 42]. Copyright: Public domain.

Figure 13.19 'Pageboy of the King'. Frame from *Stachka*, film by S. Eisenstein, USSR, 1924 [State Russian Film Archive (Gosfil'mofond)]. Copyright: Public domain.

Climax

It is obvious that the final part of *Stachka* – the execution of the workers – could have a remark from the final part of the play of Andreev as intertitles: 'corpses of the hungry are lying next to the muzzle of a huge gun, drowning in the thick twilight. And the Shadow of Death is drawn vaguely over them'.[48] Also, as in Andreev's play, the winners in *Stachka* could easily ask their victims, using the text of the play: 'So what do you have? Where did you go? What were you hoping for? We have the weapons, we have the power – and what did you have, miserable carrion?'[49]

And even the final effect of *Tsar Golod*, where the corpses of the hungry begin to raise their dead heads and open their dead mouths, whispering: 'We shall yet come! We shall yet come! Woe unto the victorious!',[50] was planned in *Stachka*. It was well known that the film should have had Trotsky's speech at the Moscow May Day parade of 1924 as an epilogue.[51] These final shots that stated the victory of the labor movement were even filmed by Eisenstein. But they were cut by the Soviet censorship because comrade Trotsky was on the Bolsheviks' blacklist by the time of the movie's premiere. So *Stachka* was released with a tragic ending instead of a happy one, as if the allegoric figure of Death from *Tsar Golod* was walking over Sergei Eisenstein's final shots. There are images of the total victory of violence and Death over the human body, often found on the canvases of Otto Dix, Max Pechtstein and Edvard Munch.

48 Andreev, *Dramaticheskiie proizvedeniia*, Vol. 1, p. 301; Eisenstein, *Izbrannyie proizvedeniia*, Vol. 6, p. 19.

49 Andreev, *Dramaticheskiie proizvedeniia*, Vol. 1, p. 302.

50 Ibid.

51 See V. Zabrodin, *Eisenstein: Popytka teatra* [Eisenstein: An Attempt at Theatre] (Moscow: Eisenstein Centre, 2005), pp. 233–235.

Figure 13.20 'Victory of Death'. Frame from *Stachka*, film by S. Eisenstein, USSR, 1924 [State Russian Film Archive (Gosfil'mofond)]. Copyright: Public domain.

Conclusions

'Over the rusty green swamp where the whole of life was in ooze, grumble and popping bubbles, stood up the weird head with a thin snake neck and unkind eyes. Everyone gasped: "There he is!" '[52] – this crucial diary note by Leonid Andreev not only indicates the constant thinking of the writer about his place in the art at the beginning of the twentieth century but also creates a verbal picture that is very close to Expressionism conceptually. The significance of this writer in Russian and world literature is still to be properly defined. The concept of 'anticipatory man' is the best explanation of who Leonid Andreev is, whose artworks are nowadays

52 L. Andreev, *S.O.S.* (Moscow: Athenium-Phenix, 1994), p. 45.

revealed as a premonition of Expressionism. The creator of *Bronenosets Potemkin* (Battleship Potemkin, 1926) Sergei Eisenstein was in absolute harmony with his time, at least in the first half of the 1920s. As this period extends, Eisenstein becomes a more significant person in the historical and aesthetic sense. He was an expert on previous periods of culture regardless of his being an indubitable symbol of the Soviet avant-garde in the 1920s. Moreover, the Silver Age's artifacts became impulses for creating his own paintings.

We have tried to prove that in 1921 Eisenstein came to work on the play *Tsar Golod* not only as a designer but also as a director who developed characters and interpreted the play in a new historical and aesthetic context. And his unrealized ideas concerning *Tsar Golod* greatly influenced his first full-length film. Studying his sketches and comparing them with certain images from *Stachka* lead to the conclusion that the eccentric costumes and make-up from *Tsar Golod* were partly used for the grotesque characters of the film. But most importantly, further analysis and comparison of the movie's and play's plots and characters reveal that the screenplay of *Stachka* is actually based on the text of Andreev's *Tsar Golod*.

It is obvious that both artworks are strongly influenced by Expressionism: the tortured and mutilated human body and consciousness exterminated by the soulless world and the new improved methods of political oppression on individuals – these are the main common themes in *Tsar Golod* and *Stachka* that are relevant to this day.

Moreover, this historical case goes on to prove that the phenomenon of the Soviet avant-garde was firmly based 'on the shoulders' of the Silver Age artists, and Futurism was not the only art movement that 'gently' moved from the pre-revolutionary age to the post-revolutionary one as it was previously stated. At the present time, Symbolist and Acmeist 'spheres of influence' on the theatre and literature of 1920s Soviet art have been found. And there is no doubt that the idea of *sobornost* (spiritual harmony) was borrowed by the theoreticians of 'Proletkult'.

Modern research in the field of 'Russian Expressionism' is proving the idea that the aesthetic foundation of revolutionary Soviet art began to form long before the historical cataclysm of 1917. We hope that our chapter is one more step in this direction.

Bibliography

Akseinov, I., *Is tvorcheskogo naslediia* [From the Creative Heritage], 2 vols (Moscow: Iskusstvo, 2008), Vol. 1.

Andreev, L., *Dramaticheskiie proizvedeniia* [Dramatic Works], 2 vols (Leningrad: Iskusstvo, 1989), Vol. 1.

——— *S.O.S.* (Moscow: Athenium-Phenix, 1994).

Eisenstein, S., 'Dikkens, Griffit i my' [Dickens, Griffith and Us], in *Izbrannyie proizvedeniia* (1968), Vol. 5, pp. 129–180.

——— *Izbrannyie proizvedeniia* [Selected Works] 6 vols (Moscow: Iskusstvo, Vol. 4, 1966; Vols 5 and 6, 1968).

Eisenstein v vospominaniiakh sovremennikov [Eisenstein in Contemporaries' Memories] (Moscow: Iskusstvo, 1974).

Filonenko, N., 'Stanovleniie i razvitiie poetiki ekspressionizma v tvochestve L.N. Andreeva 1898–1908' [Formation and Development of Expressionism Poetics in the Works of L. N. Andreeva 1898–1908], Ph.D. dissertation, Lipetskyi Gosudarstvennyi Pedagogicheskyi Universitet, Lipetsk, 2003.

Golovchiner, V., *Epicheskaia drama v russkoi literature XX veka* [Epic Drama in Russian Literature of Twentieth Century] (Tomsk: University of Tomsk, 2007).

Gorky, Maxim, and Leonid Andreev, *Gorky i Leonid Andreev: Neizdannaia perepiska* [Gorky and Leonid Andreev: Unpublished Correspondences] (Moscow: Nauka, 1965).

Kerzhentsev, P., *Tvorcheskii teatr* [Creative Theatre] (Moscow: GosIsd, 1918).

Khrenov, N., 'Vozvrashchaias' k ekspressionizmu: Ekspressionizm i russkaia kul'tura' [Back to Expressionism: Expressionism and Russian Culture], *Kul'tura i iskusstvo*, Vol. 15, No. 3 (2013), pp. 328–343.

Kovalov, O., Y. Margolit and M. Kireeva, *Sovetskii ekspressionizm: Ot Kaligari do Stalina* [Soviet Expressionism: From Caligari to Stalin] (St. Petersburg: Poryadok Slov, 2019).

Lakhno, Y., 'Dramaturgiia L. Andreeva v interpretatsii issledovatelei kontsa XIX–nachala XX veka' [The Dramaturgy of L. Andreev in the Interpretation of Researchers of the Late XX–Early XXI Century], *Vestnik Chelyabinskogo gosudarstvennogo universiteta*, Vol. 245, No. 16 (2014), pp. 66–69.

Markov, P., *O teatre* [About Theatre], 4 vols (Moscow: Iskusstvo, 1976), Vol. 3.

Shestakova, M., 'Razvitiie ekspressionisticheskikh tendentsii v romanistike L.N. Andreeva' [Development of Expressionistic Tendencies in Leonid Andreev's novels], *Vestnik SAMGu*, Vol. 112, No. 1 (2014), pp. 146–152.

Shklovsky, V., *Ikh nastoiashchee* [Their Present-Day] (Moscow: Kinopechat, 1927).

Tikhonovich, V., *50 let v teatre i okolo teatra*, 2 vols [50 Years in and around the Theatre] (Moscow: Nautchnaia biblioteka STD. Otdel rukopicei [Scientific Library of Russian Theatre Union. Department of Manuscripts], 1950), Vol. 1.

Titova, G., *Tvorcheskii teatr i teatralnyi konstruktivizm* [Creative Theatre and Theatre Constructivism] (St. Petersburg: SPB-GATI PH, 1995).

Zabrodin, V., *Eisenstein: Popytka teatra* [Eisenstein: An Attempt at Theatre] (Moscow: Eisenstein Centre, 2005).

ELENA YUSHKOVA

14 The Phoenix's Rebirth from Its Ashes: Russian Dance in the Twentieth Century

The development of dance in twentieth-century Russia was not smooth. Established traditions as well as newly invented trends were interrupted or about to be broken for reasons that had little to do with art. Politics, ideology and social problems affected the development of classical ballet, non-classical (free) and folk dance even though these kinds of art seemed to be completely apolitical, non-ideological or indifferent to social life. Nevertheless, Russia could have lost its classical ballet after the October Revolution and during the formation of the Soviet project. A decade later, in the 1930s, it could have lost those non-classical dance traditions formed before the revolution. While classical ballet was considered outdated after perestroika, free/contemporary dance was evolving rapidly.

It is too easy to suppose that traditions formed in ballet and non-classical dance were always threatened by political circumstances, but this notion is clearly superficial. Dance, like other arts, has its own logic and continuity, growing organically from its nature and defined by different laws than political or ideological ones. Being entrenched in human bodies and souls, dance cannot be easily subordinated to ideology. It always leaves room for different meanings and unexpected references to the past. It is quite difficult to erase roots, especially in ballet, which has its own strict centuries-old codification. However, politics did play a significant role in the history of Russian dance and ballet in the twentieth century.

Interactions between dance and politics became an object of study for academic research in the 1990s. Scholars working in this evolving field have done impressive work conceptualizing how such relations work by analyzing many examples from world dance history. See, for example, the works by Dana Mills (2017), Rebekah Kowal and Gerald Siegmund (2017), Andre Lepecki (2006), Alexandra Kolb (2011) and Mark Franko (1995), who note that such kinds of relations are 'intricate'[1] and 'complex'.[2] Mark Franko, one of the pioneer scholars in this field, has stressed that dance 'does not operate directly in the political sphere and thus dance is not strictly speaking political'.[3] Since dance studies appeared as a separate discipline in Russia much later than in the West (only in the second decade of the twenty-first century), there has not been a thorough observation of relationships between politics and dance in Russia and the Soviet Union. However, this analysis could open promising horizons, as we will try to show in this brief outline, and, no doubt, more work will be carried out on this topic in the nearest future.

Speaking of Russian dance in the twentieth century, we can refer to the famous formula by the philosopher Nikolai Berdyaev who noted a century ago that 'interruption is a characteristic of Russian history'.[4] Aleksandr Solzhenitsyn went further by claiming that 'the transition from pre-October Russia to the USSR is no continuation but a deadly break of the spinal cord'.[5] However, sociologist Pitirim Sorokin referred to the theory of sociological cycles,[6] which is of interest to contemporary Russian historians and political scientists nowadays (see Kåre Johan Mjør [2018] and Vladimir Pantin and V. Lapkin [2010]). Cultural historians such as Vladimir Paperny (2016) also refer to this theory, speaking of recurrent 'Culture One' and

1 Alexandra Kolb, *Dance and Politics* (Bern: Peter Lang, 2011), p. xiii.

2 Mark Franko, *Dancing Modernism/Performing Politics* (Bloomington: Indiana University Press, 1995), p. 4.

3 Mark Franko, 'Dance and the Political: States of Exception', in *Dance Discourses: Keywords in Dance Research*, ed. in Susanne Franko and Marina Nordera (London: Routledge, 2007), pp. 11–28; p. 14.

4 Nikolai Berdyaev, *The Russian Idea*, trans. R. M. French (Hudson, NY: Lindisfarne Press, 1992), p. 21.

5 Aleksandr Solzhenitsyn, *Publitsistika. Statii i rechi* (Paris: YMCA Press, 1981), p. 273.

6 Pitirim Sorokin, *Social and Cultural Dynamics* (Cincinnati: American Book Company, 1937–1941).

'Culture Two'. However, the focus of most recent research has shifted to 'the interplay between tradition and structural transformation [that] has been shaping Russian culture'.[7] Although these discussions are beyond the scope of this chapter, both notions seem to be equally applicable to dance history in the twentieth and twenty-first centuries.

Although the dichotomy 'continuity or change' related to Russian and Soviet history has been the focus of several studies over the years, historians in the 1990s did not find them appropriate and satisfying, as shown by Katerina Clark in her seminal book *Petersburg: Crucible of Cultural Revolution* promoting the 'shifts in the cultural models involving both continuity and change'.[8] Although 'there's not really one good work that goes over the whole twentieth century, that's a real gap', as the American historian Karen Petrone claims,[9] if we look at the way Western historians studying Russian and Soviet culture separate periods of the twentieth century from each other, we can see points of breaks and return to tradition. They usually consider separately pre-revolutionary Russia, Soviet Russia of the 1920s, Stalinist culture (1930–1950) (wartime is usually studied separately), the Thaw, Brezhnev's late socialism, Gorbachev's perestroika, Yeltsin's 1990s and finally Putin's Russia. Some scholars such as Clark (1966) show the transition from one period to another, outlining a mix of traditional and innovative characteristics in the arts as well as the process of their interactions.

All these frameworks can be applied to dance and ballet history, but it is also possible to look at it through the prism of another dichotomy formulated by Clark, namely, 'monumentalist versus iconoclast'[10] that was evident, for instance, in ballet. Interestingly, this social and political change influenced dance and ballet only to a certain extent. Sometimes the search for new artistic language and even tastes of sponsors (or state

7 Dmitri N. Shalin, 'Introduction: Continuity and Change in Russian Culture', in *Russian Culture at the Crossroads: Paradoxes of Postcommunist Consciousness*, 2nd edition (London: Routledge, 2018), p. 3.

8 Katerina Clark, *Petersburg: Crucible of Cultural Revolution* (Cambridge. MA: Harvard University Press, 1996), p. 1.

9 Karen Petrone, email to the author, 24 December 2020.

10 Clark, *Petersburg*, p. 26.

leaders) prevailed and became more influential and decisive. Another model for Russian dance history can be found in works by Michel de Certeau (1984) and Alexei Yurchak (2006) who wrote about hidden resistance to strict existing norms established by the authoritarian state that existed in late socialism.

Speaking of Russian dance history, we have to note that ballet historians have their own periodization in mind that differs from the one used by historians of non-classical dance. According to works by Tim Scholl (2005), Lynn Garafola (1998) and other scholars, pre-revolutionary ballet reached its peak at the turn of the nineteenth to the twentieth century, then declined and was later revolutionized by Michel Fokine and Diaghilev's enterprise. After the October Revolution, the dance form almost died but was resumed when Stalin-era high culture was established. The Cold War unexpectedly made Soviet ballet a means of cultural diplomacy – see Searcy (2020), McDaniel (2015), Ezrahi (2012), Dowler (2018); Morrison (2015) and *Dancing the Cold War* (edited by Garafola, 2017) – although its inner crisis and frozen stiff traditions again led the genre almost to a dead-end. Soviet cultural policy strove to subordinate ballet to ideology and to deprive it of aesthetic purity but failed. The new rebirth of the Russian ballet happened at the turn of the twentieth to twenty-first centuries when it flourished again, keeping old traditions and borrowing new ones.

The development of non-classical dance (called free dance) in Russia and the Soviet Union had its own highs and lows. Elizabeth Souritz (1995) and Nicoletta Misler (2011) see its beginning in the tours of the American dancer Isadora Duncan in the 1900s. This tradition developed rapidly but completely disappeared from the official arts in the 1930s, being alien to Socialist Realism based on rationality and clarity. It was restored only after perestroika, at the same time when European contemporary dance came to the country – three decades later than it appeared in Europe (the traditions of American and European modern dance were not present in Russia at all).

We will briefly consider the history of all three types of dance in order to trace how traditions and breaks have created such unique phenomena as Russian classical and non-classical dance.

Classical ballet

By the end of the nineteenth century, Russian classical ballet had attained an unprecedented success in the works of the great choreographer Marius Petipa (1818–1910). It was recognized abroad and surpassed its French and Italian counterparts, which, during the eighteenth century, had been widely acknowledged as the 'parents' of Russian professional dance.[11] For more than a century (1779–1896), a special ballet school in St. Petersburg trained about 150 professional dancers for the stage; two leading opera and ballet theatres staged masterpieces such as *Don Quixote*, *La Bayadère*, *The Nutcracker*, *The Sleeping Beauty*, *Swan Lake* and others. Nevertheless, at the beginning of the twentieth century, 'the ballet had fallen behind the increasingly rapid pace of Russian cultural life', suffering 'from its reputation as an aristocratic bauble'.[12] For the young choreographer Mikhail (Michel) Fokine, its language seemed obsolete. Deeply unsatisfied with 'old' ballet's machinery, long performances, heavy decorations, established codified language and a huge number of dancers and corps de ballet, he began working on a ballet reform. Inspired by the American dancer Isadora Duncan and the performances she gave in Russia in 1904 and 1905, he started thinking about more simplicity and spirituality on stage.[13]

Fokine's short piece *The Dying Swan*, staged for the young ballerina Anna Pavlova in 1907, had a special meaning in the Russian cultural tradition. Fokine aspired to create an ephemeral, fragmented piece, devoted to the moment of death of a fragile white bird, which is not able to survive in a brutal world. The image of the swan belonged to the Art Nouveau style,

11 A. Pleshcheev, *Nash balet* (Our Ballet) (St. Petersburg, 1886), pp. 10–20.

12 T. Scholl, *From Petipa to Balanchine: Classical Revival and Modernization of Ballet* (London: Routledge, 2005 [1994]), p. 16; pp. 10–11.

13 See G. Dobrovolskaya, *Mikhail Fokin: Russkii Period* (St. Petersburg, 2004), pp. 39–49; V. Krasovskaya, *Istoriya russkogo baleta* (St. Petersburg: Krasnodar, 2008), pp. 210–212; E. Souritz, 'Isadora Duncan and Prewar Russian Dancemakers', in *The Ballets Russes and Its World* (New Haven, CT: Yale University Press, 1999), pp. 108–114.

and the motif of death was critical for the 'decadent' art movement at the turn of the century. However, although Fokine challenged Tchaikovsky's 'big' ballet *Swan Lake*, staged in 1895 by the patriarchs of the Mariinsky Theatre, Marius Petipa and Lev Ivanov (author of the second act), he did not radically change the lexicon of the dancer. In other words, if his short lyrical piece was received as something new and revolutionary, as such it did not represent a complete break with the established canon; rather, *The Dying Swan* was Fokine's first attempt to move in a new direction within classical ballet. Unlike Isadora Duncan who had completely broken away from ballet tradition, Fokine always stressed that dancers trained in old-school techniques could express much more than a talented dilettante.[14] He used Duncan's innovations – bare feet, flexible upper parts of the body, stage clothes and classical music – in a number of performances staged in St. Petersburg: *Acis and Galatea* (1906), *Eunice* (1907), *Le Pavillon d'Armide* (1907), *The Night of Terpsichore* (1908, with a solo dance à la Duncan), *Egyptian Nights* (1908), *Dance of the Seven Veils* (1908, staged for Ida Rubinstein) and *Chopiniana* (1908, dance suite). Fokine's productions for Diaghilev's enterprise – *The Polovtsian Dances* (1909), *Firebird* (1910), *Scheherazade* (1910), *Narcisse* (1911) and *Daphnis and Chloe* (1912) – were all clearly inspired by Duncan. In this way, then, *The Dying Swan*, together with Fokine's later 'antique' or 'Greek' works, dynamized and modernized Russian classical ballet, without, however, breaking with the two-century-long tradition.

The Moscow choreographer Aleksandr Gorsky joined Fokine's ballet renovation and, like Fokine, also turned to Duncan's technique, incorporating some of her movements into his daily classes and antique ballets placing 'a greater stress on freedom of movement than he placed in his earlier ones'.[15]

With Diaghilev's 1909 appearance in the West, Russian ballet became synonymous with innovation and the spectacular. However, the success was based not only on dance but also on the joint work of painters, musicians,

14 Dobrovolskaya, *Mikhail Fokin*, pp. 43–44.

15 Souritz, 'Isadora Duncan and Prewar Russian Dancemakers', p. 105.

choreographers and dancers.[16] Another enterprise from the same period, led by Anna Pavlova, showed Western audiences a purely classical dance style.[17] In sum, the phenomenon of a new Russian ballet had a significant impact on the development of world ballet, awakening a keen interest in dance. By combining the achievements of the Italian and French schools, adding Russian lyricism and enriching rigid ballet forms with elements of Isadora Duncan's free dance, Russian ballet enriched the cultural life both in Europe and in the United States.

Having conquered the world, Russian ballet soon faced significant challenges at home. After the revolution in 1917, the great tradition was to be interrupted (see Ezrahi [2012] and Morrison [2015]). Classical ballet, which was traditionally a part of the tsar's court life, became a headache for the new proletarian state. This expensive kind of art demanded massive investments that, in a period of food and essentials shortage, could not be justified. Moreover, from a cultural perspective, the growing prevalence of the avant-garde style had the effect of making traditional ballet look even more old-fashioned. Influential Proletkult spokesmen called for the abolition of 'old' culture in general and ballet in particular because it did not fit in modern urban culture and demanded significant funding. However, thanks to Anatoly Lunacharsky, the first Soviet People's Commissar of Enlightenment, ballet survived and continued to 'transport the proletariat to a different world'.[18] Paradoxically, *Swan Lake*, *Sleeping Beauty* and other hits of 'old times' turned out to be of great interest to a non-educated proletarian audience. The ballet was to become a part of the new culture, multinational and united.[19] In other words, although it went through severe difficulties and lost many dancers, choreographers, artists and managers

16 S. Scheijen, '*Russkie sezony' navsegda* [Russian Seasons' Forever] (Moscow, 2012), pp. 212–213.

17 A. Levinson, 'Anna Pavlova i legenda Lebedya', in *Anna Pavlova; zhizn' i legenda*, ed. V. Dandre (St. Petersburg, 2003), pp. 488–504; p. 490.

18 C. Ezrahi, *Swans of the Kremlin: Ballet and Power in Soviet Russia* (Pittsburgh, PA: University of Pittsburgh Press, 2012), p. 20.

19 Elizabeth Souritz, 'Balet', in *Bol'shaya Sovetskaya Encyclopedia* (3 izdanie, 1970). Tom 2, pp. 570–572; p. 571.

(Fokine and Pavlova among others left the country), it managed to keep the repertoire and even renew it.

Despite Proletkult calls to abolish classical ballet as an obsolete art and to close academic theatres, they continued to work, and the practice of distributing free tickets brought audiences back to theatres. During the 1918–1919 season, the public (mostly workers) attended *Sleeping Beauty*, *Raymonda*, *Swan Lake*, *Le Corsaire*, *Coppelia* and *The Little Humpbacked Horse*, sitting in a cold auditorium without heat in winter.

Post-revolutionary experiments in ballet evidently demonstrate a rupture of tradition. Fedor Lopukhov staged two new ballets. The 1923 dance symphony *The Greatness of the Universe*, to the music of the Fourth Symphony of Beethoven, created a new genre of ballet – one that influenced the young George Balanchine (Georgy Balanchivadze at that time) who was a dancer in this performance. In his later career as the founder of the American Ballet, he always referred to the inspiration he had drawn from that performance, in particular, Lopukhov's innovations that were underestimated in the Soviet Union.[20] In 1924, Lopukhov staged *Krasny Vikhr* (Red Vortex) in Leningrad to music by Prokofiev and Scriabin. Depicting an image of the revolution, he used methods of revolutionary avant-garde art: 'bravery, exploration, action and aggression',[21] to create new acrobatic movements for the dancers. It had a feeling of contemporary life and expressed the spiritual freedom of a 'new' human being.[22]

In 1925, another experimental choreographer, Kasyan Goleizovsky, staged *Josef the Beautiful* in his studio, Kamerny Balet. Quite different from the revolutionary pathos, it depicted in a lyrical performance the inner life of a contemporary person. In 1927, at the Bolshoi Theatre, the performance *Krasny Mak* (Red Poppy, choreographers Laschilin and Tikhomirov) portrayed revolutionary events in China. Although generally more traditional, this ballet comprised elements of music hall dances, pantomime

20 See Elizabeth Souritz, *Khoreograficheskoe iskusstvo 20-kh godov* (Moscow, 1979), pp. 278–287.

21 John E. Bowlt and Olga Matich, eds, *Laboratory of Dreams: The Russian Avant-garde and Cultural Experiments* (Palo Alto, CA: Stanford University Press, 1996), p. 3.

22 See Souritz, *Khoreograficheskoe iskusstvo 20-kh godov*, pp. 288–298.

and divertissement. It also included the first mass heroic dance – *Yablochko* (Little Apple, sailors' dance) – which for many decades thereafter became the classic cliché of Soviet 'folk' dance, performed at every concert devoted to Soviet celebrations. For the first time, the choreographer depicted a contemporary positive female hero. For her performance, Ekaterina Geltser became one of the first ballerinas to receive the status of people's artist.[23]

Two later ballets by Fedor Lopukhov were in tune with the general line of 1930s Soviet art: *Svetly Ruchei* (1935), about the life of *kolkhozniki* (peasants working on collective farms), and *Bolt* (1931), a story of contemporary urban life and factory workers. However, regardless of their 'politically correct' content and contemporary dance lexicon, neither was successful and quickly disappeared from the repertoire. New productions of these ballets in 2003 and 2005 by Alexei Ratmansky at the Bolshoi Theatre[24] were, on the contrary, successful. The absence of any ideological prism allowed Ratmansky to reveal their genuine originality, irony and creativity. Moreover, reconstructions of ballets of different epochs had already come into fashion by that time.

Ballet in the Stalin period seems a paradoxical phenomenon. Since Stalin 'saw himself and was seen by many people as a prince – endowed with full power, wrapped in majesty, and revered by the masses',[25] and 'the Communists became the heirs of the Tsars',[26] the creation of an appropriate art was logical. Stalinist culture, which by the mid-1930s became 'a museum of Russian historical styles',[27] put classical ballet on a pedestal since it was like a type of pageant, which was needed. As Ezrahi notes, 'The Bolshoi [...] became the quasi court theater of the Kremlin, creating an unusually close relationship between the fields of politics and ballet.'[28] This is why

23 See Souritz, 'Balet', p. 571.

24 See 'Bol'shoi Teatr, Svetly Ruchei', <https://2011.bolshoi.ru/performances/61/> (Accessed 29 November 2021) and 'Shostakovich: Balet Bolt', <http://www.belcanto.ru/ballet_bolt.html> (Accessed 29 November 2021).

25 Richard Stites, *Revolutionary Dreams: Utopian Vision and Experimental Life in the Russian Revolution* (New York: Oxford University Press, 1991), p. 248.

26 Nicolas S. Timasheff, *The Great Retreat: The Growth and Decline of Communism in Russia* (New York: Dutton, 1946), p. 16.

27 Timasheff, in Stites, *Revolutionary Dreams*, p. 246.

28 Ezrahi, *Swans of the Kremlin*, p. 67.

'the companies in Moscow and Leningrad represent the tradition against which Diaghilev and Fokine rebelled',[29] and the monumentalist trend finally fought the iconoclast. *Sleeping Beauty*, *Swan Lake*, *La Bayadère* and other pre-revolutionary oeuvres were to stay in the repertoire of Soviet ballet theatres forever.

However, in the 1930s and 1940s, Socialist Realism also influenced ballet to some extent. Striving to be realistic, choreographers created the so-called dramatic ballets (dram-ballets). Based on literature, they favored pantomime over dance. The new star of the Soviet ballet Galina Ulanova, whose role in the dram-ballet *Romeo and Juliet* brought her international fame, became the symbol of Russian ballet in the 1950s in much the same way that Anna Pavlova was during the late imperial era. However, at the same time, a new type of Soviet dancer appeared: unlike the pre-revolutionary bodiless airy ballerina, expressing an abstract higher reality through her dance, new dancers such as Marina Semenova and Alexei Yermolaev stressed the materiality of the body, and endeavored to capture the heroic spirit of the Soviet people.

> Expansive movements such as powerful jumps, enabling the dancer to cover the stage in mighty leaps, corresponded to the heroic utopianism the Soviet state was propagating. Sky-borne dancer aviators covering a wide space with soaring leaps were certainly more likely to express a teleological ideology premised on the strategy of 'catch up and overtake' than dancers performing small, complex steps whose understated charm lay in accuracy and detail.[30]

That was a certain break with tradition, since technique was significantly changed and to be brought back only in the twenty-first century by the French choreographer Pierre Lacotte who staged his reconstructions of several historical ballets at the Mariinsky and Bolshoi theatres.[31]

Thanks to Stalin's personal taste and substantial state support, classical ballet became part and parcel of the Soviet cultural project recognized as

29 Ibid., p. 138.

30 Ezrahi, *Swans of the Kremlin*, p. 145.

31 Ekaterina Belyaeva, 'Premiera baleta Lakotta Marko Spada v Bol'shom teatre', 2013, <https://www.belcanto.ru/13111802.html> (Accessed 29 November 2021).

an effective tool for expressing the heroic spirit of the new human being. In many cities across the Russian Federation and capital cities of Soviet republics, state opera houses and theatres were opened. If before the revolution there were only two theatres in Russia, by 1970 there were 40, and 16 specialized colleges set up to train numerous professionals for the stage.[32] In every republic, the repertoire included both traditional old ballets and new ones based on national folklore, thereby enriching the palette of classical dance. Even during the war, the Kirov Theatre, which moved from Leningrad to Perm, produced a new ballet *Gayane*, and the Bolshoi Theatre in Kuibyshev staged *Alye Parusa* (Red Sails) – both in 1942.[33] These facts show how much this art meant for the Soviet people and their leaders. The principal theatres continued their work even during the evacuation, and the devastating effects of war did not interrupt the development of classical ballet. Loved and patronized by Stalin and other leaders, it survived, even though Socialist Realism influenced its aesthetics for the worse, and by the end of Stalin's epoch, it had found itself in 'a creative stupor', 'artistic paralysis' and even 'creative asphyxia',[34] being isolated from new trends developing in the world. However, 'conservatism in ballet didn't necessarily reflect loyalty to a regime with conservative artistic tastes. On the contrary, it could indicate a dedication to artistic and aesthetic ideals' and 'provide a defense against Sovietization.'[35] As Christina Ezrahi proves, ideology and established cultural norms could not penetrate deep into ballet aesthetic, and as the 'experience of ballet in the Soviet Union shows, the inertia of tradition could be a powerful opponent to ideological demands'.[36] This scholar cites the famous Soviet ballerina Natalia Makarova's memoirs, in which she remembers her teachers who 'had begun in the days of Petipa and Ivanov'.[37] Makarova stresses that the great ballet traditions were absorbed by the students of the Vaganova School during routine classes and the process of socialization with people from the pre-revolutionary times: 'The most

32 Souritz, 'Balet', p. 572.
33 Ibid., p. 571.
34 Ezrahi, *Swans of the Kremlin*, pp. 69; 81; 96.
35 Ibid., p. 77.
36 Ibid., p. 48.
37 Ibid., p. 82.

significant thing about the Vaganova School was very likely the daily, unobtrusive feeling of contact with the great ballet of the past, its traditions and unwritten laws, which nourished us like mother's milk. You simply could not get away from it.'[38]

While all alternative *plastique* experimental studios had been closed by the beginning of the 1930s, as we will see in the next section, the state did officially allow one alternative form of dance, which was invented by the talented dancer and choreographer Igor Moiseev. His 'folk' or even 'fakelore'[39] dances of different nationalities of the world were significantly improved with elements of ballet and acrobatics. Performed by professionals, they were very entertaining and oriented toward ordinary people living in various Soviet republics. Moiseev created his ensemble in 1937, which exists to this day. When it was originally devised, this new form clearly met the requirements of Socialist Realism: it was people-oriented (*narodnost*), joyful, energetic and optimistic. Like Soviet fine art, it depicted the countryside celebrations of happy people, and like Soviet cinema, it demonstrated the total optimism and happiness of all people. As the historian Eric Hobsbawm showed, 'inventing traditions [...] is essentially a process of formalization and ritualization, characterized by reference to the past'.[40] Turning to traditional folk art, classical ballet and acrobatics, Moiseev was able to invent a new Soviet dance tradition. The combination of characteristics important for the regime made Moiseev's ensemble suitable for official concerts and celebrations. The ensemble even became a face of Soviet culture abroad going on tours regularly from 1945 (the first tour was to Finland) and received not only recognition in many countries but was awarded the American Oscar for dance twice.[41]

These two dance forms wonderfully conveyed Soviet identity: on the one hand, an aspiration for pure perfection (in ballet), which correlated with the total glossing over of the truth, and, on the other hand,

38 Ibid.

39 See Richard M. Dorson, *American Folklore* (Chicago: University of Chicago Press, 1977).

40 Eric Hobsbawm and Terence Ranger, eds, *The Invention of Tradition* (Cambridge: Cambridge University Press, 1983), p. 4.

41 See N. Sheremetevskaya, *Tanets na estrade* (Moscow, 1985), pp. 169–177.

narodnost, a people-oriented way of perceiving reality. By the time of late socialism, both forms had become stagnant and turned into deadening official art. European and American dance trends considered bourgeois and forbidden in the USSR did not penetrate to the country. The Iron Curtain protected Soviet dance from the dangerous intervention of foreign choreographic ideas.

Only after Stalin's death, during the Khrushchev Thaw, the Soviet public had a chance to see European and American dance and *plastique* art (see Prevots [1998]). Tours by Balanchine, Joffrey, French Grand Opera, the mime Marcel Marceau and other artists and theatres broadened the horizons of Soviet dance.[42] Foreign tours by the Bolshoi and Kirov theatres brought Soviet art to the world, and again, as in 1909, Russian ballet became a sensation, showing a technique protected from modern and contemporary dance influences.[43] Soviet classical ballet, which despite the prevalence of the dram-ballet genre still had preserved a strict 'old' purity isolated from new dance trends, became an object for cultural diplomacy and in some respects a face of the Soviet Union during the Cold War (see, for instance, Searcy [2020], McDaniel [2015] and Ezrahi [2012]). Maya Plisetskaya and other renowned ballet dancers successfully presented *Swan Lake* and *The Dying Swan* as staged by Petipa and his rival Fokine all over the world. The return of the choreographer Fedor Lopukhov from underground to grand state theatres showed 'a partial rediscovery of cultural endeavors of the 1920s'.[44] His belated recognition played a great role in the development of Soviet ballet, and

> Lopukhov's emphasis on a chain of artistic continuity linking Petipa, Ivanov, Fokine, himself, and the symphonic choreographers of the Soviet cultural Thaw, and the historical roots of the debate juxtaposing drambalet and choreographic symphonism, indicate the continuity of artistic thought across periods of drastic political and social change in Russia.[45]

42 V. Gaevsky, *Divertisment* (Moscow: Iskusstvo, 1981), pp. 287–376.

43 See V. Gaevsky and P. Gershenzon, *Besedy o russkom balete. Kommentarii k noveishei istorii* (Moscow: Novoe izdatel'stvo, 2010).

44 Ezrahi, *Swans of the Kremlin*, p. 105.

45 Ibid.

However, the period from the late 1950s until the 1980s became what was termed 'the Grigorovich era'.[46] Yury Grigorovich, a young choreographer who got a chance to stage full-length productions, changed the face of Soviet ballet. 'Grigorovich's ballets infused new life into the Soviet formula of content-rich, plot driven, full-length dramatic ballets'.[47] He created many iconic performances. *Stone Flower* (1957), for example, secured his fame as a choreographer on a global scale. Based on folk fairy tales from the Urals, Grigorovich's use of pure dance was a radical departure from the Soviet genre of choreodrama with its stories of everyday life.[48] His work *Spartacus* (1968) depicted the battle between an individual and a totalitarian system. The unique, very high and expressive jump of Vladimir Vasiliev's Spartacus[49] became a metaphor for the attempt to liberate the individual from totalitarian oppression. His example was soon taken up in real life: Nureyev jumped from the USSR to the West, with Makarova and Baryshnikov following him. All of them tried to overcome the limitations placed on their creative potential in their home country. Plisetskaya's inner resistance to the regime also became symbolic.

The Grigorovich era came to an end and, from the closing decades of Soviet rule until 1996, Soviet and Russian ballet was once again in a state of decline, crippled, as dance historians have argued, by being isolated from developments in dance worldwide. Only by 2007–2008, 'the decade of dynamic developments showed its first results: new names, new performances and new hopes'.[50] A new age of dance originated in the aftermath of perestroika. It was a time of renewal (encouraged by the launching of new dance festivals) and also a time of active collaboration with some of the

46 See *Era Grigorovicha. K 90-letiyu vydayuschegosya khoreogra* [Grigorovich's Era: Devoted to the Prominent Russian Choreographer's 90th Anniversary], A. A. Bakhrushin State Central Theatre Museum Exhibition, 2016–2017, <http://www.gctm.ru/event/era-grigorovicha-k-90-letiyu-vyidayushhegosya-russkogo-horeografa/> (Accessed 29 November 2021).

47 Ezrahi, *Swans of the Kremlin*, p. 120.

48 See A. Galayda, 'Yury Grigorovich, a Living Symbol of the Bolshoi', *Russia Beyond the Headlines*, 30 December 2016.

49 See B. Lvov-Anokhin, *Mastera Bolshogo baleta* (Moscow, 1976), pp. 163–166.

50 Gaevsky and Gershenzon, *Besedy o russkom balete*, p. 3.

best Western choreographers. The dance palette was enriched owing to the talents of a new generation of stars – Diana Vishneva, Ulyana Lopatkina, Nikolai Tsiskaridze – who, despite having received their training from famous Soviet dancers, were open to innovations. A detailed analysis of this situation is beyond the scope of this chapter.

By the 2010s, Russian ballet had absorbed numerous dance trends and restored several interrupted traditions. Theatres now included authentic reconstructions of early Soviet avant-garde performances, reconstructions of Soviet classics by Yury Grigorovich, the ballets of George Balanchine, John Neumeier, Roland Petit, Alexei Ratmansky as well as pre-revolutionary ballets in the repertoire. The legacy of the Silver Age, forbidden for several decades, returned to Russia, and Diaghilev's ballets were reconstructed after years of oblivion (Andris Liepa staged several of Fokine's ballets in 1991 and 1993). As Christina Ezrahi shows,

> Russia's prerevolutionary ballet tradition was saved not because of a faithful preservation of old ballet productions but because ballet was remembered in bodies and souls, and this physical and spiritual memory was reverentially passed on from one generation to the next.[51]

Ballet is still a very popular kind of art, and even expensive tickets are not an obstacle to sold-out performances in most Russian theatres. Ballet, in general, has significantly changed in the past three decades: theatres often invite Western choreographers; Russian dancers work abroad and return to Russia; old authentic performances are reconstructed; and new ones are staged. All kinds of old and new ballet are gaining more popularity than ever. For example, the recent TV program *Bolshoi Ballet* has been a success. During the competition, several pairs of young dancers from Russian ballet theatres present their work in different styles and aesthetics; the dances are staged in collaboration with famous contemporary choreographers from many countries. This show is a testament to the fact that Russian ballet is at ease with traditional, modern, contemporary and experimental

51 Ezrahi, *Swans of the Kremlin*, p. 8.

choreography. Classical dance is 'an open system',[52] which continues to develop by absorbing numerous experiments and new trends. And it is also interesting to note that the Russian audience in the second decade of the twenty-first century still wants to be transported to a different world created by *Swan Lake*, *Sleeping Beauty* and *Giselle*. Loved by all generations, these and other romantic ballets all sell out several months in advance in major academic theatres across the country.

Free dance

Isadora Duncan's original dance helped renew ballet traditions in Russia. Derived from contemporary American and European perception of antiquity, some Nietzschean ideas, Renaissance paintings, Art-Nouveau organics and a host of other seemingly incompatible sources, its goal was to render the harmonious development of body, mind and spirit. Duncan's followers opened their studios in Moscow and St. Petersburg where they practiced dance based on this set of new principles. The most famous leader was Eli Knieper-Rabenek (Ellen Tells), whose best student, Alice Koonen, became a leading actress in Aleksandr Tairov's Moscow Chamber Theatre, combining free dance with drama in the 1900s. Other examples include Studio Heptachor in St. Petersburg (1907), Natalia Milyukova's studio of dance-drama called Chrysis (1912) and the Francesca Beata School (1913) in Moscow.[53]

This kind of dance was flourishing before the revolution, but in the early post-revolutionary years, it remained popular as numerous dance studios searched for new means of plastic expressiveness. This search was in tune with the new avant-garde art and with the spirit of liberation. Attendees of these studios were looking for a new body language and tried to express themselves in a new way, different from all kinds of canonic forms.

52 V. Uralskaya, Interview in *Dancehelp*, 22 January 2021, <https://vk.com/video-9068269_456247016?list=408bb5b7222f61442d> (Accessed 29 November 2021).

53 See Souritz, 'Isadora Duncan and Prewar Russian Dancemakers', pp. 101–104.

After 1917, despite the harsh economic conditions, even more studios appeared. For instance, the studio of Inna Chernetskaya, one of the most popular at that time, practiced dramatic rhythmo-plastique dances. She had studied in Germany with Isadora Duncan's sister, Elizabeth, and was influenced by Ausdruckstanz, a form of expressive dance.[54] She staged highly dramatic Expressionist dances and small ballets.

Lyudmila Alexeeva's studio in the 1920s, Vera Maya's studio and the Francesca Beata School were also of great interest among creative young people.[55] Vera Maya not only experimented with different styles and choreographed acrobatic dances, sometimes very stylized, but also developed folk and comic dances. Alexeeva's intention was to create her unique system of training based on gymnastics and deep penetration into musical images. In the 1930s, Nikolai Poznyakov's 'Island of Dance' attracted the audience's attention. He staged the entire ballet based on free dance.[56] Using the classical music of Chopin, Scriabin and Rachmaninov, the choreographer Lev Lukin created sensual erotic compositions. His work has often been compared to Kasyan Goleizovsky's productions, but Goleizovsky, who insisted on professional academic training, was closer to ballet (he also staged productions at academic theatres). Some studios and dancers experimented with pantomime (Rumnev, Nina Gremina). It seemed possible to catch the rhythm of the 1920s through gymnastics and acrobatics. A unique gymnastic dance was invented by Valentin Paknakh. In Nikolai Foregger's 'machine dances', people imitated the motions of pendulum, pistons and wheels.[57]

Workers' clubs and amateur theatres, affiliated with Proletkult, were interested in new movements and dance too. In 1918, Lyudmila Alexeeva staged a large pageant for Proletkult titled *Mrak, Poryv, Marsel'eza* (Gloom, Gust, Marseillaise), which depicted class struggle, revolution and the death of the heroes (the first dance to the Marseillaise was composed by Isadora

54 V. Teider, *Russky balet na perelome epoch* (Moscow, 2014), pp. 25–26.

55 Elizabeth Souritz, 'Moskovskie studii plasticheskogo tantsa', in *Avangard i teatr 1910–1920-kh godov* (Moscow, 2009), pp. 384–430.

56 Elizabeth Souritz, 'Moscow's Island of Dance, 1934–1941', *Dance Chronicle*, Vol. 17, No. 1 (1994), pp. 1–92.

57 Sheremetevskaya, *Tanets na estrade*, pp. 45–65.

Duncan in 1915). Nina Aleksandrova was the student of Emile-Jacques Dalcroze, founder of rhythmic gymnastics at the beginning of the twentieth century, which, before the October Revolution, was popularized by Prince Sergei Volkonsky. She also worked at the Proletkult club and taught at the Institute of Rhythmic Education.

Moscow Chamber Theatre dancer and actor Aleksandr Rumnev described the unprecedented popularity of non-traditional dance of many kinds in the early 1920s. He recalls that, in their spare time, young people – despite the terrible living conditions and the lack of food and clothes – moved from one studio to another, carrying small suitcases with their dancing clothes. 'Everybody danced or wanted to dance', Rumnev stressed.[58] Their thirst for self-expression through movement was stronger than basic needs; classical ballet was not suitable for that kind of self-expression, although some of the dancing people also attended studios of professional ballet dancers from the Bolshoi Theatre such as Mikhail Mordkin. Thus, the new spirit of young, liberated people in the new state presupposed the development of a special plastique: free, expressive, connecting body and mind, and based on the new rhythms of life and a new understanding of the human being.

Studios and dance schools had no special regulations and could work independently in any way they chose, especially during the first years of the New Economic Policy (NEP) – which was quite fruitful for non-canonic dance. Moreover, in the major cities, young people liked social dances of foreign origin like the foxtrot.[59] The latter fitted in well with the NEP style. The founder of free dance, Isadora Duncan, came to Russia in 1921 to open her free school for 1,000 proletarian children. The school was opened in 1922 but due to limited space could enroll only 40 students (see works by McVay [2003], Roslavleva [1975] and Yushkova [2013, 2014]).

The dance boom in post-revolutionary Soviet Russia shows that the idea of free dance and body liberation correlated with the idea of total

58 A. A. Rumnev (Zyakin) 'Gody v Kametnom teatre', 1960, RGALI, Fond 2721, opis 1, edinitsa khraneniya 35, p. 57.

59 *Natalya Stüdemann, Dionisos in Sparta: Isadora Duncan in Russland, Eine Geschichte von Tanz und Korper* (Bielefeld: Transcript Verlag, 2008).

emancipation from the old regime, old traditions, old institutions and old codified systems of movement.

In the 1920s, human movements became a subject of serious research conducted by the Choreological Laboratory, GAKhN (State Academy of Arts Sciences).[60] As archival documents show, debates at the meetings of the laboratory were heated, and scholars and practitioners often challenged classical ballet in their speeches. For instance, the scholar M. Ulitskaya argued expressing the opinion of many post-revolutionary art reformers: 'Ballet is an old-fashioned form not related to the industrial epoch.' It has such outdated qualities as 'the fantastic, eroticism, symmetry of forms, mechanistic nature and dead technique' while 'dance should embody the dynamics of the epoch, expressed in force, hardness and heaviness. It should be a dance of freed labor – industrial dance.'[61] This opinion was shared by many avant-gardists dreaming of new art.

The year 1923 became a milestone in the formation of cultural policy. The Twelfth Communist Party Congress submitted a resolution on using the theatre for the systematic mass propaganda of the communist idea. Thus, the party now demanded that theatre productions should show heroic events and feelings on stage.[62] Obviously, free dance was not suitable for propaganda, being too unpredictable and ungovernable. As anti-Western feelings gradually began to grow in society,[63], free dance, which had come from the West, seemed more and more suspicious.

Ideological pressures increased after Lenin's death, and in 1924 there were significant changes in the cultural sphere. The 'Vsemirnaya literatura' publishing house was closed; Lunacharsky summoned the theatre to go 'back to Ostrovsky'; the Soviet press attacked the State Academy of Arts

60 See N. Misler, *Vnachale bylo telo: Ritmoplasticheskie eksperimenty nachala 20 veka; Khoreologicheskaya laboratoriya GAKhN* (Moscow, 2011).

61 Tantseval'ny kooperativ Aisedorino Gore, *Rukovodstvo po primeneniyu tantseval'nogo arkhiva: Opyty choreologii, ili Kuda nas zavel 'Sovetskii zhest'* (Moscow: Muzei sovremennogo iskusstva Garage, 2020), p. 70.

62 V. Zhidkov, *Teatr i vremya: ot Oktyabrya do perestroika* (Moscow, 1991), p. 105.

63 Katerina Clark. 'Stanovlenie sovetskoi kultury', in *Amerikanskaya rusistika: Vekhi istoriografii poslednih let; Sovetskii period* (Samara, 2001), pp. 146–173, pp. 149 and 152.

Sciences, GAKhN. On 26 August, a special decree of the Moscow City Council on plastique studios was released. This document announced the closure of more than ten famous studios and appointed a communist to Isadora Duncan's Moscow School for political-educational activities.[64] Studios then became almost illegal; sensing a threat from freethinking dancing people, the state effectively declared war on them, and by the early 1930s, all studios were finally closed. Henceforth, the Soviet system prioritized mass sport and old classical ballet together with pseudo-folk dance.

Thus, the new dance tradition, which had existed for two decades across the revolutionary divide, was officially broken for more than half a century and revived only after perestroika. The non-official existence of people involved in the free dance movement was not easy; they did not get support from the state, but they kept working using every legal opportunity to teach and to develop their ideas. Figures such as Lyudmila Alexeeva who created Russian artistic gymnastics or a member of Heptakhor group, Stepanida Rudneva, who taught until her death her system of musical movement inspired by Isadora Duncan's dance, are just two examples of heroic efforts at encouraging the revival of the free dance tradition in the hope that society would, once again, be ready for it.

Contemporary dance

After the fall of the Soviet Union, free dance forms poured into the country. American modern dance, German Expressionist dance and European contemporary gave a strong impulse to the new Russian dance, while pure classical ballet was almost neglected, becoming little more than a commercial product for export. Since that time and until the early Putin era, dance was developing fast and reflected the formation of the new Russian man: freethinking, creative, open to the world, interacting with numerous contemporary trends. Contemporary dance became

64 Misler, *Vnachale bylo telo*, p. 109.

a serious alternative to ballet, which was again perceived as an old-fashioned, dead, formalistic art, unable to express the dramatic change in mentality. Contemporary dance was developed in small amateur groups but became so noticeable that the professional magazine *Ballet* wrote about it in almost every issue. Festivals of contemporary dance took place in many cities of Russia and the near abroad (the most popular was held in Vitebsk, in the former USSR republic of Belorussia). Among leaders of the new genre were several groups: the Independent Group run by Alla Sigalova, now an established choreographer, teacher and TV anchor; Gennady Abramov's Class of Expressive Plastique (Moscow); the Perm-based Yevgeny Panfilov Theatre; Tatyana Baganova's Provincial Dances in Ekaterinburg; and Aleksandr Pepelyaev's Kinetic Theatre (Moscow). By the end of the 1990s, critics were drawing attention to the high professional standards of these groups and their integration into the Russian cultural landscape.

As Gennady Abramov noted, Russian contemporary dance focuses on the search for the essence of being, of existence; it even tries to push the limits of the human body, to overcome the boundaries of consciousness, to reach the absolute.[65] Abramov explored the human body; given his background in medicine, he did this from an unusual perspective. He showed the 'miracles of plastic expressiveness',[66] presenting surprising body positions not for the sake of acrobatics, but to awaken philosophical thoughts in the audience. His premise was that ballet had lost its ability to connect movements with the inner life of the human body and spirit. Thus, his experimental performances aimed at restoring the wholeness of the contemporary human being.

> His profound, phenomenological approach to the body, his constant exploration of the cooperation and internal transformation of the body and its external surroundings

65 See Elena Yushkova, *Plastika preodoleniya: kratkie zametki ob istorii plasticheskogo teatra v Rossii v 20 veke* (Plastique of Overcoming: Notes on the History of Russian Plastique Theatre in Russia in the 20th century) (Yaroslavl, 2009), pp. 249–250; E. Vasenina, *Sovremennyi tanets: Dialogi* (Moscow, 2005), pp. 6–17.

66 Yushkova, *Plastika preodoleniya*, p. 249.

> helped him to discover new means of physical expression, and to develop an original method for their enhancement.[67]

His students continued his work after Abramov's death.

The most interesting example of the new dance movement is the work of Yevgeny Panfilov, a talented dancer-experimenter from Perm; to this day, the theatre named after him is one of the leading non-classical dance theatres. He produced many impressive and sometimes shocking performances, which his theatre has kept in its repertoire since Panfilov's early death in 2002. In 1992, he staged *Eight Folk Songs* to the music of the contemporary Perm composer Igor Mashukov. The plasticity of the dancers was sharp like the music, which was based on folk music but peppered with irony and arranged in a modern way. They aspired to convey simple, almost primitive life, naïve eroticism, and to free the folk dance from its Soviet à la Russe clichés. Challenging the polished pseudo-folk joyful acrobatic and balletic dance of Igor Moiseev, this plastique was unpolished, sometimes ugly, raw and non-acrobatic. Leg inversions differed from standard ballet practice; movements were not refined as in Western modern dance or the Judson Church experiments. It was the essence of people's life, stylized but not glamorous at all.

Panfilov's works were not limited to the folk theme. His project 'The Ballet of the Fat' attracted public attention. Parody and irony penetrated the traditional territory of absolute beauty and technical perfection. He mocked the holy of holies of the Soviet art – classical ballet – and did it with great talent and wit. Of course, his target was the formalism of the ballet, presented in numerous repetitive patterns. His very fat women were quite artful and did the usual balletic work almost professionally. They danced with slim young men in lace corsets to music from the ballet *The Corsair* and popular songs. In humiliating Soviet ballet, Panfilov was striving for freedom of expression. Not only did he protest against the strict canons,

67 Natalia Kuryumova, 'Russian Contemporary Dance', in *European Dance since 1989: Communitas and the Other*, ed. Joanna Szymajda (Abingdon: Routledge, 2014), pp. 147–161; p. 157.

but he also mocked mass culture, without ever crossing the line between good and bad taste.

In Moscow, Alla Sigalova's work focused on the intense emotions of outstanding personalities – Salome, Callas, Othello and the Russian peasant rebel Emelyan Pugachev – whose stormy lives were retold through the medium of Expressionist dance. For his Moscow Kinetic Theatre, Aleksandr Pepelyaev turned to non-choreographic literature, for example, the prose of Kafka, Cortázar, Borges and Russian absurdist writers. Pepelyaev's productions impressed critics with their strict graphic lines and a certain inner intensity. His theatre 'was born from a desire to unite the free treatment of space/gravitation in new dance with Russian psychological dramaturgy'.[68] In 2016, having worked in different countries during the past two decades, the choreographer received the Golden Mask Award for his ballet 'Café Idiot' based on Dostoevsky's novel. Tatiana Baganova from Ekaterinburg has used the palette of convulsive, irrational and spontaneous movements to capture the human being's sense of estrangement from his/her body and the absence of identity. Her *Svadebka* to the music of Igor Stravinsky has become a legend of Russian contemporary dance. In 2013, she was invited to the Bolshoi Theatre to stage *The Rite of Spring*.

All these and other notable choreographers have changed attitudes toward the human body as well as the goals of dance and the lexicon of the dancer. Their aim is to express unconscious impulses, the absence of harmony in the human soul, the sense of disconnection between man and the world, disharmonic rhythm, irony and skepticism.

> Pluralism and openness, a lack of universal canons for 'what' and 'how'; the modernist orientation toward constant novelty and relevance; the negation of all myths and ideologies; and finally, a focus on crossing and blurring boundaries of all kinds are the basic components of contemporary dance.[69]

Such features make it a significant tool for speaking about the human soul in the twenty-first century.

68 Ibid.
69 Ibid., p. 148.

By the mid-2000s, contemporary dance had become a full-fledged member of the Russian dance world. Some performances have been awarded the Golden Mask Award – the most prestigious Russian theatre award. Nevertheless, contemporary dance has not become a mainstream dance trend in Russia, and the circle of people interested in it is quite small. Moreover, despite its clear advances in the past few years, it is still in search of its identity. There are special venues in several big cities for people who work in this sphere and many specialized dance festivals. Several years ago, the Vaganova Ballet School in St. Petersburg opened a department of contemporary dance.

In 2012, two young practitioners, Aleksandra Portyannikova and Daria Plokhova, the first graduates of this department, created the dance co-operative *Aisedorino Gore* (Isadora's Grief)[70] focusing on dance performances and research of contemporary dance. In their recently published book *Soviet Gesture*, they formulated differences between classical ballet and contemporary dance. They found out that the differences are not just aesthetic but also political:

> Classical dance has been and still is an unquestionable bond for authoritarian regimes due to its practiced and transmitted set of values: strict ideological structure, cruel competition, weak horizontal connections, and solidarity. Contemporary dance developed in countries which chose a democratic way, and its practices are in tune with such human values as freedom of personality and self-expression, principles of non-violence, tolerance, and somatic-civic mindfulness.[71]

Using their logic, we could assume that the popularity of both dance genres in Russia might reveal the hybridity of the political regime with the prevalence of authoritarianism. However, the public still prefers classical ballet, although even this genre, for all its traditionalism, has undergone some notable changes.

70 See Tantseval'ny kooperativ Aisedorino Gore, <https://www.isadorino-gore.com/aboutru> (Accessed 29 November 2021).

71 Tantseval'ny kooperativ Aisedorino Gore, *Rukovodstvo po primeneniyu tantseval'nogo arkhiva*, p. 27.

Thus, all dance traditions of the twentieth century have been successfully restored in the twenty-first century, and so have their audiences. Russian dance has successfully integrated into the world context, raising new stars on par with some of the most celebrated dancers in the world.

Conclusions

During the twentieth century, traditions in Russian dance were to be broken several times. However, it turned out that the creative potential of dancers was difficult to suppress. A solid kernel continued and still continues to drive Russian dance forward today, despite constant attempts by the state to interrupt traditions or innovations or to subordinate art to ideology. People have always held on to all kinds of techniques and transmitted them to their students and followers even during the most difficult times. In this way, interrupted traditions were always revived when the 'climate' changed and conditions became more favorable. Certainly, these ruptures influenced Russian dance, diluting it to a certain extent. But openness, plasticity and constant aspiration to the excellence of the dancers and choreographers facilitated both the speedy restoration of traditions and their further development.

Christina Ezrahi in her book *Swans of the Kremlin* argues that

> Russia's prerevolutionary ballet tradition was saved not because of a faithful preservation of old ballet productions but because ballet was remembered in bodies and souls, and this physical and spiritual memory was reverentially passed on from one generation to the next.[72]

The same is applicable for the free dance that, being taught in schools, kindergartens and houses of culture, was saved although only as an amateur art. It played an important role in the development of the contemporary

72 Ezrahi, *Swans of the Kremlin*, p. 238.

dance that appeared during perestroika and was associated with freedom of self-expression and active interaction with the West.

Thus, dance history in Russia in the twentieth century is a great example of cultural continuity that, despite all attempts of the state to break traditions in favor of ideology or state interests or to establish new aesthetic norms and canons, has never been really interrupted. Like a phoenix, it has always risen from the ashes and continues to develop.

Bibliography

Belcanto.ru, 'Shostakovich: Balet Bolt', <http://www.belcanto.ru/ballet_bolt.html> (Accessed 29 November 2021).

Belyaeva, Ekaterina, 'Premiera baleta Lakotta *Marko Spada* v Bol'shom teatre', 2013, <https://www.belcanto.ru/13111802.html> (Accessed 29 November 2021).

Berdyaev, Nikolai, *The Russian Idea*, trans. R. M. French (Hudson, NY: Lindisfarne Press, 1992).

Bol'shoi Teatr, *Svetly Ruchei*, <https://2011.bolshoi.ru/performances/61/> (Accessed 29 November 2021).

Bowlt, John E., and Olga Matich, eds, *Laboratory of Dreams: The Russian Avant-garde and Cultural Experiments* (Palo Alto, CA: Stanford University Press, 1996).

Certeau, Michel de, *The Practice of Everyday Life* (Berkeley, CA: University of California Press, 1984).

Clark, Katerina, *Petersburg: Crucible of Cultural Revolution* (Cambridge. MA: Harvard University Press, 1996).

——— 'Stanovlenie sovetskoi kultury', in *Amerikanskaya rusistika: Vekhi istoriografii poslednih let; Sovetskii period* (Moscow: Samara, 2001), pp. 146–173.

Dancing the Cold War, ed. Lynn Garafola (New York: Columbia University Harriman Institute, 2017).

Dobrovolskaya, G., *Mikhail Fokin: Russky Period* (St. Petersburg: Giperion, 2004).

Dorson, Richard M., *American Folklore* (Chicago: University of Chicago Press, 1977).

Dowler, Gerald, 'Dancing through Terror', *Dancing Times*, June 2018, pp. 35–36.

Era Grigorovicha: k 90-letiyu vydayuschegosya khoreogra [Grigorovich's Era: Devoted to the Prominent Russian Choreographer's 90th Anniversary]. A. A. Bakhrushin State Central Theatre Museum, Exhibition, 2016–2017, <http://www.gctm.ru/event/era-grigorovicha-k-90-letiyu-vyidayushhegosya-russkogo-horeografa/> (Accessed 29 November 2021).

Ezrahi, Christina, *Swans of the Kremlin: Ballet and Power in Soviet Russia* (Pittsburgh, PA: University of Pittsburgh Press, 2012).
Franko, Mark, 'Dance and the Political: States of Exception', in *Dance Discourses: Keywords in Dance Research*, ed. Susanne Franko and Marina Nordera (London: Routledge, 2007), pp. 11–28.
—— *Dancing Modernism/Performing Politics* (Bloomington: Indiana University Press, 1995).
Gaevsky, V., *Divertisment* (Moscow: Iskusstvo, 1981).
—— and P. Gershenzon, *Besedy o russkom balete. Kommentarii k noveishei istorii* (Moscow: Novoe izdatel'stvo, 2010).
Galayda, A., 'Yury Grigorovich, a Living Symbol of the Bolshoi', *Russia Beyond the Headlines*, 30 December 2016.
Garafola, Lynn, *Diaghilev's Ballets Russes* (Boston, MA: Da Capo Press, 1998).
Hobsbawm, Eric, and Terence Ranger, eds, *The Invention of Tradition* (Cambridge: Cambridge University Press, 1983).
Kolb, Alexandra, *Dance and Politics* (Bern: Peter Lang, 2011).
Kowal, Rebekah, and Gerald Siegmund, *The Oxford Handbook of Dance and Politics* (Oxford: Oxford University Press, 2017).
Kuryumova, Natalia, 'Russian Contemporary Dance', in *European Dance since 1989: Communitas and the Other*, ed. Joanna Szymajda (Abingdon: Routledge, 2014), pp. 147–161.
Lvov-Anokhin, B., *Mastera Bolshogo baleta* (Moscow: Iskusstvo, 1976).
Lepecki, Andre, *Exhausting Dance: Performance and the Politics of Movement* (New York: Routledge, 2006).
Levinson, A., 'Anna Pavlova i legenda Lebedya' in Dandre, V. (ed.), *Anna Pavlova; zhizn' i legenda* (St. Petersburg: Vita Nova, 2003).
McDaniel, Cadra Peterson, *American-Soviet Cultural Diplomacy: The Bolshoi Ballet's American Premiere* (Lanham, MD: Lexington Books, 2015).
McVay, G., 'Moskovskaya schkola Aisedory Duncan (1921–1949)', in *Pamyatniki kultury: Novye otkrytiya; Pis'mennost; Iskusstvo; Arkheologiya; Ezhegodnik*, ed. T. B. Knyazevskaya and V. I. Vasil'ev (Moscow: Nauka, 2003), pp. 326–475.
Mills, Dana, *Dance and Politics: Moving beyond Boundaries* (Manchester: Manchester University Press, 2017).
Misler, Nicoletta, *Vnachale bylo telo. Ritmoplasticheskie eksperimenty nachala 20 veka: Khoreologicheskaya laboratoriya GAKhN* (Moscow: Iskusstvo-XXI vek, 2011).
Mjør, Kåre Johan, 'Smuta: Cyclical Visions of History in Contemporary Russian Thought and the Question of Hegemony', *Studies in East European Thought*, Vol. 70 (2018), pp. 19–40.

Morrison, S., 'The Bolshoi and the Revolution', in *Russian Movement Culture in the 1920s and 1930s*, ed. Lynn Garafola (New York: Columbia University Harriman Institute, 2015), pp. 4–14.

Pantin, Vladimir, and V. Lapkin, eds, *Cycles of Political Development: Prognostic Potential* (Moscow: IMEMO Russian Academy of Sciences, 2010).

Paperny, Vladimir, *Kultura Dva* (Moscow: Novoe Literaturnie Obozrenie, 2016).

Pleshcheev, A., *Nash balet* [Our Ballet] (St. Petersburg: Tipografiia A. Benke, 1886).

Prevots, Naima, *Dance for Export: Cultural Diplomacy and the Cold War* (Middletown, CT: Wesleyan University Press, 1998).

Roslavleva, Natalya, 'Prechistenka 20: The Isadora Duncan School in Moscow', *Dance Perspectives* 64, Vol. 16 (1975).

Rumnev (Zyakin), A. A., 'Gody v Kametnom teatre' (Years in the Kametny Theatre), 1960, RGALI, Fond 2721, Opis (Inventory) 1, Edinitsa Khraneniya (Item) 35.

Scheijen, S., *'Russkie sezony' navsegda* ('Russian Seasons' Forever) (Moscow: KoLibri: Azbuka-Attikus, 2013).

Scholl, Tim, *From Petipa to Balanchine: Classical Revival and Modernization of Ballet* (London: Routledge, 2005 [1994]).

Searcy, Anne, *Ballet in the Cold War: A Soviet-American Exchange* (Oxford: Oxford University Press, 2020).

Shalin, Dmitri N., 'Introduction: Continuity and Change in Russian Culture', in *Russian Culture at the Crossroads: Paradoxes of Postcommunist Consciousness*, Second edition (London: Routledge, 2018).

Sheremetevskaya, N., *Tanets na estrade* (Moscow: Iskusstvo, 1985).

Solzhenitsyn, Aleksandr, *Publitsistika. Statii i rechi* (Paris: YMCA Press, 1981).

Sorokin, Pitirim, *Social and Cultural Dynamics* (Cincinnati: American Book Company, 1937–1941).

Souritz, Elizabeth, 'Balet', in *Bol'shaia Sovetskaia Encyclopedia* (3 Edition, Moscow: Sovetskaia Entsiklopedia, 1970). Vol. 2, pp. 570–572.

——— *Khoreograficheskoe iskusstvo 20-kh godov* (Moscow: Iskusstvo, 1979).

——— 'Moscow's Island of Dance, 1934–1941', *Dance Chronicle*, Vol. 17, No. 1 (1994), pp. 1–92.

——— 'Isadora Duncan's Influence on Dance in Russia', *Dance Chronicle*, Vol. 18, No. 2 (1995), pp. 281–291.

——— 'Isadora Duncan and Prewar Russian Dancemakers', in *The Ballets Russes and Its World* (New Haven, CT: Yale University Press, 1999), pp. 101–104.

——— 'Moskovskie studii plasticheskogo tantsa', in *Avangard i teatr 1910-1920-kh godov* (Moscow: Nauka, 2008), pp. 384–430.

Stites, Richard, *Revolutionary Dreams: Utopian Vision and Experimental Life in the Russian Revolution* (New York: Oxford University Press, 1991).

Stüdemann, Natalya, *Dionisos in Sparta: Isadora Duncan in Russland, Eine Geschichte von Tanz und Korper* (Bielefeld: Transcript Verlag, 2008).

Tantseval'ny kooperativ Aisedorino Gore, https://www.isadorino-gore.com/aboutru (Accessed 27 April 2023)

—— *Rukovodstvo po primeneniyu tantseval'nogo arkhiva: Opyty choreologii, ili Kuda nas zavel 'Sovetskii zhest'* (Moscow: Muzei sovremennogo iskusstva Garage, 2020).

Teider V., *Russky balet na perelome epoch* (Moscow, 2014).

Timasheff, Nicolas S., *The Great Retreat: The Growth and Decline of Communism in Russia* (New York: Dutton, 1946).

Uralskaya V., Interview in *Dancehelp*, 22 January 2021, <https://vk.com/video-9068269_456247016?list=408bb5b7222f61442d> (Accessed 29 November 2021).

Vasenina, E., *Sovremennyi tanets: Dialogi* (Moscow: Zapasnyi Vykhod/Emergency Exit, 2005).

Yurchak, Alexei, *Everything Was Forever Until It Was No More: The Last Soviet Generation* (Princeton, NJ: Princeton University Press, 2006).

Yushkova, Elena, *Plastika preodoleniya: kratkie zametki ob istorii plasticheskogo teatra v Rossii v 20 veke* [Plastique of Overcoming: Notes on the History of Russian Plastique Theatre in Russia in the 20th Century] (Yaroslavl: YaGPU, 2009).

Zhidkov, V., *Teatr i vremya: ot Oktyabrya do perestroika* (Moscow: STD, 1991).

Further reading

Gaevsky V., *Khoreograficheskie portrety* (Moscow: Artist. Rezhisser. Teatr, 2008).

Krasovskaya, V., *Istoriya russkogo baleta* (St. Petersburg: Krasnodar: Lan' – Planeta muzyki, 2008).

Rzhevsky, Nicolas, 'Introduction', in *The Cambridge Companion to Modern Russian Culture*, ed. Nicolas Rzhevsky, Second edition (Cambridge: Cambridge University Press, 2012).

Yushkova Elena, 'Vliyanie kulturnoi politiki SSSR na shkolu Aisedory Duncan v 20-e gody', in *Vremya, vpered! Kulturnaya politika v SSSR*, ed. I. Gluschenko, V. Kurennoi (Moscow: Izdatelskyi Dom HSE, 2013), pp. 178–196.

Yushkova, Elena, 'Byt i bytie moscoskoi scholy Aisedory Duncan' [Everyday Life and Existence of Isadora Duncan's Moscow School], in *Poetik des Alltags. Russische Literatur vom 18 bis 21 Jahrhundert* (München: Herbert Utz Verlag, 2014), pp. 223–233.

Yushkova, Elena, '"Index tsitirovania" Aleksandra Rumneva: shtrikhi k portretu actera i issledovatelya', *Toronto Slavic Quarterly*, Vol. 49 (Summer 2014), <http://sites.utoronto.ca/tsq/49/index.shtml> (Accessed 29 November 2021).

Zhbankova, E., 'Iskusstvo dvizheniya' v russkoi culture kontsa 19 veka-1920-kh godov: ot esteticheskoi idei k ideologicheskoi ustanovke', Dissertation, Doctorate in Historical Sciences, Moscow: Moscow State University, 2004.

LYUDMIL DIMITROV

15 Russian Drama of the Twentieth Century as an Imported Commodity: The Transgression of Transfer

Introduction

The modern concept of the nation as a political and cultural subject, limited by the nation state, has existed *for 200 years*, and its beginning and its end are marked – literally and symbolically – by the ruin of two indicative power strongholds: the Bastille in 1789 and the Berlin Wall in 1989. In this context, theatre has survived as one of the inevitable centers of the national, and it is precisely the study of its inner procedures and condition that may answer the question 'in this unpredictable world, are the strategies of emancipating and protecting the peoples who turned out to be on the east side of Iron Curtain, effective or not?' I should clarify that in this case I allow myself to think of the Iron Curtain primarily as a theatrical metaphor: the fact that with the fall and 'rise' of this curtain in the collapse of totalitarianism, the beginning was not only our unencumbered mutual recognition, but it was also the beginning of a fruitful transgression and exchange of cultural practices along the West–East axis. That is, an active postmodern performance has begun.

The purpose of the nation is to create and reproduce a common cultural identity for all citizens of the country for the benefit of their political interests, and the drama – according to Hegel's definition – is 'a product of the already developed *national life* within itself'.[1] I quote Hegel because he is among the first classical philosophers who justified drama as

1 G. W. F. Hegel, *Sochineniya* (Moscow, 1940), Vol. 13, p. 331.

a constructive element of the nation, ensuring its fulfillment. After 1989, all the nations of Europe – ancient, medieval, new, young and even newborns – found themselves in relatively similar conditions, on the threshold (in the foreground) of a new period. In the sociopolitical sense, it is characterized by problematization and reinterpretation of factors of joint identification (about new *imagined communities*, to quote the title of Benedict Anderson's book), and in the sociocultural and narrowly theatrical sense, by *the end of the drama*. In the past three decades, theatre has become post-dramaturgical and increasingly less verbal, encouraging *the society of the spectacle* (according to Guy Debord's thesis) – a phenomenon that has led to a crisis of both personal and group identity (or simply revealed it), since the drama presumes its *imagined* perceiver until the auditorium of the theatre *materializes* it.

Whatever the changes in contemporary performance and drama, however, one thing remains constant, and it is rooted in the very essence of theatre: its reflection of the present, the search for an answer to the question of who we are and where we are going, all in the context of anxiety about identity and the preservation of the 'I'. There is, of course, a theatre of identification – a theatre that 'informs': newly written plays are staged, receiving much acclaim and awards, gradually seeking and often aggressively making their way into the national repertoire. But there is another kind of theatre, which I am talking about, and which, in fact, turns out to be significant for a particular time. It is not measured by a repertoire but by a canon, and it aims to interpret the current context and to reason in some abstract, synthesized form on the problems and prospects facing society. In favor of such an intention, plays of national drama more often are drawn upon, but any original, bold and appropriate director's concept can also be defended through a foreign text, classical or modern, if only its ideological potential is rediscovered in unexpected and specific circumstances suggested by actuality. Examples are given below. The more important question is as follows: why today, despite the ideological separation from Russia to the point of hysterical contempt, Eastern European societies do not interrupt the integration of its cultural trend in the process of their own existential remodeling.

In fact, the question is more global and has its own historical basis. More specifically, it interests me in the following perspective: how does nineteenth-century Russian drama, representing the European East, already emancipated and meriting serious world authority in the twentieth century, undertake a 'natural' strategic 'campaign' in the West with its cohort of classic authors and texts, and what happens when it comes into contact with the cultures that admit it/perceive it? How do they react? What determines the fact that, starting from Russia and penetrating to the West, the list of canonical names of playwrights – including at least eight names – is getting smaller and smaller, so that in the United States, in Canada and in most Western European cultures there is only one name left – Chekhov? Literary communication integrates at least two more authors – Dostoevsky and Tolstoy – but the theatre is limited only to Chekhov. Why? What is the most promising direction to look for an answer? And is it possible to use the Bulgarian reception of the Russian canon (located more to the west of Russia and more to the east of England) as an intermediate reference point? Throughout its conscious path from the mid-nineteenth century to the present, Bulgarian cultural memory has been formed in its fluctuating status, enriched (+) by Russian cultural influence, but also dependent (–) on it. But in two cases we also encounter a phenomenon that we can define either as *the 'import' of culture* (a voluntary act that separates the process of transgression) or as another *explosion*. In the latter case, the Russian drama, having fallen into someone else's assimilating field, is suspected of being assimilative and, interacting with it, has to initially enter the battle to defend not only its own presence, but also its identity. More precisely, is it a missionary (cultivating) role among other Slavs and Eastern Europeans, and is the environment in which it operates predictable? And is it possible in this respect to say that Chekhov smooths out this clash, and how do his plays sound outside the cultural and linguistic context that gave rise to them?

In my opinion, the choice of Chekhov is a risky business in several ways. If, relying on this author, the Russianness seeks its authenticity in a foreign environment, relying on a trustworthy, time-tested and space-tested 'means', it happens because the playwright has long overcome national borders and turned into a cosmopolitan, preserving *the Russian distinctiveness* mainly as a linguistic and attributive flavor: in the names of characters, in toponyms, realities, objects and the like. The appearance of Chekhov's plays on the non-Russian stage inevitably problematizes the process of exporting–importing–transporting text from one language to another, from one century to another, from one geostrategic space to another. And just as inevitably, in a changing cultural climate, stereotypes in a receiving cultural space are more likely to resist and seek ways to override it than to 'distance' themselves and work for it. I can state quite responsibly that the same texts by Chekhov *tell very different stories to Bulgarians, Croats, Slovenes, Hungarians, Poles and Romanians compared to those that Russians are inclined to read*. Finally, the stage is a two-dimensional transcultural mediator in the assimilation ('domestication') of Chekhov by foreign perceivers and vice versa, but this process is far from universal. It cannot be said, for example, that the same thing happens with A. N. Ostrovsky, regardless of the diligent and even biased propaganda of him as 'the most Russian playwright' on the part of the culture that gave birth to him. As for Pushkin – l'enfant terrible of the nineteenth-century theatre – he demonstrates a special, unprecedented type of dramatic thinking that remains undeveloped by stage practice. 'Boris Godunov', for example, is rarely engaged in both drama and post-drama theatre. But 'Godunov''s popularization became possible through Mussorgsky's opera, a different kind of stage art that translates drama into a different, parallel but also alternative performative language.

I am deliberately referring to playwrights, not literary critics or directors, since the latter, if they are carriers of the same cultural context as the playwright, tend to act selectively outside their environment, and their interpretations are often problematic in the assimilation of a non-Russian context. Yet, there are, of course, constant exceptions, and here I am not talking about a professional but an average viewer. But even such a figure as Eimuntas Nekrošius, according to Marina Davydova, 'is still accepted with éclat in Italy, whereas for Germany is not such an important figure'.[2] Meanwhile, it was in Germany that several Bulgarian directors unknown in Russia in the past three decades have attempted *to export* their

2 'Teatr vne polia zreniia: Maiia Pramatarova beseduet s Marinoi Davydovoi', <Post.Scriptum.ru>, 14 March 2015 (Accessed 3 April 2016).

theatrical mentality through Chekhov, and they have definitely gained admiration, successfully entering the Western cultural exchange/market of ideas. We are talking about the directors Dimitar Gochev, Ivan Stanev, Stefan Moskov and Ivan Panteleev. In addition, Margarita Mladenova and Ivan Dobchev, the creators of one of the most popular innovative theatres in Sofia – *Sfumato* – have done the same in France, where, besides them, Chekhov has been staged by Vladimir Petkov. For all of these, the author of *The Cherry Orchard* is not just a way to express themselves, but also to express in European language what concerns them as Bulgarians. I mention my compatriots, but the corresponding examples can be given with the directors of many other Eastern European countries. In this regard, I believe that what facilitates the smooth crossing of borders and functions as a kind of 'visa', legitimizing a certain spiritual causa, is a global approach to Chekhov. But to find it, the material itself must 'cede' dramatic primacy and facilitate such an adjustment. Chekhov has a unique inner abstraction, which allows for many more maneuvers, moves, directions and landmarks than other canonical Russian playwrights may have. This is in practical terms his 'internationality'.

Here I would like to emphasize once again my position with regard to the literary text: *Russia has an eternal convertible product*, much more durable and inexhaustible than oil and gas, *and this is its classical literature*; just as England constantly 'charges' the world with Shakespeare to the extent that it is no longer clear whose it is, and we often see fakes – on the stage, on the screen and in translations. But you might as well ask a similar question: who does Chekhov belong to, in fact? And in general, to what extent is this dramatic canon (even if it is Russian) 'transferable' and significant in a different, non-specific sociocultural space – whether it is Eastern or Western European? How does the current cultural situation react to it?

In an independent study of the hermeneutics of the Russian drama canon of the nineteenth century, ten years ago, I expressed the thesis that nineteenth-century Russian drama interprets a stable coordinate plot, constructed by A. S. Griboedov in his famous comedy *Woe from Wit*. It is read at the intersection of two axes: the horizontal being love, represented by Sofia, and the vertical represented by the hero, who has come from outside (Chatsky) and intervenes in the whole organism of a closed and self-sufficient society. This perspective contains the makings of the mind (intellect) and unfolds hierarchically: the supremacy of the mind over the 'overflowing' of the feelings. This plot is particularly recognized in Russian drama as *overwhelmingly Russian*. The intersection of the two axes produces *an explosion* thus forming the central conflict. The author outlines a single coordinate plot of the Russian drama, in which ideologies and cultural paradigms compete with each other to a much greater extent than individuals. Drama in Russia begins with an emphasis on the personal, to come to a kind of (empty in its essence) collegiality.

And the difficult adaptation of a character who comes from the outside is identical to attempts to introduce a new work into the canon itself. Therefore, perhaps, the Russian dramatic canon, once in a different environment, necessarily turns into a translated one. By 'translated' canon, I understand not only the linguistic re-pronunciation of the text, but also the ideas – their inevitable receptive adaptation. When watching a Russian play, a foreigner perceives it through his own self and, in addition, imposes on it a context that is different from that of the play. But he always remembers that the 'mother tongue' ('native tongue') of the plot is Russian. This is to a large extent the problem of boundaries in the theatre. And they are obviously not linguistic. Linguistic communication is just one of the many forms of theatrical language, which has recently become increasingly conventional and relegated to the background, deliberately marginalized. But this is possible in post-drama theatre. In a representation based on a dramatic text, the classical type of communication continues to function and is semantically loaded. I consider this question fundamental, as I look at the language in a broader aspect: as the main factor of the nation's existence. And the theatre is considered an immanently conservative (and in a certain sense educational) institution that is designed to preserve and develop the language in a high-level representative status.

But the canon is 'borderline' in another sense: it has a strictly defined and protected area, only allowing invasion with difficulty. As for the transgression of the Russian canon into a foreign one (e.g., into the Bulgarian one), it is carried out on the quota principle: we strive to recognize ourselves in the Other – something similar to kinship by choice. By referring to this play, we are essentially activating our identification with the culture to which it originally belongs, and we support this idea throughout the entire process of its perception since theatre is the art of psycho-optic suggestion. To paraphrase the thought of the art critic A. Natev, the cinema/screen supports the viewer's illusion that he sees only what makes sense to show him, while the theatre does just the opposite: it manipulates us, and we believe that we are witnessing something that should not be seen. More precisely, it simulatively allows the viewer to get to some 'mystery' and makes him an accomplice in its 'unraveling'.[3]

After this detailed introduction, I will demonstrate how certain aspects of what has been said operate in three performances of Chekhov's plays in different periods of the postmodern situation: Bulgarian, Hungarian and Croatian.

Three Sisters (Directed by Stoyan Kambarev, Sofia Theatre, 12 October 1998)

Three Sisters is among the few phenomena in the Bulgarian theatre whose appearance theatrical critics failed to respond to adequately and in a timely manner. Not only because it turned out to be the last play of Stoyan Kambarev, who died at the age of 44, just 20 days before the premiere. They began to write about the show problematically, analytically and consciously only some two or three years later – a period when it traveled around most of the world's emblematic festivals and received many awards. A whole decade after the end of totalitarianism in Bulgaria, the director's concept stunned the public with its insights that not only summarized what had already been experienced, and not only captured the acutely felt fatigue in society but also conjured up something far more sobering – a rejection of the future, a vacuum of expectation that hope alone was not enough to fill and make it valuable. The action takes place in a cramped, semi-dark, warped space, littered with benches and

3 Atanas Natev, *Dramatichno i dramaturgichno* (Sofia, 1967), p. 121.

railings that delineate corridors, and boundaries as well: a transient cover, much like a waiting room. In such an allegedly inconstant environment the director did not only tell the story of some hopeless cohabitation, or rather, enchanted circling, where any manifestation of refinement, spirituality and knowledge is unnecessary luxury, but also added the biography of three sisters, about whom in reality we know nothing. Or, to be precise, we know details that hide their inner world rather than reveal it. According to Tatiana Shah-Azizova,

> you are surprised by the strength of the Bulgarian performance; its persistence and preservation. Apparently, in addition to timely appearance and a bright national colouring, something deeply personal was embedded in it – without this there is no modern Chekhov. And if you look deeper, you can distinguish something else: a certain root basis inherent in the Chekhov Theatre in general and in this play in particular. The form of the performance, precise and conventional, creates a sense of the endless bustle of life, which nothing can stop. Mobile life, life in great haste, life with no mundanity [...] People here are not free, they are tightly entwined, move chaotically and incessantly – it is a kind of whirligig, aimless, Brownian motion. But these people are completely alive; there is no shadow of aloofness between them, nor between the audience and the actors.[4]

The only non-living (not in corporeal form) but 'resurrected' spirit was the spirit of the director. At the end of the performance, when all the actors come out one by one along the narrow corridor, literally passing in a string, there is a strongly rotating turnstile at the back of the stage, behind whose glass doors streams a dazzling light against the background of increasingly amplified music. Eternal waiting, the Holy Spirit coming from the promised land, from which no traveler returns.

4 Tatyana K. Shah-Azizova, 'Teatr Chekhova: istoriia; geografiia; lichnotsti (Zametki)', in *Dialogi s Chekhov: 100 godini po-kesno* (Sofia, 2004), p. 25.

Ivanov (Directed by Tamás Ascher, Katona József Theatre, Budapest 2004)

In the production of *Ivanov* by the Hungarian director Tamás Ascher, the action takes place in the 1960s, the most ferocious (after the events of 1956) time of totalitarianism in Hungary – the beginning of the Kadar era: it is bad taste and ironic, metaphorical and, if you like, metonymic counterpoint of the Russian aristocracy in shambles. Also, it is located in a space paradoxically reminiscent of *Three Sisters*: a filthy, disgusting depressing interior that resembles a staff canteen, a warehouse, a waiting room next to the doctor's office and the snack bar of a sanatorium with chaotically piled chairs at one end (somewhere in the critical writings there even appears an association with a cave); there are doors on the walls gaping into other representative spaces that we are never allowed in. And if the effect of the situation is not grotesque, then it can easily be perceived as ominously (neo)gothic. The parallel is clear: the festering environment of a nest of aristocrats, slowly drowning in the swamp of equalization – the Soviet shadow over the Eastern Bloc, the stagnation era. When at such a moment – the period of planned socialist economy – elderly 'bourgeois' ladies start talking about currency rates, stocks, bonds, mortgages and banking transactions, they really begin to look like crazy people, settled in a nursing home for those with irreparably sclerotic memories. By changing context, but preserving Chekhov's dialogue, Ascher achieves a wonderfully powerful and incredibly funny scene that reveals the tragedy of language, but this time a word-by-word language atrophied into logorrhea, which is anachronistic in relation to place and time. This is unlike other plays by Chekhov – *The Seagull*, where there are no actions; *Three Sisters*, where a duel and deployment of the military is being prepared; *The Cherry Orchard*, where bargaining and cutting down of cherry trees are expected, an event (wedding) is expected in *Ivanov*. When the hero tells Sasha that he is dying, she defiantly takes out a cigarette and starts randomly flicking the ashes everywhere – what is to come has already happened, cinders and ashes are a hint of dying, of demise. And no rejoicing is possible. Committing suicide at the finale, the well-built Ivanov (actor Erne Fekete) falls and breaks open one of these doors with his body, and a strong light suddenly spills out. With his head, like his mind and with his consciousness, he is already 'there', and the torso (body) stays here. Almost the same metaphor as in Sofia's *Three Sisters*: an open path through a tunnel into the unearthly at a time of personal and bodily destruction.

Three Sisters (Directed by Ivica Kunčević, the Croatian National Theatre, Zagreb, 10 March 2006)

In Ivica Kunčević's *Three Sisters*, the first thing that makes an impression but patiently awaits its interpretation (a defense by its director) in the course of the performance can be hastily but mistakenly classified as 'undeveloped stage space'. The huge stage seamlessly 'absorbs' a small amount of furniture and scanty props, hinting more at the interior of the house than revealing it. The sisters, who seem to be waiting for guests for Irina's nameday, sink into a soft, colorless sofa until they are invisible, and this feeling of 'loss' in space cannot be compensated for either by a standard-sized piano or by a huge table set for a much larger number of people than sit down at it (an echo of the time when 30–40 people came to the house). Irina is in white, Masha is in black, and Olga is in 'conciliatory' grey. This greyness strangely 'separates' the three sisters from the audience and imposes a kind of 'filter' on them, through which they begin to resemble the heroines of a black-and-white film. This keeps the viewer feeling that something has happened a long time ago, which is almost irrelevant; it is a story with a famous ending, recorded once and for all on film. And what is especially important: however audacious such an approach to this play may sound, it is the depersonalization (repression, even in the psychoanalytic sense) of the sisters which is the effect sought and defended by the director.

This is not a play about three sisters who dream of going to Moscow, but never get there. This performance is emphatically masculine – even in quantitative terms, there is a preponderance of male characters over female ones. This can be seen in the unifying costumes: all the characters are dressed in military style and as if they are always waiting to be mobilized. Against this background, stylized elements of the invariable paramilitary style are gradually beginning to appear in the sisters' clothing: double-breasted blouses and jackets, familiar to us from officer jackets and overcoats. The female world is losing its identity and is increasingly being contaminated by the male world. *Three Sisters* is the play with the strongest presence of 'military' themes in Chekhov. Kunčević tells the drama and trauma of a modern-day Croat who recently survived perhaps the most ridiculous and insane war in history. On a purely human level, society has diverged from all that is natural, logical and desirable, and has lost it all in the name of some chimerical ideas, goals and promises. And why exactly the battery is transferred, what causes its dislocation – this not-fully-clarified motivation in the text of the drama generates a complete virtual-associative complex of meanings, accurately, intelligently and multilaterally implicated in the performance. Some, of course, are emphasized, while in others, the director is delicately opposed to Chekhov. He seeks both agreement and controversy with the public: is it true, is it possible to explain his own fate in this way? Is Chekhov right that what happened to us was inevitable?

In the Balkans, outside forces have always dictated the 'daily routine', but each house has its own formal master: it is a matter of honor to manage one's own space. In the end, there are only huge chests on the stage, containing all the unnecessary equipment, like coffins waiting to be lifted by the order of some regular Fortinbras. In desperate convulsions, the sisters are entwined in a living chaotic tangle, rising and falling, but, alas, they cannot overcome matter and free themselves from bodies that are already completely unnecessary to them. A ridiculous human comedy in a Croatian style, in the context of which it does not matter where exactly Balzac was married.

Bibliography

Hegel, G. W. F., *Sochineniia* (Moscow: Poligrafkniga, 1940), Vol. 13.

Natev, Atanas, *Dramatichno i dramaturgichno* (Sofia: Nauka i izkustvo, 1967).

Shah-Azizova, Tatiana K., 'Teatr Chekhova: istoriia; geografiia; lichnotsti (Zametki)', in *Dialogi s Chekhov: 100 godini po-kesno* (Sofia: Fakel, 2004).

'Teatr vne polia zreniia: Maiia Pramatarova beseduet s Marinoi Davydovoi', 14 March 2015, <Post.Scriptum.ru> (Accessed 3 April 2016).

Translated by Nikita Khmarenko

MARGARITA ODESSKAYA

16 Russian Classics in the Mirror of Vasily Sigarev's Remakes

'The past fervently looks at the future'

The process of sociocultural modernization is usually connected with the total destruction of the existing system of paradigmatic constants. In such interim periods as the turn of the century, a certain reassessment of the basic values and priorities inevitably happens. This process can be explosive or gradual. Appeals to the past and its interpretation provide ways to understand and conceptualize the present. 'A finished process', as Yu. M. Lotman writes, 'is substituted by its model.'[1] This model represents a kind of initial substance, consonance of consciously transformed information about fiction, historical and cultural context, 'spirit of the age' and a certain canonized cliché of the author's image.

Why a remake?

In recent decades, since the turn of the twentieth to the twenty-first century, strategies of remaking have achieved, let us say, genre expansion in

1 Yuri M. Lotman, *Semiosphere; Culture and Explosion; Universe of the Mind: Articles, Research, Notes* (St. Petersburg, 2004), p. 25.

drama and theatre. Remake in literature is one of the ways to reevaluate the cultural inheritance of the past, to demythify – and also a way to actualize the text, to transform it and to make it fit into the contemporary realia. Remake is one of the ways of stylization, of expressing the author's attitude to someone else's text. Remake competes with parody. Remake represents the structural model of a text within a text: a new contemporary text with a clearly enunciated author's opinion on a 'predecessor's cultural complex intervenes in the old canonized text of one particular era. 'The transfer from one system of semiotic realization of the text into another', according to Lotman, gives birth to new ideas, 'accentuates the ludic quality of the text, emphasizes its ludic nature – an ironic, parodic and theatrical meaning'.[2] Stylization, ludic quality and staging are major components in remakes of nineteenth-century classics. We believe that under the conditions of rapid collapse of the 'socialist' paradigm at the end of the twentieth century, remake plays a significant role in reactualizing cultural values as well as in interpreting and reinterpreting classical examples in modern times.

This chapter will analyze the remakes of one of the leading contemporary dramatists and directors Vasily Sigarev's *The Blizzard* and *Alexei Karenin*, and their on-stage interpretation.

About Vasily Sigarev

Vasily Sigarev (born 1977) is a post-perestroika dramatist and director. His works refer to an interim period, time of ethic and aesthetic paradigm change. His play *Plasticine* made him famous, being staged in many theatres around the globe. Sigarev has received many awards as a dramatist, theatre and film director, including an Evening Standard Award in 2002 in Great Britain. Sigarev believes that his play *Plasticine*, which addresses universal and eternal human issues, had the ability of being

2 Ibid., p. 66.

adaptable to the directors' national culture. 'When a performance was staged in London, my play was specially adjusted to it. As a result it was staged as a play about Englishmen. I think that is right. Bears, *balalaika* and *valenki* are definitely not the thing. Just because it's bad taste. To stage a play about yourself – that's the right thing.'[3]

Sigarev is engaged in adaptation himself: he adjusts classics to the present day, the contemporary reader and, most of all, to the contemporary audience. He betakes himself to world renowned fiction such as *Boule de Suif* by Maupassant, *The Blizzard* by Pushkin, *The Viy* by Gogol, *Perfume: The Story of a Murderer* by Süskind and *Anna Karenina* by Tolstoy. Many of them are staged in theatres both by the author himself and by other directors. Undoubtedly, the remake is a challenge to the clichés and stereotypes that overgrow the artistic text, as well as the image of the creator of this text during its functioning in a particular social environment. The 'socialist' paradigm assumes a set of stereotypes of perception of Russian literature and writers as its representatives. The images of the 'little' and the 'superfluous' man, the 'positive hero', the themes of the struggle against social evil and injustice, the education-oriented tendency of Russian literature, its humanistic and revolutionary spirit – these are some of the cliché-ideologemes that are formed in the minds of readers and viewers of the era of socialism. In the post-perestroika period, there is a process of fetishization of these clichés, which appear as dead dogmas.

Sigarev reinterprets the classics all over again.

The Blizzard

The Blizzard was Sigarev's first remake, which he wrote as a student. In one of his interviews, he admits that the first time he visited the theatre was during the premiere of his own play *The Blizzard*: 'I had just finished

3 Anton Sazonov, 'Vasily Sigarev: "Ne ochen" udobnaia dlia prodiucerov istoriia. Mogut vsekh peresazhat' [Not a Good Story for Producers. Everybody Can Be Arrested], *Snob*, 28 August 2012, <https://snob.ru/selected/entry/52144>

my first year of theatre. And when I came to Kolyada, I had read only one play, *The Cherry Orchard*. Perhaps, right now, the theatre needs such virginity and innocence more than ever. It needs to be cleared of clichés, of platitudes, of the garbage that has cluttered it.'[4]

We should not forget that Pushkin's work 'The Blizzard' is very parodic and ludic. In it, Pushkin travesties both the literary cliches of the 1830s, and the life situation that imitates literature. The plot of 'The Blizzard' – a story with a romantic kidnapping of the bride, allusions to the French novel, a secret wedding, ominous prophetic dreams, the image of a young provincial lady with 'sad meditations in her look, and, in her hand, a small French book' – was created on the basis of a real story known in Pushkin's times, in which the characters who have read romantic works execute a secret wedding. The escape of Countess Stroganova with poor Count Fersen was 'the biggest social scandal of 1829'. 'The story of secret meetings and correspondence, as well as many real details, Pushkin used in the story "The Young Peasant Woman", the second story told to the author by the young woman K. I. T.'[5]

Vasily Sigarev, without deviating from the plot basis of Pushkin's 'The Blizzard', creates a play in which he presents a certain concentrate of impressions from Russian literature of the nineteenth century. The author follows the text of Pushkin's work, but includes additional scenes and characters in his play, for example, the ball scene and the girl K. I. T., who becomes Masha's confidante and helps with her escape. K. I. T. flirts with Cornet Dravin, and together they witness Masha's secret wedding. In Sigarev's play, K. I. T. is interwoven with the parody plot of a French courtly novel. And at the same time, Masha's parents – provincial landowners – resemble either Masha Mironova's parents from *The Captain's Daughter* or Gogol's old-world landowners but their speech was flavored with a large number of colloquialisms that they resemble the Prostakovs family (the Simpletons) from Fonvizin's comedy *The Minor*.

4 *Teatralnaia Afisha*, 21 May 2003, <http://www.teatr.ru/docs/tpl/doc.asp?id=605>

5 Antonia Glasse, 'Iz chego sdelalas' "Metel'" Pushkina [What Pushkin's 'Blizzard' Was Made of], *NLO* [UFO], 1996, p. 14 [Глассе Антония, 'Из чего сделалась "Метель" Пушкина', *НЛО*, No. 14, (1996), C].

By easily switching between styles and breaking down the barriers between language constants in the play, Sigarev makes the quote from Griboedov – 'and does the mixing-up of languages still reign? High-French low-Russian conversation?' – become a kind of indicator of the behavior model of the era, reproducing the genre of comedy of errors, on which Pushkin's story is based. Thus, a blizzard is symbolic not only of the bad weather that has mixed everything and determined the fate of the characters, but also of something that cannot be defined and that messes up people's minds as well as mixes languages, styles and even eras. It is as if we ourselves are caught in a blizzard that has mixed styles, epochs, points of view and interpretations. It is no accident that Sigarev's play opens with reflections on fate:

> Oh, fate, fate, fate! Without a doubt, you are the most mysterious lady in the world. The most mysterious and the most unpredictable. You weave such ironies of your own into our humble paths that they turn into nutritious food for the ardent minds of the artists of the word. Sometimes one doesn't know if you're joking or if you're showering us with your strange whims with some special, incomprehensible intent.
>
> Or maybe you don't exist at all?
>
> No, you do exist!
>
> I know that you do. Otherwise, there would be no other explanation for your cruelty.
>
> Oh, fate, fate, fate.[6]

Allusions to modern times in Sigarev's play are also actualized by linguistic means. So, while talking about a priest who is supposed to marry Masha and her groom, Dravin says the following in modern, coarse street language:

> Even this one (nodding his head in the direction of the iconostasis) does not even marry for 'thank you' – he's wangled five rubles, a scrounger! No doubt – he'll get drunk! I recognize them, rabble, by their beards – they're all sticky with wine. He'll get drunk, if he hasn't done so already. Surely he will.[7]

6 Vasily Sigarev, *Blizzard: A Play in Two Acts; Based on the Story by A.S. Pushkin of the Same Name*, <http://vsigarev.ru/doc/metel.html>

7 Ibid.

Sigarev's *The Blizzard* on stage

Sigarev's play *The Blizzard* has been staged in many theatres in Russia. In Perm, at the theatre with the distinctive name of 'Theatre-Theatre', the play was staged by Alexei Logachev in 2013 on the small 'Hammer' stage. The performance was built on a postmodern game with the audience, with texts and with literary and school interpretations of a work of art: that is, with all those cultural layers that overgrow texts in the process of their functioning and perception by readers and audience.

On the back wall of the stage, there hangs a portrait with familiar curls and sideburns, but the sideburns are reddish and the face is not Pushkin's. But who is it? This is Vasily Sigarev – the author of the remake of 'The Blizzard'.

Sigarev's play in the 'Theatre-Theatre' is a conversation about literature and literary interpretations in which writers and characters talk about art. And so Pushkin himself appears on the stage, all in white with fiery sideburns, as does Gogol,[8] whose 'Tale of Captain Kopeikin' is woven into the postmodern text of Sigarev's play *The Blizzard*. Thus, one can find all three writers on stage – two of them are chatting casually while the third is watching.

Pushkin's text is transformed into Gogol's, and merges with it. Gogol's Petersburg and noses appear on stage, forming a united carnival action, in which both the author and his characters participate.

Conventional interpretations of the writers' works are included in the text of the 'Theatre-Theatre' performance. In the play, there is also an example of a conventional school interpretation of a literary text. A teacher appears on the stage; she does not understand modern art but tries to judge

8 Galina Rebel enters into a polemic with the interpretation of Sigarev, who considers the appearance of Gogol on the stage justified, since this interpretation is more akin to Gogol's sarcastic spirit than to the good-natured irony of Pushkin in his story. See Ребель, 'Метель'; G. Rebel, '"Blizzard": Theatrical Dreams about Pushkin and Gogol through Sigarev', *Filolog*, No. 25, <http://philolog.pspu.ru/module/magazine/do/mpub_25_522>

it according to other laws. She is genuinely perplexed and horrified by all the substitutions and 'distortions' of the original text. And Gogol, standing next to her on the stage, silently watches from his centuries-long distance.

This example of the reactualization of a classical work provides an opportunity to observe the chain of transformations of a literary text and the stages of rejuvenation of the old meaning-generating structures in the new text: first Pushkin, who plays with models of literary clichés that have become obsolete and also travesties a real-life plot that imitates literature; then there is Sigarev, who writes with a new layer based on the old Pushkin text, fetishizing the established patterns of perception of Russian literature of the nineteenth century and adapting the literary text to the linguistic and stylistic realities of today and, finally, the stage adaptation of Sigarev's play – a theatrical metatext, a commentary on the entire cultural complex of perception of the literary text and its creator.

How *Anna Karenina* was transformed into *Alexei Karenin*

Vasily Sigarev's play *Alexei Karenin*, like other plays written by the young playwright and director based on famous works of Russian and foreign literature, is intended for performing in the theatre. According to the laws of the genre, this is a truncated work compared to the novel. The playwright focuses only on the love triangle, the relationship between Anna, her husband Alexei Karenin and Anna's lover Alexei Vronsky. As the name suggests, the focus of the playwright's attention is not Anna, but her husband Karenin.

L. N. Tolstoy's *Anna Karenina*

Anna Karenina, a novel by Leo Tolstoy, centers on the tragedy of a woman caught in a whirlwind of passions, who has lost her integrity and is faced with a choice between feelings and marital duty, between love and motherhood. Leo Tolstoy showed that one crime – the sin of adultery – entails another – suicide; he made his heroine suffer, leading her into a moral impasse. The moral law, the violation of which entails retribution, is the moral center of the novel. By introducing the name of the heroine in the title and abandoning the original title 'Two Marriages' (when it would be obviously contrasting two storylines, two families), Tolstoy emphasized the dominant role of Anna, whom he judged and punished, defending the honor of female virtue and painting the devastating and destructive power of passions.

Exquisitely beautiful, seducing and humiliated, morally and physically crushed, free, defying moral dogmas and at the same time falling into the mousetrap of secular morality and hypocrisy, Anna aroused conflicting feelings among readers. The first readers of the novel were immediately divided into two 'parties': 'defenders' and 'accusers' of Anna. Even then, in the nineteenth century, over Tolstoy's moralizing, Nekrasov ironically responded to the novel with an epigram:

> Tolstoy, you have proven with patience and talent
> That a woman should not have affairs
> Either with a sub-chamberlain or with an aide-de-camp
> When she's a wife and a mother.[9]

But who exacts justice? And who is a victim?

Although it would seem that the epigraph to the novel 'To me is vengeance, and I will repay' directly speaks about the retribution received by Anna for her sins, nevertheless by selectively quoting a passage from the Epistle to the Romans, Tolstoy makes readers doubt the understanding of its final meaning in the context of the entire novel. After all, Anna's last wish before committing suicide is to punish Vronsky, to avenge her humiliation. And then it turns out that she commits another sin, taking on the right to punish, to take revenge. For the Epistle, if you read the whole of verse 19, it contains a warning against the desire for revenge: 'Beloved, never avenge yourselves, but leave it to the wrath of God, for it is written,

9 N. A. Nekrasov, *Collected Poems* (Moscow, 1946), p. 325.

"Vengeance is mine, I will repay, says the Lord."' (Romans 12:19). Thus, by quoting an incomplete epigraph, Tolstoy gives readers the freedom to interpret the meaning of the novel and the behavior of the characters.[10]

From *Anna Karenina* to *Alexei Karenin*, based on the story of some theatre and film adaptations of *Anna Karenina*

Although there are a great many cinematic and stage versions of *Anna Karenina* in Russia and abroad, according to some critics and even directors, Tolstoy's works do not lend themselves to being adapted to the screen. This is the opinion of Lev Annensky, for example, and the director Franco Zefirelli, known for his adaptations of literary and opera classics, agrees with him. 'Cinema is too weak an art form for the genius of Tolstoy', says the famous Italian director. Nevertheless, Tolstoy's genius instigates more and more attempts to comprehend and interpret his works.[11] Most

10 There were many attempts to unveil the mystery of the epigraph. Fet, Dostoevsky, Veresayev and others provided their own interpretations. See V. A. Zhdanov and E. Ye. Zaidenschnur, 'The Story of the Creation of the Novel *Anna Karenina*', in L. N. Tolstoy, *Anna Karenina: The Novel in 8 Volumes*, ed. V. A. Zhdanov and E. Ye. Zaidenschnur (Moscow: Nauka, 1970), pp. 817–820.

11 Here is how Tomasz Glantz, a professor at the Humboldt University, explains the appeal of *Anna Karenina* to cinema: 'I think that cinema has so often turned to *Anna Karenina* not so much because the melodrama is at the centre. This, of course, is attractive, but there are thousands of such stories. And the cinema has turned to *Anna Karenina* quite often [...] And this is really something that has almost no analogues. I do not know of another classic Russian novel that has been adapted 25–30 times in the relatively short history of cinema, if you count all the TV adaptations. Just a huge number of film adaptations! And it seems to me that the attraction is based precisely on the proximity of cinema as a certain phantasm, and the intensity of the phantasm that Tolstoy builds, focusing not on social circumstances, not even on any plausible psychology, but on the problem of an altered state of consciousness.' See 'On the Centenary of Leo Tolstoy's Death: Anna Karenina as Cultural Phenomenon and Heroine of Mass Culture', Radio Svoboda, 5 December 2010, <www.svoboda.org>.

writers and directors are attracted to the adultery in the novel *Anna Karenina*, and while it would seem that the topic should be exhausted, the interpreters keep finding new angles, open up hidden meanings, thus making the work immortal. It is impossible not to agree with the statement of Roland Barthes, which has probably become almost an axiom today, that having created his masterpiece, 'the author dies', and the work continues to live according to its own laws, independent of the creator, and the work is born anew with each new reading. And in this sense, the legend that Vladimir Nabokov tells in his lectures is indicative about how Tolstoy, shortly before his death, takes a novel from the shelf, starts reading it and gets carried away, and this turns out to be *Anna Karenina*.

L. A. Barash writes:

> The director is well aware that the consciousness of the modern viewer is completely different from what the artist expected, say, in the nineteenth century. The viewer's consciousness can be based on a completely different picture of the world, other life and aesthetic realia. For this reason, the artist's 'message' should be supplemented, expanded, and brought closer to the present.[12]

Modern interpreters of Tolstoy's work expand the scope of the canonical text, update what is implicitly contained in the text, change the emphasis, bringing to the foreground the periphery of the original work.

In Soviet times, the image of Anna as a heroic figure was formed. This is how it appeared in the production of V. I. Nemirovich-Danchenko (Moscow Art Theatre, 1937). In the performance of Alla Tarasova, Anna suffocated in an atmosphere of secular morality and hypocrisy, not wanting to sacrifice sincere feelings: she died even before she threw herself under the train. The sympathy of the audience was on the side of Anna, and her portrait – a clipping from a magazine – decorated communal apartments, dormitories and so on.

Not only in the USSR, but also abroad, the image of Anna was canonized as a woman challenging and opposing everything and everyone – the secular society with its hypocrisy, the robot-like husband, the lover who

12 L. A. Barash, 'Interpretation of the Classics in Postmodern Culture', *Pushkin Herald* (Leningrad State University), No. 3 (2016), p. 248.

turned out to be not up to par . This is the image of Anna Karenina that was played by Vivien Leigh (1948); such an image, consonant with the idea of female emancipation, was established by the middle of the twentieth century.[13]

The performer of the role of Anna in the famous film adaptation of Aleksandr Zarkhi (1967), Tatyana Samoilova, spoke in an interview about her understanding of the character of the heroine as follows: 'Anna is a liberated woman who protests against prim hypocrisy and is free in the manifestations of her honest, righteous feelings.'[14]

The image of Karenin was relegated to the background, serving as the foil for a free heroine – a victim of hypocritical morality. The actor who played Karenin had to make the audience believe that Anna could not continue to live with her husband. This is how the actor Nikolai Khmelev represented Anna's husband on the stage of the Moscow Art Theatre. Here is how the image of Karenin created by the actor is described in a review of those years by the critic I. Bachelis:

> Karenin. The dry, rigid figure of a dignitary; a gray face with a web of drooping sideburns; ears spread out like Pobedonostsev's; a raspy, croaking voice; an angular, cutting gesture … […] What N. P. Khmelev showed on stage is stunning. Such a performance, such a complete actor's image in all the smallest details, we have not seen for a long time. With unexpected force, Khmelev showed a lifeless figure we did not know when reading Tolstoy.[15]

The image of Karenin in this interpretation illuminated and exalted Anna.

Nikolai Gritsenko in the 1967 film adaptation, according to the general opinion of critics and viewers, played the role of Karenin successfully. He harped upon the unsympathetic features of the hero's appearance and behavior – a raspy voice, an unpleasant crunching of fingers, a frozen facial

13 See Sergei Aksenov, 'Anna Karenina after Tolstoy', *Znamia*, No. 2 (2010), <https://znamlit.ru/publication.php?id=4186>.

14 Ibid.

15 I. Bachelis, 'Anna Karenina, Premier in the USSR, Gorky Moscow Art Theatre', *Komsomolskaia Pravda*, 22 April 1937. Cited in *Moscow Art Theatre in Russian Theatrical Criticism 1919–1943*, Part 2: *1930–1943* (Moscow, 2010), p. 257.

expression. Perfectly recreated on the screen, the portrait of a robotic man did not evoke sympathy in the audience.

Giving a retrospective assessment of the film *Anna Karenina* by Aleksandr Zarkhi, and most importantly, telling the story of the film auditions for the role of Karenin in this film adaptation, film critic Pyotr Bagrov noted that Nikolai Gritsenko played the role of Karenin grotesquely, 'with gusto' and

> in general opinion, became almost the main ornament of the picture. However, he did not play the Karenin that Tolstoy described, but the one that Anna sees and the one about whom school essays are written: 'He is not a man, but a machine, and an evil machine when it gets angry.'[16]

Looking at the unique materials of trial filming of actors for the role of Karenin preserved in the *Gosfilmofond*, among several contenders – Nikolai Cherkasov, Innokenty Smoktunovsky, Yevgeny Yevstigneev, Andrei Popov – Bagrov highlights Cherkasov, who, in his opinion, is the most convincing in this difficult role. Here is how Bagrov describes the image he created during the trial filming:

> Cherkasov played an old man who loves his young wife ecstatically, understands the doom of this love and holds on to the decency of the world as the inner core – here it is not a goal, but a means of survival. The painful tension which Gritsenko and Smoktunovsky do not have in the least bit (the stiffness is obvious, but it is completely organic), and which restrains Popov to the end, in Cherkasov is almost beyond his strength. And in a conversation with Vronsky at the bedside of his dying wife, his voice breaks off. He is the only one of the four who has truly forgiven Anna.[17]

The film critic believes that Karenin is almost a key figure in Tolstoy's plan. In fact, this interpretation of the character is not without meaning, if we take into account that, in Tolstoy's world, the ability to forgive is learned by favorite characters who have passed through a difficult path of life trials.

16 P. A. Bagrov, '*Anna Karenina*: Rehearsal', Belye Stolby Film Festival (19, 23–28 February 2015), Catalogue (Moscow, 2015), pp. 62–64.
17 Ibid., p. 64.

The psychologically complex characters of Tolstoy in the aforementioned stage and cinematic versions were presented somewhat one-sidedly, which, of course, is inevitable in any interpretation. If we turn to the history of the creation of the novel, which is the subject of the work of V. A. Zhdanov and E. E. Zaidenshnur, we will see that Tolstoy himself hesitated in the process of creating the nature of his characters, and they did not immediately acquire psychological depth and ambiguity. The image of Alexei Karenin in the original plan was different from the one that turned out in the final version of the novel. Alexei Aleksandrovich Karenin – a St. Petersburg dignitary who adhered to deep principles – in the original version was 'a soft man, and he was defeated by the injustice of life'. He had

> the misfortune to wear on his face too clearly the sign of heartfelt kindness and innocence. He often smiled a smile that wrinkled the corners of his eyes, and therefore had the appearance of a learned crank or a fool, according to the degree of intelligence of those who judged him.

In St. Petersburg, at the railway station, when meeting Anna, in the early versions, he is described as 'a good-natured man who deeply loves his wife'.[18]

Such aspects of Karenin's personality as his confusion, weakness and insecurity, which manifest themselves with special force after he forgives his wife and even her lover, and again finds himself abandoned, touch the readers of the novel. Several chapters in the novel are devoted to the feelings of the rejected and offended virtue of Karenin:

> He could not now reconcile his recent forgiveness, his emotion, his love for his sick wife and someone else's child with what was now happening, that is, with the fact that, as if as a reward for all this, he now found himself alone, disgraced, ridiculed, useless and despised by everyone.[19]

18 Zhdanov and Zaidenschnur, 'The Story of the Creation of the Novel *Anna Karenina*', p. 814.

19 L. N. Tolstoy, *Collected Works*, 12 vols (Moscow, 1959), Vol. 9, p. 83.

These so humanly understandable experiences of Karenin were until recently muted in productions and film adaptations. But inevitably there was a revision in the emphasis placed by the interpreters.

And then in 1997 there was a new American film adaptation of the novel directed by Bernard Rose with Sophie Marceau in the title role. For this actress, the behavior of a woman who left a child for the sake of a beloved man was not entirely understandable, and in an interview (*Premiere* magazine, No. 2, 1997), she quite clearly expressed her opinion regarding the characters of the novel and to the tragic conflict:

> The real victim of this story is Karenin. He's the only one who doesn't have a choice. The only one who forgave. And the only one who will be left alone with his life, with his memories, with his misery. He won't commit suicide, he won't go to war. He loved this woman, really loved her.[20]

In the same film, as Sergei Aksenov notes, Anna's drug addiction was emphasized.

Vasily Sigarev's *Alexei Karenin* and Viesturs Meikšāns

Vasily Sigarev's play *Alexei Karenin* (2011)[21] is a new attempt to look at the relationship of the characters of Tolstoy's novel from a different perspective . Sigarev's play is tragifarce. The conflict is equally likely to happen between spouses united in an unequal marriage in the nineteenth, twentieth or twenty-first century. Vasily Sigarev is interested in the consequences of Anna's action, not so much for herself as for her husband, an elderly official of high rank, a lover who, having found himself in the position of an unloved, rejected spouse, has lost all his strength. With piercing depth, the playwright shows the hopelessness of the tragedy of Karenin,

20 Cited in Aksenov. 'Anna Karenina after Tolstoy'.

21 Vasily Sigarev, *Alexei Karenin. A Play in Two Acts*, *Ural*, No. 8 (2011), <http://magazines.russ.ru/ural/2011/8/si11.html>.

the reason for which, according to Sigarev, is old age. In a conversation with his son, he confesses: 'I, Seryozha, am only to blame for being old, and far from being a Samson. I'm only to blame for worrying. I'm only to blame for not being strong and full of vim, Seryozha.'[22]

In the play, based on the novel, both the outline of the work and the relationship of the characters among themselves are very carefully preserved. The playwright gives a special sharpness to the essence of their characters in a concise form. Sigarev's likes and dislikes are obvious. If Anna rather resembles Chekhov's heroines from the stories 'Anna on the Neck' and 'The Grasshopper', then Karenin, whose feelings most occupy the playwright, in his confusion and even some incompatibility with reality, is closest to Tolstoy's first novel versions of this character. Countess Lydia Ivanovna, in her religious hypocrisy, is an almost grotesque figure.

In 2012, on the Small Stage of the Moscow Art Theatre, Karenin was staged based on Sigarev's play, directed by Viesturs Meikšāns and designer Reinis Sukhanovce. Very concise and symbolic scenography conveys the atmosphere of what is happening on the small stage. Of great importance in the performance is the wall, which constantly changes its appearance. A wall separates Karenin from his wife's world: this is a transparent wall in Karenin's dacha, where he comes in the hope of establishing relations with Anna, but in that space behind the glass partition he has no place, he is not expected, and he has disturbed the idyll unfolding in nature with a beautifully mown lawn. The antlers hanging on the lawn wall clearly indicate his position.

In the end, Karenin finds himself cornered: he beats against the walls of misunderstanding. A person who has lived by his work and ideas about family happiness is like a madman. The space of the stage very accurately characterizes the psychological state of Karenin – his loneliness, isolation, lack of understanding by others. A glass wall separates him from the madhouse, which is only a step away. Behind this wall, nurses who look threatening appear to subdue violent patients.

Anna's confused world with her premonitions, dreams and superstitions is conveyed very wittily in a scene with a homegrown psychic whom

22 Vasily Sigarev, *Alexei Karenin*, <http://magazines.russ.ru/ural/2011/8/si11.html>.

Karenin visits for a session. The psychic broadcasts Anna's thoughts, which he hears on the phone. This tragic scene highlights the total misunderstanding between the spouses and their inability to talk to each other directly, without intermediaries.

Lydia Ivanovna, fulfilling her Christian duty in the desire to protect Karenin and Seryozha from the immoral woman Karenina, causes unambiguous associations with modern distorted ideas about the role of the church in society. Actualizing and strengthening the theme of psychological impact on the individual, the director may want to say that the church, like a psychiatric hospital, is a strong lever of influence. Intimidating nurses and clergymen are played by the same actresses.

Did the playwright and the creators of the modern version of Anna Karenina manage to express all that complex conglomerate of thoughts and feelings laid down in the novel by the author? Of course, they did not. But by showing the relations of the characters from a different perspective, polemically emphasizing a different essence of the characters and the relations between the characters, the interpreters confirm to us the opinion of the inexhaustibility of the meanings contained in Tolstoy's immortal work.

So, returning to the topic of cultural explosions, we can see that they inevitably occur with varying degrees of intensity and frequency at the intersection of epochs and during periods of revaluation in society. The examples we have considered reflect the life of a literary text in time and demonstrate a chain of literary explosions, collisions of different texts within one text and the generation of new meanings. Yu. M. Lotman characterizes this process as 'a constant process of "aging" of various ways of meaning generation' and of compensation due, on the one hand, to the introduction of the 'new, previously forbidden', and on the other hand, to the rejuvenation of 'old meaning-generating structures'.[23]

23 Lotman, *Semiosphere*, p. 26.

Bibliography

Aksenov, Sergei, 'Anna Karenina after Tolstoy', *Znamia*, No. 2 (2010), <https://znamlit.ru/publication.php?id=4186> (Accessed 20 April 2023).

Bachelis, I. '*Anna Karenina*, Premier in the USSR, Gorky Moscow Art Theatre', *Komsomolskaia Pravda*, 22 April 1937. Cited in: *Moscow Art Theatre in Russian Theatrical Criticism 1919–1943*, Part 2: *1930–1943* (Moscow: Artist. Rezhisser. Teatr, 2010), p. 257.

Bagrov, P. A., '*Anna Karenina*: Rehearsal', Belye Stolby Film Festival, 19 and 23–28 February 2015, catalogue (Moscow: B/I, 2015), pp. 62–64.

Barash, L. A., 'Intepretation of the Classics in Postmodern Culture', *Pushkin Herald* (Leningrad State University), No. 3 (2016), p. 248.

Glantz, Tomasz, 'On the Centenary of Leo Tolstoy's Death: Anna Karenina as Cultural Phenomenon and Heroine of Mass Culture', Radio Svoboda, 5 December 2010, <www.svoboda.org>.

Glasse, Antonia, 'Iz chego sdelalas' "Metel'" Pushkina' [What Pushkin's 'Blizzard' Was Made of] *NLO* [UFO] (1996), p. 14 [Глассе Антония, 'Из чего сделалась "Метель" Пушкина', НЛО, No. 14, (1996), C].

Lotman, Yu. M., *Semiosphere; Culture and Explosion; Universe of the Mind: Articles, Research, Notes* (St. Petersburg: Iskusstvo-SPB, 2004).

Nekrasov, N.A., *Collected Poems* (Moscow: Gos. izd-vo Khudozhestvennoi literatury, 1946).

Rebel, G., 'Blizzard': Theatrical Dreams about Pushkin and Gogol through Sigarev, *Filolog*, No. 25 (2013), <http://philolog.pspu.ru/module/magazine/do/mpub_25_522> (Accessed 31 March 2023).

Sazonov, Anton, 'Vasily Sigarev: Not a Good Story for Producers. Everybody Can Be Arrested', *Snob*, 28 August 2012, https://snob.ru/selected/entry/52144 (Accessed 18 April 2023).

Sigarev, Vasily, 'Alexei Karenin. A Play in Two Acts', *Ural*, No. 8 (2011), http://magazines.russ.ru/ural/2011/8/si11.html (Accessed 21 April 2023).

——— *Blizzard: A Play in Two Acts; Based on the Story by A. S. Pushkin of the Same Name*, http://vsigarev.ru/doc/metel.html (Accessed 23 March 2023).

Tolstoy, L. N., *Collected Works*, 12 vols (Moscow: Gos. izd-vo Khudozhestvennoi literatury, 1959).

Zhdanov, V. A., and E. Ye. Zaidenschnur, 'The Story of the Creation of the Novel *Anna Karenina*', in L. N. Tolstoy, *Anna Karenina: The Novel in 8 Volumes*, ed. V. A. Zhdanov and E. Ye. Zaidenschnur (Moscow: Nauka, 1970), pp. 817–820.

Translated by Nikita Khmarenko

Bibliography

Notes on Contributors

ELENA ARTAMONOVA, Ph.D., is a violist and researcher who has published extensively on the history of the viola and of twentieth century music and culture in Russia, France, Serbia, Poland, the United Kingdom and the United States. Her co-edited volume *Russian-British Intercultural Dialogue: Russian Music in Britain, British Music in Russia* (2020) received international praise. Elena is Lecturer and the Deputy Director of the Research Centre for Russian Studies at University of Central Lancashire (UCLan), UK, and a member of the UCLan Research Centre for Migration, Diaspora and Exile (MIDEX), UK. She is also a member of the Editorial and Expert Council of the peer-reviewed academic journal *Art & Culture Studies*, Russia, and her research has been presented at many international conferences. She is a recording artist of the Toccata Classics label, and her CDs with the first complete viola works by Grigori Frid, Alexander Grechaninov and Sergei Vasilenko have received high critical acclaim.

OLHA CHERVINSKA, D. Litt., is Professor and Head of Department of Foreign Literature and Literary Theory at Yuriy Fedkovych Chernivtsi National University, Chernivtsi, Ukraine. She is Editor-in-Chief of the academic journal *Pytannya Literaturoznavstva/Problems of Literary Criticism*, member of the editorial board of the Czech academic journal *Modern Russian Studies* and Academic Coordinator of the International Poetological Conferences in Chernivtsi as well as the organizer of the corresponding editions. She has published widely on literary theory and Russian literature, and she is the author of *Acmeism in the Context of the Silver Age and Traditions* (1997), *Pushkin, Nabokov, Akhmatova: Metamorphosis of the Russian Lyrical Novel* (1999), *Arguments of Form* (2015) and *Dialogue: Pro Dostoevsky* (2021, jointly with R. Dzyk).

LYUDMIL DIMITROV, Ph.D., is Professor of Russian Literature, Faculty of Slavic Studies, at the Sofia University, St. Kliment Ohridski. He is a member of the Union of Translators in Bulgaria, Bulgarian PEN and the International Dostoevsky Society (IDS). From 2005 to 2010 and from 2014 to 2019, he was Lecturer in Bulgarian Language, Literature and Culture at the University of Ljubljana, Slovenia. He has authored several scholarly monographs, textbooks and books, and has over 300 publications to his credit in Bulgaria, Russia, Poland, Czech Republic, Slovakia, Turkey, Italy, Great Britain, Latvia, Serbia, Slovenia, Slovakia, Romania, Spain and United States. The Union of Slovenian Literary Translators gave him their highest award, the Janko Lavrin Prize (2017), and the Union of Translators in Bulgaria have honored him for his overall work in 2020 and for his outstanding achievements in translating the Slovenian poet France Prešeren's work into Bulgarian in 2021.

ELENA V. GLUKHOVA, Ph.D., is Senior Researcher at the Gorky Institute of World Literature, Russian Academy of Sciences. Her research interests and numerous publications encompass Russian literature and culture at the turn of the nineteenth and twentieth centuries; heritage and biographies of Silver Age writers such as Andrei Bely, Alexander Blok, Viacheslav Ivanov; Russian literature during the First World War and Revolution; the narrative of the female ego-document; mythopoetics of Russian Symbolism; ego-document studies; and prosody. She is the author of '"Estate Topos" of Russian Symbolism in the Ego-Documentary prose of Andrey Bely' (2020), 'Motifs and Images of the Vocal Cycle of F. Schubert's "Winterreise" in the Context of the Autobiographical Mythology of Andrei Bely' (2019) and 'The Philosophy of Vladimir Soloviev as the Intertextual Source at Viacheslav Ivanov's "The Tale of Tsarevich Svetomir"' (2016). She was the head of project and a member of the editorial board of 'Andrei Bely's *Aaron's Rod*: Works on the Theory of the Word 1916–1927', *Literaturnoje Nasledstvo*, Vol. 111 (2018).

VLADIMIR GOLSTEIN was born in Moscow, Russia, and educated at Columbia and Yale Universities, United States. He has taught at Oberlin College and Yale University, and he is Associate Professor and Chair of the Department of Slavic Studies at Brown University, United States. He is the author of *Lermontov's Narratives of Heroism* (1999), *Svetlana*

Aleksievich – The Voice of Soviet Intelligentsia (2015), and the co-editor of *Dostoevsky Beyond Dostoevsky* (2016). His scholarly interests embrace Russian culture, religion, film and poetry, of the past two centuries, and his scholarly articles address such diverse Russian figures as Pushkin, Gogol, Tarkovsky and Tsvetaeva. His essays on current political affairs have been published by *Forbes*, *The Nation*, *Al Jazeera*, *RT* and *Antiwar*. He is also a frequent participant in various political TV shows discussing US and Russian foreign politics and culture.

GALIMA LUKINA is Vice-Director of the Federal State Institute for Art Studies and Professor of Music History at the Russian State Specialized Arts Academy in Moscow. She has a higher doctorate in Art Studies, and has published three monographs and over 70 research articles in English and Russian. She is a member of the editorial boards of journals such as *Artistic Culture, Art Education and Science* and *Cultural Heritage of Russia*. Her research interests include the history of Russian music, the legacy of the composer Sergey Ivanovich Taneyev, philosophy of music and problems of music education. She has edited and co-edited a substantial number of collective volumes and is the author of *Creative Heritage of Sergey Taneyev in the Light of the Russian Spiritual Tradition* (2015), *The Idea of Sobornost in Choral and Symphonic Works of S. I. Taneyev* (2004) and *Methodology of Teaching Solfeggio for Visually Impaired and Blind Children in Children's Music School: Scientific and Methodical Manual* (jointly with V. I. Lisovoi, 2017).

ALEKSANDR A. MEDVEDEV, Ph.D. (Philology), is Associate Professor and Head of Department of Russian and Foreign Literature at Tyumen State University, Tyumen, Russia. His research interests include Russian literature of the nineteenth and twentieth centuries (Fedor Dostoevsky, Vasily Rozanov, Mikhail Prishvin, Anna Akhmatova, Marina Tsvetaeva, Anastasia Tsvetaeva, and others) in the historical-cultural context of 'big time' (Mikhail Bakhtin); literature and ideology; ekphrasis; and comparative studies. He is the author of more than 60 scholarly publications, including 'The Prison Experience and Gulag Poems in the Work (1937–1943) by Anastasija Cvetaeva: Overcoming the "Zone"' (2021), 'Modernist Ekphrasis in Marina Tsvetaeva's Essay Natalia Goncharova: Life and Work' (2021), '"Rozanov's Layer" in the Work of Anna Akhmatova' (2021), 'The Russian Catastrophe of 1917 and Bakhtin's "Great Time" (M. Prishvin, V. Rozanov, A. Blok)' (2019), '"No One Else Got So Close to the Gospel as You": Reception of the Gospels in the Russian Franciscana of the Silver Age (D. Merezhkovsky, S. Durylin, S. Solovyov)' (2018).

MARGARITA ODESSKAYA, Ph.D., is Professor at the Russian Language Department of the Philology and History Institute, Russian State University for the Humanities, Moscow. She is the author more than 150 scholarly publications in Russia and abroad. Her research focuses on Russian literature of the end of the nineteenth century, especially on Chekhov's works, and on comparative poetics, drama and theatre. She is a member of the Chekhov Commission of the Council in the History of World Culture of the Russian Academy of Sciences, and the author of the monograph *Chekhov and the Problem of the Ideal* (2011) as well as the editor of several collective volumes. She has taught as Visiting Professor in the Czech Republic and Norway, and also interned in the United States.

SARAH OSSIPOW CHEANG is a translator and author who teaches Russian in Geneva. Her interests lie in comparative and contemporary literature as well as the Russian Silver Age. She is the author of the book *Etude sur le thème de l'errance dans l'oeuvre de Boris Zaitsev* (2011) as well as further studies on Boris Zaitsev, Marina Tsvetaeva and others; she is also a translator of works by Katia Kapovich. Sarah published widely in various journals, such as *Russian Literature* (Elsevier), *Russian Journal of Multilingualism and Education*, *Sjani – The Georgian International Journal of Literary Theory and Comparative Literature* and *Russkaya Rech'*. Her papers have also appeared in the proceedings of international conferences in Russia and Britain.

LARISA V. POLYAKOVA is a graduate of Moscow Lomonosov State University and has a higher doctorate in Philology. She is Professor and Scientific Director of the Faculty of Philology and Journalism at Tambov

Derzhavin State University, where she served as Head of the Department of Literature in 1989–2011. She has the title of 'Honoured Scientist of the Russian Federation', and her research interests include the history of Russian literature (mainly of the twentieth and twenty-first centuries) and its theoretical aspects, and philological regional studies. She has published scholarly work since 1960 and is the author of numerous scientific publications, including 17 monographs. Since the early 1990s, she has been actively studying the creative heritage of E. I. Zamyatin. On her initiative and under her leadership in Tambov, in the homeland of the writer, the International Scientific Centre for the Study of the Creative Heritage of E. I. Zamyatin was established, with domestic and foreign branches, where international Zamyatin readings are regularly held. Her latest monograph is *Prose of E. I. Zamyatin: The Artist's Historiosophical Quest* (2022).

LIDIA I. SHISHKINA is a philologist and culturologist based in St. Petersburg, Russia. A graduate from the Faculty of Philology of St. Petersburg (Leningrad) State University, she received her doctorate in Russian Literature at the Institute of Russian Literature (Pushkin House) of the Russian Academy of Sciences. Her research interests include Russian literature and culture of the first half of the twentieth century. She is the author of the monographs *The Work of Leonid Andreev in the Context of Twentieth-Century Culture* (2009) and *The Literary Fate of Yevgeny Zamyatin* (1992), and of more than 150 articles on literature and culture of the twentieth century. She is a member of the international scientific team (IMLI, IRLI, University of Leeds, University of Helsinki) for the publication of the complete works of Leonid Andreev and is currently a Professor at the North-West Institute of Management – St. Petersburg branch of the Russian Presidential Academy of National Economy and Public Administration.

NATALIA SKOROKHOD is Professor of Drama and Theatre at the Russian State Institute of Performing Arts (St. Petersburg) and Chief of the Master's Programme in Playwriting. She graduated from Leningrad State Institute of Theatre, Music and Cinema in 1986 as a theatre maker. She has received both her doctorate (2008) and higher doctorate (2021) in Art Studies. She has published *How to Adapt Prose* (2010) and *Leonid Andreev: Biography* in the series of *Lives of Remarkable People* (2013), and more than 100 articles on theatre, play and script history, theory and practice. In 2015, the Lambert Academic Publishing released her *Postdrama Analysis*. She also serves as an expert in several contemporary drama and theatre competitions. In 2022, she supervised the program of plays at the main annual festival of Russian-speaking playwrights 'Lubimovka', and in September 2022, she presented this program in VABA LAVA theatre (Estonia) as a curator.

ALEKSANDR SYCH is Professor of History and Head of the Department of World History at Yuriy Fed'kovych Chernivtsi National University, Chernivtsi, Ukraine. He is the author of textbooks, popular science books and academic articles in the field of modern and contemporary history. His research interests include various problems of world history, in particular the First World War, the French and Russian Revolutions, civilization and migration processes. He is the author of about 300 scholarly publications, including 'Post War (WWI) Central and Eastern Europe: Time of Civilizational Choice' (2019), 'On Terminology and Beyond (To the 100th Anniversary of the October Revolution in Russia)' (2017), '*My Love is the Revolution…*' (2016), 'On the Evolution of the Socio-Political System of the States of Central and Eastern Europe in the Interwar Period' (2016) and 'The First World War as a Phenomenon of Civilizational Significance' (2011). He is a member of the editorial board of *History Journal of Yuriy Fed'kovych Chernivtsi National University and Moldavian Journal of International Law and International Relations.*

OLGA TABACHNIKOVA is Associate Professor (Reader) of Russian and the founding Director of the Vladimir Vysotsky Centre for Russian Studies at the University of Central Lancashire. She is a member of several editorial boards of scholarly journals across Europe, has more than 80 academic publications on Russian cultural and literary history and is especially interested in Russian cultural continuity and history of ideas. She is the author of *Russian Irrationalism from Pushkin to Brodsky: Seven*

Essays in Literature and Thought (2015), the editor of *Facets of Russian Irrationalism between Art and Life: Mystery inside Enigma* (2016) and *Anton Chekhov through the Eyes of Russian Thinkers: Vasilii Rozanov, Dmitrii Merezhkovskii and Lev Shestov* (2010), and also the co-editor of several scholarly volumes. Olga is also a poetry translator and the author of two books of poetry (in Russian).

ELENA TCHOUGOUNOVA-PAULSON obtained her Ph.D. in Twentieth-Century Russian Literature from the Department of Theory and Methodology of Philology and Art, A. M. Gorky Institute of World Literature, Russian Academy of Sciences, Moscow. She is currently an independent researcher, residing in Cambridge, United Kingdom, who takes part in a variety of literary projects and translations. Her research interests include Russian, Ukrainian and English literatures of the early twentieth century, Ukrainian studies, history and theory of literature, American literature of the nineteenth to early twentieth century as well as Gothic and horror studies. As a textual scholar and translator, she has taken part in several editorial projects, including *Alexander Dovzhenko: Diaries* (2013) and *Alexander Blok – L. D. Mendeleeva-Blok: Correspondence* (1901–1917) (2017).

NATALIA VINOKUROVA, Ph.D., is Senior Researcher at the Central Economics and Mathematics Institute of the Russian Academy of Sciences in Moscow and a member of the Board of the All Russian Association of Women in Science and Education. She has presented papers, including plenary talks, at numerous international conferences and has also served in scientific-organizing committees. She is the author of more than 150 scholarly publications in academic journals, collective monographs and conference proceedings in Russia, Germany, Lithuania, Britain, Sweden and Poland. Her interests encompass gender studies and studies of Russian cultural continuity, and her publications include 'New Russian "Macho" between Literature and Life' (jointly with Olga Tabachnikova) in *The Palgrave Handbook on Women and Gender in Twentieth-Century Russia and the Soviet Union* (2018), and 'Russian Semiotics of Behaviour, or Can a Russian Person Be Regarded as "Homo Economicus"?', in *Facets of Russian Irrationalism between Art and Life: Mystery inside Enigma* (2016).

ELENA YUSHKOVA, Ph.D. (Art History), is an independent scholar and a dance historian residing in Russia. She has authored two monographs (including the first Russian-language monograph on Isadora Duncan). In 2020–2022, she was Research Associate at the Five College Women's Studies Research Center in Massachusetts, United States, and in 2007–2008, she was Scholar in Residence at the Kennan Institute, Woodrow Wilson International Center for Scholars. Elena has published more than 60 academic articles in Russian and foreign academic journals, collective monographs and conference proceedings, and has edited three volumes of conference papers. Her recent publications have appeared in *Journal of Russian American Studies, Dance Chronicle, Forum Modernes Theater, Toronto Slavic Quarterly, Literature of Two Americas* and *Voprosy Literatury*.

Index

CULTURAL HISTORY AND LITERARY IMAGINATION

EDITED BY CHRISTIAN J. EMDEN & DAVID MIDGLEY

This series promotes critical inquiry into the relationship between the literary imagination and its cultural, intellectual or political contexts. The series encourages the investigation of the role of the literary imagination in cultural history and the interpretation of cultural history through literature, visual culture and the performing arts.

Contributions of a comparative or interdisciplinary nature are particularly welcome. Individual volumes might, for example, be concerned with any of the following:

- The mediation of cultural and historical memory,
- The material conditions of particular cultural manifestations,
- The construction of cultural and political meaning,
- Intellectual culture and the impact of scientific thought,
- The methodology of cultural inquiry,
- Intermediality,
- Intercultural relations and practices.

Acceptance is subject to advice from our editorial board, and all proposals and manuscripts undergo a rigorous peer review assessment prior to publication. The usual language of publication is English, but proposals in the other languages shown below will also be considered.

For French studies, contact Kenneth Loiselle <kloisell@trinity.edu>

For German studies, contact Sarah Colvin <sjc269@cam.ac.uk>

For Hispanic studies, contact Rodrigo Cacho <rgc27@cam.ac.uk>

For Italian studies, contact Heather Webb <hmw53@cam.ac.uk>

Vol. 1 Christian Emden & David Midgley (eds): Cultural Memory and Historical Consciousness in the German-Speaking World Since 1500. Papers from the Conference 'The Fragile Tradition', Cambridge 2002. Vol. 1. 316 pp., 2004. ISBN 3-03910-160-9 / US-ISBN 0-8204-6970-X

Vol. 2 Christian Emden & David Midgley (eds): German Literature, History and the Nation. Papers from the Conference 'The Fragile Tradition', Cambridge 2002. Vol. 2. 393 pp., 2004. ISBN 3-03910-169-2 / US-ISBN 0-8204-6979-3

Vol. 3 Christian Emden & David Midgley (eds): Science, Technology and the German Cultural Imagination. Papers from the Conference 'The Fragile Tradition', Cambridge 2002. Vol. 3. 319 pp., 2005. ISBN 3-03910-170-6 / US-ISBN 0-8204-6980-7

Vol. 4 Anthony Fothergill: Secret Sharers. Joseph Conrad's Cultural Reception in Germany. 274 pp., 2006. ISBN 3-03910-271-0 / US-ISBN 0-8204-7200-X

Vol. 5 Silke Arnold-de Simine (ed.): Memory Traces. 1989 and the Question of German Cultural Identity. 343 pp., 2005. ISBN 3-03910-297-4 / US-ISBN 0-8204-7223-9

Vol. 6 Renata Tyszczuk: In Hope of a Better Age. Stanislas Leszczynski in Lorraine 1737-1766. 410 pp., 2007. ISBN 978-3-03910-324-9

Vol. 7 Christian Emden, Catherine Keen & David Midgley (eds): Imagining the City, Volume 1. The Art of Urban Living. 344 pp., 2006. ISBN 3-03910-532-9 / US-ISBN 0-8204-7536-X

Vol. 8 Christian Emden, Catherine Keen & David Midgley (eds): Imagining the City, Volume 2. The Politics of Urban Space. 383 pp., 2006. ISBN 3-03910-533-7 / US-ISBN 0-8204-7537-8

Vol. 9 Christian J. Emden and Gabriele Rippl (eds): ImageScapes. Studies in Intermediality. 289 pp., 2010. ISBN 978-3-03910-573-1

Vol. 10 Alasdair King: Hans Magnus Enzensberger. Writing, Media, Democracy. 357 pp., 2007. ISBN 978-3-03910-902-9

Vol. 11 Ulrike Zitzlsperger: ZeitGeschichten: Die Berliner Übergangsjahre. Zur Verortung der Stadt nach der Mauer. 241 pp., 2007. ISBN 978-3-03911-087-2

Vol. 12 Alexandra Kolb: Performing Femininity. Dance and Literature in German Modernism.
330pp., 2009. ISBN 978-3-03911-351-4

Vol. 13 Carlo Salzani: Constellations of Reading. Walter Benjamin in Figures of Actuality.
388pp., 2009. ISBN 978-3-03911-860-1

Vol. 14 Monique Rinere: Transformations of the German Novel. *Simplicissimus* in Eighteenth-Century Adaptations. 273pp., 2009. ISBN 978-3-03911-896-0

Vol. 15 Katharina Hall and Kathryn N. Jones (eds): Constructions of Conflict. Transmitting Memories of the Past in European Historiography, Culture and Media.
282pp., 2011. ISBN 978-3-03911-923-3

Vol. 16 Ingo Cornils and Sarah Waters (eds): Memories of 1968. International Perspectives.
396pp., 2010. ISBN 978-3-03911-931-8

Vol. 17 Anna O' Driscoll: Constructions of Melancholy in Contemporary German and Austrian Literature.
263pp., 2013. ISBN 978-3-0343-0733-8

Vol. 18 Martin Modlinger and Philipp Sonntag (eds): Other People's Pain. Narratives of Trauma and the Question of Ethics. 252pp., 2011. ISBN 978-3-0343-0260-9

Vol. 19 Ian Cooper and Bernhard F. Malkmus (eds): Dialectic and Paradox. Configurations of the Third in Modernity. 265pp., 2013. ISBN 978-3-0343-0714-7

Vol. 20 Kristina Mendicino and Betiel Wasihun (eds): Playing False. Representations of Betrayal.
355pp., 2013. ISBN 978-3-0343-0867-0

Vol. 21 Guy Tourlamain: *Völkisch* Writers and National Socialism. A Study of Right-Wing Political Culture in Germany, 1890–1960.
394pp., 2014. ISBN 978-3-03911-958-5

Vol. 22 Ricarda Vidal and Ingo Cornils (eds): Alternative Worlds. Blue-Sky Thinking since 1900.
343pp., 2015. ISBN 978-3-0343-1787-0

Vol. 23 Henriette Steiner and Kristin Veel (eds): Invisibility Studies. Surveillance, Transparency and the Hidden in Contemporary Culture.
388pp., 2015. ISBN 978-3-0343-0985-1

Vol. 24 Bernd Fischer and May Mergenthaler (eds): Cultural Transformations of the Public Sphere. Contemporary and Historical Perspectives.
349pp., 2015. ISBN 978-3-0343-0991-2

Vol. 25 Marjorie Gehrhardt: The Men with Broken Faces. *Gueules Cassées* of the First World War.
309pp., 2015. ISBN 978-3-0343-1869-3

Vol. 26 David Walton and Juan A. Suárez (eds): Contemporary Writing and the Politics of Space. Borders, Networks, Escape Lines.
302pp., 2017. ISBN 978-3-0343-2205-8

Vol. 27 Robert Craig and Ina Linge (eds): Biological Discourses. The Language of Science and Literature Around 1900.
448pp., 2017. ISBN 978-1-906165-78-9

Vol. 28 Rebecca Waese: When Novels Perform History. Dramatizing the Past in Australian and Canadian Literature.
272pp., 2017. ISBN 978-1-906165-84-0

Vol. 29 Udith Dematagoda: Vladimir Nabokov and the Ideological Aesthetic. A Study of his Novels and Plays, 1926–1939.
222pp., 2017. ISBN 978-1-78707-289-3

Vol. 30 Bernard Beatty and Alicia Laspra-Rodríguez (eds): Romanticism, Reaction and Revolution. British Views on Spain, 1814–1823. 342pp., 2019. ISBN 978-3-0343-2249-2

Vol. 31 Remko Smid: European Vistas. History, Ethics and Identity in the Works of Claudio Magris. 184pp., 2020. ISBN 978-1-78997-635-9

Vol. 32 Caroline Rupprecht: Asian Fusion. New Encounters in the Asian-German Avant-Garde 259pp., 2020. ISBN 978-1-78707-355-5

Vol. 33 Kenneth David Jackson: Cannibal Angels: Transatlantic Modernism and the Brazilian Avant-Garde.
410pp., 2021. ISBN 978-1-78874-038-8

Vol. 34 Olga Tabachnikova (ed.): A Culture of Discontinuity? Russian Cultural Debates in Historical Perspective.
452pp., 2023. ISBN 978-1-78997-937-4

www.ingramcontent.com/pod-product-compliance
Lightning Source LLC
Chambersburg PA
CBHW071732110726
47908CB00006B/1572

9781789979374